The Flowers of Friendship

THE
FLOWERS of FRIENDSHIP
Letters written to
GERTRUDE STEIN

Edited by DONALD GALLUP

Before the Flowers of Friendship Faded Friendship Faded

(TITLE OF A BOOK BY GERTRUDE STEIN)

1 9 5 3
ALFRED A. KNOPF   NEW YORK

L. C. catalog card number: 52–12189

THIS IS A BORZOI BOOK,
PUBLISHED BY ALFRED A. KNOPF, INC.

FIRST EDITION

"Your remark about liking to see people come and liking to see them go seems to me the true philosophy of life"

MARIAN WALKER WILLIAMS
TO GERTRUDE STEIN, JAN 21, 1930

FOR

ALICE B. TOKLAS

who was there when they came
and who knows what they meant

FOREWORD

In 1946 Gertrude Stein gave and bequeathed her correspondence and manuscripts to the Yale University Library. When the papers were being packed just a few weeks before her death, Miss Stein refused to allow Miss Toklas to destroy some almost illiterate messages sent to them in the country by their Paris concierge. "Who knows?" she argued, "Someone some day may consider these to be the most important of all." When the material arrived at Yale and was sorted, it was evident that Miss Stein must have preserved almost every letter she received, even as early as her college days.

This selection from those letters extends from 1895 to 1946, and although concierges are not represented in it, a great many other correspondents are. The number of letters printed bears no consistent relation, however, to the number actually preserved from individual correspondents, and little is to be gathered from this book concerning the length and closeness of particular friendships. There are indeed so many letters in the complete file of those addressed to Gertrude Stein—more than twenty thousand—that it would be possible to make several different selections of this size which would still be almost as representative as the present one.

In putting together this particular assortment, I have attempted to indicate some of the influences which made Gertrude Stein into the woman and the writer she became, and certain aspects of her career and of her personality. The reader will find bits of information upon a variety of subjects: her family background and her education; her taste and interest in art, her salon and the people who came there; the rapid growth of her celebrity as a personage and her long, slow struggle for recognition as a serious artist; her influence on other writers and what they learned from her; her warmth and sympathy and understanding, and her knowledge of human nature; her deep, passionate longing after glory and how she finally achieved it.

In selecting letters from her friends which shed light on
these and other points, I hoped that the resulting portrait
might prove to be one not only of Gertrude Stein but also of
the twentieth-century artist-expatriate and the problems he
faces in our time. For the particularly indulgent reader the
book may treat, incidentally, of even broader subjects: of the
growth of youth into maturity; of hopes and ambitions; of
everyday life in peacetime and in war; of friends in far places
and those near by, and how they often go away and, sometimes, come back.

*　　*　　*　　*

Because I wished to cover in a limited space such a long period and still leave no considerable gaps, I was obliged to edit
many of the letters I had chosen, omitting words, sentences,
and even whole paragraphs. I have marked such omissions,
whatever their length, by the conventional three dots (. . .);
I have made all headings uniform as to place and date, brack-
eting thus [ ] such parts as were not supplied by the corre-
spondent; I have corrected obvious misspellings without comment, except where they had some particular significance
within a letter. My translations—all from the French—are
free, although a notable single exception is provided by the
letters of Pavel Tchelitchew, he having, with extraordinary
kindness, himself revised my version of his originals. I have
deliberately included few French correspondents, however,
because I felt it unfair to represent them by English para-
phrases.

For such, and other liberties taken with these letters, I
humbly beg their writers' pardons: may the intention be considered sufficiently worthy and the realization of it nearly
enough complete to persuade them to bear me no lasting
grudge.

DONALD GALLUP

Yale Collection of American Literature
Yale University Library

ACKNOWLEDGMENTS

THE ORIGINALS of the letters printed in the following pages are to be found in the Gertrude Stein Collection of the Yale Collection of American Literature in the Yale University Library. For their permission to print these letters, I make grateful acknowledgment to the Library as custodian of the manuscripts, to Carl Van Vechten as Literary Executor of Gertrude Stein, and to the individuals and organizations listed below as owners of the publication rights.

Harold Acton; Elmer R. Verrue, for the letters of his cousin Mildred Aldrich; Joseph Alsop; Mrs. Sherwood Anderson, for unpublished letters of Sherwood Anderson, and Little, Brown & Company, for three letters reprinted from *Letters of Sherwood Anderson*, ed. H. M. Jones and W. Rideout (Boston, 1953); Edward C. Aswell; Mrs. George S. Russell, for the letter of her mother Gertrude Atherton; Pierre Balmain; Mrs. Lewellys F. Barker and the Maryland Trust Company, Baltimore, for the letter of Dr. Lewellys F. Barker; Samuel L. M. Barlow; Natalie Clifford Barney; Alfred H. Barr, Jr.; Joseph A. Barry; B. T. Batsford Ltd. and Charles Fry, for the letters of B. T. Batsford Ltd.; Sylvia Beach; Cecil Beaton; Bernard Berenson; Eugène Berman; Robert Heber-Percy, for the letters of Lord Berners (kindness of Constable and Company Ltd.); Mrs. J. Edith Colt, for the letters of her aunt Florence Blood (kindness of Lt. Col. LeBaron C. Colt); Paul Bowles; Mrs. W. A. Bradley, for the letters of W. A. Bradley; Michael Brenner; Jessie Breon; John Breon; Franklin Brewer; Joseph Brewer; Louis Bromfield; Mrs. Harmon C. Bell, for the letters of her aunt Matilda E. Brown; Winifred Bryher; Mr. and Mrs. Walter H. Buss, for the letters of Mr. Buss's sister Kate Buss; the Hon. Jefferson Caffery; Alexander Calder; Margaret Case Harriman, for the letter of her father Frank Case; Bennett Cerf; Harriet Clark Hanley (Harriet Clark); Sir Kenneth Clark; Robert M. Coates; Alvin Langdon Coburn; Jean Cocteau; Philip B. Perlman and the Safe Deposit and Trust Company of Baltimore,

for the letters of Dr. Claribel and Etta Cone; William Cook
(kindness of Mrs. Robert Cook); Aaron Copland; Katharine Cornell (kindness of Gertrude Macy); Hermitage House Inc., for the
letter of Hart Crane reprinted from *The Letters of Hart Crane*,
ed. Brom Weber (New York, 1952); Cecilia M. Cruttwell and the
Literary Executor of Maud Cruttwell, for the letter of Maud
Cruttwell; Henri Daniel-Rops; Mrs. Jo Davidson, for the letter of
Jo Davidson; Stuart Davis; Mrs. John Dewey, for the letter of
John Dewey; Mary E. Dreier and Marcel Duchamp, for the letter
of Katherine S. Dreier; Gerald Duckworth & Co. Ltd.; Katherine
Dudley; Mrs. Pitts Duffield, for the letter of Pitts Duffield; T. S.
Eliot; Dr. Emma Lootz Erving; Doris I. Ewing, for the letter of
her cousin Max Ewing; Bernard Faÿ (kindness of Alice B. Toklas);
the Hon. Mrs. Reginald Fellowes; Dudley Fitts; Mrs. Samuel J.
Lanahan, for the letters of her father F. Scott Fitzgerald; Janet
Flanner; Dr. Fletcher Hodges, for the letter of his cousin Con-
stance Fletcher; Charles Henri Ford; Janice Biala Brustlein, for
the letters of Ford Madox Ford; Dr. Leo V. Friedman; Mrs. A. P.
Diamand, for the letter of her father Roger Fry; Marion S. Gans,
for the letters of her father Howard Gans; Mrs. Harry Phelan
Gibb, for the letters of Harry Phelan Gibb; Irita Van Doren, for
the letter of Ellen Glasgow; Dr. Oliver St. John Gogarty; Mrs.
Gilbert W. Chapman (Mrs. Charles Goodspeed); Geoffrey Gorer;
Duncan Grant; Alyse Gregory; Josette Gris, for the letters of Juan
Gris (kindness of Daniel-Henry Kahnweiler); Robert Bartlett
Haas; the late Mrs. Hutchins Hapgood, for the letters of Hutchins
Hapgood (kindness of Charles H. Hapgood); Alfred Harcourt;
Norma Berger, for the letters of her uncle Marsden Hartley; Jane
Heap (kindness of Erica Brausen); Ernest Hemingway; Mrs.
DuBose Heyward, for the letter of DuBose Heyward; Nora Holt;
Lindley Williams Hubbell; Georges Hugnet; Mrs. Wellington M.
Watters, for the letters of her father Bravig Imbs; Madame Fran-
çois Baron, for the letter of Max Jacob (kindness of François
Baron); Paul R. Reynolds & Son, for the letters of William James;
Lamont Johnson, for the letters of Mr. and Mrs. Lamont Johnson
and Mr. and Mrs. Robert Claborne; Daniel-Henry Kahnweiler;
Lincoln Kirstein; Estelle Rumbold Kohn; Lady Korzybska (kind-
ness of Charlotte Schuchardt); Lady Korzybska and Charlotte
Schuchardt, for the letter of Count Korzybski; Alfred Kreymborg;

Dr. Arthur Lachman; John Lane The Bodley Head Ltd.; Nella Larsen Imes; Élie Lascaux; James Laughlin; Michel Leiris; Mrs. Lloyd Lewis, for the letters of Lloyd Lewis; Jacques Lipchitz; Harold Loeb; Clare Boothe Luce (kindness of Dorothy Farmer); Mabel Dodge Luhan; George Platt Lynes; Robert McAlmon; Henry McBride; Kenneth Macpherson; Man Ray; Henri Matisse (kindness of Pierre Matisse); Eugenia M. Fuerstenberg, for the letter of her brother Alfred M. Maurer; Henry Miller; Douglas Moore; Marianne Moore; Ella and Margaret Munsterberg, for the letter of their father Hugo Münsterberg; Dorothy Norman; General Frederick H. Osborn; Mrs. A. M. Patch, for the letter of General A. M. Patch; Francis Picabia (kindness of Madame Picabia); Pablo Picasso (kindness of Daniel-Henry Kahnweiler); Mrs. Francis Deak Pollak, for the letter of Francis Deak Pollak; Daniel Raffel; Mrs. Grant Richards, for the letter of Grant Richards; Henri-Pierre Roché; Mrs Arnold Ronnebeck, for the letters of Arnold Rönnebeck; W. G. Rogers; Sir Francis Rose; Stephen Royce, for the letter of his father Josiah Royce; the late George Santayana (kindness of Daniel Cory); William Saroyan; Julian Sawyer; Ellery Sedgwick; Dr. Edith Sitwell (kindness of Sir Osbert Sitwell); Sir Osbert Sitwell; John Russell, for the letter of Logan Pearsall Smith (kindness of Messrs. Neish, Howell and Haldane); Dr. Adele Jaffa, for the letters of her brother Leon Solomons (kindness of Aileen R. Jaffa); Maud Hunt Squire; Joseph Solomon, for unpublished letters or parts of letters of Leo Stein, and Crown Publishers for letters reprinted from *Journey into the Self, Papers & Journals of Leo Stein*, copyright 1950, by the Estate of Leo D. Stein, Deceased (New York, 1950); Oscar Samuels, acting on behalf of Mrs. Michael Stein, for the letters of Mr. and Mrs. Michael Stein; Ettie Stettheimer, for the letter of her sister Florine Stettheimer; Samuel M. Steward; Georgia O'Keeffe, for the letters of Alfred Stieglitz (kindness of Doris Bry); Donald Sutherland; Frank Swinnerton; René Tavernier; Pavel Tchelitchew; Virgil Thomson; Alice Woods (Alice Woods Ullman); Mr. and Mrs. Carl Van Vechten; Mabel Foote Weeks; Marjorie Wells, for the letter of H. G. Wells; Glenway Wescott; Max White; Mrs. A. N. Whitehead, for the letter of A. N. Whitehead; Wendell Wilcox; Thornton Wilder (kindness of Isabel Wilder); Dr. Russell Williams, for the letters of his mother Dr. Marian Walker Williams;

Dr. William Carlos Williams (kindness of Mrs. Williams); Edmund Wilson; Leonard Woolf; Joseph Hennessey, for the letters of Alexander Woollcott; Richard Wright; O. L. Zangwill, for the letters of his father Israel Zangwill.

For information and advice I am greatly indebted to many of the individuals and organizations listed above, as well as to the following:

Appleton-Century-Crofts; James T. Babb; Mr. and Mrs. Pincus Berner; The Bobbs-Merrill Co.; Adelyn D. Breeskin; Cambridge University Press; Coward-McCann; Daniel & Cruttwell; J. M. Dent & Sons Ltd.; William Einstein; First and Merchants National Bank of Richmond; Librairie Gallimard; Harcourt, Brace and Co.; Houghton Mifflin Co.; Hutchinson & Co. Ltd.; William A. Jackson; David James; Mrs. Matthew Josephson; Alfred A. Knopf; Cecil Lang; Longmans, Green & Co.; Samuel Loveman; Carlos Lynes, Jr.; Elizabeth McCausland; Mrs. Frances W. MacKay; The Macmillan Company; Townsend Miller; Oxford University Press; Ralph Barton Perry; J. M. Richards; Walter Rideout; Mrs. Bestor Robinson; John B. Rosson; Martin Secker & Warburg Ltd.; Allen Ullman; Ivan Von Auw, Jr.

I am grateful to Random House Inc. for permission to quote words and phrases from *The Autobiography of Alice B. Toklas* and *Everybody's Autobiography*.

My indebtedness to Alice Toklas and Carl Van Vechten, for assistance and encouragement, places them in a special category.

D. G.

CONTENTS

I. STUDENT DAYS (1895–1902)

1895:	*June* 10	Hugo Münsterberg	4
1896:	*Mar* 13	Leo Stein	5
	Mar 27	Josiah Royce	6
	[*Early*]	George Santayana	7
	Apr 29	Margaret Sterling Snyder	7
	Jun 2	Michael Stein	9
	Jun 19	William James	9
	Jun 29	Leo V. Friedman	10
	Oct 26	Leon Solomons	10
	Dec 6	Matilda E. Brown	11
1897:	*Jan* 20	Mrs. Michael Stein	12
	Mar 13	Francis Pollak	13
	Jun 12	Mrs. Michael Stein	14
	Dec	Leon Solomons	15
	[*Dec* 25?]	Margaret Sterling Snyder	16
1898:	*Mar* 13	Arthur Lachman	17
1899:	*Aug* 27	Mrs. Michael Stein	18
1900:	*Oct* 9	Leo Stein	19
	Oct 17	William James	19
1901:	*Jan* 2	Mabel Foote Weeks	21
	Feb 3	Leo Stein	22
	[*Dec*?]	Marian Walker Williams	23
1902:	*Jan* 30	Lewellys Barker	24

II. EUROPE BEFORE THE WAR (1903–*July* 1914)

1903:	*Oct* 29–		
	Nov 3	Emma Lootz Erving	25
1904:	*Oct* 17	Emma Lootz Erving	26
1905:	*Mar* 14	Mabel Foote Weeks	27
	Sep 2	Emma Lootz Erving	28
1906:	*Mar* 14	Estelle Rumbold Kohn	29
	Mar 30	Harriet F. Clark	30

1906:	Apr 22	Hutchins Hapgood	31
	May 10	Mr. and Mrs. Michael Stein	32
	Aug 14	Pitts Duffield	33
	Aug 17	Pablo Picasso and Fernande	36
	Oct 8	Mrs. Michael Stein	37
	Oct 28	Harriet F. Clark	38
1907:	Jan 3	Flora M. Holly	38
	May 11	Lena Lebender	39
	Jun 15	Henri-Pierre Roché	40
1908:	[Jun 13?]	Henri Matisse	40
	Jun [14]	Pablo Picasso	41
	Sep 1	Emma Lootz Erving	41
1909:	Jan 16	The Grafton Press	42
	Apr 9	The Grafton Press	43
	Jun 11	Marian Walker Williams	44
	Jun 23	Etta Cone	45
	Dec 12	Emma Lootz Erving	46
	Dec 19	Emily F. Dawson	47
	Dec 23	Alice Woods Ullman	48
1910:	Jan 4	Hutchins Hapgood	48
	Jan 28	Florence Blood	49
	May 25	William James	50
	Nov 30	Alice Woods Ullman	51
1911:	[Apr?]	Mabel Dodge	52
	[Jun?]	Mabel Dodge	53
	Sep 27	Grant Richards	53
	[Fall?]	Mabel Dodge	54
1912:	Feb 6	Henri-Pierre Roché	55
	Feb 26	Alfred Stieglitz	57
	[Mar 16]	Henri Matisse	58
	Apr 19	A. C. Fifield	58
	Jun 4	Mildred Aldrich	59
	Jun 24	Mabel Dodge	60
	Aug 12	Leo Stein	62
	Aug 29	Leo Stein	63
	[Fall]	Marsden Hartley	64

1912:	[Nov]	Mabel Dodge	65
	Nov 23	Bernard Berenson	66
	Dec 12	Mabel Foote Weeks	67
	Dec 22	Constance Fletcher	68
1913:	Jan 7	H. G. Wells	69
	[Jan?]	Marsden Hartley	70
	Jan 24	Mabel Dodge	70
	Jan 27	Frank Palmer	73
	Jan 29	The English Review	73
	Feb 13	Mabel Dodge	74
	Feb 26	Logan Pearsall Smith	75
	Feb [i.e. Mar] 5	Roger Fry	76
	Apr 1	Arnold Rönnebeck	77
	[Apr?]	Mildred Aldrich	77
	[Apr?]	Mildred Aldrich	78
	Apr 30	Alvin Langdon Coburn	78
	[May?]	Mabel Dodge	79
	[May?]	Florence Blood	79
	Jun 11	Florence Blood	80
	Jun 21	Florence Blood	80
	[Jul 1]	Bernard Berenson	81
	Aug 23	Alvin Langdon Coburn	82
	Aug 28	Henry McBride	82
	Sep 3	Henri Matisse	84
	[Oct]	Marsden Hartley	84
	Oct 17	Daniel-Henry Kahnweiler	86
	Nov 3	Alfred Stieglitz	87
	Dec 6	Arnold Rönnebeck	88
	[Dec 10?]	Marsden Hartley	89
1914:	Jan 16	Marsden Hartley	90
	[Jan?]	Leo Stein	91
	Jan 24	Oliver St.John Gogarty	92
	Jan 25	Claribel Cone	93
	Feb	Duncan Grant	94
	Feb 17	Duncan Grant	95

1914: *Feb* 18   Donald Evans   95
      [*Mar*] 29   Mabel Dodge   96
      Jul 4   Carl Van Vechten   97
      Jul 28   Alvin Langdon Coburn   98
      Jul 28   Alvin Langdon Coburn   98
      Jul 28   Mildred Aldrich   99
      Jul 29   Alfred North Whitehead   100

III. THE FIRST WORLD WAR
(*August* 1914–1918)

1914: *Aug* 8   Mildred Aldrich   101
      Sep 16   Mildred Aldrich   103
      Oct 26   Juan Gris   104
1915: *Jan* 3   Michael Brenner   105
      Jan 21   Carl Van Vechten   105
      Feb 12   Michael Stein   106
      [*Feb* 26]   Maud Cruttwell   107
      Mar 11   Carl Van Vechten   108
      Mar 23   Mildred Aldrich   109
      Jul 23   Florence Blood   109
      Dec 9   Pablo Picasso   110
1916: *Feb* 4   Michael Brenner   111
      Feb 15   Michael Brenner   112
      Sep 14   Howard Gans   113
1917: *Feb* 28   Harry Phelan Gibb   114
      Apr   Carl Van Vechten   116
      Jun 18   Howard Gans   117
      Oct 8   Leo Stein   119
      Nov 29   American Fund for French Wounded   119
      Dec 24   Lucie Leglaye   120
      Dec 26   W. G. Rogers   121
1918: *Jan* 7   Henry McBride   123
      Jan 12   Abel Leglaye   124
      Apr 12   Michael Stein   125

1918: *May* 16   William Cook   127
       May 29   Abel Leglaye   127
       [*Spring?*]   Samuel L. M. Barlow   128

IV. THE EARLY TWENTIES (1919–1925)

1919: *Oct* 25   The Atlantic Monthly   129
       [*Nov*] 25   Katherine S. Dreier   130
       Dec 4   The Atlantic Monthly   130
       Dec 14   Leo Stein   131
1920: *Apr*   Harry Phelan Gibb   132
       Apr 10   Henri-Pierre Roché   133
       Apr 15   Erik Satie   133
       Sep 6   John Lane   134
       Sep 26   Israel Zangwill   135
       Sep 30   Frank Swinnerton   135
       Oct 6   Israel Zangwill   136
       Nov 13   Henry McBride   137
1921: *Jan* 25   Jacques Lipchitz   138
       [*June?*]   Sylvia Beach   138
       Jul 14   Mira Edgerly-Korzybska   139
       [*Jul* 14]   Count Alfred Korzybski   140
       [*Summer?*]   Robert McAlmon   141
       Aug 9   Alfred Kreymborg   142
       Dec 3   Sherwood Anderson   142
1922: *Jan* 5   The Four Seas Company   143
       [*Feb?*]   Sherwood Anderson   144
       Mar 13   Sherwood Anderson   145
       Apr 1   William Cook   145
       June 5   Harold Loeb   146
       Aug 23   Juan Gris   147
       Sep 1   Mildred Aldrich   148
       Sep 11   Jo Davidson   149
       [*Oct?*]   Kate Buss   149
       Oct 6   American Fund for French Wounded   150
1923: *Feb* 22   Carl Van Vechten   151

1923: [Early?]   Mabel Dodge Sterne   152
      [Spring]   Sherwood Anderson   152
      Apr 16   Carl Van Vechten   153
      May 9   Sherwood Anderson   155
      June 5   Carl Van Vechten   156
      Oct 22   Carl Van Vechten   157
1924: Feb 10   Alfred M. Maurer   158
      Feb 17   Ernest Hemingway   159
      Mar 5   Carl Van Vechten   160
      [July?]   Jane Heap   161
      [Aug?]   Robert McAlmon   162
      Aug 9   Ernest Hemingway   163
      Aug 15   Ernest Hemingway   164
      Sep 18   Ford Madox Ford   165
      Oct 10   Ernest Hemingway   166
      Dec 3   Janet Scudder   168
      Dec 8   Mildred Aldrich   168
1925: Jan 8   The London Mercury   169
      Jan 30   The London Mercury   169
      [Feb?]   Robert McAlmon   170
      Feb 22   Jane Heap   170
      Mar 2   Glenway Wescott   171
      Apr 18   Carl Van Vechten   171
      Apr 21   T. S. Eliot   172
      [Spring]   Samuel L. M. Barlow   173
      June   F. Scott Fitzgerald   174
      June 6   Daniel-Henry Kahnweiler   175
      June 9   Robert M. Coates   176
      June 18   Daniel-Henry Kahnweiler   177
      July 4   Daniel-Henry Kahnweiler   177
      July 5   Harry Phelan Gibb   178
      [July?]   Sherwood Anderson   179
      Aug 1   Carl Van Vechten   179
      Aug 23   Man Ray   180
      Aug 24   Mildred Aldrich   181
      Oct 7   Mabel Dodge Luhan   181

1925: *Oct* 29   Harry Phelan Gibb   182
      Dec 27   Marsden Hartley   183

V. THE LATE TWENTIES (1926–1930)

1926: *Jan* 1   Edith Sitwell   184
      Mar 4   Harold Acton   186
      Mar 18   Pavel Tchelitchew   187
      Mar 26   Jane Heap   188
      [*Spring*]   Robert McAlmon   189
      Apr 15   George Platt Lynes   190
      Apr 25   Sherwood Anderson   191
      May 23   Sherwood Anderson   192
      May 25   Bernard Faÿ   193
      Jun 11   Leonard Woolf   193
      Jun 12   T. S. Eliot   194
      Jun 22   Gerald Duckworth & Co.   194
      July 2   Gerald Duckworth & Co.   195
      July 6   Avery Hopwood   195
      July 13   The Dial   196
      Oct 10   Nora Holt   197
      [*Oct*]   René Crevel   197
      Nov 20   Geoffrey Gorer   198
      Nov 30   Joseph Brewer   199
      Dec 16   Natalie Clifford Barney   200
      [*Dec* 27]   Bravig Imbs   201
      Dec 28   Juan, Georges, and Josette Gris   202
1927: *Feb* 9   Daniel Raffel   203
      Feb 18   John Lane The Bodley Head Ltd.   203
      Apr 2   Pavel Tchelitchew   204
      Apr 25   Edith Sitwell   205
      May 11   Daniel-Henry Kahnweiler   206
      May 17   Daniel-Henry Kahnweiler   206
      [*May* 25]   Avery Hopwood   207
      [*Jun* 16]   Fania Marinoff Van Vechten   207
      [*Jun* 20]   Fania Marinoff Van Vechten   208

1927:	Jun 24	Kenneth Macpherson	208
	Aug 8	Winifred Bryher	209
	Aug 19	The Atlantic Monthly	210
	[Fall?]	Sherwood Anderson	211
	[Nov 25]	Bravig Imbs	212
	Dec 1	Daniel-Henry Kahnweiler	213
	Dec 14	Mildred Aldrich	214
	Dec 25	Mildred Aldrich	215
1928:	Feb 1	Nella Larsen	216
	Feb 17	Joseph Brewer	216
	Mar 9	George Platt Lynes	217
	Apr 3	Harold Acton	218
	May 6	Pavel Tchelitchew	219
	Jun 14	Pavel Tchelitchew	220
	Jun 28	Marian Walker Williams	223
	Jul 13	Pavel Tchelitchew	223
	Jul 19	Virgil Thomson	225
	Aug 11	Alyse Gregory	226
	Dec 25	Ford Madox Ford	226
1929:	Jan 15	Sherwood Anderson	226
	Jan 31	Hart Crane	227
	[Feb 18?]	Carl Van Vechten	228
	Feb 26	Virgil Thomson	229
	Mar 27	Charles Henri Ford	230
	May 1	Stuart Davis	231
	May 24	Georges Hugnet	231
	Jun 1	Stuart Davis	232
	[Summer]	Christian Bérard	233
	Jun 25	Bravig Imbs	234
	Jul 29	Bernard Faÿ	235
	[Late Summer]	René Crevel	237
	Oct 1	Eugène Berman	238
	Nov 12	William Cook	239
1930:	Jan 21	Marian Walker Williams	240
	Jan 24	Robert Coates	241

1930: [Jan? 29] Marsden Hartley 242
July 9 Georges Hugnet 243
Nov 29 George Platt Lynes 243
Dec 18 Georges Hugnet 244

VI. THE COMING OF FAME (1931–May 1935)

1931: [Jan?] Kate Buss 246
[Jan] Bravig Imbs 247
Feb 25 Robert M. Coates 248
[Spring?] Louis Bromfield 249
Apr 8 Michel Leiris 250
May 20 Paul Frederic Bowles 251
June Henry McBride 252
Nov 10 Aaron Copland 253
1932: Feb 19 John Dewey 254
Feb 25 Lindley Williams Hubbell 254
Feb 26 The Atlantic Monthly 256
Mar 9 Alexander Calder 256
Apr 28 F. Scott Fitzgerald 257
July 8 Charles Henri Ford 257
Aug 31 Bernard Faÿ 258
Nov 13 W. A. Bradley 259
Nov 26 W. A. Bradley 259
1933: Jan 1 Sir Francis Rose 260
Feb 11 The Atlantic Monthly 260
Mar 20 The Atlantic Monthly 261
May 22 Carl Van Vechten 262
July 2 Matilda E. Brown 263
July 20 Francis Picabia 264
Aug 13 Grace Davis Street 264
Aug 20 Katharine Cornell 266
Sep 8 Carl Van Vechten 266
[Sep 16] William Carlos Williams 267
[Fall?] Maud Hunt Squire 268
Sep 19 Max Ewing 269

1933: Oct 7   Lincoln Kirstein   269
       Oct 27   Henry McBride   270
       Dec 6   Virgil Thomson   271
1934: Jan 2   Carl Van Vechten   272
       Jan 9   W. G. Rogers   273
       [Feb?]   Sir Francis Rose   274
       Feb 8   Carl Van Vechten   275
       [Feb]   Paul Frederic Bowles   276
       Mar 2   Alfred Harcourt   277
       Mar 20   Henry McBride   277
       [May?]   Sir Francis Rose   279
       June 4   W. G. Rogers   280
       Jun 12   Max White   281
       [Jul 10?]   Mrs. Charles Goodspeed   282
       Jul 26   Bennett Cerf   283
       [Summer?]   Donald Sutherland   284
       [Aug?]   Jean Cocteau   285
       Aug 4   Janet Scudder   285
       Aug 31   Julian Sawyer   286
       Sep 2   James Laughlin   287
       Oct 26   Alfred Harcourt   288
       Oct 31   Dorothy Norman   289
       Nov 11   Florine Stettheimer   289
       Nov 15   William Saroyan   290
       Nov 30   Bernard Faÿ   291
       [Dec?]   Carl Van Vechten   292
       Dec 18   Bennett Cerf   293
       Dec 29   F. Scott Fitzgerald   294
1935: Jan 18   Dudley Fitts   295
       Mar 16   Gertrude Atherton   296
       Apr 5   Lloyd Lewis   297
       Apr 6   DuBose Heyward   298
       [Early?]   Joseph W. Alsop, Jr.   298
       Apr 30   Ellen Glasgow   299

VII. THE LATE THIRTIES
(*Summer* 1935–*July* 1939)

1935:	[*Summer?*]	Sir Francis Rose	300
	Jun 21	Frank Case	301
	Jul 19	James Laughlin	302
	Jul 24	Henry Miller	302
	[*Aug*]	Élie Lascaux	303
	Sept 23	Thornton Wilder	303
	Oct 7	Thornton Wilder	305
	Oct 14	Thornton Wilder	306
	[*Dec?*]	Sir Francis Rose	308
	Dec 22	Donald Sutherland	309
1936:	[*Jan* 2]	Wendell Wilcox	310
	Jan 6	Lord Berners	312
	Feb 21	Alfred Harcourt	312
	Mar 1	Lord Berners	313
	Mar 18	Alexander Woollcott	314
	May	Sir Francis Rose	314
	May 7	William Cook	316
	Jun 26	Lloyd Lewis	317
	July 9	Samuel Steward	318
	Aug 7	William Cook	319
	Nov 16	Lord Berners	320
1937:	*Feb* 9	Lord Berners	321
	Feb 21	Lloyd Lewis	321
	Feb 28	Max White	322
	May 3	Sir Osbert Sitwell	323
	Jun 22	Carl Van Vechten	324
1938:	*Jan* 4	Mrs. Charles Goodspeed	325
	Jan 30	Max White	326
	Mar 27	William Cook	327
	Apr 3	Janet Scudder	328
	May 15	Jacques Lipchitz	329
	May 17	Lord Berners	330
	Aug 4	Bennett Cerf	330

1938:	Dec 2	Carl Van Vechten	332
	[Dec 25]	Alexander Woollcott	333
1939:	Jan 5	Sir Kenneth Clark	334
	May 14	Carl Van Vechten	335
	[June]	Thornton Wilder	336
	Jun 14	Max Jacob	337
	Jun 15	B. T. Batsford Ltd.	338
	[Jun 18–		
	20]	Thornton Wilder	338
	Jul 17	Alfred Barr	340

VIII. WORLD WAR II AND AFTER
(*August*, 1939–1946)

1939:	Aug 16	Clare Boothe Luce	341
	Oct 16	Janet Flanner	344
	Oct 17	Bennett Cerf	344
	Nov 20	B. T. Batsford Ltd.	345
	Dec 3	Lord Berners	346
	Dec 3	Natalie Barney	347
1940:	Feb 6	Bravig Imbs	347
	Mar 1	Robert Haas	348
	Mar 19	Carl Van Vechten	349
	Apr 2	Bennett Cerf	350
	Jul 18	Bernard Faÿ	351
	Jul 30	Kate Buss	352
1941:	Jan 6	Mr. and Mrs. W. G. Rogers	352
	Jan 26	Sherwood Anderson	353
	Jan 31	Natalie Barney	354
	Apr 23	Arnold Rönnebeck	355
	June 5	Lindley Williams Hubbell	355
	Sep 13	Bernard Faÿ	356
	Oct 13	W. G. Rogers	357
	Dec 27	Henri Daniel-Rops	358
	Dec 27	Francis Picabia	359
1942:	Apr 17	Edmund Wilson	359

1942: [Sep]   W. G. Rogers   360
      Sep 9   Mrs. Charles Goodspeed   361
1943: Apr 14   René Tavernier   362
      May 1   Bernard Faÿ   363
      June 23   René Tavernier   363
      Sep 10   Charles de la Fléchère   364
1944: Jan 4   Bernard Faÿ   365
      June 13   René Tavernier   365
      Sep 7   Raymond Escholier   366
      Sep 17   Lieut. Gen. A. M. Patch   367
      Oct 29   Cecil Beaton   368
      Nov 2   Bravig Imbs   369
      Nov 14   Katherine Dudley   370
      Nov 27   Sir Francis Rose   371
      Nov 29   Carl Van Vechten   372
1945: Jan 9   Katharine Cornell   373
      [Feb?]   Carl Van Vechten   374
      Mar 10   The American Ambassador to France   375
      Mar 17   Pfc. John Breon   375
      Mar 27   Bennett Cerf   376
      Apr 2   Robert Haas   377
      Apr 16   Sir Francis Rose   378
      May 27   Richard Wright   379
      Jun 21   Carl Van Vechten   381
      Jun 27   The Ground Forces Replacement Center   382
      [Summer?]   Mrs. Jessie Breon   382
      Jul 16   Donald Sutherland   383
      Jul 19   Sir Francis Rose   384
      Aug 10   Major Gen. F. H. Osborn   385
      Sep 7   Pierre Balmain   386
      Sep 24   Franklin H. Brewer   387
      Oct 15   Bernard Faÿ   388
      Oct 22   John Breon   389
      Oct 27   The Biarritz American University Theater   390
      Oct 30   Headquarters, Chanor Base Section, U.S.
                   Army   391

1945: *Nov 12*   Harold Acton   392
      Nov 19   Carl Van Vechten   393
      [Nov 30]   Joseph A. Barry   394
1946: *[Jan 11]*   Robert Claborne and Lamont Johnson   394
      Feb 14   Robert Claborne   395
      Mar 15   Virgil Thomson   396
      Mar 28   The Hon. Mrs. Reginald Fellowes   397
      Apr 15   Virgil Thomson   397
      Apr 25   Douglas Moore   398
      [Spring?] Louis Bromfield   399
      May 31?   Natalie Barney   400
      [Jul 24]   Lamont Johnson   401

* * * *

      Aug 1   Bernard Faÿ to Alice Toklas   402

INDEX   *follows page*   403

ILLUSTRATIONS

FACING PAGE

Gertrude Stein at about 19 (circa 1893)   4

Gertrude Stein in the Luxembourg Gardens (circa 1903)   26

Alice B. Toklas and Gertrude Stein at 27, rue de Fleurus (1923)   156
     (Photograph by Man Ray)

Gertrude Stein and Basket I at Bilignin (1934)   282
     (Photograph by Carl Van Vechten)

Gertrude Stein at 5, rue Christine (1945)   374
     (Photograph by André Ostier)

The Flowers of Friendship

I. STUDENT DAYS   1895–1902

Gertrude Stein was born on February 3, 1874 in Allegheny, Pennsylvania, of an upper-middle-class family of Jewish stock. Her father and his brother had been successful business partners, but they quarreled shortly after Gertrude Stein was born and her father took his family to Europe. They went first to Vienna, staying there about three years, then to Paris for a year, and finally returned to America. After a short visit in Baltimore, the family went West and settled in Oakland, California. There Gertrude Stein lived and attended the public schools until she was about seventeen. First her mother and then her father having died, she, her sister Bertha, and her brother Leo went East to Baltimore to stay with their mother's family. Leo went off to Harvard, and after a winter in Baltimore, Gertrude Stein entered Radcliffe in the fall of 1893. There she had a very good time as one of a group of Radcliffe women and Harvard men who lived closely and interestingly together. In her sophomore year she took William Vaughn Moody's English 22 and, more significantly, worked under Hugo Münsterberg in the Harvard Psychological Laboratory. There she and a Harvard graduate student, Leon Solomons, worked out some experiments in automatic writing. When the year was over, Professor Münsterberg's students presented him with a set of the writings of James Russell Lowell to show their appreciation before he sailed to spend the summer in his native Germany.

FROM HUGO MÜNSTERBERG

On board SS "Columbia," mid-ocean,
June 10, 1895

My dear Miss Stein:—

You know it is generally my principle to stay to my pro-grammes and a part of my last week's programme in Cam-bridge was to say you good-bye personally and to express my thanks to you. But this time too much came together to stand against the programme—I had to leave Cambridge with-out having seen you and not before today—just in the middle between New York and Hamburg—I can fulfill this most agreeable duty. I thank you for your part in that delightful Lowell-souvenir, I thank you for your generous contribution to the Helmholtz-memorial, but I thank you above all for that model-work you have done in the laboratory and the other courses wherever I met you. My contact with Radcliffe was in every way a most charming part of my Cambridge experi-ences. But while I met there all types and kinds of students, you were to me the ideal student, just as a female student ought to be, and if in later years you look into printed dis-cussions which I have in mind to publish about students in America, I hope you will then pardon me if you recognize some features of my ideal student picture as your own.—I hope to hear about you still often and expect the best from you.

With best regards to your friends, Miss [Adele] Oppen-heimer and Mr. Solomons,

I am very sincerely yours
Hugo Münsterberg

Gertrude Stein's oldest brother Michael, with his wife Sarah ("Sally"), had at the elder Steins' deaths assumed the position of head of the family, and was acting as guardian for Gertrude and for

Gertrude Stein at about 19 (circa 1893)

*Leo. The latter, with his cousin and Harvard classmate Fred Stein,
was traveling abroad as guest and companion of an uncle.*

FROM LEO STEIN

Mena House Hotel, Pyramids, Cairo,
Mar 13, 1896

Dear Gertrude

I've reached a stage of momentary mental collapse. Never
in my life I believe have I felt so completely dulled so intolera-
bly stupid so inanely played out. I'm glad this thing will soon
be over and may the weight of Cheops rest on my recumbent
person if I ever undertake such a job again. I rather thought
I was more completely bore-proof than I have proved to be
but "We have met the enemy and we are his'n." I didn't undertake this expedition with the expectation of finding it a
picnic but I'm afraid my sense of obligation in this case has
carried me beyond my depth. At all events we shall soon be
in Italy and there at least I shall be able to defy the foul
fiends of dullness as well as of all other things. . . .

I was going to speak of your coming to Europe this summer. . . . Now as I wrote to you last summer I know of no
pleasanter way of spending a few months than in traveling
in the low countries with an incidental three or four weeks in
Paris perhaps. If you came over on the Red Star . . . you
would strike Europe at perhaps the most favorable port [Ant-
werp] for getting a really satisfactory impression as well as in
the most delightful town that I have been in yet. From there
we could go through a number of delightful old places,
Bruges, Liége, Mechlin, etc., and then into Holland, with the
Hague, Amsterdam, Rotterdam, Scheveningen and others too
numerous to mention. If we got tired of Dutchland we could
go to Cologne take the steamer up the Rhine to Mainz and
then via Heidelberg or Frankfurt & Strassburg to Rheims &
Paris, stay there until it was time to go home but there the
opportunities are infinite. One thing that you want to attend
to in time though is a letter of credit for £200 which you want

to write to Mike about so that you can attend to the signature business. You'd better let me know as soon as you are certain what your movements will be so that I can convey to you certain other advices & directions concerning the passage Perilous. This morning . . . I climbed the big Pyramid but it was hardly worth the trouble except that it gave you a realizing sense of its size. Well so long

Leo

It was eventually decided that Gertrude and Leo would spend the summer in Italy. But meanwhile there were Radcliffe matters to occupy Gertrude Stein's attention. She was for two years secretary of the Radcliffe Philosophy Club, with the responsibility of securing guest-lecturers. Josiah Royce was Professor of the History of Philosophy at Harvard. George Santayana, Assistant Professor of Philosophy at Harvard, had at this time published his Sonnets, and Other Poems (1894); *his* The Sense of Beauty: Being the Outlines of Aesthetic Theory *appeared in 1896.*

FROM JOSIAH ROYCE

103 Irving St. [Cambridge, Mass.]
Mar 27, 1896

Dear Miss Stein:—

Tuesday is my Seminary evening, and I can therefore give no Tuesday evening before the Examination period. I shall be glad, however, to read to the Philosophy Club of Radcliffe any Thursday evening in May, at 8 o'clock. . . .

As to subject,—I read to the Boston Browning Club, the other day, a paper on "Browning's Theism." I also am preparing a paper, to be read soon at Princeton, on "The Principle of Individuation." The latter is a more technical paper, but is still adapted to a pretty general, if philosophically studious, company, on the problem, "What do we mean when we call any object an Individual?", or "What constitutes Individuality?" This problem is a pretty one, and is of practical interest to people who desire to call their souls their own.

Which one of these papers would you like? I am half disposed to offer you both, in case, upon different evenings, or for different purposes, they could be of any service to your Club, in whose fortunes I always feel a strong interest.

Yours Very Truly
Josiah Royce.

FROM GEORGE SANTAYANA

[Cambridge, Mass., early 1896?]

My dear Miss Stein

Friday evening is perfectly convenient, and you may expect me at 7:45 . . .

If you don't think the subject too vast I should like to talk about 'Faith and Criticism.'

Yours very truly
G Santayana

In the spring of 1896, Gertrude Stein, influenced by William James, decided upon a medical career. An older Radcliffe friend of hers, who had received her degree in 1895, questioned the wisdom of this decision.

FROM MARGARET STERLING SNYDER

Mt. Tabor, N. J.,
Apr 29, 1896

My dear Gertrude:

Your last letter was newsy and nice. It surprised me for I know your tendencies of *good will* to the absent rather than actual *deeds* of scribbling. But keep on as you're doing and I shall set you down as thoroughly constant.

So the summer is Italy. How happy for you to be with a brother of whom you are so fond and proud. I hope it will be unmarred in any way. Undoubtedly you will see as many funny things as beautiful, for you will be looking at the doings of people as well as the art of the galleries.

No I have no intention of trying to teach next year. I should not be strong enough to do so. This of course, has somewhat to do with what you will regard as my lack of enthusiasm concerning your J. Hopkins plan. Will it do you one bit of good as a deterrent if I tell you . . . that I now see I was one of the most deluded and pitiable of all these many young women who are aspiring after what is beyond them in our own day. My dear Gertrude, I have no explanations and no theories; I do not know enough to have. But I will say in a word that a sheltered life, domestic tastes, maternity, and faith are all I could ask for myself or you or the great mass of womankind. I overworked and overreached—too much ambition, too little faith in traditional ideals. A "career" is the last thing on earth from my desires. Now this I say not to preach to you—you are headstrong as I was and will probably have to work it out for yourself—but that when you begin possibly to waver in "being a useful member of society" in the way you have outlined you may recall my experience and my affectionate advice.

Of course everybody wants you to be useful. I frankly tell you Gertrude I doubt your fitness for what you propose. I could give you detailed reasons from what I know of your temperament and tastes and what I know of myself. It is not my purpose or place to do so. If you go through happily I shall rejoice of course. If you chose a less ambitious way to be useful I should think you more prudent. . . .

Give my love to all who are so kind . . . I shall spend the summer here.

Bon Voyage—

Yours affectionately
Margaret S. S.

FROM MICHAEL STEIN

San Francisco, Cal.,
June 2, 1896

Dear Gert.

It is now June 2nd and you had better let me know just when you are going to start and where you are going *to* so I can get your letter of credit for you. Also let me know at once what drafts you want for use before starting. Also see that all your & Leo's bills (room rent etc.) are settled before you go, so as to have everything in ship-shape. . . .

So long

Your aff Bro
Mike

At Easter, the members of his Radcliffe class had presented an azalea tree to William James, Professor of Psychology at Harvard, and at the end of this her junior year, Gertrude Stein and her classmates joined in a further gesture of appreciation to Professor James, whose seminar they had been taking. It was he who, according to Gertrude Stein, was "the important person" in her Radcliffe life.

FROM WILLIAM JAMES

[Cambridge, Mass.]
June 19, 1896

Dear Miss Stein

Your friends are too good; and their number overwhelms me, so I bow my head and accept with hearty thanks their offerings.

Gratefully yours
Wm. James

*One of the Harvard young men who shared her passion for music
wrote to Gertrude Stein just as she was about to sail with Leo for
Italy.*

FROM LEO V. FRIEDMAN

23 Irving St., Cambridge, Mass.,
June 29, 1896

Dear Gertrude,

I write to tell you good-by for somehow I could not do it
while you were here—and to wish that you may have a happy
trip. Weeks ago I felt how lonesome it would be here without
you and I hope you will return early in the fall with Leo, who
ought to be persuaded to come to the symphonies with us
next year. Good-by—God bless you

Leo.

*Leon Solomons did not return to Harvard in the fall, chiefly for
reasons of health. The report of the experiments that he and Gertrude Stein had carried on was published under the title "Normal
Motor Automatism" in the* Harvard Psychological Review *for
September 1896. A note at the foot of the first page explained that
the report was "From the Harvard Psychological Laboratory."*

FROM LEON SOLOMONS

2632 Haste St., Berkeley,
Oct 26 [1896]

My Dear Gertrude—

Was very glad to hear from you and hope you are the
same. Your brother [Michael] was apparently deeply injured
and I gave him the letter to read. Whereat he was more injured and said you never wrote him anything about your work,
and that that was what he liked to hear about. I was about to
suggest that perhaps it was because you so seldom had any

work to write about, but desisted for fear you might take it as an insult. . . .

I hope you have not given up the work on fatigue. It's a big subject, but you might as well try it as anyone else. . . . As soon as you let me know what plan you and the powers that be have decided upon, I will send on my suggestions.

Next Day—The reprints of our article have just arrived. How is it there are only nine? Did you only send me that many thinking that would be all I would want, or didn't you get the proper number? We ought to have received twenty-five. By the way has it struck you the Harvard Psych Lab has a way of getting between its inmates and the world which is indelicate to say the least? . . . To call a piece of research work done by a student who pays for the privilege of working in a particular laboratory, a contribution from that laboratory as though the *lab.* had *hired* the man to do the work, is misleading to say the least. Not the least of the advantages I will gain by working out here this year, is the privilege of appearing in the psychological world in propria persona, instead of in shadow behind the Harvard Curtain. Give my best regards to Finnie, and write soon.

Sincerely
Leon

The news of the article spread to Oakland and, through one of the teachers, to a former schoolmate of Gertrude Stein's at the Oakland High School.

FROM MATILDA E. BROWN

566 Caledonia Ave., Oakland,
Dec 6, 1896

My dear Gertrude;

If such a person still be in existence! . . . Not a word have I heard from you all these years and had it not been for Miss Wertz, who stopped me on the street yesterday and told me that she had been informed regarding your whereabouts and the wondrous fame you were earning as an all round literary-scientific critic and genius, the embodiment of wisdom etc., etc., I should have had no hopes of ever knowing anything concerning my old time friend.

Now, won't you condescend to just drop me a line or so? I shall feel so proud to be able to say "I have heard from wonderful Gertrude Stein." Let me know all about yourself—are you still *Miss* or *Mrs*? . . .

Goodbye—this is well meant even if you consider it a great liberty. How are Leo & Bertha?

Adoringly
Tillie E. Brown.

FROM MRS. MICHAEL STEIN

[San Francisco] Jan 20 [1897]

Dear Gertrude,

There is no reason in the world why I do not write more but that I have nothing to write about. Things are just about as they always were except for the baby and he is too kaleidoscopic to be put down coldly in black on white. . . .

It's too bad about Leo. I hope he's on his feet again—I did not know that he had been miserable ever since his return.

What do you mean by "going to keep house and nurse him according to all the latest medical school theories." Are you going to Johns Hopkins, or Harvard Medical School, or New York, or where? Mike and I feel quite hurt that Leon Solomons seems to know all your plans but we are in pitchy darkness. . . .

Give my love to Leo, also two of these photographs. I hope to hear from you very soon—

As ever,
Sally.

Francis Pollak had graduated from Harvard in 1896, and had entered the Columbia Law School.

FROM FRANCIS POLLAK

Summit, Mar 13, 1897

My dear Gertrude,

. . . Many thanks for the letter and the books and the inscription . . .

All in all law has been getting more interesting, mainly because I have been getting to know some of it. The sense of learning isolated facts by rote wears off when you know enough of them to make a frame to fit others in. . . .

Have you seen by the way that [William] James has out a book of essays in "Popular Philosophy," headed by the one on the "Will to Believe." I don't know what else is in the collection, but I should think that it would probably make some sensation as the first philosophic defense of Balfourianism by an American scientist of note; or I suppose for that matter, by any scientist of note. It will be interesting to see the handling it gets in the reviews. The "Will to Believe" deserves respectful treatment, if for nothing else, for the emphasis on the distinction between the ideals of the "Attainment of Truth" and the "Avoidance of Error." . . .

I haven't time for more, or news either, so Adios till June, (the Adios is by the way meant only to apply to oral conversation; I hope to write before then) and don't let the five laboratory courses weigh upon your soul.

Yours
Francis.

✳

Gertrude Stein had decided to enter Johns Hopkins Medical School in the fall, and was planning to take a summer course in embryology at the University of Chicago before she continued on to California to visit her brother and his wife in San Francisco.

FROM MRS. MICHAEL STEIN

[San Francisco] June 12, 1897

Dear Gertrude,

Mike has been intending to answer your letter ever since its arrival, but as that is as far as he will probably get for some time to come, I shall assume the responsibility myself. . . .

There certainly is nothing in the line of happiness to compare with that which a mother derives from the contemplation of her first-born and even the agony which she endures from the moment of its birth does not seem to mar it, therefore my dear and beloved sister in law go and get married, for there is nothing in this whole wide world like babies—Leo to the contrary, notwithstanding.

Well to proceed to business, Mike is very sorry that the course you contemplate taking will prevent your coming out here in the first week of July and thus taking advantage of the very great reduction made to the Christian Endeavorers.

He also wishes that you could make up your minds to board with Bachrachs or some other congenial people, while in Baltimore as he can't quite see who will run the house when you are at college and Leo reading, and he particularly wonders at your investing in house-furnishings before you are sure that you will enjoy house-keeping. If you feel it necessary to go house-keeping alone, can't you rent a furnished flat?

Of course, you know how glad we will be to see you and how anxious we are to have you see our dear little boy, but four weeks does seem a short time after coming a long distance and spending so much cash. Your financial condition after the August allowance, which you will need to pay for your course of study, will be about $300.00 on hand with $150— on Sept 1st from Mk't Str 5%s. and $300— on Oct 1st from Omnibus 6%s; then nothing until Jan 10th. again. . . .

With love to Leo, as ever,

Sally.

In the fall of 1897, Gertrude and Leo Stein took a house in Baltimore and engaged as housekeeper an elderly German woman named Lena Lebender. Gertrude, at Johns Hopkins, completed the report of her own Radcliffe experiments in cultivated motor automatism and sent it for criticism to Professor Münsterberg, and to Leon Solomons, who had returned to his studies at Harvard.

FROM LEON SOLOMONS

Cambridge, Dec [1897]

My Dear Gertrude

Your pathetic appeal at hand. Notwithstanding its obvious inaccuracies it was moving. . . . I had no intention of neglecting you, but have not written simply because I did not have your address, and always forgot to get it. Last Sunday I really did remember to get it, and have been intending to write all week—on things in general and your article for the Review in particular.

To begin then with the article . . . My general comment is that you ought to be ashamed of yourself for the careless manner in which you have written it up. I think the work is good, and well worth publishing, though if you were here in the laboratory and continuing, I would advise waiting until you had carried the investigation further. The trouble with the article as it stands is that one has to hunt around too much to find the important points,—it is as bewildering as a detailed map of a large country on a small scale. What it needs is relief, perspective. You must make perfectly clear to yourself just what you regard as the essentials of the work, and devote all your energies to bringing them out. As it is one is apt to miss the essentials in irrelevant or at least less important details. . . . Don't be afraid of leaving things out. It is the essence of good writing frequently, and art is as essential in the presentation of scientific material as elsewhere. In short don't emulate our friends the Germans, but be a little French. Of course the article as it stands is as good as most of the stuff that is published, but that of course does not mean anything to you, you want what you write to be a good deal better, and it ought. There, with your kind permission I will now drop the role of instructor in English composition, and resume that of interesting invalid. . . .

I am able to work fairly well, and though I cannot do the "study" that I would like, and which I rather expected to do, still I can go ahead with my original work, and that is what I care most about. . . . It is supper time and this letter is quite long enough as it is, so if you want the rest you will have to tell me a whole lot about you and Leo and the university.

Sincerely
Leon.

FROM MARGARET STERLING SNYDER

[Mt. Tabor, N. J., Christmas 1897?]

Dear Gertrude:

Wordsworth doesn't know any more about rich sensations of love for nature than you do. He only puts his in rhyme. Yet he is supposed to be as true a poet of nature as any we have. Well I confess I never knew a woman who knew the warm sun, the hidden stream, the tender green of spring more than you,—and I know a good many women pretty well. As a rule so much sensuous intellectuality as you have is found in men.

Yours always affectionately
Margaret Sterling Snyder.

From Harvard, Arthur Lachman had gone to Ann Arbor, and then to teach at the University of Oregon. His letter is written on paper with the printed heading: University of Oregon, Arthur Lachman, Ph.D., Professor of Chemistry.

FROM ARTHUR LACHMAN

Eugene, Oregon, Mar 13, 1898

My dear Gertrude:

As one of my personal friends, you shall be favored with a sample of my office stationery . . .

I tremble at the job of reading through your last letter, in order to discover its salient features; but friendship such as ours must not shrink or flinch at the call of stern duty. Fortunately, I took the precaution to number the pages in something like consecutive order. . . .

I am very glad to hear that you enjoy your present occupation, and that you revel in bones. . . . I should like to ask you a pile of questions about measles, whooping cough, malaria, mumps, etc., but I guess you haven't had them yet—I mean, in class. . . .

Leon [Solomons] has made up his mind to get his degree this year, an eminently sensible idea. . . .

That's all.

Arthur.

In the summer of 1899, Gertrude Stein had again visited the Michael Steins in San Francisco. Their son Allan was now three years old.

FROM MRS. MICHAEL STEIN

[San Francisco] Aug 27 [1899]

Dear Gertrude,—

. . . I went to hear Prof. [William] James last night, and enjoyed his personality immensely. His English was, also, most elegant; Leon [Solomons] says much finer than usual. Except for a slight halting in his delivery, I should call him a perfect lecturer. I only wish I knew a little philosophy for the time being. . . .

Allan and Mike are at present practising with your gun. I just asked him what I should say to you. This is verbatim: "Tell her that I want her to come here soon again, *very* soon again . . . Tell her that *I* have to tell *you* her stories. And the next time I see her she will tell me more stories—And tell her that I *love* her, and that's all"—If I could only give you an idea of the intensity with which he says *love*, you'd be tickled, you couldn't help it. . . .

With many misgivings I have just dug up the last umbrella plant you experimented on and find it a great success. There are long roots and two new shoots, so I am encouraged to experiment a little on my own hook, now. . . .

Hoping to hear from you soon again,

With love,
Sally.

Gertrude and Leo Stein and Mabel Foote Weeks, who had graduated from Radcliffe in 1894, spent the summer of 1900 in Europe. Gertrude left Mabel and Leo in Paris in September and returned to her studies at Johns Hopkins.

In Florence, Bernard Berenson had already established himself as an authority on Italian painting of the Renaissance.

FROM LEO STEIN

20 Lungarno Acciaioli, Firenze,
Oct 9, 1900

Dear Gertrude

After a long breathing spell I've at last gotten to the stage where I can force myself to attack some paper with a pen. I've been in Florence about a week . . .

I took lunch with Berenson . . . the other day. . . . He has sense there's no doubt about that. He's rather younger than I thought him—only thirty five—but he's been in Florence since he was twenty. His house is filled with beautiful old Italian furniture & hangings & he has a really magnificent art library. . . . He says that almost all recent writers on Italian Art were not only fools but thieves as well, for they take everything that they have from him and almost never acknowledge their indebtedness. . . .

What's your address?

Leo

Leon Solomons died in 1900 as the result of an infection contracted in the laboratory. William James had been appointed Gifford lecturer on natural religion at the University of Edinburgh, and held this appointment, on leave from Harvard, for two years, 1899–1901.

FROM WILLIAM JAMES

Geneva [Switzerland],
Oct 17, 1900

Dear Miss Stein,

Ever since Solomons's untimely and never too much to be regretted death, I have had an impulse to write to you, to express my sorrow to a sympathetic friend . . . I never was more startled by anything, and never was anything outwardly at least more irrational and ascribable to mere chance than such an event. Exactly what he would have done had he lived, it is impossible to say, but it would have been absolutely original and remarkable, absolutely clear, and it might have been very important. Such a mixture of a rather wild independence, with amiability; of a rather contemptuous intellectuality with breadth of sympathy; made of him a very peculiar and extraordinary character. His eagerness, daring, honesty, good spirits, and scorn of all that was nonsensical and mendacious in life were glorious. We shall never look upon his like, and seldom on his equal. . . .

I am sending this off to the J. H. U., imagining you to be there still, but sure of nothing. I hope wherever you may be, that you are well and prospering, and laying up great stores of medical erudition, whilst awaiting the day in which you can convert it into medical skill, a far greater thing. I am rather out of humour with the doctors, having, to please them, just gone through a 3rd course at Nauheim for degenerate heart and general arterial sclerosis, with no result. But my "nerves" are tougher than they were some 10 months ago (when they had acute "prostration" in consequence of the said doctors) and I have hopes of not being wholly laid on the shelf. We go shortly to Italy to pass the winter, as much of it as works, in Rome. Our address here is always care of Brown, Shipley & Co., London, S. W.

Believe me, dear Miss Stein, with warm regards from my wife,

Yours faithfully,
Wm James

Mabel Foote Weeks had gone from France to England and was studying during the winter at Cambridge. Gertrude Stein had sent her a book as souvenir of the summer.

FROM MABEL FOOTE WEEKS

18 Great College St., Westminster, S.W.,
Jan 2, 1901

Dearest Gertrude,

I am a proud and happy person tonight with my new possession. . . .

You spoke of the summer as being particularly fruitful for you. So it was for me, but I don't know whether the fruit is good or bad—anyway it is now bitter in my mouth though perhaps eternally salutary. I mean that I am embarked on interests now, that bear an undecipherable relation to the work I have always considered was mine to do in the world: larger they certainly are, and thank the good Lord, I rejoice in my diviner moments in the better perspective I have got even if it has put my own scope & activities at the wrong end of the opera-glass. It has increased my respect for all there is in the world, but diminished my respect for my own power of getting the best out of it. Now this England for instance, and London especially—I haven't a doubt that it's a mighty fine place, but I can't get at it. I could get more out of one day in London with you, than all five weeks by myself. But this verges on sentiment, which you can't stand, I remember.

The National Gallery is a glory—I am just at present absorbed in the Flemish School, and Rubens in particular. . . . I think his triumphant objectivity, and splendidly intelligent optimism are as tonic as a cold bath, or a walk over the hills. Always prescribe him, Gertrude, for any patients who have nostalgia, to alleviate, if it does not cure. . . .

I want this to go tonight, so no more—I suspect considering the unelastic temper it is enough. I am delighted with the book, but could find it in my heart to wish that you hadn't mentioned Spain. What with Leo's suggesting Greece in the Spring, and you Spain in the Summer, I find the immediate reality of Cambridge rather a come-down.

Always yours,
Mabel.

The first two years at Johns Hopkins had gone very well. Gertrude
Stein had begun some research on the brain tracts under Doctors
Lewellys Barker and Franklin Mall. But in her third and fourth
years she became bored and began to have doubts about the wis-
dom of trying to take her degree. Leo Stein was still in Florence,
and wrote to his sister on her twenty-seventh birthday.

FROM LEO STEIN

[Florence] Feb 3 [1901]

Dear Gertrude,

It rains and the wind is never weary. Florentine weather
can't easily be improved on in the direction of undesirability.
I've been meeting more people of late, lots of queer specimens, in fact one meets hardly any simple minded normal
foreigners that come here to live. Such have sense enough
to stay at home especially as far as the women are concerned. . . . I believe I'm the only American in Florence at
least so the people here tell me. I blow the American trumpet
as though it was the whole of Sousa's band that I had to work
with. Mrs. Berenson however tells me that they have decided
that my Americanism is just a bluff, that I only think that I
think that I'm an American. However I haven't any doubts
about it and believe that if things work out in America during the next fifty years as I thoroughly believe they will I shall
not become less of one even if I never set foot on the continent within that time. . . .

What is all this non-medicated rumble that issues from
your quarter—is it representative of a phase or a general condition? It would be too bad if the first person in the family
who had gone so far as to get the adequate preparation for
anything should go back on it. Well I suppose you won't, especially as there's nothing else to be done. If you had my very

superior talents for loafing it might do but you haven't so it won't. . . .

Adieu
Leo

By the way I had just finished this letter & attached the date when it struck me as singularly familiar and in a moment or two its implications occurred to me. 27, the world's shore moving fast.

LDS

❧

At the end of her fourth year at Johns Hopkins, in 1901, Gertrude Stein failed to receive a passing grade in one of her minor courses. She joined Leo in Florence for the summer and then returned to Baltimore with the idea of continuing her research on the brain tracts, though not of getting a degree. There she lived with a fellow student, Emma Lootz. Marian Walker, another Johns Hopkins friend, had got her degree, had married a doctor, Allen Williams, and was living in Boston ("Bosting"). She writes about various medical books.

FROM MARIAN WALKER WILLIAMS

3 Jay St., Bosting [Dec 1901?]

Dear Gertrude

Did you sell your Dennis? Does Emma . . . want to sell hers? Also have you a Ziegler special in English of which you want to get rid? R. S. V. P. I am in the book buying business. Did you sell Emma your Kelly?

I am delighted about your brain. . . . Am glad you've been to N. Y. Now you can come here at Xmas.

Marriage is an admirable institution. I highly recommend it if accompanied by steady work outside the sphere of home. But don't talk to me about wife & mother & whole end of woman! I wouldn't have believed you capable of it except that you are the victim of moods which at times resemble fixed ideas. . . . Tell Emma if she got married even she might be happy for a while.

Yours
M. W. W.

FROM DR. LEWELLYS BARKER

Chicago Neurological Society,
Jan 30, 1902

Dear Miss Stein:—

I have just gone through your second part with which I was more familiar because I studied these sections more thoroughly than the other set. I do not think that you have included too many drawings from sections. It seems to me that these are necessary in order to give a clear idea to the reader. Do you think that one drawing of the model will suffice? Dr. Mall's advice on that point will be valuable. I think that the photographs of the brains showing the planes of sections should be included, for they will be of special value to any research worker who wishes to identify convolutions. . . .

I think, too, that when all is brought together, you might go over it once with special reference to the literary form. I find that I am helped very much by reading an article through with some friend, who will point out sentences that are not clear, or that are not in the best form. When we are so close to our own work as we necessarily are, points of form will elude us and a second head is an aid.

I am glad you are so soon to get off to Europe. What shall you do over there? Are you to continue work on the nervous system? It would seem a pity not to, now that you have gone so far in this line of work and have so good a back-ground.

I send the manuscript by this mail.

Yours sincerely,
Lewellys F. Barker

II. EUROPE BEFORE THE WAR

1903–JULY 1914

*Gertrude Stein spent the spring and summer of 1902 in Europe
with Leo and then together they settled in England, first in the
Lake District and then at 20 Bloomsbury Square, London. There,
through the Berensons, they met Bertrand Russell and Israel Zangwill, and made other English friends. They had intended to stay
for five or six months, but Gertrude Stein found the atmosphere
depressing and returned alone to pass the winter in New York.
There she lived at "The White House," 100th Street and Riverside Drive, with Mabel Weeks, Estelle Rumbold, and Harriet
Clark. In the spring she joined Leo in Europe. After the summer in
Spain, they returned to Paris together to live permanently on the
Left Bank at 27, rue de Fleurus. There Gertrude Stein began to
write, and her first short novel, entitled simply "Q. E. D." was
completed on October 24, 1903. Meanwhile Emma Lootz had
married a doctor, William Erving.*

FROM EMMA LOOTZ ERVING

15 Haviland St., Boston, Mass.,
Oct 29, 1903

Dear Gertrude,—

Thanks for a letter from gay Paree. I'm glad literatoor
is entrancing, and I am willing to hand over any reason-

able amount if you will do me nicely in a story. I must see the job before I pay, though. I have to be a real interesting heroine. . . .

Here it is November 3d. . . . I haven't heard from those New York girls for ages, and I'm too poor to go to concerts or theatres, so I have no purple thoughts to impart.—Write again, old lady, and give my best to Brother Leo. I hope literature will continue to keep you busy.

With love,
Emma L. Erving.

The Ervings spent the next summer in Italy, where they saw Gertrude and Leo Stein in Florence, and returned to Washington to concentrate on making a success in the medical profession, which Gertrude Stein had abandoned.

922 Seventeenth St., N. W., Washington, D.C.,
Oct 17, 1904

Dearest Gertie,—

If you know now of any quick method of making money I'd like to know about it. We're spending a million dollars a minute and not taking in anything, and it makes me feel lopsided—not to say alarmed. . . . All the old practitioners . . . are cheerfully discouraging and say of course we shall starve very soon and we'd better get out while we are able. . . .

That walk thro' the hill towns was the best I ever did. Cortona & Sienna & Perugia & Assisi & Spoleto—oh goodness! I wish I was back in the sunshine. . . . My love to Leo. I enjoyed those days in Florence a whole lot.

Love to you, old lady,
Emma L. E—

Gertrude Stein in the Luxembourg Gardens (circa 1903)

Leo Stein had become interested in Japanese prints at the time of his visit to Japan in 1896, and had accumulated a good many of them there. From the prints, he and his sister proceeded to the works of the French Impressionists, and began to purchase such paintings as they liked and could afford. When they found a Manet that they wanted to buy, Gertrude Stein wrote to Mabel Weeks about selling in New York the painting by Alexander Schilling, an American artist, for which she had paid six hundred dollars several years before.

FROM MABEL FOOTE WEEKS

100th St. & Riverside Drive,
Mar 14, 1905

Dearest Gertrude,

I've been trying hard to get time and spirit at once for a letter, and now this will be just business. About the picture— I have inquired diligently, and apparently there isn't a chance of selling it before next winter. The sales are about over or would be by the time it got on here. Estelle [Rumbold] thinks that possibly the Blacks of Cleveland might like it, and will talk to them when she goes to Cleveland which will be in a few weeks. Otherwise nothing can be done before next fall, and then if you'll send it on, we'll do what we can. I hope you can get the Manet just the same. I am consumed with eagerness to see your collection. It's too bad the Schilling is so out of it. You did have a real enthusiasm for it once, but that's not to the point. I'd hate to be confronted by all my past enthusiasms, and I fancy Paris makes one grow very fast. . . .

Goodnight, Robert [Kohn] & Estelle are on their way up stairs to play checkers with me—Won't you bet on me please —I've improved.

Yours faithfully,
Mabel.

FROM EMMA LOOTZ ERVING

162 New Bond St., London,
Sep 2, 1905

Dear Gertie,—

Thanks for a letter received in Paris. . . . I went to the studio several times and sat there for quite a while, and you certainly have some lovely stuff. I was enormously interested in it. Unfortunately I went to Durand-Ruel's only once . . . but the time I did go I nearly burst with excitement. The Renoirs are ravishing, and what a lot of things there are there. Your Renoirs are bully, too, and the Cézannes. . . . It's an awfully interesting lot of painting, but it is all so new to me that I can't place it of course. Your Cézanne landscape is all right, and the Delacroix is a beauty. . . . I loved Paris and was sorry enough to leave. Anglo-Saxons kill me. The sun hasn't appeared since we came here, and life is certainly stodgy. But I like the National Gallery, and we are having a good time. . . . I hope you & Leo are flourishing. Gif him my luf —with thanks for the freedom of the studio. . . .

Love to you, old lady,
Emma L— E—

Estelle Rumbold had been one of the occupants of "The White House," in New York in 1902. She was a sculptor, and Gertrude Stein commissioned her to do a small figure as a wedding present for Emma Lootz. When Estelle married Robert Kohn, Gertrude Stein sent her a wedding gift. During that winter 1905–6, Miss Stein had finished writing three stories, to which she gave the collective title "Three Histories."

FROM ESTELLE RUMBOLD KOHN

631 West 152 St. [New York]
Mar 14, 1906

Dear Gertrude:—

It is'ent that I have not written to you many and many a time in my mind and thanked you almost every day . . . for your gift, that I did not get it all written down on paper to send to you—but it is all because I have a work shop such as I used to dream about and I can't get used to it.

I have spent a winter in it and it has lured me away from every thing. . . .

It will not be polite on your part to be surprised when I tell you Emma's marble is practically finished. I am mounting it on a wooden block, and that is not finished but the rest is. I mean to have it photographed and will send you one—good or bad so you can see what you are giving her. . . .

I would so like to take you into the shop and get you to tell me how rotten some of the stuff is. If one only really knew. You never believe anyone when they say your stuff is good and when you are told it's bad, you fight them, and don't believe that either. . . .

Some one told me you were thinking of publishing something. If you are I wonder if you feel like I do when I take the cover off of my work for the last time and let it go away— and if you do Sister I am that sorry for you. . . . You feel so lonely and so foolish for doing so little with what you know some one else could have done so much with. I hope you don't care. . . .

Good bye, with love

from
Estelle

Mabel Weeks and Harriet Clark continued to live at the White House. The Kohns and some other friends had just been there for an evening when Miss Clark wrote to Gertrude Stein.

FROM HARRIET F. CLARK

100 Street and Riverside Drive,
Mar 30, 1906

Dear Gertrude;

. . . We had a pleasant evening with them all here. . . .

We talked much about you and Leo and America with a big A. In fact the Eagle hopped from shoulder to shoulder and we gloried in our crudeness and said how great Art was always produced in the struggling youth of a country, not after it had attained an "atmosphere"; how we relied upon the mighty strength within us to produce great things and looked fearlessly at the bad things outside; and we said many more things and we sighed and agreed that you and Leo would before long see your error and come back. Then we felt better! and pretty soon we went home! . . .

When are you coming for that visit? The White House remembers you and asks after you frequently. . . .

Please remember me to your brother and sister, give my regards to Leo and with much love to yourself,

Faithfully yours
Harriet F. Clark.

Gertrude Stein's three stories, "The Good Anna," "Melanctha," and "The Gentle Lena," had been read and admired by Sarah Stein, and typed by a distant cousin, Etta Cone of Baltimore, then in Paris. Miss Stein finally got courage to send copies of them to the author-journalist Hutchins Hapgood, who, with his wife Neith Boyce (herself an established writer) and their children, was living near Florence and had known the Steins there.

FROM HUTCHINS HAPGOOD

Villa Linda, Via Poggio di Gherardi 2, Settignano,
Apr 22 [1906]

Dear Gertrude—

I have been reading your stories with a very great deal of
interest. In the essentials they seem to me extremely good—
full of reality, truth, unconventionality. I am struck with their
deep humanity, and with the really remarkable way you have
of getting deep into human psychology. In this respect, the
Negro story ["Melanctha"] seemed to me wonderfully strong
and true, a powerful picture of the relations between a man
and a woman and the inevitable causes of their separation.
The characters in all the stories are real and clearly drawn, and
the atmosphere and setting is all in tone. I really feel like com-
plimenting you highly on what is most fundamental in your
work. You have grasped some big things and have been able
to make a picture of them. They show, too, a remarkable sympathy in you. Without that, you could not have done any
work of that kind. The Negro story especially is extraordinary
in this way. It is the very best thing on the subject of the
Negro that I have ever read.

Saying all this, means of course, that in some way you have
done an artistic thing. And yet somehow you have attained
your end without any of the ordinary devices of plot, piquancy,
conversation, variety, drama, etc. Your stories are not easy
reading, for that reason. They lack all the minor qualities of
art,—construction, etc., etc. They often irritate me by the innumerable and often as it seems to me unnecessary repetitions;
by your painstaking but often clumsy phraseology, by what
seems sometimes almost an affectation of style. You may say
you couldn't have attained your effects otherwise—but I think
you could improve them much by cutting and by manipula-
tions in other ways. But that sort of thing must be left to the
author. He knows best what *moyens* he can avail himself of.
The gist of my criticism is: *au fond*, they are excellent—super-

ficially irritating and difficult and I fear to most people un-
attractive.

I fear you will have difficulties with the publishers; partly
for the very idiotic but real reason that they are not the right
length, and partly (and this the most important) because to
get their real quality, patience and culture are demanded of
the reader. . . . I think that . . . you will surely find an ulti-
mate publisher, but it may take you a long time. [Pitts] Duffield is the most likely man to get into the quality of your
work, that I know; and, if he likes it, he is less likely to allow
strictly commercial reasons to interfere with his publishing it,
than many others. I will gladly write him, if you like, and call
his attention to what I think the great excellence of your
work. . . .

Your stories really have a remarkable amount of quality
and they would certainly be successful if publishers and public
were what they ought to be. Perhaps they will be anyway.

Auf Wiedersehen

Hutchins Hapgood

Gertrude Stein wrote Hapgood at once to send the stories to Duf-
field.

Meanwhile the San Francisco earthquake had made it necessary
for the Michael Steins to return abruptly to America to look after
their property in California.

FROM MR. AND MRS. MICHAEL STEIN

2321 Linden [Baltimore],
May 10, 1906

Dear Kids

We got to N. Y. yesterday morning, and . . . here at
5 p.m. and had a glorious reception. We had a good deal
of mail, the most interesting being from Theresa who sees
Mathews every day. Our houses she says are practically all

right; but the chimneys are gone and will have to be rebuilt perhaps all the way down necessitating tearing open the walls to reach them. Mathews had Leiten, the contractor, out with men at once, and covered up the holes that the chimneys made in falling through the roofs so that the rain would not injure the interiors. . . . We telegraphed at once for answers to the questions I asked in my Paris letter, and we will wait here for the replies. I am more and more convinced that we will have to go out there *very* soon. In one of Mrs. Samuels' letters she mentions that we can rent the living room of the flat below hers. Simon [Stein] was burnt out and went to camp in the Hecht house, which had been abandoned, then had to leave that as it was rented for business purposes, and is now on Sutter St. . . . We have been overrun here with people and tonight hold a grand reception. . . .

[Mike]

Dear Gertrude,

The first person we saw after Hortense & Jacob [Moses] was Lena [Lebender] who came here de suite. She's all reconciled to your staying over there & now, & instead of wishing Leo a bad tummy is going to save up to take a trip over to see you. . . .

Much love
Sarah

FROM PITTS DUFFIELD

Duffield & Company, New York,
Aug 14, 1906

Dear Miss Stein:

We have all been reading your Three Histories with lively interest, and I am chagrined to find that quite three months have passed since the manuscript arrived. I know this may seem an unconceivable time to wait . . .

But to report at last:—we hardly see our way clear to making you any offer of publication for "Three Histories." The book is too unconventional, for one thing, and if I may say so, too literary. Where one person would be interested in your application of French methods to American low life, a hundred, ignorant of any sense of literary values, would see only another piece of realism; and realism nowadays doesn't go. This, at any rate, would be our unfavorable prognosis.

To make up for our delay I shall be glad to see that the manuscript is sent to Miss Holly, the literary agent, if you say so. In that case I suggest that you cable to us* the one word "Holly." Our cable address is Fox-field, New York.

Yours very sincerely,
Pitts Duffield

*at our expense [*Duffield's note*]

Gertrude Stein cabled Duffield to turn the manuscript over to Miss Holly.

The story "Melanctha" had been composed while Gertrude Stein walked back and forth between 27, rue de Fleurus and Montmartre, where she posed some eighty times for her portrait by the young Spanish painter Pablo Picasso. She and Leo had bought some of his pictures and had been introduced to the artist himself by their French friend Henri-Pierre Roché, whom Miss Stein called the "general introducer."

Picasso's earliest letters, in a French strongly influenced by Spanish, are addressed to Leo rather than to Gertrude Stein, and it was to Leo that he wrote in August 1906 just after having returned from spending the summer at Gosol in Spain. The picture he was working on was the large composition Peasants and Oxen now in the collection of the Barnes Foundation in Merion, Pennsylvania. Fernande Bellevallée (later Olivier), who was with Picasso then, added a note addressed to Gertrude Stein. Both Pablo and Fernande were devoted to the American newspaper comics, "Little Jimmy" et al., which Gertrude Stein sent them regularly.

FROM PABLO PICASSO AND FERNANDE [TRANSLATED]

[Paris] Aug 17, 1906

My dear friend Stein

I received your letter and the money, thank you.

I worked at Gosol and I am working here. I'll show you all that and talk with you about it when I see you. Each day becomes more difficult and where can one find calm? I am working on a painting of a man with a little girl; they are carrying flowers in a basket, and beside them are two oxen and some wheat—something like this: [*see preceding page*]

My best remembrances to your sister and to you from your friend

Picasso

I doubt that you will be able to work out the meaning of Pablo's letter, but it seems to me best to leave the original as it is, in this more or less fantastic French. I am very much disappointed, *Miss* Gertrude, at not having received *Little Jimmy* at Gosol, but you must know that in Spain one never receives anything which appears useful or interesting to the postal authorities, for in such cases they confiscate everything for their own use.

As for my English!!! pointless to speak of it to you.

Kindest regards
Fernande

It was from the Autumn Salon of 1905 that Gertrude and Leo Stein purchased their first Matisse, the Femme au Chapeau. *The Michael Steins already owned several pictures by this artist, and they had left most of them with Leo and Gertrude in May, taking three small ones with them to the United States. One of these was the controversial portrait of Mme Matisse of 1905, which the Steins called variously "The Green Line" or "Woman with a Green Nose."*

FROM MRS. MICHAEL STEIN

San Francisco, Oct 8, 1906

My dear Gertrude:—

. . . I have had a pretty hot time with some of the artists
. . . You see, Mikey sprang the Matisses on one just for fun,
& since the startling news that there was such stuff in town
has been communicated, I have been a very popular lady; it
has not always been what Albert Meyer used to call "pleasant."

Oh, Albert Bender has been our most faithful & devoted
—as always . . . but his devotion hardly stood the test of the
'femme au nez vert.' . . . Upon his demand, I assured him
that perhaps he'd better spare himself this test, as I knew his
belief in my infallibility was something very dear to him.
"No," he said, "I shall *never, never, never* say, as others have,
that you are crazy." Well—he saw it—for two minutes he was
speechless—then he meekly inquired—"But don't *you* think
you're crazy?" . . .

Have been called to the telephone six times during this
effort—six more invitations, accepted 'em all—going morning,
noon, afternoon, evening, night—it's rather amusing—and I
do love to show my clothes; they always create such a sensation!

And, oh, the slang. Gertrude, it's great.—I don't understand most of it;—but when I do, I wonder—as I do at most
everything. . . .

Good-bye,
Sarah

In 1905 and 1906 Matisse had painted a large decoration, the Bon-
heur de Vivre, which, after its exhibition in the Salon of 1906, Leo
and Gertrude Stein hung for him in their atelier at 27, rue de
Fleurus. In the collection then taking shape, the etchings that
Gertrude Stein had purchased in her earlier days in the United
States seemed to have little place.

FROM HARRIET F. CLARK

100 Street and Riverside Drive,
Oct 28, 1906

My dear Gertrude,

. . . I really didn't neglect the etchings and am awfully sorry that up to date only two, the Zorn and Hayden, have been sold. The enclosed draft represents them. The whole collection has been to every dealer in town but no one will buy them as they are not the popular things. . . . I shall be glad to keep charge of them if you wish it or to try to dispose of any others for you at any time, only really, it is only decent to let a fellow know what you want, or at least paid for things —otherwise one is simply at the mercy of the dealer . . .

With much love
Harriet F Clark

Miss Holly was meanwhile having difficulty with Gertrude Stein's stories.

FROM FLORA M. HOLLY

156 Fifth Avenue, New York,
Jan 3, 1907

Dear Miss Stein:—

I have been delayed in writing you because I have been having trouble with my eyes, and all reading was forbidden for a number of weeks. I have at last gone over your manuscript, but it was very difficult to decipher it as the typewriting is so faint. I doubt very much if I could find a publisher who would consider these three stories for book publication. They seem to me to be more character sketches than anything else, while the characters themselves would not appeal to a large audience. I suppose you know that a publisher wants to feel sure that a book will sell from three to five thousand copies before he cares to undertake it for publication. On the other hand, these stories, if taken separately would be too long for magazine pub-

lication. Miss Roseboro' is still with McClure's, and I will
send the manuscript over there as you suggest, and if she is
not interested I will notify you at once in order that you may
advise me as to the further disposal of the material.

Very sincerely yours,
F. M. Holly

FROM LENA LEBENDER

Baltimore, May 11, 1907

Dear Miss Gertrude,

I wrote you a long time ago, did not [have] any answer. I
do not know if you received it or not. I received your beautiful present, and value it very highly. I felt very much disappointed when Mrs. [Michael] Stein told me you had decided
not to return to this country as I would love dearly to be with
you. My health is not very good. I have to go twice a week to
the Doctor, my head troubles me very much. I still have my
little home, try to do the best I can but have a hard struggle
at times—but still it is my own little home. Mrs. Stein told
me she would let me know when she would go abroad again
and I crocheted you a pair of bedroom slippers to take over.
One day in market I met Mrs. [Bertha Stein] Raffel. She told
me Mrs. Stein had [been] gone over a month. I met Mrs.
Moses last week; she promised to let me know if any one is
going over there so I could send them. How is Mr. Leo, is he
still busy painting? He promised to paint my portrait when
he returns but I am afraid I will be an old woman before he
returns. I hope you will soon write me a long letter, you have
no idea how much I would like to see both of you. Miss Gertrude I will bid you both good bye. . . . Give my love to Mr.
and Mrs. Stein and the young gentleman.

Yours Respectfully
Lena Lebender.

Jack & Rags send love.

The stories were being shown to other friends in Paris, among them Henri-Pierre Roché, who had introduced Leo Stein to Picasso.

FROM HENRI-PIERRE ROCHÉ [TRANSLATED]

[Paris] June 15, 1907

I have read—very slowly—the story of Melanctha Herbert, and Jeff and the others.

I like the broad narrative manner and the great simplicity of style. I was often surprised by the unity of simplicity that you maintain naturally in the characters and yet give nuances and complexities.

I have certainly never read anything like it. The effect is strong, direct, and one feels oneself very near your humanity. And it is also refreshing, like something natural and new.

There were indeed moments when I felt worn out and bored—when I found that the fine narrative sweep became chaotic—when I wanted to shut the mouth of such and such a character with my fist so that he could no longer talk like that—but later on I became naïve again and in accord with the story.

You have found your mode of expression very well. I shall be eager to see what you are writing now.

[*Unsigned*]

Henri Matisse sent a post-card from Dieppe.

FROM HENRI MATISSE [TRANSLATED]

[Dieppe-Rouen, June 13? 1908]

Solitude is to the spirit what diet is to the body. (Vauvenargues)

Solitude in a charming place, gentle in color and freshness, and from which I send you my regards.

H Matisse

FROM PABLO PICASSO [TRANSLATED]

Paris, Sunday, June [14], 1908

My dear friends

Every day I've wanted to write you and don't think ill of me if I haven't written, for I've been working very hard for some time. The big picture is coming along but what effort it costs and along with it I am painting other things. I am happy and fairly calm. . . .

All the Independents have left for the south; we are alone here. Fernande and I see only the Champs de Mars painters.

At the end of the month I shall go to see your brother [Michael] because I very much need help.

Greetings to you both and all my friendship

Picasso

The Ervings were spending the summer in Norway.

FROM EMMA LOOTZ ERVING

Bergen, Sep 1, 1908

Dear Gertie,—

You might think it about time I was writing to you perhaps. To say that I have been absorbed this summer is to put it mildly. You see I hadn't been here for nine years and I had a lot of back time to make up—and the result of it all is somewhat dismaying for I discover that I so hopelessly belong over here that it almost makes me sick to think of going and living in America again. . . .

Now my happy days are over and we go back to work. I

think that mental equilibrium I wrote you about may have
been due to the fact that I finally got really interested in my
work. If I get more work I hope the state of mind will return.
Curious how as we grow older we discover the truth of all the
foolish platitudes that we have heard since we were infants.
Work really is the answer to a good deal. It's the damned emotions that ruin us females. . . . Tell me what you are doing,
Gertie, & give my love to the family.

Love from
Emma L— E.

*Viola Roseboro' of McClure's Magazine had not been interested
in Gertrude Stein's stories, and the manuscript was sent to Mabel
Weeks. Miss Weeks did her best to find a publisher, but was
obliged finally to turn the stories over to another friend, Mrs.
Charles Knoblauch. Mrs. Knoblauch took the manuscript to the
Grafton Press, a firm that specialized in private printings, and
there the stories were at last to be published—at their author's
expense.*

FROM THE GRAFTON PRESS

New York, Jan 16, 1909

Dear Madam:—

We are sending you under separate cover two sets of gal-
ley proofs of your book. . . . My proof-readers report that
there are some pretty bad slips in grammar, probably caused
in the type-writing. I think, either you ought to go over these
yourself very carefully correcting them all or else allow us to
have some one do it here. We would make the charge, of
course, as little as possible . . .

It just occurs to us that perhaps you might have this editorial work done in Paris and if so would refer you to Mr.
Alvin F. Sanborn, 61 Rue Lepic, Paris. He is an expert editor
and has done a great deal of extremely satisfactory work for
us. If you would like to have the work done under your own

eyes, and of course, this would be the proper way, you can not do any better than to ask Mr. Sanborn's help. He is extremely reliable in everything that he undertakes.

Yours very truly,
F. H. Hitchcock

Gertrude Stein made no effort to get in touch with Mr. Sanborn, but he went to 27, rue de Fleurus one day to see her, only to be told quite emphatically that the stories were to be printed exactly as Miss Stein had written them. She did, however, accept some suggestions made by Mr. Hitchcock: when the book appeared early in the fall, its title was Three Lives: Stories of the Good Anna, Melanctha, and the Gentle Lena; *and though there was no intro-duction, the dust-wrapper quoted Mrs. Hapgood (Neith Boyce) and her husband.*

New York, Apr 9, 1909

Dear Madam:—

Owing to my having been out of town a good deal lately I have only this week been able to read through all your proofs. After I had done this I asked Mrs. Knoblauch if she would not come and talk the matter over with me. She was kind enough to do this and I think now I understand your position in the matter. The corrections will be made exactly as you have marked them. It does not seem to me that you need any fur-ther proofs but if you wish them we will send them to you.

In regard to the title I want to suggest "Three Lives" as being much more descriptive for what you have written. I would prefer not to use "Three Histories" for two reasons. The first that it is much too formal and the second that I do not want it to get confused with my real historical publica-tions. Mrs. Knoblauch liked "Three Lives" and I hope you will also.

As the sub-title I would suggest "Stories of The Good Anna, Melanctha, and The Good Lena." With these titles I can make an attractive title page and the words exactly describe what is in the book, which is in my opinion a very desirable feature in the title of a book. . . .

I suggested to Mrs. Knoblauch that it would help the book a good deal if we came out openly and stated your ideas and why you have written the book in the way you have. She thought that perhaps Mrs. Hapgood would be willing to write such an introduction if you are willing to have it. A name like . . . Mrs. Hapgood's . . . perhaps better known hereabouts than yours . . . would go a great deal towards arresting the attention of the casual examiner of the volume and causing him or her to sit down and read it. . . .

I want to say frankly that I think you have written a very peculiar book and it will be a hard thing to make people take it seriously, but I want to assure you that I shall do all I can under the circumstances to please you and Mrs. Knoblauch in the matter.

Yours very truly,
F. H. Hitchcock

FROM MARIAN WALKER WILLIAMS

748 Asylum Ave., Hartford, Conn.,
June 11, 1909

My dear Gertrude—

I am so devoured with envy of that reprobate of a Mabel [Weeks] who is calmly sailing over the summer seas on her way to visit you that there seems nothing for it but that I should sit down and tell you about it. Why is it not you who are sailing homeward instead? What is the use, pray, of my going on producing a fine baby every two years on purpose for you to play with, if you don't come home and play with them? You haven't an objet d'art in your whole collection that can [come] up to either of them—but perhaps you are so behind the times that you didn't know that we had two. . . .

By the way, in an idle moment I read the book on sex [Weininger's *Sex & Character*] which you said exactly embodied your views—the one by the Viennese lunatic. It struck me that you made a mistake in your statement—it was evidently before not after he wrote the book that he went insane. We had a considerable amount of fun, however, in calculating the percentage of male and female in our various friends according to his classification. But he was really a very half-baked individual. . . .

How's Leo? And how is his painting? Am more than anxious to see your book when it comes out. Let me know as soon as it is on the market. . . . Allen would send his love if he knew I was writing. As ever—

Marian W. W.

Miss Etta Cone and her sister Dr. Claribel Cone of Baltimore were in Paris, and it occurred to Gertrude Stein that Etta Cone, having made the first typed copy of the manuscript, might be willing to help finance the publication of Three Lives.

FROM ETTA CONE

[Paris] Monday, June 23, 1909

My dear Gertrude,

I do indeed appreciate your kind thought of me in realizing my personal pride and interest in your "Three Lives."

I simply have to face the truth and that is, that I am seriously considering putting all I can spare of what I have left of my income in a Renoir painting. This, with other expenses somewhat heavier than usual are handicapping me a bit this year. . . . We have engagements for Tuesday evening & regret extremely that we cannot come to you. Perhaps one day next week or the latter part of this.

Yours as always
Etta

※

*Even without Etta Cone's financial assistance, Gertrude Stein con-
tinued with her plans to publish* Three Lives, *and the first copies
were placed on sale in September 1909.*

FROM EMMA LOOTZ ERVING

922 Farragut Square, Washington, D. C.,
Dec 12, 1909

Dear Gertie,—

It seems to be about the time of year when I write letters
to people, and I have meant to write to you for a long time
anyhow. I had a bully visit from Mabel [Weeks] at Thanksgiving and we had considerable conversation about your book
—also the one she has in manuscript. Mother read Three Lives
& she says "Gertrude Stein has a great gift, if she is willing to
use self control and not despise her readers. I am very much
impressed. Nobody could have told Lena [Lebender]'s life
better." . . . Your theory of form, or expression or whatever,
has a sort of gruesome fascination—and gives finally, perhaps,
the effect you want to give—but I don't believe it is the right
thing yet. You have something to say all right, Gertie, tho' I
don't agree with much of it. In Melanctha I get so balled up
with my own observation of the drama that I am incapable
of seeing it straight, but I'm powerful interested in the work-
ing-out of your theory. . . . I'm reading Henry James with
great enthusiasm—in that new [New York] edition that he has
personally so immensely supervised. I like book people vastly
better than world people. The life of the average Washington
woman makes my blood curdle. Bless you, Gertie, and my
love to Leo.

Yours,
Emma L— E—

To help publicize Three Lives *in England, Gertrude Stein had four copies of the book sent to her friend Emily Dawson in London, requesting her to see that they got to certain well-known British authors.*

FROM EMILY F. DAWSON

39, Cheyne Court, Chelsea, S. W.,
Dec 19, 1909

Dearest Gertrude—

I'm very *nearly* lost to shame but still my Conscience did give an uncomfortable squawk when your card came! Yes, I did have the books, four of them from the N. Y. publishers, and yet I'm still waiting waiting to find the best way of sending 'em to Wells & Shaw & Galsworthy & Arnold Bennett! Oh, Gertrude, thou'rt right, the Anglo-Saxon is a curious beast, for I've loaned the copies thee gave me to 4 or 5 very critical, very discriminating & clever English friends from whom I wanted special introduction letters to the 4 Olympians above-mentioned. But though every one of my friends has admired the stories & has labelled you a genius & a Creator & all sorts of things all my hints avail nothing so far as sending the volumes on to the real big people is concerned. . . . Right after Xmas, I shall send them myself with a letter of my own . . . I wish I could see you—& forgive me all my muddlesomeness . . . for I'm ever your very loving

E. F. D.

Alice Woods Ullman, an American writer and hostess, had been to see Gertrude Stein with the Infanta Eulalia of Spain, and had recommended Romeike as the best press-clipping agency. In her comments on the pictures, she refers to a nude by Félix Vallotton,

*to Matisse, and to Picasso. Alice Toklas had early this year come
to share the apartment at 27, rue de Fleurus with Gertrude and
Leo Stein.*

FROM ALICE WOODS ULLMAN

1, Rue Chernoviz, Passy,
Dec 23, 1909

Dear Miss Stein,

This was the most satisfactory establishment that I had to
deal with. As nearly as I can remember their terms are five
dollars for 100 reviews. We had a very nice time chez vous
yesterday. HRH finds you are *delightful*, all of you, but your
pictures 'horrors!' She was very amusing on the subject of the
pictures. Extraordinary woman. She took me to the Cassa-
Mirandas after we left you. They are a great collection of
Monticellis, Bouchers, etc. What a world Paris is!

I was personally much interested in the pictures you have,
though unconvinced. I like the nude on the white sheet, and I
saw the colour in the Matisse things, but the Spaniard's things
mmm—I'm sure I do not at all know what. But pictures aside,
it was a great pleasure to see you & your brother again & I hope
you'll let me come again. What a beautiful young woman you
have stopping with you! . . .

Yours ever,
Alice Woods Ullman.

FROM HUTCHINS HAPGOOD

Short Hills, New Jersey,
Jan 4 [1910]

Dear Gertrude—

I have been intending to write you for a long time past
. . .

I don't believe your publishers have done at all well by
your book. I did not know that it was published until long

after it appeared. . . . I have seen no reviews and no advertisements. . . .

I wish I could drop in now at 27 Rue de Fleurus and have
a long chat with you & Leo. I can't even begin to tell you about
my present inside existence. It would take me a long time to
hitch it on to my spiritually far-distant Paris & Italy state.
Many things, some important, have happened to me since I
saw you—you would, with your sympathetic understanding,
notice the effect of them—but I cannot convey it in a letter.

With Love to you both

Hutch.

Miss Florence Blood occupied the Villa Gamberaia in Florence.

FROM FLORENCE BLOOD

Sachino par Bidart (Basses Pyrenées),

Jan 28, 1910

Dear Miss Stein—

I am delighted to hear that you are to spend part of the
summer at Fiesole. I shall be back in Florence in the early
spring & expect to remain till December. I was driven away
from Gamberaia by the death of my beautiful beloved dog.
It may sound sentimental but I could not remain there any
longer without him. I hope to go to Paris soon, & look forward
to seeing you with much pleasure. . . .

Remember me very kindly to your brother & with best regards for yourself,

Believe me

Sincerely yours

Florence Blood

William James had of course received from Gertrude Stein a copy of Three Lives, *followed by a letter and a volume of Charles Péguy. James had become emeritus from Harvard in 1907, and in 1908 had lectured on philosophy at Oxford. He died just three months after the following letter was written.*

FROM WILLIAM JAMES

Bad-Nauheim, May 25, 1910

Dear Miss Stein,

Your letter has been forwarded to me here, while the Péguy volume doubtless waits for me at home. I will surely read it on my return.—I passed a week at Paris 10 days ago, and thought of you and your brother a good deal. I should have sought a meeting had I known of your address. My circulatory organs have been running down very fast during the past year and a half, and I am in hopes that the course of baths which I have begun here, may arrest the progress in the wrong direction, even if it doesn't cause time to roll backward in its flight & restore its youthful elasticity to my aorta. "Youth's a stuff will not endure."

I have had a bad conscience about "Three Lives." You know (?) how hard it is for me to read novels. Well, I read 30 or 40 pages, and said "this is a fine new kind of realism—Gertrude Stein is great! I will go at it carefully when just the right mood comes." But apparently the right mood never came. I thought I had put the book in my trunk, to finish over here, but I don't find it on unpacking. I promise you that it shall be read *some* time! You see what a swine I am to have pearls cast before him! As a rule reading fiction is as hard to me as trying to hit a target by hurling feathers at it. I need *resistance*, to cerebrate!

How is the wonderful Matisse and his associates? Does he continue to *wear*? My wife and I will probably return to England through Paris by the middle of July, and if so we shall

certainly look you up. My address is simply Bad-Nauheim
until the end of June, after that "c/o Coutts & Co., London"
will be safer.

I hope that you are well—I warrant you to be sufficiently
happy! Please give my cordial regards to your brother, & believe me, dear Miss Stein, yours always faithfully

Wm James

Having finished writing Three Lives *in 1906, Gertrude Stein had
begun immediately a long series of studies for her monumental
"history of a family,"* The Making of Americans. *By 1910, the
manuscript had almost reached completion, and parts of it were
already being shown to friends.*

FROM ALICE WOODS ULLMAN

1, Rue Chernoviz, Passy,
Nov 30, 1910

Dear Gertrude,

. . . I'm bowled over with your book: it's the biggest conception imaginable but, dear girl, you are making for 'lonesomeness'! Of course it's going to be the finest thing there is
to gain, that lonesomeness. And you'll have with you *the few.*
It is beautiful: and, if that were reasonable, I'd have more than
ever for you of admiration. Do you mind if I read it very
slowly? I am enjoying it so at a snail's pace, reading & re-read-
ing as I go. If you are in a hurry to have it back I'll go faster,
but I hope you aren't!

Yours ever,
Alice Ullman.

*Mabel Dodge had met the Steins in Florence where she and her
husband Edwin owned the Villa Curonia. On a visit to Paris, Mrs.
Dodge had been taken to Gertrude Stein's by Mildred Aldrich,*

and had carried away part of the manuscript of The Making of Americans *to read.*

FROM MABEL DODGE

Villa Curonia [Arcetri, Apr? 1911]

Dear Miss Stein—

You must have been expecting to hear from me because you have been so much in my mind of late. When I left you in Paris I had to go . . . [to] Nice . . . then on arriving here I was ill with neuralgia & toothache, so that only these last days have I been able to plunge into your MSS. To me it is one of the most remarkable things I have ever read. There are things hammered out of consciousness into black & white that have never been expressed before—so far as I know. States of being put into words the "noumenon" captured—as few have done it. To name a thing is practically to create it & this is what your work is—real creation. It is almost frightening to come up against reality in language in this way. I always get—as I told you—the shivers when I read your things. And your palette is such a simple one—the primary colors in word painting & you express every shade known & unknown with them. It is as new & strange & big as the post-impressionists in their way &, I am perfectly convinced, it is the forerunner of a whole epoch of new form & expression. It is very morally constructive for I feel it will alter reality as we have known it, & help us to get at Truth instead of away from it as "literature" so sadly often does.

One cannot read you & still go on cherishing the consistent illusions one has built up about oneself & others.—

Well, anyway, all that I may say of it is inadequate. I feel awfully strongly about it. I've not yet quite finished it. May I keep it a few days & then send it? I will be so glad to see you when you come. Let me know when you are here. Bring some more of it with you, will you?

Always sincerely yours, with the *greatest* admiration.—

Mabel Dodge

Shortly after her arrival in Florence for the summer, Gertrude Stein had tea at the Villa Curonia, where Constance Fletcher, the playwright, was a guest.

> Villa Curonia, Via delle Piazzole, Arcetri
> [June? 1911]

Dear Miss Stein—

I want to send you a few words to tell you how much you were appreciated the other day. *Why* are there not more *real* people like you in the world? Or are there & one doesn't attract them? Miss Fletcher & I both felt as though we had been drinking champagne all the afternoon . . . You said so many significant things that everything everyone else said sounded trivial & insincere! I am *so* sorry that I am going away so that we can't have more talks together, but please don't forget me & let me see you sometimes in Paris.

I am *longing* for your book to get born! It will probably be a moral earthquake to me, as the other was quite a shock.

I hope you'll have a nice summer—

> Sincerely yours,
> Mabel Dodge

Gertrude Stein hoped that Three Lives *could be published in England, and she sent a copy to Mrs. Grant Richards with the suggestion that if her husband was not interested in publishing that, there were unpublished manuscripts available.*

FROM GRANT RICHARDS

> 7, Carlton Street, Regent Street, S.W.,
> Sep 27, 1911

Dear Miss Stein,

The book that you were kind enough to send to my wife with the idea that we should publish it I have read with great interest. I fear, however, that it would not have much chance of success in England. The fact that it is made up of three stories is, unfortunately, a great barrier to its popularity. For some reason, with which I have no sympathy, libraries and booksellers in this country will do nothing to help collections of short stories or a book that contains more than one story. Moreover, there is the question of scene and atmosphere, both in this case so very American that the ordinary English reader would be a little at a loss. The work has interested me and I should be very glad if you would let me see both the "volume of short things" of which you write as being finished (in spite of the prejudice that I have mentioned above) and also the long book that will be finished in a few months.

Believe me, dear Miss Stein,

Very faithfully yours,
Grant Richards

❦

Mabel Dodge reported on events at St. Moritz. Bernard Berenson and Charles Loeser—whose Cézannes were among the first that the Steins saw—had quarreled many years before.

FROM MABEL DODGE

Palace Hotel, Maloja, Sunday
[Fall? 1911]

Dear Miss Stein—

I suppose you are back again in Paris & hard at work—are you? I cannot resist sending you a "line" to tell you of the remarkable dénouement at which I assisted yesterday! We had driven over to St. Moritz for lunch in company with Loeser, & as we drove thro' the town whom should we see but "B. B." who saw *us* but didn't catch sight of our companion! He hailed us & ran after the carriage, so Edwin & I tried to stop it & hop out in time to speak to him before he caught up to it & so avoid an unpleasant encounter! But the carriage was slow in stopping & B. B. swift in arriving & presently there he was at our carriage step directly in front of Loeser whom he *only* then noticed. I shivered for what would happen! To my amazement he pulled off his hat & put out his hand & said "How are you Loeser," & they *shook hands!* Then we had some talk together—he all trembling & *quite* pale—& then drove off. "The first time in fifteen years," said Loeser meditatively! . . .

Aff. yrs.
Mabel D.

H.-P. Roché, who had been enthusiastic about Three Lives, *wrote frankly about some of the later writing (probably portraits) that Gertrude Stein had given him to read.*

FROM HENRI-PIERRE ROCHÉ

[Paris] Feb 6, 1912

Dear Miss Stein,

The other day you told me about this girl at Vendôme's Tea Room.—Was she an actress?—No. Not even that.—It was a good story. I had a good laugh. Then, suddenly, you say it again, shorter, but the same.—You spoil my laugh. I ask myself: "Why does she say it again? Is it for me as evident in her writings as in her sayings that repetition is bad?"

I get home, read one of your writings, & answer "yes" to myself.

I re-read that writing. I altogether some times love it, and things in it. "– – – – it is a diamond mine?—but all the work of digging, finding, cleaning, polishing the stones remains to be done—too much sand is left."

I get angry with you to spoil it for me by those d – – – repetitions, by so many words duplicate. Many repetitions have great purpose and efficiency, but they have a sea of sisters, which I think, have perceivable meaning for nobody but you.

I start reading your style only when I feel very strong &
want in a way to suffer.—After a few minutes I am giddy, then
sea-sick, though there are islands to be seen.—It is no river,
no sea, c'est une inondation l'hiver dans la campagne.

More and more your style gets solitary—the vision remains
great, and the glory of some occasional pages.—Rhythm? oh
yes. But that sort of rhythm is intoxicating for you—it is something like – – – – –

Quantity! Quantity! Is thy name woman?

Of course it is very enjoyable to let oneself go & write
heaps—but – – – Why don't you finish, correct, re-write ten
times the same chaotic material till it has its very shape worthy
of its fullness? A condensation of 60 to 90% would often do?

Do you know any one, (human not literary) who, without
knowing you, or the models of your portraits, or both, has
understood something in them?

Melanctha is great in my memory. I was quite at home
with her, though I had already some toil. I thought your style
would concentrate, it has enormously expanded.

The last things stand upon the strength of your personality. Far from your eyes, they fall to pieces.

Your own right faith in yourself shakes other people's
doubts about your ways of expression—they probably do not
tell them much in front of you?

Are not you after all very lazy?

With frankness, humility and perhaps huge stupidity

Yours very sincerely

H P Roché

*Mrs. Knoblauch had continued her efforts to find a publisher for
Gertrude Stein's work and turned to Alfred Stieglitz, who, with
his Photo-Secession Gallery at 291 Fifth Avenue, had already established himself as a willing champion of new ideas in art and
literature.*

FROM ALFRED STIEGLITZ

291 Fifth Ave, New York,
Feb 26, 1912

My dear Miss Stein:

Your friend has undoubtedly written you that she has placed your MSS on Matisse and Picasso in my hands. They interest me hugely and I feel as if I would like to publish them. I am not in business, and therefore cannot afford to pay for the privilege, should you be willing to extend it to me. My idea would be to have a few Picasso's and a few Matisse's reproduced as illustrations to accompany your text, and to publish text and pictures in a special number of Camera Work, the official organ of the Photo Secession. Naturally I'd let you have 100 or 200 copies for yourself so that you could use them as you see fit. I intend putting a price on the publication which I hope will cover the costs of printing, binding and mailing. Should there be a surplus, which I doubt for I have never experienced such a thing with any of my attempts in the publishing line, it will naturally be divided equally between you and the Secession. You may also rest assured that I shall be exceeding careful in the proof-reading as I realize the special significance of extreme care in this instance. You have undoubtedly succeeded in expressing Matisse and Picasso in words, for me at least. It is for that reason that I am desirous of sharing my pleasure with others.

With kindest regards to yourself and to your brother.

Yours sincerely,
Alfred Stieglitz.

Matisse sent a post-card from Tangier—a view of Soco Chico, showing the Café des Postes and the Hôtel de l'Univers.

FROM HENRI MATISSE [TRANSLATED]

[Tangier, Morocco, Mar 16, 1912]

I send you the most Parisian corner of Tangier, as well as our greetings. The weather has been fine for three weeks and I have taken advantage of it to work: painting is always a very difficult thing for me—it's always a struggle—is that natural? Yes, but why so much trouble? It is so fine when it comes easily. Regards to Leo when you write to him.

Your devoted
H Matisse

❧

Someone had suggested Fifield in London as a possible publisher for some of Gertrude Stein's advanced writing. His reply was written in a burlesque of her style.

FROM A. C. FIFIELD

13, Clifford's Inn, London, E. C.,
Apr 19, 1912

Dear Madam,

I am only one, only one, only one. Only one being, one at the same time. Not two, not three, only one. Only one life to live, only sixty minutes in one hour. Only one pair of eyes. Only one brain. Only one being. Being only one, having only one pair of eyes, having only one time, having only one life, I cannot read your M.S. three or four times. Not even one time. Only one look, only one look is enough. Hardly one copy would sell here. Hardly one. Hardly one.

Many thanks. I am returning the M.S. by registered post. Only one M.S. by one post.

Sincerely yours,
A. C. Fifield

❧

*Gertrude Stein and Alice Toklas left Paris that spring for Spain.
There they received a letter from their American friend Mildred
Aldrich, who had been living for several years in Paris.*

FROM MILDRED ALDRICH

23, Rue Boissonade, XIV, June 4, 1912

Dear girls:

I never meant to let so long go by without writing you a
decent letter, but, as usual, I have been bothered & tormented
by all sorts of nagging little disappointments. I must be very
wicked if there is any truth in "No rest for the wicked" or is
it the "weary"? All the same I have followed you along your
route—Burgos, Avila, Valladolid to Madrid & envied you every
moment. Your card of Goya's "Family" of poor Charles IV
came this morning. . . . Théophile Gautier said of the family
group that it looked "like a grocer's family that had won the
big lottery prize." . . .

Mabel Dodge is in town and is coming to tea Friday afternoon. I do wish that you could be here too.—I had a long, most
amusing letter from Harriet [Levy], still at Mt Carmel. Her
description of that resort of all geniuses was amusing and Will
Irwin, who was here last week, added delightfully to it when
I met him Wednesday night at a little dinner Mrs Fiske gave
at Foyot's. Perhaps you, Gertrude, know who Irwin is? He is
a great friend of the [Hutchins] Hapgoods & has done some
bully work in Collier's. You would both have liked him. It was
his first visit to these parts. He is from San Francisco & we
call him "Young Lochinvar" because he "came out of the
west," & conquered New York—just rode away with it as Scott's
hero did with the lady so fair. He can tell stories better than
I can. Ha, ha! . . . Well, this is all you'll have time to read.
Even this seems taking too much time from the imbibing of
culture. . . .

Love to you both
Mildred

Oh, during the museum concours here, "Pentecost" the English choral societies sang in the Place Hôtel de Ville & of course sang "God Save the King" among other things. It was printed on the programs "God *Shave* the King." Isn't that altogether lovely—every way? How the late Edward would have enjoyed it.

In Florence at the Villa Curonia, there was, as usual, hardly a dull moment.

FROM MABEL DODGE

Florence, June 24 [1912]

Dear Gertrude,

I am missing you very much. How much nicer it would be if you were here. We are having an exceptional time just now, & you would love it. We have been having a *great deal* of "spook." The Jo Davidsons are here, Florence Bradley an American actress, Mary Foote a portrait painter, & a tutor—(football player of 22). All these people have been haunted by our ghost. And I not at all. I almost believe I have hypnotised the whole lot of them. It has been screamingly funny. They have seen, heard & felt all sorts of things. . . . Before sleeping the other night they all saw, in the hall, a large brass platter reel from side to side on the table & make an awful clatter. I had to read the *Bible* to them all to quiet them down. We wanted to read the Sermon on the Mount & no one knew where to find it, so Davidson opened it to read a chapter au hasard, & of course it was all about persecution of the jews & he was still more frightened & thought the spook was in that too. The chapter ended up by a description of adultery which was *really* irrelevant. Then they went to bed, two Davidsons & the tutor, in beds they had pulled on to my terrace. I was waked up in an hour, in my room just inside, by screams &

weeping & I heard Davidson saying "My God! My God! I can't stand this." I got up & went out & found that really their bed had been lifted up & down under them, while their candle was still lighted & he was reading & another clattering of metal like the brass platter made sounding just by the bed. I've *never* seen people so petrified! He was nearly out of his head. He said he *had* to get out of the house, & yet he dared not go to his room & dress! I said we'd all go with him! I felt he had to be saved! I had tried making them all three (the tutor was just as scared!) do deep-breathing exercises out there but it did no good. So we all solemnly marched into his room (the knob of his door came off in his hand which only added more terror!) & the tutor held up a large bath towel & Mr. D. hastily clothed himself behind it. Then *he* accompanied the tutor while *he* dressed & they went out, Davidson having kissed his wife passionately goodby & left her behind with the spook & me & Miss Bradley. These two *both* got into my bed & we three lay like saints on tombs perfectly straight out, there was so little room, until morning, no one sleeping a wink.

The next day I had a priest come & spend a night in the "haunted room" to see what *he* would do. He read prayers till five & saw nothing but said he thought he'd better perform the service of exorcism the next night. So he came with a porridge bowl of Holy water & an olive branch & we made a pageant thro' all the rooms while he exorcised & blessed all over. Miss Bradley laughed with nerves during it which scared her so she said she was going to sleep down on the loggia. Friendship & all that were quite forgotten! With all those newly blessed beds to sleep in no one offered to accompany her. We all went to bed, but at 2— she came hastily up, for the spook, driven out of the upstairs rooms, had gone down to the loggia & groaned twice *just beside her*! No more sleep that night for anyone except *me* who had locked my door! At dinner last night Mrs. Davidson suddenly left the table & dashed into the garden. We paid no attention but she came back soon & had hysterics saying someone behind her chair had pushed her out

of the room. A general panic ensued, which resulted in the
two Davidsons & Miss Bradley leaving in hot haste *for Rome*
on the 11.20 last eve. So there we are. That's what happens
when you come to the Villa Curonia for a good rest & vacation!

Of Florence the news is slight. . . . Loeser is laid up, in
his villa, with varicose veins . . . Miss Fletcher is in Venice,
the [Paul] Drapers are in London, [Arthur] Acton is as Acton-
ish as ever . . . I took all my party to Miss Blood's last Sunday which rather flustered her. She cannot easily handle large
masses of mixed humans. She gave us tea & said "Now do go
& see all the garden & then come back & say goodby!" . . .
The Berensons have left. I am well & happy & can't get enough
sun. Write *yr* news.

Love,
Mabel

FROM LEO STEIN

Florence, Aug 12, 1912

Dear Gertrude,

Last night I dined at the Dodges' and met Loeser there.
He was perfectly amiable and our conversation was exactly
what it has always been. What pictures had I bought recently
etc. etc. . . . Today Miss Blood took me to see the Berensons' garden. She takes a wicked delight in showing it to people, and it certainly is the most vulgar beastly horror that can
be imagined. Everything's bad in design and carried out with
an utter lack of taste & sensitiveness. . . . Miss Blood whose
favorite occupation is making fun of the taste and artistic
sensibility of the great connoisseurs is going to take me to see
Loeser's villa on Thursday. She says it is not as bad as B. B.'s
but that it's bad enough to be worth showing. Also Loeser
took her copy of Fabbri's Cézanne with the row of trees for

the original & after having admired it & congratulated her on having it said and now let me see your copy. . . .

So long
Leo

❧

Gertrude Stein and Alice Toklas returned to Paris from Spain at the end of August and found that a new Renoir had appeared on the walls.

Florence, Aug 29, 1912

Dear Gertrude

I've received your letter from Paris. That Renoir head which is as fine as of them there be happened to be at Bernheim's (I had previously seen it at Hessel's). The price was exactly the same as I had paid for the 2 landscapes. As I didn't care much for the smaller landscape I told the Bernheims that I'd give them the little landscape for the same price as I'd paid for it & the other half of the money. They said yes & so it was. . . . I'm afraid you don't look very sharply. All the Renoirs & Cézannes, the Manet & Daumier have been cleaned & varnished. I never had seen what the Cézanne landscape was like until it was cleaned. The light yellows & the sky have become something entirely different. I suppose you got that letter that I wrote you about that Hessel exchange proposition on Cézannes. If not ask Mike about it so that you don't make a break if you should meet Hessel. . . .

Miss Blood is going to America this winter. Loeser is to be married . . . Otherwise there is no news that I know of. I had a marvellous moonlight auto ride with the Dodges a few days ago & with Miss Blood & family to Firenzuola, but I prefer either horseback or foot as a means of traveling. Autos are all right if you want to go somewhere or if you want speed for its own sake but I don't want to get anywhere in particular & in the country I don't find any need of rapid motion, so I've had enough; I'm going to take to my legs again.

So long
Leo

FROM MARSDEN HARTLEY

18, rue Moulin de Beurre
[Paris, Fall, 1912]

Dear Miss Stein,

I write to ask if I might have the privilege of again seeing the paintings you have which I enjoyed seeing in the Spring before you left for Spain. It is possible that you are not prepared for your usual Saturday evenings or you may have given them up—in which case if it were agreeable to you—any time at all would be most agreeable to myself. A German sculptor [Arnold Rönnebeck] an intimate friend quite longs for the privilege—might he be included? I did not get to see the albums of Picasso drawings the one hour I was there and this you were kind enough to offer me for a time in the fall. I hope by this time you have received a copy of the special number of Camera Work of Alfred Stieglitz from the Photo-Secession of New York where, as one of the few young painters struggling toward individual expression, I have twice exhibited. It seems to me a very worthy presentation of your interpretation of the two artists concerned. I think your articles very interesting. They seem to get as close to the subjects in hand as words can go.

May I then be bold and ask for this real favor, for myself and for my friend who finds Picasso as impressive as I myself do?

I thank you in advance for the same and await your disposal.

Sincerely yours
Marsden Hartley.

You may remember me best as a friend of [Lee] Simonson's who went to your place with Carlock.

During the early autumn, Gertrude Stein had spent a few days at the Villa Curonia, and while there had written a portrait of her hostess. Mabel Dodge had had this printed locally, bound in Florentine paper, and circulated among her friends.

FROM MABEL DODGE

Villa Curonia, Via delle Piazzole, Arcetri
[Nov 1912]

Dearest Gertrude—

I must snatch a lucid moment when "argument is clear" to tell you that I consider the "Portrait" to be a master-piece of success from my (& your) point of view *as* a portrait of *me as* I am to others! When I repeat to you some of the comments you will see that their application to *me* is absolutely perfect. I keep still & let people talk. What they see in *it* is what, I consider, they see in me. No more no less. . . . My English friend Mrs. Napier (to whom Kipling dedicated "Plain Tales from the Hills" as "The wittiest woman in India") writes "it is bold effrontery to do this sort of thing" (*If* she knew *me*!!!) Others say (as they would of me! they know *so little* they *are* saying it of me!) "there is no beauty in it." Someone else says "would not one of the only five or six (literary) forms have done to express this in?" . . . Muriel [Draper] who is here & who makes me feel more like *mush* & seems to me more like a dogbiscuit herself than ever says "Ducie Haweis & I wanted to wire from London 'We understand *the cover*(!) We *know* that' "—

Someone else says "it is all a confusion—things do not seem to follow each other out of each other" . . . No one (but me!) can remember a line in it to quote without referring to it! In fact it is so faithful a portrait as, I think, to produce about the same effects as myself were the truth always said! I think it better & better as time goes on & they say more & more things. Some days I don't understand it, but some days I don't understand things in myself, past or about to come! When I tell people that my "precious coherence" is in it they roar never having perceived any in me! When I say it seems to me "middleclass, confused, & rather sound," Edwin laughs with contempt at my daring to even mention the word "sound" in connection with myself not to mention *it*!

Good by—best love—
Mabel.

The copies of Camera Work *for August 1912, which Stieglitz had sent, at last arrived in Paris, and Gertrude Stein began to distribute them.*

FROM BERNARD BERENSON

I Tatti, Settignano (Florence),
Nov 23, 1912

Dear Gertrude Stein—

My cordial thanks for the pamphlet full of extraordinarily fine reproductions of Matisse's & Picasso's. In a moment of perfect peace when I feel my best I shall try again to see whether I can puzzle out the intention of some of Picasso's designs.

As for your own prose I find it vastly more obscure still. It beats me hollow, & makes me dizzy to boot. So do some of the Picasso's by the way. But I'll try try again.

We are having a beautiful autumn, & I am doing a bit of work, & a great deal of looking at pictures, books, & some reading. Our visitors are gone, & we are quite alone, & indeed I hope we shall be till spring. Oh, I forgot, Santayana is coming next week.

My love to Leo.

Very sincerely yours
B. Berenson

Both Camera Work *and the* Portrait of Mabel Dodge *went to Mabel Weeks in New York.*

FROM MABEL FOOTE WEEKS

Barnard College, Columbia University, New York,
Dec 12, 1912

Dearest Gertrude,

For two weeks and more I've been trying desperately hard to write to you, and now if only no one invades my office hour, I shall manage it. Thank you so very much for sending me your things. I had already bought the magazine, and May [Knoblauch] had lent me the Portrait, but I will send my copy of the Matisse & Picasso to Harriet [Clark] who is pining for stimulation in the Middle West though she apparently has everything else that heart could desire. The Portrait I am very glad to own though I should be disingenuous if I said I either understand or enjoy it. It puzzles me because in it you seem to have gone back on the principles that have guided you in your other writing and that were bringing you to such a point of success. For the other things do seem very successful. The Matisse more than the Picasso to the mind of one who really knows nothing about either. But in the Portrait you seem to be doing something entirely different, and I feel rather sad because it evidently marks your taking of a path in which I can't follow you. I shall, I suppose, have to adopt Leo's course and simply not read you, and considering the pleasure I've had in reading you in the past I am naturally cast down. This isn't criticism, I admit; only a definition of limitation. I'm long past trying to make myself over and I'd have to, to enjoy the Portrait I am afraid. . . .

To get my precious copy of your Matisse and Picasso, I had to have an interview with Stieglitz. . . . I suspect him of something of a pose in his interest in the new things, because he is so pitifully eager to shock people with them. When he found that I knew the work of Matisse & of you, at least to the extent of not being in the least shocked, his face fell ludicrously and he lost all interest. What he dotes on is a chance to harangue some astounded soul. . . . However I really am grateful for without him we shouldn't have the few chances we have to see these things. . . .

Ever yours,
Mamie Weeks.

The number of Camera Work *continued to create a stir in Italy.*

FROM CONSTANCE FLETCHER

Palazzo Capello, Rio Marin, Venice,
Dec 22 [1912]

I must tell you, dear Gertrude, about your book. Incidentally, I, too, can *see* the Picassos. Some of them are more Egyptian than Egypt. A dozen cubes—& the result is something august. . . . But Matisse—. No. I'm not in that game yet. But I must tell you of how you have revolutionized a solemn sitting of the Professors of the Belle Arti! One of them asked & asked until I, reluctantly, lent you for a day. Then you were carried off & read aloud at a "seduta" & fought over, & ramped over, & stormed over, & considered as something between a prophet & a bombshell. Several of them know English: the others, I am told, clamored for a translation. At all events, the whole sitting was devoted to you. They did 'no other

work that day.' It must have been a scene. I wish we could
have witnessed it.

Thank you—at last!—but thank you a thousand times for
sending it to me. I like the way it is written so much better
than the M[abel]. D[odge]. Portrait. I feel the rhythm in this.
I feel the expression.

How are you all? Here, life has been rather knocking me
about. Think of everything most foreign to your smiling calm:
—that's been my lot. But, my dear Gertrude, does Memnon
understand why the sandtracks shift & disappear? He sees it
happen: but can he understand? . . .

We have had four or five weeks of wonderful blue skies,
green moving water, & gorgeous pageantry of sunsets. Today,
a sea fog blots out the world.—And you? I think of you in
a Paris shining with the nouvel an. Are there new pictures?
Have you heard good music? I went on an expedition the
other day to see some Longhis, just sold, & disappearing forever from the old yellow boudoir for which they were painted.
Charming, artificial things:—as attractive & as pathetic as old
dancing-tunes.

My love to you,
Constance.

At last Gertrude Stein succeeded in getting a copy of Three Lives
*into the hands of one of the four English writers whom she had
hoped to interest in her work in 1909.*

FROM H. G. WELLS

17, Church Row, Hampstead [Jan 7, 1913]

Dear Miss Stein

I have just read *Three Lives*. At first I was repelled by your
extraordinary style, I was busy with a book of my own & I
put yours away. It is only in the last week I have read it—I
read it with a deepening pleasure & admiration. I'm very grate-

ful indeed to you for sending it to me & I shall watch for your
name again very curiously & eagerly.

Very sincerely yrs
H. G. Wells

FROM MARSDEN HARTLEY

[Paris, Jan 1913?]

My Dear Miss Stein—

I have your note this morning and shall be most happy to
dine with you on Friday at seven. With your invitation came
a short letter from Stieglitz with no special news. . . .

Maybe you'll have more news of the great [Armory] show.
The "new spirit" gods how omnipotent they are. The Indians
always said the "great spirit," but the New York Indians have
to invent a "new" one.

Yours sincerely
Marsden Hartley.

❦

*Mabel Dodge returned to America late in 1912, taking with her the
remaining copies of her* Portrait, *and established her headquarters
in New York at 23 Fifth Avenue. She had news of the Armory
exhibition.*

FROM MABEL DODGE

Atlantic City, Jan 24 [1913]

Dearest Gertrude—

Behold the above address. I am here for two or three days
. . . just getting over . . . nervous prostration. But in the
midst of nerves we are in mad excitement just the same. . . .

I hadn't been in New York long before I found out why
I had come. I had been waiting to find out! There is an exhibition coming off the 15 Feb to 15 March, which is the most

important public event that has ever come off since the signing of the Declaration of Independence, & it is of the same nature. Arthur Davies is the President of a group of men here who felt the American people ought to be given a chance to see what the modern artists have been doing in Europe, America & England of late years. So they have got a collection of paintings from Ingres to the Italian futurists taking in all the French, Spanish, English, German—in fact *all* one has heard of. This will be a *scream*! 2000 exhibits, in the great armory of the 69th Regiment! The academy are frantic. Most of them are left out of it. . . . Somehow or other I got right into all this. I am working like a dog for it. I am *all for it*. . . . There will be a riot & a revolution & things will never be quite the same afterwards.

Now I have been talking a great deal about the Gertrude Stein portraits . . . So one day the man who has charge of all the press work . . . asked me if I would write an article for him. He said that two or three art magazines had offered their whole February numbers, to be made up exclusively of stuff about the show . . . I told him I couldn't write him an article about any special artist or movement because while I believed in the whole thing & was giving all my time & energy to helping on the show, still it was the *idea* of it all that interested me more than anything . . . the relation of it *all* to all that is going on everywhere in spots, *here* in painting, there in some little isolated sheltered girl (Ruth Draper), here in politics, there in literature. Then he flung up his hands & exclaimed "Oh! I'm all up in the air about this post-impressionistic literature—now this Gertrude Stein!—" I said—"Well, you believe that there is too much smell of death in most of the painting you know. You want the new spirit. You want fresh life. Why don't you see that you can apply that to words? Words originally in primitive man were pure sound expressing directly an emotion. That is some time since. The life has gone out of them, their meaning is lost, blurred—Gertrude Stein—" "Why don't you write me an article about Gertrude

Stein's post-impressionism," he broke in. "I'll have a shot at
it if you like" I said. "All right, have it ready by Monday noon,
will you?" (This was Saturday.) "Certainly" I agreed, as tho'
I'd done it all my life!

Now, my poor darling Gertrude, I have written an article
called "Speculations" somehow drawing a comparison between
you & Picasso & it is going to come out in some art magazine
in February & be on sale for a month at that show unless they
change their minds, because they accepted it! . . . I don't
mind telling you that I am petrified at having done it & in
my dreadful *dead* language! At the same time, as you per-
ceive, it *will* make your name known by & large, as the writer
of "post impressionistic literature" which is my only consolation & then perhaps Mitchell Kennerley who likes innovations
will get out a small book of portraits or something. . . .

So there Gertrude is my confession. *I* am your faithful &
incomprehending Boswell. If I dare, I'll send you some copies.
I don't know what it's going to be in yet! The cheaper the
better as *more* people will buy it!! I couldn't have stood it
without the show over here. Now I feel of use—& am. . . .

I had a party the other night all made of artists & art critics
with a dash of social reform & anarchists. Picabia the Spanish
[*i.e.* Cuban] Picasso was there with a nice wife. Charlotte
Becker has named him Pi*cubi*a, which all have adopted!

I have some more letters & parodies of the portrait. *Many*
people have it now. All my letters come to Mrs. Mabel Dodge
where last year they came to Mrs. *Edwin* Dodge—that's what
you've done for one thing! Let me know *all* about your English experiences. . . . I feel things are moving. Anyway I'm
shoving! But promise beforehand to *forgive* my article, won't
you?

Ever yrs,
Mabel.

In an effort to interest English publishers in her work, Gertrude Stein went to London in January 1913. Among the firms which she visited was that of Frank Palmer.

FROM FRANK PALMER

14, Red Lion Court, Fleet Street, London, E.C.,
Jan 27, 1913

Dear Madam,

I have read through a portion of the MS which you gave me on Friday, but I regret that I cannot make you any proposition concerning the same. I say I have only read a portion of it, because I found it perfectly useless to read further, as I did not understand any of it. I have to confess to being as stupid and as ignorant as all the other readers to whom the book has been submitted.

I herewith return the MS.

Yours faithfully,
for Frank Palmer.
K. W.

FROM THE ENGLISH REVIEW

London, Jan 29, 1913

Dear Madam,

I really cannot publish these curious Studies.

Yours very truly,
Austin Harrison,
Encl.   Editor.

The situation in New York was apparently quite different.

FROM MABEL DODGE

23 Fifth Avenue, Feb 13 [1913]

Dearest Gertrude,

You are just on the eve of *bursting*! Everybody wherever
I go—& others who go where I don't say the same thing—is
talking of Gertrude Stein! There is an article about you coming out in the N. Y. Times this Sunday & the editor sent a
young man around to see me & talk about you as he (the ed.)
had got hold of a copy of yr portrait of me & he said he *must*
get hold of it all *first* as it was new, etc., etc. I had met the
young man who came to see me about it, at dinner, & found
him temperamental . . . but rather nice! So I got Hutch[ins
Hapgood] to be here—this was yesterday—when he came so
that between us we could try & get something into him that
wouldn't make it seem a mere *pie*. So he arrived & we talked
at him & he couldn't understand a word we said but he carried away the portrait & a photograph of *me*(!) & my promise
to get him some of *you*. I telephoned Mabel Weeks & your
cousin Mrs. [Howard] Gans & secured a variety (one sitting
on a sundial!) & sent them to the young man. His name is
[Carl] Van Vechten. So on Sunday you will be in the Times
& Monday the show opens where they will sell that idiotic
article of mine on you! And now Stieglitz is trying to get the
Portrait away from Dubois who took it for his April number,
because Stieglitz says he *must* have it. It was very funny the
other day, just after I left Stieglitz's where I had been for the
first time he turned to Jo Davidson & said "Now I understand
the portrait perfectly, now I've seen her!" Just as *easy*!!! *Picabia*
the painter is here & very intelligent & understands it all perfectly. I asked him to write down what he said & I will send it
to you. I will give him a letter to you as you & Leo will *both*
(strangely enough) like him. . . .

I have done myself proud in the way I have distributed
those Portraits . . . I have been expecting a letter from you
lately. Let me hear what you hear. . . . Love to Alice & Leo.

M. D.

Logan Pearsall Smith, the essayist and critic, a friend of Constance Fletcher's, had undertaken to place one of Gertrude Stein's manuscripts with the Oxford Fortnightly.

FROM LOGAN PEARSALL SMITH

Ford Place, Arundel, Feb 26, 1913

Dear Miss Stein,

I sent on your MS. to the Oxford paper, but the editor writes that he is afraid it is rather too long for them, as their paper is not a very large one. They would very much like however, to have something shorter, & have asked me to ask you whether this is possible. They suggest printing the portrait of Miss Fletcher—shall I send this on to them, or will you let them have something else? I don't suppose it would do to print Miss Fletcher's name, but they might print the initials C. F.

I am going abroad next week for a month or two, but if they may have the Miss Fletcher, & you will let me know at once, I can forward it to them before I start—I have the MS. here. If however you wish them to have anything else, it would be better to send it direct to The Editor, Oxford Fortnightly, Holywell Press, Oxford.

Yours sincerely
L. Pearsall Smith

Roger Fry, the English critic and painter, had agreed to try to help in the matter of publication. He was in this year organizing the Omega Workshops for the production and sale of applied art.

FROM ROGER FRY

Durbins, Guildford, Feb [*i.e.* Mar] 5, 1913

My dear Miss Stein,

I've wanted to write but been too busy & lazy in between-whiles and I knew you would understand. . . . I've seen [John] Lane at last after many misses. . . . He's not read 3 Lives yet (his eyes are bad) but I've made him promise to have it read to him by a clergyman's wife! I *think* he'll publish it. I've also approached Methuen about the other things. He's interested & I shall take them over to him at Haslemere as soon as I get a spare day. I've been going round the provinces lecturing—Leeds & Liverpool. English Provincial life is a very strange & exotic thing. I feel as tho' I were in another planet when I get into it. They listened to me with deep attention & remained as far as I could see profoundly unmoved & unconvinced. Do you know the effect of Picasso's Tête d'Homme (the one with G. R. on it) as lantern slide is simply amazing. The increase of scale & the intensity of light & shade make it a most impressive thing. But the difficulty with an English audience is that they haven't got the sensibility to form. They'll take one's ideas as pure ideas but they can't fit them on to the pictures at all.

My decorating scheme goes along well. I've got orders already for stuffs & painted furniture but as yet cannot get a house to start in.

I've a lecture to-morrow or I'd go on talking. You know what a great pleasure it was seeing you here. You must repeat your strange adventures into England.

Yrs. very sincerely
Roger Fry.

FROM ARNOLD RÖNNEBECK

16 rue du Saint Gothard [Paris] (XIV),
Apr 1, 1913

Dear Miss Stein,

A friend sent me this clipping from a Berlin paper. It is a "criticisme" of Kandinsky's prose-poems "Klänge" which appeared lately.

I send it you because I think that the three or four samples which are reproduced might interest you. They show rather well Kandinsky's intentions in using the *word* itself as a pure interior sound (Klang)—and how, thus applied, it loses its quality as a name of a certain object.

I have been very glad indeed that I could read your latest portrait (R[obert]. D[elaunay].) How flattered the model would be if he would know it in all its intensity!

With kindest regards

Faithfully yours
Arnold Rönnebeck.

FROM MILDRED ALDRICH

23, Rue Boissonade, XIV, Sunday [Apr? 1913]

Dearest Gertrude:

I was so sorry you could not come to Janet [Scudder]'s & so was every one. I want you to come to tea one day next week, but I am not quite sure of the day—probably Thursday—will let you know as soon as I can arrange it.—I am expecting [James] Stephens, the Irishman who wrote "The Crock of Gold" & I want you and Alice for the afternoon that he comes.

It may interest you to see him even if you did not care for his book. He is a rare creature. . . .

> Affectionately
> Mildred

23, Rue Boissonade, XIV, Monday [Apr? 1913]

Dearest Gertrude:

I am expecting that Stephens will join me chez-vous, about nine Wednesday evening. . . . I have taken the liberty of asking my old friend Henry McBride, art critic of the Sun, who has just seen Roger Fry, to join me also. I hope this is all right. . . .

> Much love
> Mildred

FROM ALVIN LANGDON COBURN

Paris, Apr 30, 1913

Madam Stein

I am greatly interested in modern painting, and have heard, as who has not, of your splendid collection of paintings by Matisse. I am therefore writing to inquire if it would be possible for me to see it?

I first became interested in the work of the modern school through my friend Mr Max Weber of New York whose work you no doubt know, and about twenty of whose paintings are in my collection, which I would consider it a great honour to show you if ever you are in London where I live.

You may even have seen some of my own work in photography?

Trusting that I am not asking too great a favor I remain

> Yours very sincerely
> Alvin Langdon Coburn

FROM MABEL DODGE

[New York, May? 1913]

Dear Gertrude

This letter is brought to you by Carl Van Vechten—he can tell you all about your succès here—he wrote one of the columns I sent you, the one that said your work, sociologically, was like the orchid!

Hope to see you soon.

Hope you'll like Carl. Hutch & I do.

Ever yrs,
Mabel Dodge at the Villa Curonia.

Gertrude Stein did portraits of many of her friends and acquaintances, among them Miss Blood of the Villa Gamberaia in Florence. The second sentence of this "Portrait of F. B." begins "There is no squeak," and there is a reference, later on, to "the distaste of pink pepper." The "wild card," referred to in the second letter, was a post-card reproduction of one of Picasso's paintings used by Guillaume Apollinaire in his Les Peintres Cubistes, *which had recently been published in Paris.*

FROM FLORENCE BLOOD

Grand Hôtel de Londres, Paris, Saturday
[May? 1913]

Dear Miss Stein

Oh! dear Miss Stein—oh! am I really like that & what—oh! what does it mean? I feel like a person who has rushed eagerly to the looking glass to see themselves with new eyes, but alas alas, all the familiar landmarks have been quite swept away—eyes, mouth, hands, feet, & the rest, all gone!—I feel convinced you know me better than I do myself & if your knowledge is contained in these leaves do do give me the key—

You say there is no squeak, but I wish you could have heard the one I gave when I came to the pink pepper. Oh! dear Miss Stein tell me what it all means!!

With all thanks

Affectionately yrs
Florence Blood

Gamberaia, Settignano, Firenze, June 11 [1913]

Dear Miss Stein—

Thank you for your wild card—I had seen the same in Apollinaire's book—what strikes me most about the latter is what good fun he must have had in doing it—also what charming faces all those Cubists have. Next to Aviators they are the nicest things going. But why is not Picasso's portrait in the book? he too has such a charming countenance.

I have a great favor to ask of Miss Toklas. Would she be so awfully kind as to make me another copy of *"my portrait"*? In all this travelling about & *lending,* I seem to have mislaid it or even quite lost, for hunt as I may it can't be found. I should be so grateful, & thanks to her d'avance! . . .

Aff't'ly—
F B

Gertrude Stein and Alice Toklas were at that time planning a trip to Spain and the Balearic Islands. Miss Stein sent the second copy of her portrait to Miss Blood.

Gamberaia, Settignano, Firenze,
June 21 [1913]

Dear Miss Stein—

Many thanks for the portrait—though I don't understand it yet I felt quite lonely without "the taste of pink pepper."

And so it is drama you are doing now? Oh! dear, oh! dear & shall I miss it all?

What takes you to those distant islands, & what language is Miss Toklas learning at Berlitz to pave your way? My ignorance is such that I don't know what lingo they speak there or to whom they belong. I wonder sometimes how I get on at all, I know so terribly little. Here it is as usual very beautiful. I am alone with plenty of time for thinking things over, but I have so far made no discovery worth recording.

If any of those charming looking Cubists come my way do send them to see me. I am in all summer long on Sunday, & should welcome something young & fresh & cubistic very warmly.

The people here are so horribly dull!

The Berensons had left before I arrived & really though they are neither young or fresh or cubistic they are the best the place affords & when they have gone what is there?

Tell your brother he owes me two postcards!

Affectionately yrs

F B—

FROM BERNARD BERENSON

[Hotel Ritz, Paris] 9. a.m., Tuesday
[July 1, 1913]

Dear Gertrude,

I should love to see you & Matisse but my only free evening is Friday. If you could manage to transfer yr. feast to that evening & let me know by tomorrow morning at latest I should be a happy man.

Ever yrs.

B. B.

Alvin Langdon Coburn, who had now met and photographed Gertrude Stein and seen the Matisse paintings, was continuing his efforts on behalf of her writing in England. Roger Fry did not, however, write an introduction, nor did Gerald Duckworth publish the projected book.

FROM ALVIN LANGDON COBURN

Thameside, 9 Lower Mall, Hammersmith,
Aug 23, 1913

Dear Miss Stein:—

Very many thanks for your two letters . . .

I saw Duckworth the other day and he had just received your letter and was on the point of answering it. You have probably heard from him before this. He told me that he had asked Roger Fry, through a friend, to write the introduction to your book, that Fry had replied that he would like to do it but that he must first write to you for your permission to do so. If he has not done so I suggest you write to him (Fry) and then Duckworth will go ahead with the book. . . .

Yours with kindest regards
Alvin Langdon Coburn.

Before she left for Spain, Gertrude Stein had discussed the possible production of some of her short plays with Henry McBride, art critic of the New York Sun, whom she had met through Mildred Aldrich.

FROM HENRY McBRIDE

Restaurant Weber, 21 & 23, Rue Royale, Paris,
Aug 28, 1913

Chère mademoiselle:

The Café Weber provides blank writing paper also, and some consider it the more chic, but I am purposely using the printed sheets to prove I really write it here. Deficiency of style in café-letters is not criminal.

You will be writing yours behind slatted windows in semi-but translucent darkness and the *helados* will put you in a good humour and the domino-players a topic to write upon if you have no other. . . .

Have seen Mick (your Mildred) once or twice. Once at James Stephens' and he read aloud to us some of his things. It was the first I had heard of his and I liked 'em. One called the "Three Penny Bit" not yet published, is sure to make you laugh. His short sketch "Horses" is in the newest "Nation" (English) and whether Stephens knows it or not, it is "Post."

I am disgusted, really, at not seeing you again. I wanted to read those plays over again and talk with you about them. That man Willis Polk of San Francisco is already returned to Paris. He is Chief of the Architectural Commission for the Fair, and has some influence in a general way I imagine. I told him that the Fair should stage your plays, and that Society that plays out in the Forest should know of you. To do the gentleman justice, I must say, his eyes sparkled at the idea. . . . In the meantime, I still think they should be done next winter in New York, and if they are done, I hope I shall be allowed to help. If you see anything in the Fair, let me know and I'll nab Polk. He gave me the idea that the San Franciscans would love to be up to date or a little ahead of it, if possible.

I'm in Paris—33 *ave. d'Antin*—until Sept 6, sailing on Rochambeau. After that in New York in care "The Sun." I think I shall have to bore you by writing occasionally. Like my friend Mr. Polk, I should like to keep up-to-date. Wishing you luck with the Palms of Murcia and kindest regards to your charming friend whose name I can't spell.

Yours most sincere,
Henry McBride.

FROM HENRI MATISSE [TRANSLATED]

[Bellencombre, Seine-Inf., Sep 3, 1913]

Dear Mademoiselle

Where are you?

. I don't think you let me have your traveling address and I was waiting to answer until you had given it to me. I hope you are happy with your season, and that even so we shall soon have the pleasure of seeing you again. Picasso has taken up horseback-riding and we ride together to the astonishment of many! Why? Painting goes slowly but well. A line from you would give us pleasure.

Regards

H. M.

Marsden Hartley was having financial troubles. Earlier, when Gertrude Stein had insisted upon paying twenty dollars for a drawing of his which he wanted to give to her, it had been agreed that the money would be regarded as an emergency fund that Hartley would call for when he really needed it. It was this money, plus an equal amount as a gift, which Miss Stein had just telegraphed him in Berlin.

FROM MARSDEN HARTLEY

Nassauischestr. 4, Wilmersdorf, Berlin [Oct 1913]

My Dear Miss Stein,

I have your letter this morning & want to thank you profoundly for your telegram & for the money—& for your kind support generally. The money has averted a nasty situation. Your warmth and interest contribute highly to my welfare. . . .

I had a letter this morning also from Rönnebeck saying

he had seen you all & was so glad for it, and that you talked over my situation with him . . . I had told him that I knew some people in N.Y. with heaps of money. Well I know them in a far off way as far as money goes. They bought two of my still-lifes, and it was on this money and on $500— which Arthur B. Davies gave me personally that I lived in Paris. My only connection with these people is through Stieglitz, that is on the money side. . . . I owe him everything for the success of the past . . . And . . . for all this time I have been one of his spiritual & practical cares. Steichen was his first one—he fostered him through every namable vicissitude to success as a photographer and alike as a painter. The same with John Marin the water color man, who is really wonderful in that medium. Then myself. You see I actually want to end these responsibilities for him & for myself. For this reason alone I have thought my presence with the pictures would effect a decent connection. . . . Apart from all this, a good talk with Stieglitz privately as a friend on all matters would be valuable to him and me. Then there is Davies too, who has silent con-nections—a wealthy woman who I really think bought some-thing & gave him all or part of the money he gave me. I never have known. I only know that this very quiet and lovely per-son came often to my show at "291" & took me to Mrs. Have-meyer's house to see her collection among which are nine Cézannes—very fine over all—that was my first actual glimpse of him. It was from his water colors that I got most inspira-tion as expressing the color & form of "new places"—those you have & others at Bernheim's. I write you all this—too much at length—only because I think you should know a lit-tle more of facts & backgrounds about me. . . .

However you will be bored to death—by this time. If I were sitting with you in 27, it would all be but one of my conversations. . . .

As to your idea to have Stieglitz print your play with me in it and reproduce some of my work, I think it simply splen-did & I would love it, and I think that all we would have to do would be to suggest it, for I know he would be very sympathetic to the idea. Suppose you suggest this to him in a letter soon & I will mention it too. . . .

My very best wishes to you always—the same to Miss Toklas. . . .

Always your friend
Marsden Hartley

At about this time Leo and Gertrude Stein, because of their disagreement about Picasso's later work and for other reasons, decided to maintain separate establishments. Leo planned to settle in Italy near Florence. Between them they agreed that he should have some of the smaller Cézannes and all of the paintings by Renoir and Matisse, with the exception of the latter's Femme au Chapeau, while Gertrude would retain other Cézannes, including the large Portrait d'une Femme and all of the Picassos. The details had not been completely worked out, but Gertrude Stein and Alice Toklas were considering moving from 27, rue de Fleurus.

With Leo no longer a member of the household and with the prospect of war in Europe, Gertrude Stein was forced occasionally to sell pictures, though she did not cease buying new ones. The important Picassos sold in 1913 to the dealer Daniel-Henry Kahnweiler, who was now handling the output of Picasso and most of the other Cubist painters, were purchased from him by the Russian collectors Schukin and Morosoff, and are now in the Museum of Modern Western Art in Moscow.

FROM DANIEL-HENRY KAHNWEILER [TRANSLATED]

Galérie Kahnweiler, 28, Rue Vignon,
Oct 17, 1913

Mademoiselle,

I have the honor of confirming our conversation of yesterday.

You are selling me three of your Picassos, to wit:

The young girl standing on the ball

The large composition in pink
The woman with the linen

For these three pictures I am paying you 20,000 francs in cash, plus the new Picasso called "The man in black."

I enclose herewith, as we agreed, a check for 20,000 francs payable January 15, 1914. I should be grateful if you would let me know that you have received it.

Yours very sincerely,
Kahnweiler

FROM ALFRED STIEGLITZ

291 Fifth Ave., New York, Nov 3, 1913

My dear Miss Stein:

Hartley has undoubtedly let you know that I have thought it wisest to have him come over here with his pictures. He has kept me fully posted as to your opinion of his work. Of course my main idea in bringing him over here is to bring him into touch, if possible, with some people who might take sufficient interest in him and his work to give him the opportunity to return to Berlin without the constant worry of money. . . . I hope that his work, his presence—not for the purpose of explaining anything, Heaven forbid—and my great faith in his ability, may bring about what he and his few intimate friends most wish for.

I wrote to Hartley in my last that it might help him for you to write a few words for his catalogue. It is really for this purpose that these lines are dictated. Of course should you decide to write, it would have to be done at once and mailed to me at once, as I wish to show the Hartley pictures virtually by November 20th or 22nd so as not to keep him here any longer than absolutely necessary. Times are terrifically hard over here. . . . Then too, one must remember that there is no real feeling for art, or love for art, in the United States as yet. It is still considered a great luxury; something which is really not necessary. And all this in spite of the so-called interest in old masters and the millions spent for them by people like Altman and Morgan. Was not Altman the landlord of our little "291"? Did he not double the rent virtually on the day on which he bought the property and incidentally bought a new Rembrandt? Did he ever know that "291" was fighting tooth and nail, single handed, in this vast country of ours, for the very thing he thought he loved? Of course I could have gone to him and taken the case before him and I suppose we would have had rent free. But I don't do things that way. I don't believe in going to the people with hat in hand begging. It may be too idealistic, too unpractical, this method of mine. But just like Hartley insists, as does every real artist, on developing his self expression in his own way, I insist on doing things in my own way. . . . I have created conditions in which occasionally something happened for others. And I shall continue doing this for others as long as I can. . . .

With kindest regards,

Cordially,
Alfred Stieglitz.

FROM ARNOLD RÖNNEBECK

3 Offenbacher Str., Berlin-Friedenau,
Dec 6, 1913

My dear Miss Stein,

There has been the intention—and all that time—and no time at all! The *intention* to write you was not sufficient for the realisation. Still, since I am here I am still more at your place than [when] I was in Paris. And it is a strange feeling to place oneself into a very distinct atmosphere—to be in thought just *there*—without knowing *where*. Of course the local situation is not so important for the spiritual process. But it is a kind of puzzle to me to imagine you and Miss

Toklas and all the living things in your house at another place than rue de Fleurus. Perhaps you did not move yet—or did you? And has your brother gone to Florence? I suppose you kept all of Picasso's pictures. Poor Pablo has been sick? Kahnweiler mentioned it to me when he sent me a photograph some time ago. I hope he is "out of danger." . . . I miss it terribly, to suddenly see him come along the boulevard . . . with his almost unreally shiny eyes and the passionate rrrrrr when he speaks . . . I am thankful for every news that comes from Paris. After all I feel interiorly at home *there*. The change is certainly good for me. And the brightness and "up-to-date-hood" of Berlin quite wonderful too,—but: *there has been Paris!* . . .

No news from Hartley yet. Did *you* hear of him? . . . My very best regards to Miss Toklas, to Picasso and his charming little madame. When I have the time I shall try to give him something of "The Portrait of M[abel]. D[odge]." in French, —as I promised him. To yourself the kindest regards of yours very sincerely

Rönnebeck

FROM MARSDEN HARTLEY

291 Fifth Ave., New York [Dec 10? 1913]

My Dear Miss Stein—

I have wanted to write you something. I have been here two weeks. It is an eternity. I want to go home. I am homeless here. New York is an inferno . . . My pictures are in the toils of the customs . . . and one is so helpless with it all. I just hang around from day to day in an utterly strange place. It is good to see the few I like so much—Mabel Dodge—Hapgood—Stieglitz & a number of others whom I like & [who] like me, but I feel as if I never want to come again. It is fatal to anyone who wants to create and be. . . .

How are you both? Have you found a new place or are you still at 27? I wonder much. I hope the new place will be what you thoroughly like & you will be contented. I should like much to hear from you here. My very best wishes to you always.

Yours,
Marsden H.

Stieglitz sends best wishes also.

Hartley's next communication revealed a changed situation in New York. His opening sentence is a slightly adapted version of the beginning of the Portrait of Mabel Dodge at the Villa Curonia.

[New York, Jan 16, 1914]

Dear Gertrude S.

The days are wonderful & the nights are wonderful & life is pleasant. The show is open, four are sold, one year is secure —I want two years' freedom. The artists are all elated & enthusiastic & the people say queer & interesting things. It all seems to start up new phases of emotions in people. I shall write as soon as I can, more at length. Two lovely long letters from Rönnebeck this morning. I got your fine letter also. I am with Mabel Dodge daily & she is simply great. Heartiest good wishes to you & Miss T. always,

Marsden Hartley.

The final details of the division of the collection of paintings and drawings between Gertrude and Leo Stein were now being settled. Miss Stein and Miss Toklas had almost made up their minds to take an apartment over the Palais Royal gardens, but eventually decided to remain at 27, rue de Fleurus.

FROM LEO STEIN

27 Rue de Fleurus [Jan 1914?]

Dear Gertrude

It's impossible simply to answer yes or no to your note because there are a number of mistaken beliefs affirmed to which a mere yes or no would not satisfactorily fit.

In regard to the value of the [Japanese] prints which you had owned, with the exception of the few bought from Bing & Hoyashi & the triptych from N. Y. the value is inconsiderable. If I make something substantial out of the sale it will be with the Harunobus, Kuninagas, Chinchos etc. that I got afterwards. . . .

The Cézanne apples have a unique importance to me that nothing can replace. The Picasso landscape is not important in any such sense. We are as it seems to me on the whole both so well off now that we needn't repine. The Cézannes had to be divided. I am willing to leave you the Picasso oeuvre as you left me the Renoir & you can have everything except that I want to keep the few drawings that I have. This leaves no string for me, it is financially equable either way for estimates are only rough & ready methods, & I'm afraid you'll have to look upon the loss of the apples as an act of God. I have been anxious above all things that each should have in reason all that he wanted and just as I was glad that Renoir was sufficiently indifferent to you so that you were ready to give them up, so I am glad that Pablo is sufficiently indifferent to me that I am willing to let you have all you want of it. I should not have taken the Spanish landscape in the first place if I had not supposed that your interest in the later things had rendered it of minor importance. Since this is evidently not the case I shall not only propose but shall insist with happy cheerfulness that you make as clean a sweep of the Picassos as I have of the Renoirs with the exception of the drawings which I want to keep partly on account of their actual delightfulness & partly on account of the personal note. But then with the exception of the presentations there is among them I think nothing of special importance to you. You'll take the little still life, the gouache head & the little bronze.

I very much prefer it that way, & I hope that we will all live happily ever after & maintain our respective & due proportions while sucking gleefully our respective oranges.

Leo

Harry Phelan Gibb, the English painter, had borrowed a manuscript of Gertrude Stein's to lend to his friend Oliver St. John Gogarty, who had helped to arrange a show of Gibb's pictures in Dublin in 1913. One of the friends for whom Dr. Gogarty wanted a copy of the Portrait of Mabel Dodge *was James Joyce.*

FROM DR. OLIVER ST. JOHN GOGARTY

15, Ely Place, Dublin,
Jan 24, 1914

Dear Miss Stein:

I should have answered your letter long ago and apologised to you for making it necessary for you to write to me for your M.S. but things were so upset that I had no opportunity to do so until this moment.

I [am] glad to have an autograph letter in spite of the fact that I obtained it unworthily. I send on your M.S. by registered post to your Paris address. I wonder if your good nature would not be overtaxed by my requesting a few copies of "The Portrait of Mabel Dodge at the Villa Curonia"? I want one or two for my friends.

I am incompetent to offer an opinion on a form of Art so new as yours. We had an old standing example of the medium being used for its own sake in the Law! Phelan Gibb paid us an explicit visit. Will you soon come so far away from the centres of culture as to visit Dublin? . . .

Please send a post card to say that your M.S. is safe. I shall forward it . . . and Believe me to be:

Yours sincerely

Oliver Gogarty.

FROM DR. CLARIBEL CONE

The Marlborough [Baltimore, Md.] Sunday midnight,
Jan 25, 1914

My dear Gertrude:

I received your nice letter a few days ago and am much interested to know that you and Miss Toklas have found a satisfactory home. . . .

A few evenings ago, Friday, Etta and I had guests for dinner. After dinner I slipt out to go to a "medical society meeting." After I got out a few steps I changed my mind (it was then 9:10 p.m.) and went to McCoy Hall where I remembered that [William] Chase the artist was to talk on Whistler. . . . As a matter of fact I got to the meeting (having walked!) in time—9:25 p.m.—to hear the peroration so to speak—the closing anecdotes—amusing it is true but "closing"—about Whistler—and then—from the speaker—"But then I have promised to tell you of some of the new movements in Art"— so he began with an opening sentence on the "Cubists, Futurists, Post-Impressionists." When he launched into "Matisse" I thought he was going to tell us something about Matisse when he—here it is, I wrote it down as he said it, he chose to give us Matisse in this guise: "There is a Gertrude Stein a sister of a man of considerable means who is buying Matisse's works and making him known. Each one of these paintings is a gold brick to the owner" etc. "Gertrude Stein has written an appreciation of Matisse and says:" (he picked up the—it did not look like Camera Work—I think it must have been a paper in which your sketches of Matisse & Picasso were quoted in full. He began) "One was quite certain—etc." He

read on and on—and although he did not put the commas
(imaginary) exactly in the right places, sitting as I was in the
back part of the hall it sounded very well—all did not agree
with me however, but I thought so. He read a large part of
your sketch of Matisse. The next day another mention was
made of you in the Baltimore Sun . . . I hope you got the
letter in which I thanked you for your nice Picasso photograph. Let me thank you again most sincerely, and do keep
me posted as to what goes on—as I shall you—as I get information as to your fast-growing American fame. . . .

  Love to you and *all*.

Sincerely
Claribel Cone

*Duncan Grant, the English painter, was a cousin of Lytton
Strachey, who had introduced him to the Bloomsbury group of
artists and writers in London. At the Steins', some years earlier, he
had seen for the first time the paintings of Pablo Picasso. In 1914,
Grant was designing the costumes for Jacques Copeau's production of* Twelfth Night *at the Vieux-Colombier in Paris. The material for these costumes was produced by Roger Fry's Omega
Workshops.*

FROM DUNCAN GRANT

On board the Carthage, Feb 1914

Dear Miss Stein
  When I was in Paris you very kindly said you would take
me to see Picasso. I shall be in Paris from Monday night next
for about a week at the Hôtel de l'Univers et du Portugal, Rue
Croix des Petits Champs. Will you please write to me there
to say if it is possible or not? I believe when I last saw you I
left behind the post card you gave me of the Bull fight. I hope
I may get it again.

Yrs sincerely
Duncan Grant.

Hôtel de l'Univers & du Portugal, Paris,
Feb 17, 1914

Dear Miss Stein

I should very much like to come to lunch with you on Friday next Feb. 20. I am sorry not to have dated my letter.

Yours sincerely
Duncan Grant

Donald Evans, the American poet, was a friend of Mabel Dodge's and Carl Van Vechten's, who worked at this time as copy-reader on the New York Times. *He had established a publishing firm to issue his own and his friends' books, naming it after a lady of his acquaintance, Claire Marie Burke. Allen Norton, whose book of poems is referred to, was editor of the brief-lived little magazine* Rogue.

FROM DONALD EVANS

Claire Marie, Publisher, East Fourteenth Street, No. 3, New York,
Feb 18, 1914

Dear Miss Stein:

I should very much like to publish in volume form the plays of yours that Mrs. Dodge has told me about. Will you let me do it?

I can give you a book of more distinguished appearance than any other publisher in America and I can also get more publicity for it. I think Mrs. Dodge said she sent you my two recent volumes "SONNETS FROM THE PATAGONIAN" and "LITTLE WAX CANDLE" so you can judge what my formats are. My public also is the most civilized in this country.

I can offer you 10% royalty on the first 500 copies sold and 15% on all after that.

Mr. Van Vechten told me he thought you might not wish

the plays published before you had them produced here. My bringing out the volume, my dear Miss Stein, would not in any way hurt the producing value; in fact, it would stimulate interest in their production in the theatre. . . .

Mr. Norton's new book of verse is dedicated to you. I will have a copy sent you. Will you let me have an answer as soon as possible because I should like to get your book out in the early spring if you let me have it?

Faithfully yours,
Claire Marie

Gertrude Stein did not wish the plays published before they had been produced, but she sent to Donald Evans instead a group of three manuscripts "Food," "Objects," "Rooms" to which she gave the collective title Tender Buttons. *Evans agreed to publish the volume and a contract was signed.*

FROM MABEL DODGE

[New York] Sunday, [Mar] 29 [1914]

Dearest Gertrude—

This is going to be a letter.

Now in the first place. About your stuff. I cabled you *not* to publish with D. Evans after having a long talk with E. A. Robinson who is our "dark poet" here, & who knows more about things than most people. He knows Evans & believes in his ability but he thinks the Claire Marie Press which Evans runs is absolutely third rate, & in bad odor here, being called for the most part "decadent" & Broadwayish & that sort of thing. He wrote Evans to get out of it, to chuck it & stop getting linked up in the public "mind" with it. I think it would be a pity to publish with him *if* it will emphasize the idea in the opinion of the public, that there is something degenerate & effete & decadent about the whole of the cubist movement which they *all* connect you with, because, hang it all, as long as they don't understand a thing they think all sorts of things. My feeling in this is quite strong. . . . Best love to you & Alice . . .

Yrs.

M— D.

Despite Mabel Dodge and E. A. Robinson, Gertrude Stein did not withdraw her manuscript, and Tender Buttons *in due course appeared, bound in canary-yellow boards with a green label. Soon after its publication, Carl Van Vechten was in Paris. He and Fania Marinoff, the actress, whom he took to see Gertrude Stein, were married some three months later.*

FROM CARL VAN VECHTEN

American Express Co., 11 Rue Scribe, Paris,

July 4, 1914

Dear Miss Stein,

I'm in Paris for a few days with the latest gossip about Tender Buttons, Mabel, Hutch, and everybody.—I hope I can see you, and I should like to bring over a little Russian called Fania.—I'm stopping at the Hotel Fribourg, 46 Rue de Trévise.

Sincerely

Carl Van Vechten

In July 1914, Gertrude Stein made another trip to London to interview publishers. Alvin Langdon Coburn did his best to smooth the way for her and hoped to arrange a meeting with Henry James.

FROM ALVIN LANGDON COBURN

Thameside, 9 Lower Mall, Hammersmith,
July 28, 1914

Dear Miss Stein:—

It occurred to me this morning that it would be a good idea
to arrange a meeting with my friend J. P. Collins of the Pall
Mall Gazette, as he edits the best book page in any London
paper, so I phoned him.

He had just been reading some American reviews of "Tender Buttons" and was delighted by the prospect of a chat with
you. I at once sent you the wire and I am glad you can see him
tomorrow (Wednesday) at 12. noon.

You will find Collins a delightfully clever Irish journalist,
with a well developed sense of humor.

No word from James yet. I hope he is not abroad.

Let me know if there is anything else I can do.

Yours with best wishes
A Langdon Coburn.

Thameside, 9 Lower Mall, Hammersmith,
July 28, 1914

Dear Miss Stein:—

Alas, I have just received the enclosed telegraph from
Henry James. Perhaps another year when you are over he will
be in town and we can make an arrangement for a meeting.

It looks as if the dear man were ill again. He is never well
for long at a time these days. Anyway I have done my best,
and we will hope that he will be in town and well the next
time you come this way.

I hope you have a pleasant chat with Brother Collins, as I
am sure you will.

Yours very sincerely
Alvin Langdon Coburn.

While Gertrude Stein was in London, extensive alterations were made at 27, rue de Fleurus.

FROM MILDRED ALDRICH

La Creste, Huiry, Couilly (S. et M.),
July 28, 1914

Dearest Gertrude:

I was glad to get a wave of the hand from you and to know that you had done your best to "look like a genius." I hope you got your effect "over the footlights" as we say in the theatre. Pretty soon you must be turning your sandalled feet in the direction of renovated "27." . . . [James] Stephens went back to Dublin this morning with his family and thereby hangs a tale which I will tell you when I see you. . . . [His] new book "Demi-Gods" is on the press and may come out any day now. I am awaiting it with impatience as I am . . . "Tender Buttons."—I have not been able to do much work in my garden for three weeks and the fruit, owing to strong winds and wild rains, is simply rotting on the ground. You must come before my plums are finished. I have three kinds. The pansies still flourish and I [have] big dark daisies and Reine Marguérite & golden rod everywhere not to mention weeds growing in quaint profusion. . . .

Affectionately
Mildred.

Gertrude Stein and Alice Toklas had met the philosopher Alfred North Whitehead and his wife through English friends and, their business in London completed, they accepted an invitation to spend a few days in the country.

FROM ALFRED NORTH WHITEHEAD

Seventeen, Carlyle Square, Chelsea, S. W.,
July 29, 1914

Dear Miss Stein

We are immensely looking forward to seeing you and Miss Toklas on Friday afternoon at our Wiltshire Cottage. The best train leaves Paddington at 5 p.m. and arrives at Marlborough at 7.2, where I will meet you at the station. You change at Savernake, where you arrive about 6.30. At Paddington you must be careful to get into the 'Savernake slip'; the rest of the train does not stop there. Please excuse my wife for not herself writing; we are in the agony of changing our London house. The address of our cottage is Sarsen Land, Lockeridge, nr. Marlborough.

Very sincerely yrs
A. N. Whitehead

III. THE FIRST WORLD WAR

AUGUST 1914-1918

*The outbreak of the war in August made it temporarily impossible
for Gertrude Stein and Alice Toklas to return to Paris. News from
France came in long letters from Mildred Aldrich—letters which
paralleled part of her later book* A Hilltop on the Marne.

FROM MILDRED ALDRICH

La Creste, Huiry, Couilly (S. et M.),
Aug 8, 1914

Dearest Gertrude:

I am all right—quite comfortable—well taken care of, and
so heart full of love of the French that I feel as if I had done
all their heroic things myself. . . . I cannot tell you what
it has been like, from the day I ran up the road to the old
grange at the top of the hill to read the government procla-
mation of the mobilization to this morning when the news
comes that Belgium, unaided, had repulsed the German
invasion at Liége before the French and English could reach
them. It was sad seeing the men go, but the women were so
wonderful: Day after day whole families went by my gate
toward Couilly, and women and children came silently back

alone. There was none of the "show-off" I remembered so well in my childhood when Northern regiments started south —no drums, no flags, no marching in the streets. Men—rich and poor together—gentlemen & peasants—were simply packed into the trains. There was a little sob-broken cry from the women and children on the platform, as the train started, of "Vive l'Armée" and a shout from the men hanging out of the windows & waving their hats and caps of "Vive la France"—that was all. . . .

Everyone worried about me—there was no need. I am on the line to the frontier & have really seen more of the actual preparations than they have in Paris, although they have had the excitement of seeing a city paralyzed & the quiet departure of thousands. I see all the aeroplanes, sometimes six a day that pass between Paris & the frontier, and even those that go from the frontier to the coast. The food question has been hard,—for three days no bread—& even now no butter, no sugar, no petrol, but what of that? All that will be changed as soon as the army is mobilized & provisioned—that is the important thing. I am ardently hoping that with England, France, Russia & Belgium shoulder to shoulder in a great cause, with Italy sure to *have* to come into line, with United States as arbiter, if even her navy does not have to come in on account of the treatment of Americans shut up in Germany, we are going to see the most civilized great war in history. Germany & Austria are surrounded—they can be reduced by siege and famine without the awful bloodshed that must otherwise follow. I hope ardently this is to be the policy. If you were here, and I wish you were, I should "*orate*" until your ears tingled. . . . I've heaps to talk about, but I'm so occupied idolizing France that I am incoherent. Do get back if you can. Much love to you both.

Mildred Aldrich.

La Creste, Huiry, Couilly (S. et M.),
Sep 16 [1914]

Dear girls:

Today, for the first time since August 30 I have received my mail. All our communications have been cut from that date to today—railroad, telegraph, bridges everything, for perhaps you know I have been inside the battle zone. For seven days—from Thursday noon, September 3 to Wednesday noon September 11—how many days is that?—I was within sight and hearing of the smoke and the cannonading, and just before noon on Saturday September 5 the battle advanced into that plain before my garden and for eight hours right under my eyes they pounded their heavy artillery and ended just after dark by shelling the plain and retreated leaving all the towns and villages in sight . . . in flames, and four thousand unburied Germans on the field. . . . Arrangements had been made, if worse came to worst, to take me through the firing line to safety, and I determined to stick. I stuck, and the Germans did not get to the Marne. . . . But I'll tell you all about it later—all the stories of the soldiers, and of the battles, and of me feeding and cleaning, and serving cigarettes to the boys, and in spite of my almost collapsed condition, swearing that I would *not* get *demoralized*, and proving it by putting on a white dress every day, and white shoes and stockings and black ribbons in my hair in honor of the boys that were dying within sight of my door. I feel now that I shall never be able to look out on that plain again with the joy it once gave me, but one of the officers said "When the war is over, and peace is dearer and more consoling to you than you ever dreamed it could be, you will soon learn to look out there with pride instead of pain." Perhaps he's right—but not yet. . . .

Much love to you both,

Mildred.

The war had made a bad situation for many of the artists, particularly those like Juan Gris, the Spaniard, who had been dependent upon Kahnweiler, for the latter, as a German subject, had had to take refuge in Switzerland and could not send funds to Paris. Gertrude Stein had purchased two of Gris's paintings from Kahnweiler just two months before the outbreak of the war.

FROM JUAN GRIS [TRANSLATED]

Collioure, Oct 26, 1914

My dear Miss Stein—

I have just received your money-order for which I thank you very much.

We are very much embarrassed in other respects for, if we have to leave this family with whom we are staying, it seems risky to me to return to Paris with things as they are and in such a financial situation as I am.

Here in the country with what you have sent us we shall be able to get along for more than a month longer. But to return to Paris having spent more than half of your check on the trip seems a little mad to me. Tell me what you think.

Thank you again for your great kindness.

With best wishes,

Juan Gris

Michael Brenner, then in Europe, and R. J. Coady in New York were planning to secure pictures for sale at their Washington Square Gallery. Brenner had discussed with Gertrude Stein various projects, one of which concerned Juan Gris.

FROM MICHAEL BRENNER

Amiens, Jan 3, 1915

Dear Miss Stein

I got your letter the one wishing for a happy year so the other letter you mention regarding Gris must have gone astray.

I have written you the surprise Gris's letter caused me. I am sure he very well understood that he was to let me have all his pictures that is after you had your choice and in a previous letter expressed his satisfaction at the decision he had come to which was à faire des affaires avec moi. So why this sudden change and the discovery of resources through his parents? And now I get a letter from Kahnweiler thanking me for my kindness to poor Gris and confirming he says what Gris told me that he (Kahnweiler) will reimburse me after the war the 60 francs a month that I am kind enough to advance to him (Gris). This is pretty funny and I would enjoy it as a joke had I not also received a letter from Coady who is in a wretched state over the situation. It's true by this time he must have received the stuff you sent him but it's little compared to the program we had planned and had announced. . . .

I've been to the front where it's as fascinating as a game of chance.

Thanks for good wishes. Mine's the same.

Michael Brenner

FROM CARL VAN VECHTEN

210 West Forty-fourth Street [New York]
Jan 21, 1915

Dear Gertrude Stein—

Since The Trend has gone its way I have taken your four sketches to several "literary agents" to see what can be done, but they say they can do nothing with "work so advanced."

Still there is talk at present of a new revue to be called *New York Mornings* or something of the sort. They may be appreciative of the four sketches. Matisse has reached the Montross Galleries—in other words become old-fashioned, but Picabia and Picasso are still exhibiting at Stieglitz's. . . . Marsden Hartley is still in Berlin. [Charles] Demuth gets letters from him. Hartley does not seem to know that there is a war. He speaks of working away, and plans exhibitions this Spring in Vienna, Buda-Pesth, and in New York next fall. . . .

I am writing all the time—I suppose you are too. If you like I'll send the four sketches back to you, or else I'll keep them until an opportunity turns up, and that may be soon. Please remember me to Miss Toklas, and Fania sends greetings to you both.

As ever,
Carlo Van Vechten.

In order to secure funds at this time, Gertrude Stein sold her only remaining Matisse, the Femme au Chapeau, *to the Michael Steins.*

FROM MICHAEL STEIN

Agay (Var), Feb 12, 1915

My Dear Gertrude

Enclosed you will find draft for $2000— Will send you the other $2000 in the early part of March.

For the present the picture had better remain at your place, as it is covered by your policy. Should you want to leave earlier let me know and I'll send the second draft to you to Spain.

Do you plan to leave your Cézannes in your studio when you leave? If not put the Femme au chapeau with them.

Yours affectionately
Mike

Saint Raphael

P.S. When I got to the Bank the man who signs drafts was away for the day, so am sending my cheque, which your bank will take for encaissement.

Yours
Mike

❧

Maud Cruttwell, the art historian, was an English friend from the early days in Florence.

FROM MAUD CRUTTWELL

Hotel Pavillon, San Remo [Feb 26, 1915]

Dear Miss Stein & Miss Toklas,

Here I am feeling very gay & trying to forget that the planet is at war. All my friends are here & we have a splendid time, the weather beautiful. I'm going to pay all my expenses at the tables & I've won already. . . . I'm very glad to be here, so glad that if I can win a little money I shall stay on for a bit. Why don't you come? You might pay the expenses at Rouge et Noir like me—like I hope to do at least. The only thing I regret are my visits to you & those I do regret very much.

Yours very sincerely
Maud Cruttwell.

Later: All my winnings gone, alas!

❧

Someone had told Gertrude Stein that the magazine Rogue, *which Allen Norton was editing, was not a proper medium for the publication of her work, and she cabled Carl Van Vechten to withdraw a manuscript that he had sold to Norton. When she received the check in payment for her contribution, she relented.*

FROM CARL VAN VECHTEN

210 West Forty-fourth Street,
Mar 11 [1915]

Dear Gertrude Stein—

Your cablegram arrived too late as *Rogue* is already published and it includes *Aux Galeries Lafayette*. I am sending it to you with your other three manuscripts by registered post —and in this letter I am enclosing a cheque for *Aux Galeries Lafayette*. I am sorry that I have given something to Norton —if you didn't want me to—but you wrote me to get you an agent and an agent, of course, would sell to anyone he could sell to—even a newspaper. Naturally I thought this would be all right. . . . Everyone admires *Aux Galeries* tremendously. I read it aloud with great effect! and I am frequently asked to do so. I am excited and interested about the tales you are writing and about your departure from Paris. Where are you going? We may go to Italy or Spain this summer. Fan at present is in Florida acting in a lurid moving picture drama in which the principal scene seems to be a jaunt in a boat with a *crazy* sailor. I do nothing but write and go to masked balls as Heliogabalus. All salutations to you and Miss Toklas, and so does Avery Hopwood!

Always
Carlo V. V.

In March a German zeppelin had got through in the night to Paris. Gertrude Stein, writing in her studio, had heard it, but no bombs were dropped. Shortly afterwards, she and Alice Toklas left Paris for Spain and Mallorca.

FROM MILDRED ALDRICH

La Creste, Huiry, Couilly (S. et M.),
Mar 23, 1915

Dearest Gertrude:

Well I am glad you heard the damned thing since it got there, just as a matter of experience, but I'll be hanged if I understand how, with the big aerial fleet that the allies have, it crossed their lines, much less got back safely. That is a mystery. They are fort those g—— d—— bosches. Yesterday we had a cantonment de regiment here—reinforcements going to the Reims section—in fine spirits and condition. . . . Things are beginning to grow in the garden, though I have not done much work yet & it looks a little naked, but in a few weeks it will be better. No cannon heard here for several days & I am that glad. . . .

Affectionately
Mildred Aldrich

FROM FLORENCE BLOOD

Sachino, Bidart (B.-Pyr.), July 23, 1915

Dear Miss Stein—

I was so delighted to get your little letter. Often I have wondered why you had given me no sign. It is evident you did not receive my card which I sent you at Xmas telling you of my whereabouts & my doings.

I have been here since last October. We came here my friend & I & turned her house into a hospital for convalescent soldiers & I have managed the whole concern since it has opened now over eight months. We have forty-five beds, a resident doctor, four sisters, a chaplain, & innumerable servants. I boss them too! & never have I had the feeling of doing a job as well. Every faculty I have is used to its utmost, & all I do is absolutely within my line. . . . This whole experience has been most interesting & I consider it a great privilege to have had work to do in these awful days. . . .

How I should enjoy a good talk with you! Perhaps you will write me a real letter & tell me what you think of all this madness. I wonder if you are serenely writing for a few initiated those extraordinary essays & portraits? You will have to add a postscript to mine, since this new phase of my career! . . .

Remember me to Miss Toklas, & believe me dear Miss Stein,

> Yours affectionately,
> Florence B—

Fernande and Picasso had separated and Eva had taken Fernande's place; but Eva was now sick, and she died shortly after the following letter was written. Beffa was acting as caretaker at 27, rue de Fleurus while Gertrude Stein and Alice Toklas were away. The painting of a harlequin which Picasso mentions is now in the collection of the Museum of Modern Art in New York.

FROM PABLO PICASSO [TRANSLATED]

> 5 bis, R. Schoelcher, 14e., Paris,
> Dec 9, 1915

My dear Gertrude,

I have just had word from you. Don't be surprised that I have not written you since you left. My life is a hell—Eva has been continually sick and grows worse each day and she has been in a nursing-home for the past month. This is the end. My life is not very gay. I hardly work at all. I go to the nursing-home and I spend half the time in the métro. I have not had the heart to write you; I've thought of you—you know that—I even asked Beffa when I met him for news of you.

Even so I have done a painting of a harlequin which in my opinion and in that of several people is the best that I

have done. Rosenberg has had it. You shall see it when you
return. And so my life is well-filled and, as always, I do
not stop.

Greetings to Alice and my best to you

Picasso

Write me

FROM MICHAEL BRENNER

Washington Square Gallery, 47 Washington Square, N. Y.,
Feb 4, 1916

My dear Miss Stein

I was pretty glad to get your letter I assure you and Miss
Toklas's greetings believe me. God, but things from Europe
smell sweet to me now and words from across are full of
mystery. . . .

We have sold three of Picasso's drawings, a couple of Gris's,
a couple of Derain's and where things are sold the part due
to the artist is immediately sent to him. Some of the small
things we have invested in ourselves. We sold all the gallery's engravings, sold another of my drawings at a good
price. We've got a beautiful place now, next door to where
we had started, the most pleasing gallery in New York; there's
one drawback, but that a big one—it's too far downtown.
We'll overcome that if we can hang on long enough, if there's
any future at all for art in New York we'll come into our
own. . . .

When I left Paris, Derain had not yet been at the front,
was stationed somewhere in Normandy. I suppose you know
of Braque being wounded, Doucet killed. . . . Léger stretcher
bearer at the front, Apollinaire brigadier of an artillery
company.

Gris was in Paris when I left, working more or less. I suppose you get news from Picasso directly, in his last to me he

signed himself Professeur de dessin—I suppose he teaches
drawing to orphaned children, he's done some beautiful
work lately. . . .

I wonder if we shall meet in Spring. I'm not sure of being
able to get back. Does all your writing belong to one publisher, have you got a bit of verse you could give us? This is
a secret—Coady expects to start a magazine. We've got some
stuff that you would consider of the best—it need not be
verse. . . .

As always sincerely yours,
Michael Brenner

❧

Washington Square Gallery, 47 Washington Square, N. Y.,
Feb 15, 1916

My dear Miss Stein

Coady and I have been wanting to produce [Ambroise]
Vollard's book on Cézanne in English, we can get backing
for such a venture. There would be considerable profit on the
sale of an edition of one thousand copies which is not too
much to expect with the Cézanne boom now on in this
country. Vollard had once, in the course of a conversation,
pleased at the idea of his book being published in English,
offered to sell the rights to an English edition together with
the plates and cuts that went to make up his own edition.

I know some one here who can translate Vollard's style
perfectly, making it as delightful reading in English as is the
original in French.

I am sending you a specimen translation together with
the original.

Our wish is that if you like the translation, to say as much
to Vollard, it would go a long way to renew his interest which
may have lagged and make him agreeable.

In case he's no longer interested in an English edition of
his book we would like to get permission to run a transla-

tion of the book as a serial in the magazine. So if you can see your way to writing to Vollard telling him that we have submitted a specimen translation to your approval, of your approval, (if so it proves) and maybe hinting of our devotion to Cézanne, it would be of great help to us.

I introduced a new artist to New York named [Diego] Rivera; soon after another gallery took him up. It's very flattering but I wish we were getting richer a little more quickly. I hope I'm not making a nuisance of myself to you.

With my best greetings always sincerely yours

Michael Brenner

The Vollard plan did not materialize, while another scheme of Coady's—to publish a Stein manuscript, "Letters and Parcels and Wool"—also ran into difficulties and the book was never issued. The magazine did, however, appear under the title Soil, *and included a piece by Gertrude Stein, "Mrs. Th——y."*

Gertrude Stein and Alice Toklas wanted to do something for the war effort and returned from Mallorca to offer their services to the American Fund for French Wounded, the chairman of which in Paris was Mrs. Isabel Lathrop. The A. F. F. W. needed vehicles, and Gertrude Stein wrote to some cousins in New York to see what they could do.

FROM HOWARD GANS

Woolworth Building, New York,
Sep 14, 1916

Dear Gertrude:

Your letter to Bird, in which you asked us to try to collect funds for a Ford motor van, reached us just as I was about to go to a military training camp at Plattsburg, conducted by the regular army as part of a preparedness propaganda.

Before leaving I had time only to write letters to the

more available of my friends, from whom I hoped to get the
$450.00 necessary to supplement the $100. I was contributing myself, to cover the cost of delivering the car to you. On
my return from Plattsburg, however, I find that the total
collected is just half the necessary amount, and I shall have
to do some more soliciting. . . . I hope, however, to raise
it within the next couple of weeks, and as soon as I succeed
I will forward the car, and let you know. . . .

Bird and I are thirsting for a chance to come abroad
again, and are praying for the end of the war for that as well
as the usual reasons. However, I don't want it to end until it
ends right. My guess is that somewhere around '18 or '19 we
may be able to come over. I suppose there is no chance of
your following Leo's example by revisiting your native shores,
so as to give us a glimpse of you before that time?

Cordially yours,
Howard.

❧

*An old friend from London days was the English painter Harry
Phelan Gibb. Gertrude Stein was convinced that he and Juan
Gris were the two artists of her generation who would be discovered after they were dead. At this time, after a certain amount
of success with the showing of his pictures in Dublin, Harry Gibb
had fallen upon bad days.*

FROM HARRY PHELAN GIBB

47 Church St., Chelsea, Feb 28, 1917

My dear Miss Stein,

I have written to you twice. I sent you a catalogue of my
show about 3 weeks ago & after that a post-card & yet have
not had a word from you. I can assure you at this time a letter would be quite a blessing. I am having a very bad time
indeed. Tho' it is miles ahead of anything I have ever done,
in fact I made nothing less than a superhuman effort & I *know*

I am justified in telling you how much I went ahead. . . . Well the "Critics"? have made a dead set against me & will not even come to see my exhibition. It is nothing less than sinful. I never knew such damned cruelty. Of course I treated them as tho' they didn't exist, which they don't in the real sense of the word. That is I merely sent them a catalogue, had no "Press" day, no whiskies & sodas & wine . . .

If you saw my show, I think it would nearly bring tears to your eyes. I had great expense, had to have the Gallery specially decorated . . . then the catalogues were most expensive. I have thrown my whole efforts into it. Of course it may be a bit soon to "cry out," it has been open one third of its "run," but I feel it is "doomed"—

[Jacob] Epstein is having the "run" of his life. He is proclaimed the greatest sculptor Britain has ever produced, in fact the greatest sculptor the *world* has ever seen since "Phidias." Whereas, as you know, all he has is sensuous quality plus a sucré, which wins the appreciation of my intelligent countrymen & women. . . .

I hear Wyndham Lewis is having great success in New York—strange, isn't it, he seems to me to have nothing to say whatever, but does a very slippery & shallow kind of thing with no meaning. Is he really having such a big success as I am told? . . .

I wish you could be over here to encourage me. Today I feel desperate, it seems so impossible to move this city on one's own back. . . . Please give my remembrance to Miss Toklas.

> Yours most sincerely,
> Phelan Gibb

In April 1917, the United States entered the war against Germany, and Carl Van Vechten reported upon events in New York.

FROM CARL VAN VECHTEN

151 East 19 Street [New York],
April—of a Thursday [1917]

Dear Gertrude Stein,

Almost everything is happening here, besides our going
to war. Sarah Bernhardt has been operated on at the age of
seventy-three and had several kidneys removed. A day or two
after she sits up in bed and eats spinach, a vegetable which
had been denied her for two years previously. She plans to
begin another farewell tour of America in August, and is
really intending to put on the whole of L'Aiglon. . . .

Isadora Duncan is dancing the Marseillaise and Tschaikowsky's Marche Slav, with a symbolic reference to the Russian revolution, to packed houses. People—this includes me
—get on the chairs and yell. Then Isadora comes out slightly
covered by an American flag of filmy silk and awakens still
more enthusiasm. It is very exciting to see American patriot-
ism thoroughly awakened—I tell you she drives 'em mad; the
recruiting stations are full of her converts—by someone who
previously has not been very much interested in awakening it.

Then there is the Salon des Independents (so to speak
—at least), which has already had two scandals. The first
concerned the rejection by the board (which is not supposed
to have the power to reject anything) of an object labelled
"Fountain" and signed R. J. Mutts. This porcelain tribute
was bought cold in some plumber shop (where it awaited the
call to join some bath room trinity) and sent in. When it
was rejected Marcel Duchamp at once resigned from the
board. Stieglitz is exhibiting the object at "291" and he has
made some wonderful photographs of it. The photographs
make it look like anything from a Madonna to a Bud-
dha. . . .

Fania [Marinoff] has been appearing in Wedekind's "The
Awakening of Spring." At least she appeared in it once. Then

the police stepped in and now all concerned are awaiting a decision from the bench of the Supreme Court.

I am writing. My new book [*Interpreters and Interpretations*] is finished, but it will not appear until fall. We do want to see Paris again soon. I have a feeling that the war will last a very long time; everybody is so anxious that it should stop, but it won't. I should like to see you run a FORD. Perhaps I will yet.

All felicitations and salutations to you both from us,

Carlo V. V.

❧

The Ford car arrived in good time and was christened "Auntie," after Gertrude Stein's Aunt Pauline, "who always behaved admirably in emergencies and behaved fairly well most times if she was properly flattered." For the A. F. F. W., Gertrude Stein, Alice B. Toklas, and "Auntie" went to Nîmes.

FROM HOWARD GANS

Woolworth Building, New York,
June 18, 1917

Dear Gertrude:

Your very welcome picture card representing the "Aunt Pauline" with you in the background served to add an additional prick to my conscience, which has become tender over my failure to answer a postal received from you some months ago exhibiting you in the unfilial proceeding of sitting on Aunt Pauline. . . .

It is mighty good to hear from you and to know that you are on the job and doing something that really counts tangibly toward the Allies' success. . . .

Over here things are in a good deal of a turmoil. Even to those of us who can think of little other than the War and its progress and consequences, the whole thing seems very distant; and none of us, I fear, are gripped by it and stimulated by it as we should be. . . . However, there . . . is some satisfaction in knowing that the "Liberty Loan" is out of the way, and that, on the whole, the results are satisfactory. For, considering the short time that has elapsed since the President of the United States was telling the country that the fight on the other side was a struggle between madmen, with the implication that the two sides were equally mad, and since he was telling us that the thought of preparedness was pure hysteria and that it was quite impossible to contemplate our being drawn into the conflict, it really should be considered rather as a tribute to the alertness of the American mind to find that there are two million people ready to take the matter sufficiently seriously to subscribe to one of the largest, if not the largest, single loan that has ever been floated. This may sound like an eaglet's scream, but really it is an apologia. . . .

Leo . . . is psycho-analyzing and being psycho-analyzed, philosophizing and perambulating; also, he is writing things that are being published. And, of course, everything he writes justifies itself through the detachedness and clarity of its viewpoint. (I am reminded here that the clarity is only perceptible to the elect, through an interjection of my stenographer to the effect that so much of his writings as she had typed for him have not impressed her as particularly clear, and that if other people did not understand them any better than she did they would not carry far.) Of course, it is to be said that he has not achieved the capacity of writing for the general public. He says that his great ambition is to say what he has to say in such manner as to get it published in the Saturday Evening Post. . . .

Everybody sends love, as do I, with wishes of more power to your elbow.

Cordially yours,
Howard.

Leo and Gertrude Stein had not corresponded since his departure for Italy, but from the United States he sent her an item which turned up in the family archives.

FROM LEO STEIN

Nantucket, Oct 8, 1917

In a letter of Rachel's dated Vienna Nov. 28, 1875 "Our little Gertie is a little Schnatterer. She talks all day long and so plainly. *She outdoes them all.* She's such a round little pudding, toddles around the whole day & repeats everything that is said or done."

Leo

FROM THE AMERICAN FUND FOR FRENCH WOUNDED

Paris, Nov 29, 1917

Dear Miss Stein:—

Mrs. Lathrop received your interesting letter and asked me to take the matter up, because she is obliged to leave this week for America.

We also received your wire yesterday, reading: "Can anything be done immediately about X Ray installation for chief Hospital. Borrowed installation has been reclaimed. Seriously wounded from Italy expected daily. 1500 to 3000 francs asked for installation.—Urgent need.—Rest of sum has been secured.—Directors and doctors make special plea for American help.—Please wire provisional answer Hotel Luxembourg.—Nîmes.—STEIN.—TOKLAS."

We took the matter up immediately with the American Red Cross and learned that the Directrice of the hospital called on them 4 days ago and that they have already taken up the subject of the installation.

The letter from the "Econome" about the details of the

installation required which you enclosed in your note we
handed to the Red X, as they needed the information contained therein. They assured us that the matter was under way
and would be pushed as fast as possible and we wired you,
last night, to this effect.

The question of supplies for the needy in villages is a
special matter that we would have to take up as a new departure. At the moment, we have not any funds or supplies
for this particular purpose.

How are you off for supplies? Have you received our envois?

Very sincerely yours,

. . . Secretary

FROM LUCIE LEGLAYE [TRANSLATED]

Nîmes, Dec 24, 1917

Miss Gertrude Stein

I want to thank you for your generous gift to my husband: please believe that in returning the pocket-book which
you lost he only did his duty, and you owed him nothing for
the service; thank you then on behalf of our children for
whose Christmas we were able to buy some sweets.

We are evacués from the Meuse district; my husband
was discharged because of lung trouble contracted at the
beginning of the war; my son is in the army at 17, and hopes
soon to get into aviation since he is a mechanic.

May I ask you a favor for him, since he did not dare ask
it himself: would you be his war-godmother? If this is impossible, please excuse my presumption in asking this for my
son whose address I give below.

Respectfully yours

Lucie L.

for her son Abel Leglaye

    19th Artillery

    64th Battery

    in garrison at Nîmes (Gard).

❧

Although they were working primarily with the French, Gertrude Stein and Alice Toklas occasionally met American doughboys in their travels. W. G. Rogers, nicknamed "The Kiddie," came from Springfield, Mass. His first letter had been addressed to Miss Toklas.

FROM W. G. ROGERS

Somewhere in France, Dec 26, 1917

My dear Miss Stein,

I trust this second letter following so closely on the heels of the first one won't discourage you. But I hasten to repeat that if you answer about a third of my letters you will gain a golden seat in Heaven and will have done much more than your share. But you see, I am sick. I've read Shakespeare, and Browning, and Jules LeMaître, and lots of other things; but I can't read all the time and so I write. Having had so much time for it, I've now gone all the way around the "roster" and it is unfortunately your turn again. . . .

I asked our mechanic about the knock in your Ford. He said that if it wasn't due to the carbon, it was probably a broken bearing in your driving rod. Get the car going fast, and then, leaving it in gear, put on your foot brake. If that makes it knock, it is one of the afore-mentioned bearings, and ought to be fixed—in Paris. Also, you absolutely should *not* touch the carburetor. Put it in one place and then leave it alone. That is final, and comes indirectly thru the man in charge of setting up all the Ford ambulances used by the U. S. in France,—a man whom Ford is paying several thousand dollars a year for so doing; and directly thru our mechanic. Thirdly, the only possible reason I could find for its starting with difficulty when hot was that you had too rich a mixture. In the summer you ought to be able to get along on *less* gas than in the winter.

I trust that advice will help you out. It came from experts who really know about all there is in a Ford. You had better be careful about that knock; to let it go might wreck the car "Pauline," I think you called it; a trip to Paris might be very wise.

And now that I'm this far I'll go on with a tale of our merry Xmas. We feasted on goose, as the main dish. I don't think we dined quite as well as we did Thanksgiving Day, but we had more fun. I took my life in my hands, bundled up, & went to the café we had hired as a banquet hall with the others. We had a real *Tree*, including candles and presents. . . . So it was a very merry time, altho there were several fellows away in hospitals or on duty and two on permission at Nice. Then, having spent all the preceding afternoon, half the night, and all Christmas morning translating and typewriting Dickens' Christmas Carol, that was read to them in the evening. So everyone went to bed happy, and some a bit dizzy.

The best part of it is, that our Xmas packages from the States probably won't get to us for a month and a half, according to the newspapers. Sometime ago there was an article in the Lit. Digest about delivering every package to our "boys in the trenches" on Christmas morning. To expedite matters, the government asked that all such packages be marked "Christmas" very plainly. As a result of that, every such package has been held up in New York and quite possibly none of them have left there yet. Unfortunately, trusting but deceived relatives sent all my boxes plainly marked, and I fear the cigarettes will rot before I see them.

Possibly I have written quite enough; anyway I can't afford more than two sheets of paper for one letter so I'll close. Please remind Miss Toklas that her turn comes next; console her for it; and pay her my deepest respects.

Ever despairing,
W. G. Rogers.

Gertrude Stein wrote a portrait of Henry McBride, entitled Have
They Attacked Mary, He Giggled. (A Political Caricature),
which was printed by Frank Crowninshield in Vanity Fair, *though
it had to be cut slightly. Mr. McBride had the complete piece
printed privately as a separate pamphlet, decorated with a drawing of him by Jules Pascin, and circulated it among his friends.*

FROM HENRY McBRIDE

358 West 22, New York, Jan 7, 1918

My dear Gertrude Stein:

You didn't send me a Christmas card this year! True, I
didn't send one to you. But then I never send them to anyone, and you always do. It is clear we are becoming estranged!
It is probably my fault. But I will reform. I will make New
Year's resolutions. I made New Year's resolutions last year,
however; and nothing much happened. You can't understand
why I don't write letters, can you? You didn't understand
why I sent the portraits of me, (or I should say 'you and me')
to everybody before I sent them to you, the authoress of the
work? I am sure I don't understand that myself. I am in the
peculiar position of being an entirely virtuous person whose
life is a succession of acts of villainy! . . .

How did you like the portrait? I have the Mms. of your
portrait of Braque, which I mean to publish somehow, if
possible. It might not be a bad idea to collect all of your
portraits and make a little book of them. I hear good words
spoken of your "Three Lives" from all sorts of places. You
are by no means forgotten, although you must understand,
that nothing in the way of art that requires people to re-
adjust their faculties, has any chance here. . . . Poor Jacques
Copeau is here with his Théâtre du Vieux Colombier doing
the most beautiful things in his theatre, and no one goes to
see them, and the few that do, sit like uncomprehending

little wooden blocks. His Molière stuff is gorgeous, done before Gordon Craig simplified backgrounds, in grand colors.

Give my kindest regards to Alice. It's hopeless I can't recall her last name. I was forced once to refer to her as Alice in the public prints lately. Isn't that shameful? But what can you do when you have no memory? I was chagrined the other day to read that wisdom was "learning well remembered." In that case I shall never be wise, for I never remember anything. . . .

But just the same I'm always yours

Henry McB

I'll send you some more *portraits*!

The principal duty of a "war god-mother" was to send letters and parcels to her soldier god-son.

FROM ABEL LEGLAYE [TRANSLATED]

Nîmes, Jan 12, 1918

Mademoiselle

. . . Thank you very much for the warm clothing and thank you too for the little flag. I shall take good care of it and shall wear it when I go up to the front convinced that it will bring me good luck. I hope that this spring under the protection of your flag and with the support of your compatriots we shall recover our poor country, where the Germans left us only homes in ashes. I was fourteen when we had to flee before the massacre of the Germans who were burning the countryside. It is all engraved on my memory; I shall never forget it; and we shall also not forget all that you have done for us.

Yours respectfully,

Abel Leglaye

At about half-past eleven on the night of January 30th, the Germans began the bombardment of Paris.

FROM MICHAEL STEIN

Montigny-sur-Loing, *S et M,*
Apr 12 [1918]

My Dear Gertrude—

Sally & I went up to Paris yesterday for the first time in a month. . . . The cannon which had been silent for several days gave us a chance until four o'clock and began just as we were leaving the Am. Express Co for the Gare de Lyon to take the train back. . . . Of course I gave Beffa the key to the Atelier & showed him how to arrange the pictures. We both looked over the situation carefully he & I, and decided that the Pavillon was better than the Atelier much more solid & with a joint wall against the main building. So he will put most of the pictures in the Pavillon against the wall with a nail in the floor to prevent the stacks from slipping. . . . In the Atelier all the furniture is moved back away from the sky light and all ornaments laid down flat.

Then I did a thing which I had been pondering over for several days before going to Paris and which I weighed carefully in all its respects. I took the [Cézanne] Baigneurs, the [Cézanne] Fumeur, & the Manet, made a good package of them and on our way to the Gare left them at the Am. Ex. Co. who will place the package in a wooden box and send it to you—insured for forty thousand francs. At Nîmes you can have it stored in the Safe of the branch of the Credit Lyonnais and at least you will have them where they need cause you no anxiety. Please let me know at once when you receive the package, and don't forget to put *Seine et Marne,* you did not in the last letter. The Cézanne portrait I could not send without rolling it as the PLM is absolutely closed to Messageries—only small packages can go; but should you desire it, I arranged with Beffa so that he knows the picture. He saw it put in the closet & promised to save it in case anything happened. I also arranged with the Am. Express Co. in case I wrote to them that they would have their expert packer call for it, take it off the chassis, roll it and box it and send it to you insured for the amt. we should indicate. Only the Insurance does not begin until it is in the hands of the Railroad. There is no way of covering it while being handled in Paris. I am also looking into the matter of cannon insurance. The rate is fixed but the companies can't be compelled to accept the insurance, and if the bombardment should become intense, of course the Companies would bust. I tell you it's no cinch arranging and deciding things these days. Of course as regards personal possessions the only danger is an actual hit, as luckily they do not experience the nervous strain that humans are subject to and Paris is quite large and has lots of empty spaces. The shells are not nearly so bad as the air torpedoes and so far are not incendiary. . . .

Please let me know if you get this letter. . . .

Love from
Mike.

In the early days, Mildred Aldrich had introduced Gertrude Stein to William Cook, an American painter, and his French wife Jeanne. They had been in Mallorca at the same time as Miss Stein and Miss Toklas in 1913. Later, in Paris, Cook had worked for a brief period as a taxi-cab driver, and it was he who taught Gertrude Stein to drive her Ford. In 1918 Cook had joined the A. E. F., and Miss Stein was sending him, now and then, copies of the magazine Argonaut.

FROM WILLIAM COOK

32nd Aero-Eng. Sqdrn., American Ex. Forces, France,
May 16, 1918

Dear Friends—

Your letter came yesterday and I was glad to get it and the photos. . . . There is really so little to write about here in camp. If the war lasts another couple years, I guess we'll be reduced to writing a form post-card—for lack of any news. . . .

The Argonauts are great fun. I have to read most of the editorials twice—why I don't know. Maybe you can guess. If there are no politics in the army it does seem that there still are some outside. Jeanne is conserving the food supply of her hard-pressed country by sending me roast chicken that never ceases to arrive in an advanced state of decomposition. The French are so economical. . . .

My best to you both,

Always
Cook

FROM ABEL LEGLAYE [TRANSLATED]

Postal Sector 118, May 29, 1918

My dear God-mother

I am writing to give you my news which is not bad just now and I hope yours is the same. I am now in the trenches and have been for three days; it isn't too bad. We are attacking just now; the cannon fire a good deal, they don't stop. I am to carry munitions at night and barbed wire, with two horses and a caisson. The cannon balls whistle but I am already used to that and I am not afraid. Two of my comrades were wounded yesterday not far from me; one was hit five times and the other had a light wound; their horses were killed. At night one doesn't sleep very much because the German planes come to bombard the batteries; I should like to be able to chase them.

The food is very good at the front. We have good bread,
a litre of wine and brandy.

I shall close for today, sending you my respectful good
wishes and thanks.

Your god-son
Abel L.

*Another American whom Gertrude Stein and Alice Toklas had
met in their travels was Samuel L. M. Barlow, then stationed with
the U. S. Intelligence Service in Marseille.*

FROM SAMUEL L. M. BARLOW

33 Rue Grignan, Chez Mme. Ouvière, Marseille
[Spring? 1918]

Dearly beloved Ladies,

This fly-leaf note-paper is due to the Crise de Papier—
and of course over here one can't have the family crest or
x Fifth Avenue at the top. It isn't done in the army. But if I
wait any longer for respectable note-paper you might never
know just how much I enjoyed our motor trip through
Provence—the Towers of Aigues Mortes, Arles, Pont du Gard
and Avignon. The little arch at San Rémy and Les Baux
are always popping up in my mind's eye—and constantly
the delight of that trip relieves the strain of the Battle of
Marseille. Really I am grateful and I had such a good time
and you were both so nice. . . .

I got back more or less on time—weary but O so satisfied.
If you knew how I had yearned to see all those lovely places!
Now all that remains is a Château near Perpignan.

Let me know if you come this way and I will show you
the ruins here—mostly human.

Very sincerely yours
Samuel L. M. Barlow

IV. THE EARLY TWENTIES
1919–1925

For several years, with Mildred Aldrich's example before her, Gertrude Stein had cherished the hope of having her work appear in the pages of one of the most conservative New England magazines. She misread the signature of the editor as Ellen Sedgwick and consequently addressed him in her reply as "Miss."

FROM THE ATLANTIC MONTHLY

Boston, Oct 25, 1919

My dear Miss Stein:—

Your poems, I am sorry to say, would be a puzzle picture to our readers. All who have not the key must find them baffling, and—alack! that key is known to very, very few.

Yours faithfully,
Ellery Sedgwick

H.-P. Roché continued in his role of general introducer and brought Katherine Dreier, who the following year, with Marcel Duchamp, founded the Société Anonyme, which was to do so much to advance the cause of modern abstract art.

FROM KATHERINE S. DREIER

Hotel Brighton, 218 rue de Rivoli, Paris,
[Nov] 25 [1919]

Dear Miss Stein—

Roché asked me to let you know whether Marcel Duchamp as well as I would be free to come to your studio on Friday at half past four. So I am writing to say that we are all 3 coming with much pleasure.

I am glad to know you for many reasons, but also because I believe you too are a friend of Mary Knoblauch's. Mary has shown real courage these past years by upholding the American right of freedom of speech.

Looking forward with much pleasure to Friday, believe me

Sincerely
Katherine S. Dreier.

FROM THE ATLANTIC MONTHLY

Boston, Dec 4, 1919

Dear Miss Stein:—

I thank you for your letter and for the manuscript, which I shall try to read myself within the next few days.

Your letter, however, seems to show me that you misjudge our public. Here there is no group of *literati* or *illuminati* or *cognoscenti* or *illustrissimi* of any kind, who could agree upon interpretations of your poetry. More than this, you could not find a handful even of careful readers who would think that it was a serious effort. Pardon me if I say this. I am talking quite seriously, and am trying not to be critical but to be reasonably helpful. You will, however, doubt my statements, as is your right, and so I am inclined to say that I will print your poem on Ireland, together with your letter, and let The Atlantic's public be judge and jury. I have a department in the magazine for discussion, much of it for intelligent discussion, and quite apart from the humorists who will spend their foolish wits upon it, we shall have an opportunity of serious rejoinders. There is, I think, nothing in your letter to the printing of which you will take exception, and it will serve admirably to explain the discussion which has arisen between us. . . .

Pardon my candor, which is invited by your own, and believe me

Very truly yours,
Ellery Sedgwick.

The lady to whom you write is evidently the result of an imaginative rendering of my masculine name. I apologize for my own cramped & careless hand—

Ellery Sedgwick.

FROM LEO STEIN

Settignano, Dec 14 [1919]

Dear Gertrude

I sent you a note from N. Y. before I left as I found that the antagonism that had grown up some years ago had gotten dissipated and that I felt quite amiable, rather more so even than I used to feel before that strain developed. It's rather curious, the change that has come over me in the last month or so. You know all those digestive troubles & most of the others that I had, I eventually found to be merely neurotic symptoms & all the time in America or at least intermittently during all that time I was trying to cure the neurosis. But they're damned hard things to cure & it was as it was with the digestive cures always up and down, till recently I was in almost utter despair. Then, indirectly through Harriet [Clark] as it happened, I got on a tack that has led to better states. This has finally led to an easing up & simplifying of most of my contacts with things and people and bro't

about a condition where it was possible to write to you. . . .
"The family romance" as it is called is almost always central in the case of a neurosis just as you used to get indi-
gestion when we had a dispute. So I could tell pretty well
how I was getting on by the degree of possibility I felt of
writing as I am doing now.

It's a curious thing to look back upon one's life as I do
now as something with which I have nothing to do except
to stand for the consequences because it was really a pro-
longed disease, a kind of mild insanity. . . . Unfortunately
my first attempts at psychoanalysis did not work satisfactorily, every little advance was countered by as great a relapse.
If it hadn't been for that I might have had a successful time
over there. . . . Georgiana [King] wanted me to give a
course at Bryn Mawr but unfortunately I couldn't risk it as
I didn't know what minute I might shut up like a trap &
the course come to an end. I'd like to have found out though
whether some notions of mine about teaching are practi-
cable or not. I suppose that I shall write about them this
winter but I'd like to have been able to put them to the test.
I'm going to Algiers in about a week where my address will
be Poste Restante. My regards to Alice

Leo

*In 1920, things had still not improved for Harry Phelan Gibb. He
asked for news of* The Making of Americans, *which was still unpublished.*

FROM HARRY PHELAN GIBB

Hotel Lecadre, Rochefort-en-Terre, Apr 1920

Dear Gertrude,

It is very kind of you to go & see the studio. I was very
afraid it would be 'no go,' still I have far from given up hope.
I feel quite certain something will turn up for us this autumn.

For I cannot go back to England. The thought puts me in a dreadful state. It is hopeless. . . .

Any news of your book? Really *it must* get published. I feel it is quite a bit of very bad management somehow a large publication has not happened long ere this. But it needs, or rather you need some business man to do this. For its success I have no doubt whatever. Think of all those who have copied you. It makes my blood boil & they get a hearing too! . . .

Ever very sincerely,
Harry Phelan Gibb

FROM HENRI-PIERRE ROCHÉ [TRANSLATED]

99 Boulevard Arago, Paris—14e.,
Apr 10, 1920

Dear friend,

Thanks for your note. . . .

Do you want me to come to lunch, or just for coffee, with Marie Laurencin and Erik Satie, or only one of them,* on Friday the 16th?

Your
H P Roché

*say whom [*Roché's note*]

Erik Satie, the French composer, had first been brought to the rue de Fleurus by Picasso.

FROM ERIK SATIE [TRANSLATED]

Arcueil-Cachan, Apr 15, 1920

Dear Miss —

Roché has told me of your kind invitation, & . . . . it is impossible to accept . . . . Yes . . . .

. . . . I who would so have liked to come! What a shame! Poor me!

How gay it will be!

What to do? . . . .

. . . . . I am writing to Roché. Perhaps he will find a solution, ... a formula: he is so clever in his way, good old fellow!

Let's wait and see . . . .

. . . .

Thank you, Mademoiselle; best wishes to the exquisite Marie Laurencin,

from
Erik Satie

P.-S.—*At the last minute:*
I am free!
   I am coming!
      Until tomorrow!

John Lane had imported some copies of Three Lives *for publication in England in 1915. In 1920, he was at last persuaded to reprint the volume. Complimentary copies were sent to Israel Zangwill and Frank Swinnerton, among others.*

FROM JOHN LANE

The Bodley Head, Vigo Street, London, W.1,
Sep 6, 1920

Dear Miss Gertrude Stein,

Next week I am publishing your "THREE LIVES." I think you told me that you had some Press influence in England. Was it not to Roger Fry you wished copies sent? Anyone you can think of I shall be pleased to send copies to, and enclose any letters you like to write to my care. If you have journalistic friends here, they will be of help just now, I am sure. I am looking forward with much interest to the reviews. I thought we had better publish the book as it stood, rather than make any alterations. If this book goes all right, we can then do something together in the near future.

Yours very truly,
John Lane

FROM ISRAEL ZANGWILL

Far End, East Preston, Sussex,
Sep 26, 1920

Dear Miss Stein,

Thank you so much for sending me your "Three Lives." You were misinformed if you were told that I did not "like" your privately printed volume, if by that was meant the portrait of somebody at an Italian villa. It made me tremble for your reason, and I am not sure it was not a joke palmed off on me by the cynical Pearsall Smith. I cannot yet read your new book—I am up to my neck in proofs of my own new book, "The Voice of Jerusalem"—but a glimpse is quite enough to see that your latest art method is not inconsistent with sanity. I shall take the book abroad with me, where I am going in about a fortnight, and will honestly let you know my impression.

With kind regards to yourself and your brother,

Sincerely yours,
Israel Zangwill

FROM FRANK SWINNERTON

London, W.C.2, Sep 30, 1920

Dear Miss Stein

Thank you so very much for sending me a copy of 'Three Lives.' I am very proud to have this, and to renew acquaintance with Melanctha and the other suffering human beings whom you have drawn and exemplified with such extraordinary penetration.

Yours sincerely
Frank Swinnerton

❧

FROM ISRAEL ZANGWILL

Far End, East Preston, Sussex,
Oct 6, 1920

Dear Miss Stein,

I have had time to read your first story before leaving England, and as the others seem to be of the same texture, I can at once give you my opinion. The measure of my failure to appreciate your other work is the measure of my appreciation of this, which seems to me a very considerable literary achievement, full of subtlety and originality, and revealing a beautiful sympathy with humble lives.

The only faint rufflements I found in reading "The Good Anna," came from the split infinitives, which, although I am not a purist, exceed the necessities of language (e.g. "to very clearly see," page 53); from the trick of spelling German, etc. with a small "g"; from not having been told early enough that it was a Southern American town; and, finally, from a feeling of discrepancy between the image of Miss Mathilda as a large comfortable lady, and her image as an active tramper. But these are mere specks in a real work of art. So I tender you my respectful congratulations and renewed thanks for sending me the book.

I am only passing through Paris this time, but I am returning six months hence, when I shall hope to see you, if you are still there.

Please convey my kind regards to your brother, and believe me,

Sincerely yours,
Israel Zangwill

FROM HENRY McBRIDE

The Coffee House, 54 West Forty-fifth Street, New York,
Nov 13, 1920

Dear Gertrude:

Your letter which doesn't breathe fire and brimstone as I expected (and deserved) has just come. Also Three Lives. I read it through again with the same empressement as before. I don't review books but I'll try to sneak a little announcement of it into my page.

Last spring I dined with Walter Arensberg & [Marcel] Duchamp and we talked of a new book of your things and the best way to put it over etc. My opinion was that you ought to print it privately at your own expense and once a thousand volumes were printed they could be sold somehow. I think in the end it would pay for itself. You see you are handicapped by writing in a language that is behind in the arts. *There is a public for you but no publisher.* . . . For all that, a writer who already has so many followers as you have is safe in assuming the expense of publishing. Only don't be impatient. Let the books that don't sell at once wait in your trunk and every new book you get out helps sell the old ones. . . .

I was to have written this last spring but I collapsed seriously and my feeble correspondence stopped automatically . . . If you come across any amusing art things in the papers kindly clip them out and send 'em along. There is absolute famine of news here.

With love, toujours
Henry McB.

Gertrude Stein one day on the street encountered Jacques Lipchitz, the Polish sculptor, whom she had known slightly. He had

just finished his bust of Jean Cocteau. Later in the spring he did a portrait head of Gertrude Stein and became himself the subject of one of Miss Stein's portraits. She enjoyed posing for him, she said, because he was an excellent gossip and was able to supply the missing parts of several stories.

FROM JACQUES LIPCHITZ [TRANSLATED]

54, Rue du Montparnasse, Paris,
Jan 25, 1921

Dear Madame,

Will you give me the pleasure of coming to see me on Thursday the 27th at about three o'clock, with Miss Toklas? I should like to show you my last statuette to get your opinion of it which I value highly.

Hoping to see you then,

Respectfully yours,
J Lipchitz

Sylvia Beach had established her American bookshop in Paris and given it the name "Shakespeare and Company." She was a principal agent in mixing nationalities, and her shop became a meeting-place for Americans in Paris. It was in the summer of this year that Miss Beach asked to bring the American novelist Sherwood Anderson to see Gertrude Stein.

FROM SYLVIA BEACH

Shakespeare and Company, 8 rue Dupuytren, Paris (6e.),
Thursday [June? 1921]

Dear Miss Gertrude Stein,

Would you let me bring around Mr Sherwood Anderson of Poor White and Winesburg Ohio to see you say tomorrow evening Friday? He is so anxious to know you for he says you have influenced him ever so much & that you stand as such a great master of words.

Unless I hear from you saying NO I will take him to you after dinner to[morrow] night.

> Yours affectionately
> Sylvia Beach

❧

Mildred Aldrich had before the war introduced Gertrude Stein to Mira Edgerly, who had had a considerable success in making miniature portraits of fashionable Europeans. "The Edgerly," as her friends called her, had in January 1919 married Count Alfred Korzybski, the semanticist, and was eager to help launch his new book Manhood of Humanity—The Science and Art of Human Engineering. *To Miss Stein, Count Korzybski sent four copies.*

FROM MIRA EDGERLY-KORZYBSKA

> El Mirasol, Santa Barbara, California,
> July 14, 1921

My dears—

Alfred is sending a book and its accoutrements that explain itself—and is writing all the rest.

I felt it would be so much more secure that they would land safely to their destination by passing through your hands. In helping Alfred with the book I have had one wonderful year playing with people who really think, really feel & really know . . .

I hope we are not putting on you what may prove a burden.

Surely by the autumn I will have tidied my affairs & we will be over. I am hungry to see you.

As [Mildred] Aldrich described me as "the altruistic enthusiast in search of a great mission" I've found it all in Alfred, and am more happy than I thought a human was capable of registering. I'd adore hearing from you.

> Yours faithfully, affectionately
> Edgerly-K.

FROM COUNT KORZYBSKI

Fifth Avenue Bank, New York
[July 14, 1921]

My dear Miss Stein:

Encouraged by my wife, I have taken the liberty to send to you 4 [copies of my] book and some literature about it. . . . I was told to proceed directly to the business end; with your kind permission that's what I will do. . . .

One of the books with a dedication is for you, the three others are for the French, German and Italian translations.

In England I have sent the book . . . to Professor Alfred Whitehead . . . hinting only that I would like to be published by the Cambridge University Press. If he will like the book he will push it; if not he won't. I did not ask him to do so.

In France I have sent a copy, the publicity and a short letter to Professor Henri Bergson, without asking him anything, of course he MAY be of very great value if he would like to help. I also sent two copies of the book to Professor Benoy Kumar Sarkar from India . . .

Till now the book has proven to be a good base for bringing people together and I look forward with hope that it will continue to be so. . . . If you will like the book, and feel like pushing this work you could do a great amount of help in giving the books to proper people and trying to find out the reactions of Bergson, Whitehead, Sarkar. If their reaction is favorable, and you would all come together, well in such case the work would begin strongly at once. . . .

I feel strongly that the highest type of scientists would be the most desirable translators, the selection of words being very difficult and of the most vital importance. As to the conditions, we do not know anything about the publishing in Europe, and we would have to rely on the best judgment of our friends. . . .

Thanking you in advance for all your kindness and troubles caused by the books and this letter, I wish to express my deepest gratitude

Yours faithfully
Korzybski

Contact, *a literary periodical edited by William Carlos Williams and Robert McAlmon, made its debut in December 1920. The first number, reproduced from typewritten copy, contained contributions from, besides the editors, Marsden Hartley and Marianne Moore.*

FROM ROBERT McALMON

351 West 15th St., New York [Summer? 1921]

Dear Miss Stein:

I enclose a Contact for you. Through Marsden Hartley, and Mrs. Knoblauch—I believe, he said—we have some of your Ms., and don't know whether to use it or not. It doesn't mean much to me, but a whimsical emotion now and then at some neat phrase, or an irony upon unfinished thought, and situation. Of course it is not necessary, and it is very kind, at times to forget the slavery of sequence, logic, and of the "natural." . . . I take your work—how shall I say, seriously, or at least with a potential or suspended respect. I don't get it, and believing that you have conviction to go on in your manner, simply have a waiting frame of mind.

Will you talk a little about your method for us, to permit us—if we publish some of your things—to be able to back ourselves in doing so? We shall not publish anything because it is exotic—new tricks are too easy. But after going over "England" and "Mrs. Th——y," I'm ready to believe that you're experimenting valuably. . . .

Yours sincerely,
Robert McAlmon

*Kate Buss had introduced Alfred Kreymborg, the American poet,
and his wife to Gertrude Stein. Kreymborg's first book, Apos-
trophes (1910), had been printed like* Three Lives *by the Grafton
Press. The Kreymborgs, in turn, introduced Harold Loeb, who was
then editing the periodical* Broom.

FROM ALFRED KREYMBORG

Casella Postale 63, Como, Aug 9, 1921

Dear Miss Stein:

This is by way of a lame effort of thanking you for your
recent hospitality. 27 Rue de Fleurus has gone and will continue far in our memory.

We are contented as mice with cheese here. I know of
no experience richer than dawdling about with the na-
tives. . . . We shall miss you and a few others in Paris, but
after all, there is an occasional mail. And one is able to work
here, normally, just as one eats or breathes. There is no cor-
rosive effort necessary.

I haven't heard from Loeb as yet. I trust he has called
on you?

With every good wish from 2 to yourself and Miss (whose
name I dread mis-spelling),

Faithfully,
Alfred Kreymborg

*The Ernest Hemingways came to Paris, bringing a letter of intro-
duction to Gertrude Stein.*

FROM SHERWOOD ANDERSON

Chicago, Illinois, Dec 3, 1921

Dear Miss Stein:

I am writing this note to make you acquainted with my
friend Ernest Hemingway, who with Mrs. Hemingway is going

to Paris to live, and will ask him to drop it in the mails when
he arrives there.

Mr. Hemingway is an American writer instinctively in
touch with everything worth while going on here and I know
you will find Mr. and Mrs. Hemingway delightful people to
know. . . .

Sincerely,
Sherwood Anderson.

Did you get my note about the introduction?
Love to Marsden Hartley.

*Harry Gibb, Henry McBride, and other friends were eager that
Gertrude Stein should publish a volume of her short manuscripts.
Kate Buss, a New England journalist and poet who had interviewed Miss Stein, was just then having her* Studies in the Chinese Drama *published by the Four Seas Company in Boston, and
Mr. Brown of that company—to whom Gertrude Stein gave the
nickname "Honest-to-God"—agreed to undertake* Geography and
Plays, *though at Miss Stein's financial risk. Sherwood Anderson
had consented to write a preface for the book.*

FROM THE FOUR SEAS COMPANY

168 Dartmouth Street, Boston,
Jan 5, 1922

Dear Miss Stein:

I am sure that Sherwood Anderson's explanatory preface
for your book will be very helpful, not only as an aid to the
general reader but also to us in marketing. . . .

I am glad to enclose contracts providing that we will make
an edition of 2500 copies at a cost of only $2500, and that
we will pay you a royalty of 15%, and in addition that we will
pay you $1.00 a copy on every copy sold of the first edition,
which will bring you back the return of your investment. . . .

As soon as we have completed the arrangements I am

sure you will be glad to send me a short biographical sketch of yourself, which we can use to great advantage in our preliminary publicity, and I find we can use very satisfactorily several photographs of an author. Many special magazines and journals are glad to print photographs of interesting authors, even when they do not print many reviews.

I assure you that even if we never succeed in making any great amount of money on this book, we appreciate the value of having your name on our list, and you may be sure that we shall not lose the opportunity offered by such an unusual book to get special publicity and comment.

Yours sincerely,
Edmund R. Brown

FROM SHERWOOD ANDERSON

708 Royal Street, New Orleans [Feb? 1922]

My Dear Gertrude Stein—

I was delighted to get your letter of today and to hear that arrangements are made for the publication of the book.

I was afraid you might have changed your mind about having me write the introduction and had you done so I should have been quite upset. It's a literary job I'd rather do than any other I know of. I'll get at it very soon and send it along.

Someone told me you were off Americans, that you had become bored with them and that frightened me too. "I'll bet she'll put me in with the rest of the mess and chuck us all," I thought.

In the January Dial Paul Rosenfeld had an article on my own work in which he spoke of the influence on myself of first coming across one of your books, at the time they [were] raising such a guffa over here. I'd like you to see the article but hav'n't it here.

I came down here about a month ago and am living in the old French Creole quarter, the most civilized place I've found in America and have been writing like a man gone mad ever since I got off the train.

You will hear from me with the introduction very soon.

Your Sincere admirer.

Sherwood Anderson

Chicago, Illinois, Monday, Mar 13, 1922

My dear Gertrude Stein:

Of course, I understood what you said about your disliking Americans was only fun. I am delighted that you are delighted with the preface. Any way, I knew what I wrote was sincerely felt. I have no doubt but that the Four Seas will get it as I sent it some time ago.

I had a charming letter from Mr. Hemingway, stating how glad he is to know you. I, myself, will not get to France this year, although the Lord knows I would like to be there this Spring.

With love

Yours very sincerely,

Sherwood Anderson

William Cook had taken a job with the American mission in the Near East.

FROM WILLIAM COOK

Tiflis, Apr 1, 1922

Dear Friends,

This is the Paris of the Caucasus. It is rather nice. The streets are large, wide and seem to have been very well kept. It is a place where much money has been spent. Probably the residence town of the oil men in other days.

We came up in a box car from Batoum. It was a very pleasant trip. Two nights and a day and a half. Seemed something like the army again. The first night was rather amusing as we stopped at every station. At first it was a bit exciting as before every stop we were surrounded by a real live howling mob. Of course we were in the dark and keeping quiet, in hopes that our car would not be invaded. There [were] people all over the train on top and on the bottom and on all the sides. The crowd however were very nice. When we found out what it was all about we calmed down and went to sleep. It seems that the people had come down from the country to get their seed corn and were taking it back on their backs. Naturally it is to them a matter of life and death and they were all for getting on that train. At every stop our car was opened and when our convoyer explained that we were the American mission they melted as if by magic and stormed another car. They were most peaceable and gentle if anything. Of course the noise was considerable and in a strange language it was a bit impressive at first. . . .

My best to you both,
Cook

Harold Loeb had eventually written to Gertrude Stein and had bought a manuscript of hers for publication in his magazine Broom, *of which early numbers were published in Rome. Miss Stein's contribution was printed in three instalments.*

FROM HAROLD LOEB

Broom, 68, Via Leccosa, Roma (9), Italy,
June 5, 1922

Dear Miss Stein,

Please forgive our withholding this remittance until "If You Had Three Husbands" was completed.

I regret that we have heard little report of its reception

from New York. Waldo Frank and Matthew Josephson have remarked on it enthusiastically—the average American in Rome asks why is it printed? Probably you are used to such reactions.

I look forward to seeing you on my next visit to Paris, as I remember with pleasure our two talks.

Kind regards
H. A. Loeb

✿

With the arrangements completed for the publication of Geography and Plays, Gertrude Stein and Alice Toklas left Paris in their Ford, "Godiva," to spend the summer, fall, and winter chiefly in Saint-Rémy. The misunderstanding with Juan Gris in 1914 had led to Gertrude Stein's not seeing him for a number of years, but in 1921, she wrote him a note of congratulation on a recent exhibition of his pictures, and a reconciliation ensued.

FROM JUAN GRIS [TRANSLATED]

8 rue de la Mairie, Boulogne sur Seine (Seine),
Aug 23, 1922

My dear friend—

Thank you for your very kind letter. . . .

I'm working a great deal, a great deal too much, and am somewhat disheartened with painting. With pictures it's the same as with roulette: you try often and win rarely. Even so, I think I've won once or twice of late. Sometimes I have the desire to do nothing, to think of nothing absolutely, but it is too difficult. If I do not work I get despondent. For me work is repose and repose is restlessness. Happy are those who know how to do nothing without being restless.

I do not remember whether I told you that on the 15th of next month I am going to the hospital to undergo a delicate operation. I shall have at least two weeks in bed. This obligatory vacation does not appeal to me, above all because of the indiscriminate mixing of the hospital.

Looking forward to reading you soon, my dear friend. Regards to you both

Your
Juan Gris

Through the efforts of the Steins and other friends, Mildred Aldrich was eventually awarded the Legion of Honor for her books about France and the war. She had just received the decoration when she wrote to Gertrude Stein and Alice Toklas.

FROM MILDRED ALDRICH

La Creste, Huiry, Couilly (S. et M.),
Sep 1, 1922

Dearest girls:

Thanks for your letters and telegram. Of course I am for the moment overwhelmed and terribly timid. This is the last thing I ever thought of—it is not only far from any dream I ever had—it is outside in the most absolute way of any thought or any ambition I ever had. I'll try and get used to it before you return and to recover from the impulse I have when any one looks at me to cover it with my hand. . . .

I am glad you are having such a fine time, and I only wish I could [send] some of my wonderful early pears to you. I never eat one without thinking of you. The early ones will be finished before you return—and so will the abundance of tomatoes.

This is all the news I have—and it is not much news to you. . . .

Affectionately
Mildred.

Gertrude Stein had met Jo and Yvonne Davidson through Mabel Dodge many years before. In 1922, Jo Davidson did a seated statue

of Gertrude Stein, and was himself the subject of a Stein portrait.
This was finally published not in the Century Magazine but in
Vanity Fair in February 1923, and was accompanied by a photo-
graph of the Davidson work.

FROM JO DAVIDSON

Hotel Brevoort, New York, Sep 11 [1922]

Dear Gertrude,

I have just received your letter, and have written to Kate
Buss but I have no other photos except the ones Man Ray
took. The plaster came out fine and Yvonne is going to send
it to the Salon d'Automne.

I am hammering at the Century Magazine to publish your
portrait of me, and illustrate it with my portrait of you. I hope
to succeed—they are so dam timid—that it's awful. If they
should turn me down, I'll try elsewhere.

My job here is finished and I am only waiting for the
bronzes to be cast. Which means another 3 or 4 weeks.

What a hell of a job it is to put things over. It simply has
nothing to do with one's work . . . I am just aching to get
back to Paris & get to work. New York always affects me that
way. So in a way it's a good thing. . . .

My very best to you and Alice and don't forget Godiva.

Yours

Jo.

FROM KATE BUSS

44 Bradlee Road, Medford, Massachusetts [Oct 1922?]

Dear Gertrude,

Do you recall New England winds? How they howl in
October as though December were a fact—as I suppose it is;
today is such a one. . . .

I am wondering if you have, but of course you have, seen

the delightful things [Sherwood] Anderson says of you in a recent New Republic. Rich, nice imagery, individual, I think you must be pleased with it. . . . I telephoned Honest [-to-God Brown] two days ago. He says your book will appear about the tenth of November—wasn't April or March, the date you first terrified him with? . . . WHAT a slow business getting published is. . . .

Just had a letter from you written at St. Rémy which sounds as though you had had several cocktails. It was gay and rhythmic and inconsequential . . .

I should like to know how you know there is no demarcation between your thinking and your unthinking mind. I don't see how you CAN know that. Do give me a further boost in that direction. I seem SUCH a dunce! Maybe I am . . .

Much love, and you ARE a dear.

Kitty

FROM THE AMERICAN FUND FOR FRENCH WOUNDED

Paris, Oct 6, 1922

Madame:

We have been requested by the French Government to transmit to you—with their grateful memories for your generous and devoted collaboration—the Médaille de la Reconnaissance Française, that was conferred upon you some time ago.

Kindly acknowledge its receipt to us . . .

Yours faithfully
American Fund for French Wounded
Paris Depot

Geography and Plays *at last appeared in January 1923, and a copy was sent at once to Carl Van Vechten in New York. He asked*

about the still unpublished "history of a family," The Making of Americans.

FROM CARL VAN VECHTEN

The Colonial Inn, Fairhope, Alabama,
Feb 22, 1923

Dear Gertrude,

The book is lovely, and I thank you. I adored the *Nations* & *Marcel* & one or two of the plays are too divine. *Me* especially I like, but I had seen that before. How nice, nevertheless, to be in a big book by Gertrude Stein. But I *always* put you in my books. You are in the next one, The Blind Bow-Boy, which comes out next August when I shall send you a copy. Madel [Dodge] will not like this book. She is not in it. What has become of *The Family*? I want to show the ms. to my publisher [Alfred Knopf]. It has occurred to me that the time is getting ripe for its publication now that you are a classic & have Imitators & Disciples! Please do something about this!

You probably have seen Avery [Hopwood] and I am sending you one or two others later. Have you read Ronald Firbank? You should. His last one, The Flower beneath the Foot, published by Grant Richards in London, will do. I am sending him your book to Bordighera, he will love it.

I am sending you a (bad) photograph of Florine Stettheimer's new portrait of me. Perhaps you can tell something even without the colour. She has also done Marcel [Duchamp]. Get him to get you a photograph of it. . . .

By the time this letter reaches you I will be back in New York again.

Tout coeur,
Carl Van Vechten

🌸

Avery Hopwood, the playwright, author of such plays as The Gold Diggers, The Demi-Virgin, *and* The Bat (*the latter with* Mary

Roberts Rinehart), had been sent to Gertrude Stein by both Carl Van Vechten and Mabel Dodge Sterne. He presented Mrs. Sterne's letter.

FROM MABEL DODGE STERNE

[Early 1923?]

Dear Gertrude,

This is to introduce Mr. Avery Hopwood. I don't need to tell you about him & his pursuits because, as usual, you will know more about him in two minutes than I could in two years!

Yours,
Mabel.

Gertrude Stein had written a piece "Idem the Same: A Valentine to Sherwood Anderson," which Jane Heap had agreed to publish in the Little Review.

FROM SHERWOOD ANDERSON

[Reno, Nevada, Spring 1923]

Dear Friend,

Got your note yesterday and just recently have been thinking about you a good deal. You see, in this book [*A Story Teller's Story*], on which I am at work, I am trying to make a kind of picture of the artist's life in the midst of present day American life. It has been a job. So much to discard. Have never thrown away so much stuff. I want to make it a sort of tale you see, not a preachment.

Also I have to find out if I can what really affected the fellow. There isn't any doubt about you there. It was a vital day for me when I stumbled upon you.

But also there was and is something else. There was not only your work but also your room in the house there in Paris. That was something special too. I mean the effect on myself.

You would be surprised to know just how altogether American I found you.

You see, dear friend, I believe in this damn mixed-up country of ours. In an odd way I'm in love with it. And you get into it, in my sense of it quite tremendously.

I've been checking over things and people that have meant most. You, Jane Heap, Dreiser, Paul Rosenfeld, Van Wyck Brooks, Alfred Stieglitz. That about nails the list. It is a list that would make Jane sputter with wrath perhaps. She is an arbitrary one—that same Jane.

What I have to figure is just the people who have given me fine moments. I've an idea that's what counts most.

Well you'll see the book some day. I'm glad Jane is going to publish the Valentine. I like it because it always stirs me and is full of sharp criticism too.

Am sitting right here in a desert as big as God until I get this book done . . . Then I'll shift to something else and I hope some of these days my shifting will bring me to your door again.

With love,
Sherwood

❧

Following his suggestion, Gertrude Stein had sent Carl Van Vechten the first three volumes of the manuscript of The Making of Americans *to show to Alfred Knopf. She had just written "A List. Inspired by Avery Hopwood." Mabel Dodge Sterne, in Taos, New Mexico, had divorced Maurice Sterne, the painter, and married a full-blooded Indian, Antonio Luhan.*

FROM CARL VAN VECHTEN

151 East Nineteenth Street, New York,
Apr 16, 1923

Dear Gertrude,

Three volumes have arrived. Please don't send any more until you hear from me. When Mary Knoblauch had the set

I read a little in the first volume but now I have read it *through* and my feeling is that you have done a very big thing, probably as big as, perhaps bigger than James Joyce, Marcel Proust, or Dorothy Richardson. Knopf won't be back until the middle of May. I don't know what he'll make of it. You see the thing is so long that it will be hellishly expensive to publish, and can one expect much of a sale? I mean, to the average reader, the book will probably be *work*. I think even the average reader will enjoy it, however, once he begins to get the rhythm, that is so important. To me, now, it is a little like the Book of Genesis. There is something Biblical about you, Gertrude. Certainly there is something Biblical about you. I liked the passages about fat people, and washing, and religion, and old man Hersland certainly emerges complete from this first volume.

There is another thing, the type is so dim in this copy, and there are so many errors in spelling, etc. that it is much harder reading than it would be in print. I shall explain these things to Knopf. I wonder what he will make of it? Hope for nothing until we find out. I am sure, however, that, if not now, sooner or later this book will be published.

The [Stettheimer] portrait is not very big, and I am thinner now. The colour is important. The picture is more about me than of me. You are right about the curtains; they are the stroke of genius in the picture.

I am also interested in what you say of Raquel Meller. I have heard so much about her, and she is coming to America in a year or so. So many people come to America after they have tired Europe of themselves, but you and I *started* in America. And that is more important for America than Raquel Meller and the Russian Ballet are important for America.

Which of Avery's plays did you rearrange? Was it the Gold-Diggers or The Demi-Virgin? I am crazy to see it!

Marinoff and I send our love to you and Miss Toklas,

Carlo Van Vechten

✳

Sherwood Anderson had sent Gertrude Stein a copy of his Many
Marriages, *published in February of this year, and she had written
to him about it.*

FROM SHERWOOD ANDERSON

[Reno, Nev.] May 9, 1923

Dear Gertrude Stein—

Your letter found me out yesterday. Am still out in the
far west—in the desert country and I surely did think I had
written you recently. There must be a letter—somewhere—
on the road to you.

I got the book—with the charming Valentine—about two
weeks ago—someone forwarded it.

And now I have this letter of yours about the book.

Do you know I think it the most clear-headed criticism
I've had and that you have its weaknesses and good points
about rightly sized up.

It's a job—for an American—with the damned Anglo-
Saxon blood in him, to become quite impersonal, but I've
a hope I'm going toward it.

I cut out of New York about the time your book and my
own were published and did not see the comments on either.

I felt like work and wanted to work and did not want to
be thinking much about the job done—for good or evil.

Then I got out here and the painting impulse got me and
I've been fairly swimming.

For one thing I'm doing a quite frankly autobiographical
book [A *Story Teller's Story*]—(that may take something of
the tendency to be too much interested in self out of me)—
unload it—as it were.

Then I am getting a book of tales—call it "Horses and
Men," ready for book publication this fall. There are, I fancy,
some good things in it.

I am dead set on getting to Paris next year and do hope I shall make it and that you will be there. If you aren't I'll look you up—where you are.

I believe I'm getting some things in painting. I get up early—write in the morning—tear around for two or three hours and then settle down to paint. It excites me, even more than writing—it's such a holy gamble—for me anyway.

I've a long novel at work in me but I shall not get to that until next fall or winter.

Am delighted you are working. I'd fancy, what you are doing means more to more people than you know.

With love,
Sherwood.

FROM CARL VAN VECHTEN

151 East Nineteenth Street, New York,
June 5, 1923

Dear Gertrude,

[Edmund] Wilson, the young man on Vanity Fair says A List ["inspired by Avery Hopwood"] is too long and wants to cut it. He seeks my permission but I have written him that . . . he must communicate with you. He adores the whole thing, but says that the mechanics of V. F. prohibit publishing manuscripts of that length.

There is no news as yet about your [Making of] Americans, and no further news from Mabel [Dodge Luhan] . . .

I'll be sending you my new book [The Blind Bow-Boy] in about a month. I have just finished the first draught of a new one [The Tattooed Countess], to be published next year.

I do not know what has happened to Avery, except that he wrote me that now that Mabel had married an Indian he saw no reason for returning to New York before June.

Alice B. Toklas and Gertrude Stein at 27, rue de Fleurus (1923)

On your note, I conclude: "Perhaps America, well yes, perhaps America! That's *us!*"

Love to you and Miss Toklas,

Carlo V. V.

The Blind Bow-Boy appeared and Gertrude Stein wrote a second portrait of its author, entitled "Van or Twenty, Years After." This was later printed in the Reviewer *for April 1924.*

151 East Nineteenth Street, New York,
Oct 22, 1923

Dear Gertrude,

Mabel [Dodge Luhan]'s letter about The Bow-Boy almost knocks me flat. She identifies herself with Campaspe, which, of course, she *isn't:* says it's the most perfect character in fiction: "showing the perfect equilibrium which results from a soul in utter conflict." Not a word about the chief! and to this day I don't know how to spell her FIFTH name.

The new portrait I liked very much, although as yet it is little but meter and rhythm to me. More will come later. It is a little difficult for me to *ask* Vanity Fair to publish it as it is about *me* but I thought, as occasion offers, I might show it to an editor or two and perhaps one of them might ask me for it. Would you mind if it were published elsewhere than Vanity Fair?

There is news about the History of a Family at last. Knopf thinks the best thing to do is to issue a circular, which he plans to do a little later, telling something about the book and inviting subscriptions. If he gets enough he will go ahead. I think this is an excellent plan. If he does the book he wants to do it *beautifully* and that will cost money: three or four volumes of large type, with possibly portraits of you by David-son, Picasso, etc. as frontispieces. And signed by you. This will all cost money and it will probably be necessary to charge $25

for the set! Therefore, before plunging, it seems advisable to
see how many copies he can sell in advance by subscription.
The whole idea of publishing a novel of this length all at
once is so novel, the book itself is so original, that I should
not be surprised to find collectors leaping for it. Let him, however, take his time; if he does it he will do it better than any
one else. . . .

With much love,
Carl Van Vechten

*Alfred Maurer, the American painter, had been an habitué of the
Stein salon in the early days, but Gertrude Stein had heard from
him rarely in later years.*

FROM ALFRED M. MAURER

Feb 10, 1924

My dear Gertrude

Sherwood Anderson wanted me to send you this clipping,
he thought the terror part of meeting you might be of interest.

If I were in 27 rue de Fleurus I could talk my head off,
mine is a story no fountain pen can write, so some day.

Until then my love to you and Alice

Comme toujours
Alf

*Ernest Hemingway had gone to Canada to work on the Toronto
Star, but in January 1924, he returned to Paris. Ezra Pound had
invited him to help Ford Madox Ford with his Transatlantic Review, then being financed chiefly by John Quinn, the American
lawyer, collector, and patron of letters. Hemingway lost no time
in suggesting to Ford that he print Gertrude Stein's The Making
of Americans in the new periodical.*

FROM ERNEST HEMINGWAY

[113, rue Notre Dame des Champs, Paris] Sunday p.m.
[Feb 17, 1924]

Dear Miss Stein—

Ford alleges he is delighted with the stuff and is going to call on you. I told him it took you 4½ years to write it and that there were 6 volumes.

He is going to publish the 1st installment in the April No. going to press the 1st part of March. He wondered if you would accept 30 francs a page (his magazine page) and I said I thought I could get you to. (Be haughty but not too haughty.) I made it clear it was a remarkable scoop for his magazine obtained only through my obtaining genius. He is under the impression that you get big prices when you consent to publish. I did not give him this impression but did not discourage it. After all it is Quinn's money and the stuff is worth all of their 35,000 f.

Treat him high wide and handsome. I said they could publish as much of the six volumes as they wished and that it got better and better as it went along.

It is really a scoop for them you know. They are going to have Joyce in the same number. You can't tell, the review might be a success. They'll never be able to pay 9,000 times 30 francs tho.

Your friend
Hemingway.

Carl Van Vechten had had Gertrude Stein's "An Indian Boy" printed in the Reviewer, *a periodical published in Richmond, Virginia, where his own "second portrait" also eventually appeared. Plans were being made for the publication by Kahnweiler of the "Gertrude Stein Birthday Book," with etchings by Picasso, for whose son the book itself had been written. Jo Davidson's article about Gertrude Stein had been published in* Vanity Fair.

FROM CARL VAN VECHTEN

151 East Nineteenth Street [New York]
Mar 5, 1924

Dear Gertrude,

I've not written you for such a long time because I've been so busy & I've had nothing to write you about *your* business—nor have I yet. Knopf has not spoken again. You see he has been moving—& getting out his *new* magazine, The American Mercury—and what not. Presently, I will speak to him again. If he doesn't do The History of a Family somebody some day will: I feel sure of that. Don't send the other volumes until I ask for them.—As for your wonderful portrait of me—[Frank] Crowninshield who has had it ever since you gave it to me at last decided that Vanity Fair had been publishing a good deal of your work & so he would lay off awhile —a stupid decision. But I have sent it elsewhere—& it will be published, I am sure. The Indian garçons in the Reviewer have created a sensation. I am sending one to Mabel [Dodge Luhan].

My new book, The Tattooed Countess, is all done & the proofs read. It will appear in August. Now, I am getting together a book of musical papers, & I have two introductions to write for other people's books.

Of course, I must have the Gertrude Stein birthday book as soon as it is out. I like Joe Davidson's thing about you & so does most everybody else. It is, however, lacking in humour & I think of that as a very essential part of you, but nobody else who writes about you seems to get this. Anyway . . . I salute you!

Carl Van Vechten

Harold Stearns, an American journalist friend of Ernest Hemingway, was acting as an agent for Horace Liveright in Paris. At his

request, Gertrude Stein cabled Carl Van Vechten to get the first
three volumes of the manuscript of The Making of Americans
away from Alfred Knopf and turn them over to Liveright. But
Liveright finally decided not to publish the book.

Meanwhile, there was some question as to whether even the
printing of the book in the Transatlantic Review *would continue,*
for the withdrawal of John Quinn's financial support had created
serious difficulties for the periodical. Lady Rothermere was at this
time financing the publication in London of the Criterion *under*
T. S. Eliot's editorship. Gertrude Stein and Alice Toklas had left
Paris to spend the summer in Belley.

FROM JANE HEAP

Samois, Sunday [July? 1924]

Dear Gertrude Stein:—

Yesterday Juan Gris and I decided that we'd devote an
entire number of the L[ittle]. R[eview]. to his work—don't
you want to write a word about him for the occasion? He is
giving me 20 photographs and co-operation with Kahnweiler.
I like him very much.

I have our story all laid out—am coming to Samois this
week to put it in shape to send off to America.

I wish I could tell you how many things my hours at your
house mean to me. My kindest greetings to Alice and yourself.

Jane Heap.

Later—

I have talked to Lady Rothermere—and if the Transatlantic
fails, we are going to arrange to have your "novel" transferred
to the Criterion and continue—!

Yours

jh

Robert McAlmon and Winifred Bryher were planning the Con-
tact Collection of Contemporary Writers. This was published in

the following year and contained Gertrude Stein's "Two Women."
Ford Madox Ford, Ernest Hemingway, Marsden Hartley, James
Joyce, and Ezra Pound were among the other contributors.

FROM ROBERT McALMON

Château Riant, Territet, Suisse [Aug? 1924]

Dear Miss Stein:

We want to get out a book of various writers—samples—
for continental distribution. It'll be a conglomeration, because
some names will come in simply for their 'public' value, and
to aid the sale of the book. . . . We have about a list of
thirty five we want to get, and then we'll print the book, for
pre-spring, if we can manage it. Will you send along something to me for inclusion? Not to exceed 5,000 words if
possible.

Bryher got hold of your *Three Lives*; and I read it through
first. The second story was amazing; a *clarified* Dostoevskian
depiction of niggers. It gave me an entirely different and
larger view of your work, though I had been getting that
quality out of the T. A. Review story. Bryher was as struck
with it as I. I wish I had an ability to get down, critically
what I felt about the story, for all of the articles I've seen
on you insist too much on a quality you undoubtedly have,
that of refreshing the language, and of sensitizing it, but it
strikes me they don't dwell enough on the zip of intelligence,
and whoop of personality power, you get into "The Making
of Americans;" and "Melanctha." But I can't find myself
interested enough in educating the public to use my mental
energy trying to put into terms what I think you've done.

Do send me in something—or several things—for the
book. . . . Of course a bit out of The Making of Americans,
taking from away further on—where by its location the expected death of the T. A. will mean that we print it first—
would do, but I'd rather it were a complete short story.

Yours sincerely,

R. McAlmon

❧

FROM ERNEST HEMINGWAY

[Paris] Aug 9, 1924

Dear Friend—

Well the news is that the transatlantic is going on.

I have a friend in town who (or whom) I got to guarantee Ford $200 a month for six months with the first check written out and the others the first of each month with an option at the end of 6 mos. of buying Ford out and keeping him on as Editor or continuing the 200 a month for another six months.

That of course was not good enough for Ford, who had hitherto stayed up all night writing pneumatiques and spent 100s of francs on taxis to get 500 francs out of Natalie Barney and that sort of business. Once the grandeur started working Ford insisted on 25,000 francs down in addition and then as the grandeur increased he declared he wanted no money at all till October if Krebs [Friend], this guy, could guarantee him 15,000 francs then! It is a type of reasoning that I cannot follow with any degree of sympathy.

I got Krebs to back the magazine purely on the basis that a good mag. printing yourself and edited by old Ford, a veteran of the World War, etc. should not be allowed to go haywired. Now Ford's attitude is that he is selling Krebs an excellent business proposition and that Krebs is consequently a business man and the foe of all artists of which he Ford is the only living example and in duty bound as a representative of the dying race to grind he Krebs, the natural Foe, into the ground. He's sure to quarrel with Krebs between now and Oct. on that basis and Krebs was ready with the ft. pen and check book. . . .

When Ford told me, the day you . . . left, that the next number was in doubt and he was sending no M.S. to the printer in any event, I decided to hang onto your M.S. as he was threatening to bring out a quarterly which was pretty vaporous as he had about decided to use the death of Quinn as an excuse to kill off the Magazine. Jane Heap was trying to fix it up with the Criterion, Major Elliott and Lady Rothermere's paper, and I didn't want to have to get it away from Ford and then give it back and gum up everything in case he did pull off a quarterly and the Criterion didn't come through. Jane might have been able to work it at that but the Major is not an admirer of yours and I don't believe Rothermere could make him print it if he didn't want to. I don't believe Jane's drag would be strong enough to make Rothermere force a fight on the question.

At any rate now there will be regular and continuous publication and after all that is better than embalmed in the heavy, uncut pages of Eliot's quarterly. . . .

> Always
> Ernest Hemingway.

[Paris] Aug 15 [1924]

Dear Friend—

I wrote you to the house a few days ago. You've probably gotten it by now. . . .

The able bodied directors of the transatlantic meet today to elect Krebs President. He is going to be president and pay all the Bills. He has breakfast every morning at Ford's and things are going smoothly. I am so glad it is going on being published with a minimum of worry now because it was too awfully bad to think of busting off publishing the long book regularly. . . .

I have finished two long short stories, one of them not much good, and the other very good and finished the long one I worked on before I went to Spain where I'm trying to do the country like Cézanne and having a hell of a time and sometimes getting it a little bit. It is about 100 pages long and nothing happens and the country is swell, I made it all up, so I see it all and part of it comes out the way it ought to, it is swell about the fish, but isn't writing a hard job though?

It used to be easy before I met you. I certainly was bad, gosh, I'm awfully bad now but it's a different kind of bad. . . .

Ernest Hemingway.

FROM FORD MADOX FORD

the transatlantic review, 29, Quai d'Anjou, Paris (4e),
Sep 18, 1924

Private.

Dear Miss Stein,

I have just got your letter of the fifteenth. I am very sorry that you have had to wait for your cheque. The business management has passed, to my immense relief, out of my hands into those of a capitalist who is a little slow in parting with money but who *will* part immediately. I have had immense trouble in re-starting the review and it is only just beginning to run smoothly again, but, at any rate it runs, looks as if eventually it might really pay. . . .

As for the novel: Hemingway when he first handed me your manuscript, gave me the impression that it was a long-short story that would run for about three numbers. It was probably my fault that I had that impression. Had I known that it was to be a long novel I should have delayed publishing it until my own serial had run out and should then have offered you a lump sum as serials are not accounted so valuable as shorter matter. I do not get paid for my own serial at all, neither does [Ezra] Pound for his.

Hemingway now says that you have been offered what he calls real money by the *Criterion* for the rest of *The Making of Americans* so I really do not know how to deal with the situation. Apparently your book consists of three or four novels. In that case, if the *Criterion* really is offering you real money I suppose you could let them have the second novel and rook them all that you possibly can. I should be very sorry to lose you, but I was never the one to stand in a contributor's way: indeed I really exist as a sort of half-way house between non-publishable youth and real money—a sort of green baize swing door that every one kicks both on entering and on leaving.

You might let me know your private reflections on the above in a letter marked *private*. And would you, in any case, let me know the full length of your book and its respective parts? I will then stir up the capitalist to make an offer which you can compare with the *Criterion*'s. . . .

With kind regards, I'm yours

Very faithfully
[*Unsigned*]

FROM ERNEST HEMINGWAY

[Paris] Oct 10 [1924]

Dear Friend—

. . . The next batch of Making of Americans has come and I am correcting it today. Will go down to the office as they did not send the original ms. with it.

By the way did you ever . . . get a letter from Ford marked private and confidential and not consequently to be revealed to me in which he said I had originally told him that the Makings was a short story and he had continued to publish it as such only to have me again tell him after six months that it was not a short story but a novel, in fact several novels? He had a number of other lies in this letter which he hoped I would not see and the gist of it was that he wanted you to make him a flat price on the first book of the novel as serials are paid for at a lower rate than regular contributions like six month long short stories etc.

I don't know whether he ever sent it—if he did you might tell him you will talk it all over on your return.

I have had a constant fight to keep it on being published since Mrs. Friend conceived the bright idea of reducing the expenses of the magazine by trying to drop everything they would have to pay for. . . . Krebs' latest idea is to have all the young writers contribute their stuff for nothing and show their loyalty to the magazine by chasing ads during the daylight hours. Ford ruined everything except of course himself, by selling the magazine to the Friends instead of taking money from them and keeping them on the outside as originally arranged. Now the two Friends feel that . . . the only way to make a Go is to stop all expenditure. So I believe the magazine is going to Go to hell on or about the first of Jan and in that case I want you to get your money fairly well up to date and to have had the Makings appear regularly straight through the life of the review.

When you consider that the review was dead, that there was never going to be another number and that Ford was returning subscriptions in August (this Ford has forgotten and Krebs never knew) it is something to have it last the year out. . . .

Well this had better stop. The weather is fine here now. I've been working hard. . . .

Always yours,
Hemingway.

Mildred Aldrich was in financial difficulties. Her friends were trying to raise money to help her and to establish a memorial after her death. It was she who had introduced Janet Scudder, the American sculptor, to Gertrude Stein.

FROM JANET SCUDDER

70 bis, rue N. D. des C. [Paris]
Dec 3, 1924

Dear Toklas-Steins,

I don't like the name of "Amies Mildred Aldrich" because it is not American. And we should have to have two names, each entirely different from the other—the French name and "Friends of Mildred Aldrich" which sounds awfully like charity.

I am perfectly stuck on the poetic flow of the sound of "Mildred Aldrich Memorial." They are beautiful words that swing together and to frenchify the title, we only have to add one little e whenever we want to. Why don't you ask Mildred tomorrow how she feels about it herself? "Foundation" sounds awfully rich and magnificent because of Foundation Rockefeller, etc.

If I were Mildred and were having this thing done to perpetuate my memory, I should want it frankly called even before my death by its real name. It's simple and direct, explains our desire to do her great honor, and has a lovely sound. Also it's awfully important to have a name that absolutely expresses the purpose of an association and a name easily remembered.

I got a contribution yesterday at a tea party, don't know how much yet. . . .

Affectionately,
Janet

FROM MILDRED ALDRICH

La Creste, Huiry, Quincy-Ségy, S. et M.,
Dec 8, 1924

Dearest Gertie:

I look a bit like the wreck of the Hesperides this morning—witness my handwriting—but that is my fault—and I am all at sea. The bank sent me out 520 francs in bills this morning and no sign of the source, and that upsets me. I know by my experience with Morgan & Harjes Co two months ago that I shall gain nothing by asking who sent it—so there I am. My grandmother taught me that it was "more blessed to give than receive." Life taught me that it was a darned sight easier & my mother taught me that grace was a prettier virtue than gratitude, so—God give me grace to accept—gracefully, as I am rather weak in gratitude. One thing I learned yesterday which was a wonderful uplift—that people were to live on the place when I was gone. . . . I should love to think of young people enjoying what I have loved—especially young painters, for the country is paintable. This is a scrawl—forgive it. . . .

Affectionately
Mildred.

The struggle continued to get the manuscripts published.

FROM THE LONDON MERCURY

London, E. C. 4, Jan 8, 1925

Dear Madam,

We shall of course be pleased to consider any thing you may care to submit to us, provided that it does not exceed 7000 words in length.

Yours faithfully,
J. C. Squire
Editor.

London, E. C. 4, Jan 30, 1925

Mr. J. C. Squire very much regrets that he doesn't understand Miss Stein's two stories.

*At last Gertrude Stein persuaded Robert McAlmon to undertake
the long-deferred publication of* The Making of Americans *in the
series of Contact Editions, which had already included his own
book* Village *and Hemingway's* Three Stories & Ten Poems.

FROM ROBERT McALMON

29, Quai d'Anjou, Île Saint-Louis, Paris
[Feb? 1925]

Dear Miss Stein:

Here is the preliminary announcement of the book. When
it gets under way we'll get out a sheet of press notices on it,
but for the time being this general announcement which is
going out, for the whole lot of books, had better be confined
to just a statement that it is to be published. I'll draft a contract for you to sign. . . .

I liked your comments on Village.

Yours sincerely,
McAlmon

*Meanwhile, Jane Heap had agreed to act as a kind of agent for
Gertrude Stein's work in New York, where she had opened the
Little Review Gallery.*

FROM JANE HEAP

24 East Eleventh Street, New York,
Feb 22, 1925

Dear Gertrude Stein:—

Don't think that I have been remiss about your manu-
scripts, if I have seemed to be so about writing to you. New
York is always so hectic on one hand and slow on the other.
Boni and Liveright have had "The Long Gay Book" and
"Three Lives"—for months, trying to decide. I have called and

written but they hesitate. . . . [B. W.] Huebsch has taken months to answer me in regard to the publication of the "Making of Americans." It is as if they waited for some occult sign. But we'll do what we planned yet. . . .

I want to come to Paris in May—if I can make it. I have many plans. My gallery is attracting a lot of attention. All is well.

It is very nice to hear from you—give my greetings to "Alice"—and I am,

Always yours,
Jane Heap—

After attending the University of Chicago, Glenway Wescott had lived chiefly in Europe. He had published a small book of poems, The Bitterns, *in 1920, and a novel,* The Apple of the Eye, *in 1924.*

FROM GLENWAY WESCOTT

Hotel Savoy, 30 rue de Vaugirard, VI.,
Mar 2, 1925

My dear Miss Stein,

Almost two years ago Miss Loy very kindly presented me to you. I have now returned to Paris, and am writing to ask if I may call upon you again, at a time that will suit you best. It would be a great privilege and a great pleasure.

Yours sincerely,
Glenway Wescott

FROM CARL VAN VECHTEN

150 West Fifty-fifth Street [New York]
Apr 18, 1925

Dear Gertrude,

The announcements of The Making of Americans arrived and I was thrilled; I am scattering them about where I think they will do the most good. And I am waiting with tremors of excitement for the book. And, of course, I am awaiting the volumes illustrated by Juan Gris and Picasso with enormous interest too. It seems to me that with the dawning of another year all the world will know of your glory!

You didn't say if you had received RED, which I sent you. Presently I'll be sending you Firecrackers, my new novel, and I have been arranging a book of essays called Excavations which is to come out next January. . . . In the meantime I'm sending you Fania [Marinoff Van Vechten], who sails on April 29 on the Aquitania and will be in Paris towards the end of May. If you are moving about write her . . . and tell her where you'll be, as she wants to see you. Also Alfred and Blanche Knopf are going over and I'm giving him a letter to you. We may get The Making of Americans done over here yet!

Don't forget me,
Carlo

Jane Heap had brought Lady Rothermere and T. S. Eliot to see Gertrude Stein on November 15, 1924. Mr. Eliot in the course of conversation said that if he ever printed anything of Gertrude Stein's in the Criterion *it would have to be her most recent work. As soon as her guests had departed, Miss Stein wrote a portrait of T. S. Eliot entitled "The Fifteenth of November," and sent it off to the* Criterion. *It was finally printed, after further delays, in the issue of the periodical for January 1926.*

FROM T. S. ELIOT

London, Apr 21 [1925]

Dear Miss Stein

I must apologise most humbly for the long delay, due to my and my wife's severe illness. I no longer, of course, have any claim on your poem, but I should like to use it. That would

have to be in October, as the unexpected receipt of two contributions from people whom I promised to print as soon as
possible, has jammed the June.

I am immensely interested in everything you write.

Hoping that we may meet again before long.

Sincerely yours,
pp. the *Criterion*
T. S. Eliot

*Samuel L. M. Barlow recalled his meeting with Gertrude Stein
and Alice Toklas in Nîmes and the conducted tour of the sights
of the country which they had given him.*

FROM SAMUEL L. M. BARLOW

EZE Village, A. M., France [Spring 1925]

Dear Miss Stein,

Provence—you brought me here, you lifted my eye-lids
upon Les Baux, you fed me by the waters of the Rhône, you
initiated me with the white dust of Liguria and shot me with
arrows of cypress, olive, and fig—it is seven, eight years gone
and you have forgotten, but I have stayed—returned rather—
where you left me, a Provençal. The Ford, Miss Toklas, Nîmes
—and one memorable day from Aigues Mortes to Avignon—
and your infinite kindness.

Will you not come this summer and stay in my old ram-
part a thousand feet over the sea—and for a few days recap-
ture, remake, confirm what to me was a real inspiration?

Ever sincerely yrs,
Samuel L. M. Barlow

*Just before Gertrude Stein and Alice Toklas left Paris to spend the
summer in Belley, Ernest Hemingway introduced them to the*

young American novelist F. Scott Fitzgerald. Gertrude Stein had read his This Side of Paradise *shortly after it was first published in 1920, and said of it that it "really created for the public the new generation." Fitzgerald gave Miss Stein a copy of his most recent novel* The Great Gatsby, *and from Belley she wrote him a letter praising both books and likening him to Thackeray.*

FROM F. SCOTT FITZGERALD

14 Rue de Tilsitt [Paris], June 1925

Dear Miss Gertrude Stein:

Thank you. None of your letter was "a bad compliment" and all of it "was a comfort." Thank you very much. My wife and I think you a very handsome, very gallant, very kind lady and thought so as soon as we saw you, and were telling Hemingway so when you passed us searching your car on the street. Hemingway and I went to Lyons shortly after to get my car and had a slick drive through Burgundy. He's a peach of a fellow and absolutely first rate.

I am so anxious to get *The Making of Americans* & learn something from it and imitate things out of it which I shall doubtless do. That future debt I tried so hard to repay by making the Scribners read it in the *Transatlantic* & convinced one, but the old man's mind was too old.

You see, I am content to let you, and the one or two like you who are acutely sensitive, think or fail to think for me and my kind artistically (their name is not legend but the word like it), much as the man of 1901, say, would let Nietche (sp.) think for him intellectually. I am a very second rate person compared to first rate people—I have indignation as well as most of the other major faults—and it honestly makes me shiver to know that such a writer as you attributes such a significance to my factitious, meritricous (metricious?) *This Side of Paradise*. It puts me in a false position, I feel. Like Gatsby I have only hope.

Thank you enormously for writing me.

Scott Fitzg—

Gertrude Stein continued her practice of disposing of old pictures in order to buy new ones. The painting by Marie Laurencin referred to in the following letter was a group portrait of Pablo and Fernande Picasso, Guillaume Apollinaire and Marie Laurencin, and was traditionally the first picture this artist ever sold.

FROM DANIEL-HENRY KAHNWEILER

Galérie Simon, 29 bis, Rue d'Astorg, Paris (VIII)
June 6, 1925

Dear Miss Stein,

I hope you had a nice journey down to Belley and you are feeling well there. I have had the photo of the Laurencin picture made, and asked [Alfred] Flechtheim, how he could buy it. He told me that the old Laurencin paintings have not so much amateurs, these asking for new ones. Still the same, he is ready to buy it.

Juan [Gris] tells me that you want to buy one of his new pictures, the "Tapis vert," one of the two big pictures he painted just now. Perhaps we could make the two things together. What I could do, is this: against your Laurencin I could give you that Gris picture, and Fr. 3000.—(three thousand francs) ready money. I hope that my proposal agrees you.

Kindest regards from us all to you both.

Believe me, dear Miss Stein
Yours sincerely
Kahnweiler

Gertrude Stein had met and become interested in the writing of a young American, Robert Coates. She lent him a number of her large collection of the novels of Anthony Trollope in the paperbound Tauchnitz edition.

FROM ROBERT M. COATES

Giverny—par Vernon, Eure, June 9, 1925

Dear Miss Stein,

I don't know why you go south. Though your letter reached me about a week ago, it has been so hot that I simply haven't answered it. . . .

Your letter makes me wonder suddenly if your maid remembered my leaving a package of Trollopes about six weeks ago. I brought them over to deliver to you, but you were out, so I left them with her. Two volumes that I hadn't read then, I still have—"Can You Forgive Her?" I'm sending them immediately.

A few days after I had your letter, my only rich friend came down here for a few days. So I gave him a copy of the Mildred Aldrich folder, and a long talk about it all. I am glad things are working out properly with her.

And I thank you very much for the Trollopes. And I regret so much not having seen you before your leaving. I'm working . . . on my novel. Suddenly, the other day I decided to finish it, which seems to be the hardest part. The book when finished ought to be full of surprises for the reader. It certainly has been for me.

Please let me know if you get the two Trollopes safely. I had trouble reading your address. And if you want me to look up the others.

Very sincerely,
Robert Coates—

The Laurencin picture was eventually purchased by the Cone sisters, and Gertrude Stein suggested an early painting by André Masson as a possible exchange for the Gris.

FROM DANIEL-HENRY KAHNWEILER

Galérie Simon, 29 bis, Rue d'Astorg, Paris,
June 18, 1925

Dear Miss Stein,

Many thanks for your kind letter. I am very glad the Laurencin was sold so well.

As to the Gris, certainly I would exchange against your Masson Still-Life, but the price of the Gris being much higher than that of a Masson of the same size, I am obliged to ask you, if you want to make that exchange, to give me a thousand francs, with the Masson.

Here everybody is well. Even Gris is in a very pleasant state of mind, without any "cafard." The only unpleasant thing is my hay-fever—it's awful with that dry weather.

With kindest regards from us all to you both

I am, dear Miss Stein

Yours sincerely

Kahnweiler

The Picasso engravings for the "Birthday Book" were still not forthcoming, and despite Kahnweiler's optimism, the planned edition did not appear.

Galérie Simon, 29 bis, Rue d'Astorg, Paris,
July 4, 1925

Dear Miss Stein,

Many thanks for your kind letter. About the Birthday-book, Picasso is to give us the engravings when he comes back from the South, and I don't think that a "period of unreliability" is to interfere. I hope to issue the book at the end of the year.

. . . Poor Odette Masson has been ill . . . but now she is feeling better. Masson himself is fine. So are [Elie] Lascaux and my sister-in-law [Mme Lascaux]. Juan [Gris] is doing well, too. He intends not to leave Boulogne, as his work is getting on very well, and he is afraid to go somewhere else being not certain to work as well there.

I am glad to tell you that his pictures are now selling exceedingly well: lots of people that did not like him, till now, are liking them, and buying them, too. At last, success has come.

With kindest regards from us all to you both

Always yours sincerely

Kahnweiler

But although success was coming to Gris, it showed no signs of favoring the English artist Harry Gibb.

FROM HARRY PHELAN GIBB

Desolate, Brendon, N. Devon,

July 5, 1925

My dear Gertrude,

I was delighted to get your letter. It was like you to write & try to give me courage. I need it badly. . . . What a grand thing it would be had I some one like you here, or some one [one] quarter as good—but no, I have no one. . . .

I find you have had a great influence on many of the story writers, some of whom have really got something worth while entirely through you. I think this should be some return, some satisfaction to you. For it means that you have done good & shown a road clearly which is so well worth treading. . . .

Harry

The magazine Ex Libris *for March 1925 contained reviews by Gertrude Stein and Ernest Hemingway of Sherwood Anderson's autobiographical* A Story Teller's Story. *Hemingway's own* In Our Time *was to be published in New York in September by Boni and Liveright.*

FROM SHERWOOD ANDERSON

[Troutdale, Va., July? 1925]

Dear Gertrude Stein—

I got your fine letter the other day and today got the magazine containing the reviews written by you and Hemingway. I am putting in a note for him. Do not have his address. I wrote a crackerjack review for the jacket of his book and will review it when it comes out. Have already asked one of the bigger reviews to save it for me.

Note also the announcement of your new book. Am crazy to see it.

Have decided to leave Huebsch and am going to Liveright, the same people who are doing the Hemingway book. They made me a generous offer for my books for the next five years and got them.

Have just finished the new novel. I think it is good. Will call it Dark Laughter and Liveright will publish it in the fall.

Your review of Story Teller was great. I loved it. You always manage to say so much and say it straighter than anyone else I know. Bless you for it.

Guess we'll stay here this summer as we want to get our new house underway. It's going to be fun to fix up a place of our own. If it gets too hot we'll run off to the mountains.

Lots of love,
Sherwood Anderson

FROM CARL VAN VECHTEN

150 West Fifty-fifth Street [New York],
Aug 1, 1925

Dear Gertrude

This letter preludes the approach of two of the nicest people left in the world: Essie and Paul Robeson. But you know already what I think about *that*!

My affection to you,
Carlo

FROM MAN RAY

31 bis, rue Campagne Première, Paris,
Aug 23 [1925]

My dear Miss Stein—

I am sending out the photos to Miss Buss, today.

Your photo has appeared in this month's Vanity Fair very effectively. If you haven't a copy, I'll send you mine. Another publication "Shadowland" has just written me that they will publish the photo of the interior, next month. So you see I am doing my share to keep the pot boiling. I hope your book will have a grand success.—As for me I am still at it, producing quite a lot, since there is nothing else to do in Paris, or rather since that is the best thing one can do here.

Matisse has been to my studio and I have gotten several good studies of him. One morning while he was here, André Breton dropped in, and I listened to a very amusing discussion. I thought it delicious to hear Matisse speak of drawing hands that look like hands and not like cigar butts. Breton, expecting to find a sympathetic iconoclast found himself facing an instructor in painting! And as they talked, it seemed to me that two men were speaking entirely different languages. It's simple enough to learn a language, but to make oneself understood———! However, at the end, Matisse told me he enjoyed the talk immensely, not having spoken for seven years!

I wish you the pleasantest of times. My regards to Miss Toklas.

Cordially
Man Ray

FROM MILDRED ALDRICH

La Creste, Huiry, Quincy-Ségy, S. et M.,
Aug 24, 1925

Dearest Gertrude:

I should probably agree that the title page was pretty if you had sent it, which you did not.—I am surprised that the proofs have not killed you,—I should have succumbed after the page proofs, in addition to which if any one ever let me read proof sheets it would cost me more than any book royalties ever produced. I never in my life was able to see how a thing was going to look or sound until I saw it in print. Then my one idea was to pull it all to pieces. That is why I have never glanced at my books but superficially and it was enough and to spare. . . . Glad you are both well.

Love
Mildred

FROM MABEL DODGE LUHAN

Taos, New Mexico, Oct 7 [1925]

Dearest Gertrude—

I remember so well leaving Paris with your big mms in my hands;—in the station I dropped it—it was open—I was reading it as I got on the train—the train jerked—some pages dropped under the wheels—Oh dear—What a horror! And now it's printed. I am so anxious to have it, but have lost the address—and anyway I want you to write in it—so can you get me a copy & send it C. O. D. as I also don't know the price of it.

I have been working on an autobiography since last December. The first vol. is finished—called "Background"—just the first 22 years until I went to Italy. It is not to be published

but put away until a few people are dead! But I am going to
let some people read it. Do you want to? Willa Cather &
Carl V. V. & some others who have seen it say it's the best
record of that period in America ('80 & '90) ever done. Anyone who reads it must give me a criticism to bury with it in
the Safety Deposit box to be unearthed in better days. Do
you want to or *da?*

Rönnebeck has been here this summer, & has just come
in & sends his best regards. I *wish* I could see you again. I
want to hear your *laugh.* Will you get those publishers to send
the book soon? I'll review it for Vanity Fair or something.

Write me a nice long letter & tell me about yourself.

With the same affection as ever (in spite of the *terrible*
things you said to Neith & Hutch [Hapgood] about me—that
I was a "sweet woman from the middle west." You won't
think me so sweet if you ever read the Memoirs though!)

Affectionately
Mabel. (Luhan)

❦

*Printing complications delayed the publication of the book and
Gertrude Stein did not receive her copies until the end of October. One of the first of them went to Harry Gibb.*

FROM HARRY PHELAN GIBB

3 Manor Studios, Flood St., Chelsea S.W. 3, London,
Oct 29, 1925

My dear Gertrude,

You can have no idea how delighted I am to have your
book. How splendid! You have done it this time—there can
be no more resistance, for it means you have conquered
"them." Your victory is secure, and thank God it is not a
"moral victory," for there is nothing so damnably intolerable
as "moral victories." Of course I have not had time to do
anything more than dip into many parts of it, but as *you* know

it is easy to know—only a few pages tells you when there is something remarkable & great . . .

Now what about the sale in England? . . . I feel sure everything should be done to bring it before the English people. This is an age when everything must be done, besides it ought to be done. And I am only too willing & too proud to do anything. Please let me know.

I know quite a number of people here are greatly interested in your work in quarters which might surprise you. . . .

Do please write & tell us about what has been said & about yourself. We are always talking about you. You are the bright spot in our lives.

With love from us both

Yours sincerely
Phelan Gibb

I am quietly slipping into oblivion.

FROM MARSDEN HARTLEY

Vence (Ain), Dec 27, 1925

My dear Gertrude—

I received yesterday—the day after Xmas—your card inviting me to the [Paul] Robeson party at your house. Having been here in Vence since the last of August, I was of course unable to be present—but I've seen the Robesons twice at Villefranche finding him a most attractive person. . . . Vence is a truly agreeable place but it's always the same—where one is is not the place one wants—for it's a few people one likes that make the place. . . .

I hear your big book is out, and I am waiting for it to come from Sylvia Beach's. I hope it has great success dear Gertrude . . .

As always
Marsden—

V. THE LATE TWENTIES

1926–1930

Edith Sitwell had met Gertrude Stein, and had, she thought, persuaded her to come to lecture at Cambridge. Miss Stein did eventually reconsider her decision and made the trip to England in May of this year. Miss Sitwell had attempted to persuade Leonard and Virginia Woolf to publish an edition of The Making of Americans *in England.*

FROM EDITH SITWELL

22, Pembridge Mansions, Moscow Road, W.2.,
Jan 1, 1926

Dear Miss Stein,

I should have written ages ago to thank you for your kind letter, but was laid up with a wretched form of influenza. First of all, I must tell you how bitterly disappointed I am,—and the Cambridge people will be—that you are not able to accept this invitation. I wish very deeply that you had been able to do so, because I do feel that your actual presence in England would help the cause. It is quite undoubted that a personality does help to convince half-intelligent people. Would it not be possible for you to come over in the summer for a stay? . . . If I work up Oxford, and University College, London, as well as Cambridge, to invite you to lecture, wouldn't you then reconsider your decision, and, perhaps, come to London sometime in the summer?—I am still working hard at propaganda. It is miserably disappointing, Virginia Woolf not taking the book.—However . . . . A great writer like yourself is absolutely bound to win through. There can't be any question about it. Meanwhile, of course one does hate the insults. . . .

I hope you are not allowing the trials to which every pioneer is subjected, to prevent your doing a tremendous amount of work.—And by the way, has Tom Eliot put your portrait of him in the Criterion yet?

Alas, I don't see much chance at the moment of coming to Paris, because work, for one thing, keeps us here. We had been hoping to come,—but apart from everything else, I have got a good many lectures coming on.—In which, as you may imagine, I shall lose no chance of doing propaganda work for you. It is very disappointing about Paris; I had been hoping for long talks with you. And for this reason, I shall take the first opportunity I have for coming. But I don't know, quite, when that will be.

Do, if you can, reconsider this question of coming over here and helping in the invaluable way that only you can, with the propaganda.

Helen [Rootham] and I send you and Miss Toklas all our heartiest best wishes for the New Year. And may we soon meet again.

Yours always
Edith Sitwell

There are *many* fresh admirers.

FROM HAROLD ACTON

10, Oriel Street, Oxford, (and Christ Church),
Mar 4, 1926

Dear Miss Stein,

My friend Edith Sitwell tells me that probably you will sojourn in England during the month of April, May, or June, in the course of which you will favour Cambridge with a visit. May I invite you to do Oxford a similar favour? This is on behalf of a literary society of which I have fulfilled the office of President and which I can call together at will for so great an occasion. I do not feel I need much introduction (perhaps you will remember me as a child) the eldest son of Arthur Acton, of Florence, the happy possessor of divers "autographed" numbers of "Camera Work" with articles by yourself about Matisse and Picasso, and of the "Portrait of Mabel Dodge at the Villa Curonia."

Granted that there are more intelligent young men in Cambridge than in Oxford at present, there are still more than a few who would be more than disappointed, seriously grieved, if you paid such an honour to a rival university while leaving Oxford to wallow in an almost-deserved oblivion.

Come then, when it is most convenient to yourself, you have but to name the date: the room shall be prepared, the members and the guests shall be bidden.

Yours very sincerely,
Harold Acton.

Gertrude Stein had met the Russian painter Pavel Tchelitchew in Paris through Jane Heap in the spring of 1926 and had become interested in his pictures. In March 1926, Tchelitchew left on a trip to Africa.

FROM PAVEL TCHELITCHEW [TRANSLATED]

[Grand] Hotel Moderne, rue Constantine [Tunis]
Mar 18 [1926]

Dear Miss Stein and Miss Toklas

Here we are in Tunis after a rather long trip on the water
—a trip which I like the least in the world. Marseille is very
very beautiful—we saw it on a marvelous day. After that we
took the boat which was tacky as anything. It seems the sea
was fairly calm but I wonder what a rough one would be like.
I've crossed a good many times in my life but I think that the
boats I took were larger, for I was never in such despair as
this time. All these balancings affect me morally even more
than physically, for I do not get sick; but this indecision with
the movement of the boat and the feeling of being shut up
in a box without being able to get out—why does one balance
to the left and then to the right irregularly and why not always
to the left or to the right?—That put me into such despair
that I did not want to see or understand anything, not understanding the essential problem. . . .

All that is made up for in Tunis. The city is extremely
beautiful, all white, so that it is only against the sky that one
can see the houses and the people, the white is so bright that
we had to buy dark glasses and we are like two owls at present.
There is a wonderful simplicity in the people and their life
here, their point of view is straight and naive, but the naivete
is serious. . . . The surrounding country is very lovely. I am
not completely sure that I can work at this hotel, I think not,
but I shall try then to rent two rooms somewhere, for ours
are a little too small and not very light because of the color
of the walls . . . The costumes of these people are very beautiful and very simple. The Arabian women wear white except
for a black mask over the face covering all but the eyes. The
mask is a kind of veil. The Jewish women are so fat that I
can't tell you their dimensions; they are specially fed to be fat
for otherwise the men would not marry them. . . .

The only thing is that I do not yet know what I must paint —it is all so different here—nothing reminds one of Paris. I think that one must wait.

Actually I do nothing, I eat, drink, and sleep—that's all. We shall become fat like the Jewish women of Tunis very quickly! We took some photographs but they didn't come out very well. Well, enough of this joking. It's too bad that you are not here. That would be so wonderful and interesting. There is so much to tell you but I am so stupid because of the sun and from doing nothing that I cannot put my thoughts in order. Write us a line. We hope that some of our photographs will be good and we shall try to send them.

Good-bye and don't forget us. Best to you,

Pavlik

Jane Heap continued her efforts in New York to market Gertrude Stein's writing, and had half-seriously suggested to Miss Stein that she offer the manuscript of The Making of Americans *to Dr. A. S. W. Rosenbach, the bookdealer, who had two years earlier purchased the manuscript of Joyce's* Ulysses *in the sale of John Quinn's collection.*

FROM JANE HEAP

Little Review and Little Review Gallery, 66 Fifth Avenue,
New York, Mar 26, 1926

Dear Gertrude Stein:

. . . I saw Chas. and Albert Boni this a.m. They will make a contract and send you an advance royalty check for $100 on "Three Lives." They have had such unfortunate business dealings with Bob [McAlmon] that they won't risk another cent. They were forced to pay a fine of $180.00 on their 100 copies of the big book, because he would not send them an invoice from the consul. They have sold 85 copies—so you see what could be done. They want me to pick up all the copies still existing and to bring them over. Will you find out just how many can be had, where the others are placed (in what book-shops), and what he will take for the lot? Let me know and I will see if we can get the money. Of course, you would have to buy them in, he would suspect everyone else.

Everyone advises us not to sell the mss. of the big book— now. I have tried to see Rosenbach but he is busy buying pages of the Gutenberg Bible, for millions of dollars the page. "Money is tight because we had a panic or something on the Exchange." . . .

Many greetings—
J. Heap.

❦

Although Robert McAlmon had published The Making of Americans, *there had been a series of disagreements between him and Gertrude Stein. He never carried out his threat to pulp the remaining copies of the book, but its distribution was hardly satisfactory from the standpoint of either author or publisher.*

FROM ROBERT McALMON

12 rue de l'Odeon, Paris [Spring 1926]

Dear Miss Stein:

Contrary to your verbal statements that you would help rid us of your volume, you have done nothing. The Dial review I got for you. The Irish Statesman review, came from a book sent them at my instructions. Books were sent to people you asked to have them sent to. Ten books were given GIVEN you. You *asked* me to take on the book. You knew it was a philanthropic enterprise as the Ms. had been some twenty years on your hands. There is no evidence of any order having come in through your offices except from your immediate family, and Mr. Whittaker; the family, one judges, mentioned in the book. You were perfectly ready to go over my head, not too honestly, and ask the printer to ship 400 of the books to a Paris Agent without my knowledge. I do not forget quantities I say in my letter; and you did the asking but two days after I had said definitely "NO."

If you wish to purchase the rest of the books you may do so. It has been on the market for six months and there is no evidence that it will sell. As the Three Mts. Press is now non-existent, and any publishing I do will be as a private person, using the name Contact, and as Mr. Bird is out of it, I do not choose to bother storing a book of that size, when its author so warily fears we might get back a portion of the amount paid for it.

Incidentally the whole publishing of the book was GIVEN you, at your request, quavering. No attitude on your part will delude me into believing that you did not know at the time it amounted to that. Incidentally you have never been financially incapable of putting your book before the public if *your* art is of prime importance to you. If you wish the books retained, you may bid for them. Otherwise, by Sept.—one year after publication—I shall simply rid myself of them en-masse, by the pulping proposition. . . .

Yours very truly,
R. McAlmon

George Platt Lynes had conceived the idea of printing a short piece of Gertrude Stein's, Descriptions of Literature, *in a series of publications which she had named "As Stable." The brochure was decorated with a drawing by Pavel Tchelitchew.*

FROM GEORGE PLATT LYNES

Englewood, New Jersey, Apr 15 [1926]
(the day that makes me nineteen)

Dear Miss Stein:

Descriptions of Literature goes to press day after to-morrow and will be ready for distribution by the first May. Subscriptions are coming in well, and I am putting a number (fifty or so) in bookshops in New York, Philadelphia and New Haven. I have received only two subscriptions from the people on the list you gave me. Miss Etta Cone subscribed for five copies and Mr. Howard Gans for one. And that is almost all of that. . . .

Now for my news. There really is none except that I am working at Brentano's . . . I am in the OLD and RARE Dept. Of course I do all the dusting but that really does not matter. Besides that I tutor four evenings a week and spend much time on being AS STABLE. Please remember me to Miss Toklas.

Sincerely,
George

Sherwood Anderson at last acknowledged receipt of his copy of The Making of Americans. *He refers to Hemingway's short story "The Undefeated," which had appeared in the magazine* This Quarter.

FROM SHERWOOD ANDERSON

New Orleans, La., Apr 25, 1926

My dear Gertrude Stein:

I just received your letter in the midst of packing up to go away to the country. We have got a little farm up there and are going there to spend the summer.

Your new book came when I was away lecturing and got put away with a lot of other books and was sent up to the farm with the lot, where it has been resting peacefully ever since. One of the reasons I am so anxious to get up there is that I may dip into the book.

Yesterday I saw a little story of Hemingway's in the Quarter. It was a beautiful story, beautifully done. Lordy but that man can write.

I am having the Notebook published this spring. A rather

slight thing I think but I am going to send you a copy when it comes.

We have our plans all made for coming to Europe in the fall, perhaps as late as November. I am up to my eyes in a new novel and that, with the mess of getting packed and getting off to the country, has kept me pretty much up in the air. It will be great fun to see you again.

I am going to write you about the book as soon as I get up to the farm and get settled.

With love,
Sherwood

Troutdale, Va., May 23 [1926]

My files are all packed and your exact address is in them. I shall write you today but may not be able to send this for a week. I had saved your book for the quiet of the country and have been dipping into it. I find the same music I always find in your prose, the thing that always stirs me in everything you write. The music is only more complete, more sustained. I know of no other way to express what I mean. I sent you my Notebook. It is a fragmentary thing.

When I got up here I got at once into a new novel. That has absorbed me. I keep your book here on my desk. I steal from it.

My cabin is beautifully located in the half wild hills. I hope to stay here about eight months of the year, the rest of the time in civilization, New York or Europe now and then if I can afford it. As you know I am hoping for a sight of Paris and you this fall. It depends on how my money holds out. . . .

Much love
Sherwood Anderson

*With René Crevel, the French writer, Gertrude Stein went to tea
at the house of Bernard Fay, then a young professor at the University of Clermont-Ferrand; but Miss Stein found that Mr. Fay
and she did not then have anything in particular to say to each
other. They were later to become the best of friends.*

FROM BERNARD FAŸ [TRANSLATED]

11, rue Saint-Florentin, May 25, 1926

Mademoiselle,

I have read eagerly everything that you have written and
it would be a great pleasure to make your acquaintance.

Would you be good enough to come to tea here at my
house on next Friday at 5:30? The tea will be modest but the
joy you give me will be great.

Respectfully yours,

B. Faÿ.

*It was at the suggestion of the Sitwells that Virginia and Leonard
Woolf decided to publish the Oxford-Cambridge lecture over their
Hogarth Press imprint.*

FROM LEONARD WOOLF

The Hogarth Press, London, W. C. 1,
June 11, 1926

Dear Miss Stein:

We should very much like, if possible, to publish the address which you delivered at Christchurch in our Hogarth
Essay series. Would you allow us to consider it? If you
would let us see the MS. we would then be able to make you
a definite offer with regard to terms.

Yours sincerely
Leonard Woolf

The lecture, along with four shorter pieces, was published in a volume entitled Composition as Explanation. *Circumstances did not permit its prior publication in the* New Criterion.

FROM T. S. ELIOT

London, June 12, 1926

Dear Miss Stein,

Many thanks for your letter. I am indeed sorry to have been absent from England and unable to swell your triumphant progress, but I hope that we may meet again in Paris. I should be most interested to see your Oxford and Cambridge lecture, although I am afraid it would be impossible to use it in THE NEW CRITERION at any rate for the next six months. But I hope that you will let me have the pleasure of reading it.

Yours very sincerely,

T. S. Eliot

Alvin Langdon Coburn had tried in 1913 to persuade Duckworth to publish a volume of short pieces by Gertrude Stein. The English visit thirteen years later stirred up new hopes, but they in their turn came to nothing.

FROM GERALD DUCKWORTH & COMPANY

[London] W. C. 2, June 22, 1926

Dear Miss Stein,

Many thanks for your letter of the 19th. We have carefully reconsidered the question of publishing Portraits and Prayers but I am sorry to say we still think we could not get enough sales for it to justify the venture. Personally I am sorry not to be your publisher, and hope some one else will prove more enterprising.

With kind regards

Yrs. sincerely

T. Balston

July 2, 1926

Dear Miss Stein,

We have reconsidered the question very carefully, and I'm sorry to say that we still think the publication would be too speculative, financially, for us to undertake it in these very difficult times. I think you would be surprised to know how very small is the circulation in England of the more intellectual novels and poems in spite of the considerable publicity they get in the Reviews etc. To publish a novel successfully, it is necessary for us to sell at least 1500 copies.

Do believe me that I'm very sorry for this decision & that I appreciate your kindness in giving us a fresh opportunity to consider it.

Yrs. sincerely
T. Balston

FROM AVERY HOPWOOD

[Capri] July 6 [1926]

Dear Gertrude;—

If your thoughts ever wander in my direction, you may wonder, while they wander, whether I have gone into The Great Silence.—On second thought, however, you probably no longer associate silence with me.

I was ill again, in Paris, then my mother arrived, & we went off to Aix-les-Bains—from there to Venice—& now we're here in Capri—for a few days more—then I'm going to Perugia, to superintend the 700th anniversary of St. Francis, at Assisi!

I shall be back in Paris, briefly, in September, & if you & Alice are there, then, I hope that I may take advantage of your invitation to take "tea—*just tea!*"

My love to you both
Avery

The English lecture was offered to the Dial *through a friend of
Miss Stein's, and was printed in the October number. Marianne
Moore, then Managing Editor, had written a very favorable review
of* The Making of Americans *at the time of its publication.*

FROM THE DIAL

New York, July 13, 1926

Dear Miss Stein:

Miss Mabel Ulrich has allowed us to see your article COM-
POSITION AS EXPLANATION which we should much like to publish, if we might know that it would not appear previously in
another magazine. Could you permit us to have it for use in
The Dial's November issue?

Should you permit us to have the article, will you be so
good as to give us some slight biographical data for our Contributors' Notes—as for instance data concerning place of
birth or other information that seems to you suitable? Unless
you would prefer to have us look up such detail as you might
direct us?

The letter which I received from you was a very great
pleasure. The reading of THE MAKING OF AMERICANS was one
of the most eager and enriching experiences that I have ever
had, and uncontent as I was with my comment upon it, that
the review could at all meet with your acceptance enhanced
the pleasure which I already owed to you.

Sincerely yours,
Marianne Moore

*Carl Van Vechten had sent Nora Holt, the Negro musician and
entertainer.*

FROM NORA HOLT

Bon Séjour Hotel, 19 Ave Wagram [Paris],
Oct 10, 1926

Dear Miss Stein—

I have, resting in my writing case, a letter to me from Carl Van Vechten telling me of you, also one introducing you to me. I came to your apartment once this summer bringing these letters but you were in the country.

I hope this finds you back in Paris, and I await your summons as to when I may call.

I hear from Fania and Carl at intervals and I just wrote them telling them that I am again doing the unexpected, Carl loves it you know, appearing at a night club. I can hear him saying to Fania, Rita Van Doren and some others, What will she do next?

I open at the Prado, Les Nuits du Prado, 41 Ave Wagram, Thursday night Oct 14th, in a group of songs at the piano. A very chic place and I think an innovation—no dancing.

Well, what a long letter and we haven't met. I shall wait patiently.

Very best wishes—
Nora Holt.

René Crevel was a friend of Pavel Tchelitchew. "He was young and violent and ill and revolutionary and sweet and tender, and Gertrude Stein became very fond of him." To him she had promised to give a letter to the English anthropologist Geoffrey Gorer, whom she had met in Cambridge. Crevel wrote in his own special version of English.

FROM RENÉ CREVEL

6 Rue de la Muette [Paris, Oct 1926]

Dear Miss Stein,

You are too good to think of me. And I think [of] you very much. I am in Paris now, and I will be happy to see your friend of Cambridge. The summer was fifty-fifty. Not very good, not very bad, not lyrical. I have worked. But I cannot say how is the work. My book of last summer will be published in fifteen days.

And the boys? How are the boys Pavelik and Allen [Tanner]? Say their my good (pensées) and when Pavelik will return at Paris (when?) I want ask from he a drawing for a little philosophical book what I will publish this winter at Marseille. It's a winter book, if it was a summer book I would publish in the mountains.

I have seen this summer at Antibes an American poet, Archibald Macleish (wonderful and poetical name) and a curious fellow Scott Fitzgerald. Curious and poor fellow. A boy. He has a wonderful wife, you know her, I think, but what this young, charming and spirituel people has in the hed (tête)? I cannot say, but I want [to] speak about that with you and Miss Touclas, when, for my great joy, you want go to Paris.

I write like a pig.

Pig is a pig.

Crevel is Crevel.

Say the more good things for Miss Touclas and the two boys, and for you not polish things like in the end letter, but Real and Respectuous things like

Always   René

René Crevel René

FROM GEOFFREY GORER

20 Jesus Lane, Cambridge, Nov 20, 1926

Dear Miss Stein,

I feel I should like to thank you for having been the cause of my making the acquaintance of so charming a person as René Crevel. He passed a couple of days here, and I only hope that he received as good an impression as he produced. His

lecture—I don't know if you have seen or heard it—has produced an enormous amount of discussion.

I want to come to Paris to see him about the middle of
next month, & I hope I may come & see you then.

Again very many thanks.

Yours sincerely
Geoffrey Gorer.

*Joseph Brewer, with the firm of Payson & Clarke Ltd., had shown
interest in the possible publication by his firm of a volume of short
pieces by Gertrude Stein.*

FROM JOSEPH BREWER

18 East Fifty-third Street, New York,
Nov 30, 1926

Dear Miss Stein:

This is only a hasty note to say that I have received your
letter and the Ms. of "Useful Knowledge" both of which I
am extremely delighted to have.

I have only just got back to New York and am in the
throes of getting straightened around again after my absence.
Please forgive me therefore, for seeming rather curt, but this
is intended by no means to be a letter. I only want you to
know that your Ms. arrived safely. I am longing to get at it,
and shall as soon as ever I can. I find I have a very sympathetic
listener in one of my partners, at least, and so I am bold
enough to be hopeful of publication. Well, we shall see. It
was extraordinarily nice meeting you and I look forward to
a renewal of our acquaintance as soon as ever it is possible.

Yours ever,
Joseph Brewer

Natalie Barney, the "Amazon" of Rémy de Gourmont's Lettres à l'Amazone, *was devoted to the cause of improving Franco-American literary relations. Her salon was famous in Paris.*

FROM NATALIE CLIFFORD BARNEY

20 rue Jacob [Paris], Dec 16, 1926

Dear Gertrude Stein,

The other night "au Caméléon" I realized how little the French "femmes de lettres" know of the English and Americans and vice versa (orful expression—only such clichés remain!) I wish I might bring about a better "entente," and hope therefore to organize here this winter, and this spring, readings and presentations that will enable our mind-allies to appreciate each other. As you will see, by enclosed card, je fête à mes prochains vendredis les 2 femmes qui m'ont si aimablement et humouristiquement exposés—and "Colette" has promised to act a scene from her "Vagabonde" which is to appear later in a theatre in Paris. I should like to add at least one Anglo-Saxon to this first group, and thought that *you, presented by yourself* would make a good representation —and balance the French trio. Will you! Shall we? And may I announce you, in the invitations I am sending out Saturday for either the last Friday of January—the 28th—or the 4th of February? Wasn't the 4th of February celebrated in some way by Americans in history, if so we must surely cling to that date! I'm at home, dans l'intimité, to-morrow Friday all afternoon and we could talk it over, or I could drop in and see you (if you don't come here to-morrow) this Saturday about 3.30 or 4 o'clock.

Hoping my "petit projet" may meet with your approval and receive your participation. With affectionate greetings to you and your friend, in which Romaine Brooks joins me—

Yours most appreciatively

Natalie C. Barney

le 7 Janvier pour fêter Madame Aurel
le 14 Janvier pour fêter Madame Colette . . .
le 21 Janvier: Lucie Delarue-Mardrus . . .

Bravig Imbs, a young American trying to become a writer in Paris, had been taken to the rue de Fleurus by Choura Tchelitchew, Pavel's sister. Gertrude Stein and Alice Toklas accepted his invitation.

FROM BRAVIG IMBS

Hotel du Caveau, V rue de la Huchette, Paris V,
Monday [Dec 27, 1926]

Dear Miss Stein:—

Mr. [Elliot] Paul and I are going to give a Grand High New Year's Tea at the Caveau next Friday afternoon and you and Miss Toklas are most cordially invited.

Mr. and Mrs. [Sherwood] Anderson, Pavlik [Tchelitchew] and Allen [Tanner] have been invited and these are all, so I am sure we will all have a regularly gay time.

Please send me a 'pneu' if you and Miss Toklas can come and I will call for you on Friday at 4:30 p.m.

Most sincerely yours,
Bravig Imbs

Juan Gris, now in very bad health, had recently finished his lithographs for Gertrude Stein's A Book Concluding with As a Wife has a Cow a Love Story, *to be published by Kahnweiler. He, his wife Josette, and his son Georges sent Miss Stein and Miss Toklas a decorated Christmas greeting.*

FROM JUAN, GEORGES, AND JOSETTE GRIS [TRANSLATED]

Dec 28, 1926

My dear friends,

I wish you a Happy New Year and I hope that you are going to celebrate its arrival. We shall do nothing, for I stick very closely to my regime and the least upset harms me. Especially now that I'm beginning to feel better (the fact that my temperature is now normal proves it) I do not want to lose all that I have gained just for a big dinner.

I'm suffering now mostly from attacks of asthma which come the moment I lie down and force me to sit in an armchair for two or three hours. As you see, I have actually all that is necessary for happiness.

I'm working, not for long but regularly each day. I am not dissatisfied but as yet there is too little.

I did not think I was capable of leading such a sober, regulated and solitary existence. Save for a short daily walk after lunch, I have no other distraction. And the worst of all is that I am getting used to this and am going to become a savage.

I'm waiting impatiently for the book, but it does not come. Have you it already?

Success with your work, dear Gertrude. I hope you are both well. Best wishes from all three of us

Juan Gris

Georges

I send you my best wishes for the New Year.

Josette

Daniel Raffel was the son of Gertrude Stein's sister Bertha. He became the subject of a portrait "Dan Raffel a Nephew," published in Transition.

FROM DANIEL RAFFEL

Les Glycines, Rue Jules Chaplain 15, Paris,
Feb 9, 1927

Dear Aunt Gertrude,

My wife and I are in Paris on our way back to America. We were very sorry not to have seen you the last time that we were here in the summer of 1926, when you were in the country.

I should like to renew the acquaintance of which, due to my tender years, I have but one faint memory. You were explaining to me the difference in method, quite unreal, of removing the tonsils from the throats of little boys and of little girls. As a result of your explanation I still have two healthy tonsils.

I am looking forward with pleasure to seeing you again.

Yours sincerely,
Daniel Raffel.

The Oxford-Cambridge lecture seemed to have turned the tide for Gertrude Stein in England. Even the John Lane firm asked to republish Three Lives, *a boon which Miss Stein granted.*

FROM JOHN LANE THE BODLEY HEAD LTD

London, W. 1, Feb 18, 1927

Dear Madam

You will remember that in 1924 we returned you the plates of "Three Lives" and cancelled the contract, since at that time it seemed impossible to arouse any interest in your book in Great Britain. Since then, however, there seems to have been a growing interest in your work and we are wondering whether, if the plates are still in existence, you would care to make a contract with us to print and publish a new edition. If so, we should be very pleased to make an agreement with you.

Yours faithfully

B. W. Willett

Director

Pavel Tchelitchew was traveling again in North Africa. The "error" of Elliot Paul's to which he refers was the printing of Miss Stein's "An Elucidation" in the April 1927 number of Transition, *with some words set in the wrong order. The error was corrected by reprinting the contribution separately and issuing it as a supplement to the number.*

FROM PAVEL TCHELITCHEW [TRANSLATED]

Philippeville, Algérie, Apr 2 [1927]

Dear friends Gertrude and Alice

After a not very pleasant voyage we have been here just eight days. The crossing was bearable, the food terrible, the sky gray; when at last we reached land we were very happy! The country is splendid here, very green, very rich, not at all exotic; it reminds me very much of Belley, except that the presence of the sea gives it all something unexpected. Spring is at its height and is lovelier here than in France: foliage of all colors, trees of all kinds, lots of flowers in the fields. We think often of you and believe that the country would please you a great deal with its beauty and tranquillity. Most of the Arabs are poor and dirty, but the Arab girls are very pretty, even beautiful; one sees them taking the sheep and the goats to pasture. Sometimes the landscape becomes completely biblical. . . .

And what is your news? Write us a line. You know that in spite of all our faults we love you a great deal and think of you often. How did [Elliot] Paul correct his error? He has sent

us nothing yet, it is probably not yet corrected. Well, dear
friends, we send you all our friendship and affection.

Yours

Pavlik

P.S. Coming through Marseille we saw the whole group,
Berman, Bérard, etc. Bébé almost died of astonishment when
I was nice to him; he couldn't understand it at all. I had a
good laugh.

P.

❧

FROM EDITH SITWELL

22, Pembridge Mansions, Moscow Road, [London] W. 2,

Apr 25, 1927

My dear Gertrude,

You can imagine my delight at receiving "An Elucidation"
in print. As you know, I have it in typescript, and it has been
most valuable to me in lecturing etc. And now I am so happy
to have it in printed form. Thank you so much for sending it
to me.—Your reputation grows every day, it seems to me. It
is such a happiness to me to see this happening, under our
eyes, as it were.

By the way, I'm having my own new book sent to you from
the publishers. It contains a Variation on a theme from "Accents in Alsace." I do *hope* you will like it.

One of my greatest friends, Alvaro Guevara, has come,
with his mother, to live in Paris. He is a painter, and also
writer, of real genius,—not one of these dear little intellectu-
als. It would be a great kindness to me, and a great kindness
to him, if you would allow him to go and see you and Alice.
And yours is such a fine atmosphere. It would be an awful
thing if a man with a mind like his had to have it fretted away
by the vulgar little clothes-moths that sit drinking and pre-
tending to be geniuses in the cafés. His address is Hotel Windsor Étoile, 14 Rue Beaujon.

I shall see you, I hope, at the end of May, when I *trust* I shall be in Paris, though only for a day or two, to see Sachie's ballet.—Sachie now has a son, born on Good Friday. He is too sweet for words, and just like Osbert to look at.

I do hope you and Alice are very well. I am longing to see you again. On Wednesday I go to Florence, travelling straight through. My address will be: Castello di Montegufoni, Montenagna, Val di Pesa, Firenze. Helen [Rootham] and I send you both our love.

Yours ever
Edith

Juan Gris became worse during the early months of 1927, and died on May 11. He was buried two days later. Gertrude Stein's tribute to his memory, "The Life and Death of Juan Gris," was printed in Transition *in July. Gris was usually addressed as Jean by his friends although Gertrude Stein had always called him Juan.*

FROM DANIEL-HENRY KAHNWEILER

Galérie Simon, 29 bis, Rue d'Astorg, Paris,
May 11, 1927

Dear Miss Stein,

Poor Juan is very low. The doctor believes the end very near.

Yours,
Kahnweiler

[TRANSLATED]

Galérie Simon, 29 bis, Rue d'Astorg, Paris,
May 17, 1927

Dear Miss Stein,

I have just read your very moving article. One senses in it so well how much you loved our poor Juan. No one was better qualified to write about him than you. And I am certain that no one will express better than you have done what we have lost in him.

Thank you also for having mentioned me so kindly. I am happy with it. What merit did I have? That of loving Jean: I was not alone, for you, too, loved him.

Your
Kahnweiler

❧

FROM AVERY HOPWOOD

Hotel Chambord, 123 Avenue des Champs Elysées, Paris,
Wednesday [May 25, 1927]

Dear Gertrude & Alice:—

Monday, the 28th, is my birthday. That date has also, this year, been made Whit-Monday, in my honor. My natal day, however, will assume its true splendor only if you will both dine with me, that evening. It will be a nice, quiet dinner (I am once more "un agneau") & there won't be any other guests, unless you wish to bring someone—& you don't have to give me any presents, as you in yourselves will be gifts enough.

Do say that you will come, & tell me at what time I shall call for you.

Your nice, quiet little
Avery

❧

FROM FANIA MARINOFF VAN VECHTEN

[Paris] Thursday [June 16, 1927]

My dears

Here I am once more, but only because I'm sailing from France June 25th. I would so love to see you both again before I depart and Miguel Covarrubias wants very much to

meet you. When can you be seen? I'm at the same Hotel
Littré and will come to see you any time you suggest but to-
morrow, and I hope it may be soon.

Fania

[Paris] Lundi [June 20, 1927]

Alright lady dear
   Covarrubias and I will be chez vous demain à cinq heures
and I for one will be very glad to see you both again.

Fania

*Through Robert McAlmon, Gertrude Stein had met Hilda Doo-
little ("H. D.") and Winifred Bryher. The latter, having divorced
McAlmon, had married Kenneth Macpherson, and with him was
publishing* Close Up.

FROM KENNETH MACPHERSON

POOL, Riant Château, Territet, Suisse,
June 24 [1927]

Dear Miss Stein,
   I am sending you under separate cover a copy of my latest book POOLREFLECTION, and the first issue of CLOSE UP, a
monthly magazine to deal with films from the artistic, psychological and educational points of view. I hope you will
enjoy both of these but especially CLOSE UP which I am editing and which I believe will be welcomed by the greatly increasing numbers of people who are coming to regard films as
a medium for the possible expression of art in its most modern
and experimental aspects.
   I consider you have done more toward the advancement of
thought in art than almost any other writer. Apart from
which, one derives a real and stimulating pleasure from your

writing. I really want to ask now if perhaps some time you would send a poem or article for CLOSE UP in which this development of experimental art is concerned. You will see that H. D. has written a charming poem PROJECTOR, which has this bearing upon form in the films. The most modern tendency seems so linked up in this way and the kind of thing you write is so exactly the kind of thing that could be translated to the screen that anything you might send would be deeply appreciated.

Our terms are two guineas for a poem or short article, three guineas up to three thousand words, our limit. The intention is to form a kind of debating ground for distinguished minds, in contemporary thought and art, and to go on from there.

With compliments and best wishes,

Kenneth Macpherson

Gertrude Stein sent a manuscript entitled "Three Sitting Here," which was printed in the issues of Close Up *for September and October 1927.*

FROM WINIFRED BRYHER

CLOSE UP, Riant Château, Territet, Suisse,

Aug 8 [1927]

Dear Miss Stein,

Thank you so much for your letter and good wishes. I am very happy you like CLOSE UP, for I have always, from the time I read "Three Lives" and met you, valued your opinion very highly. And I look forward to seeing you again, in the autumn.

Your manuscript arrived this morning and excited us both. It is one of the finest things you have done, I feel. There is a great feeling of depth and continuity about it, like a short but perfect novel. I am sorry it has to be split up into two numbers but we feel it unwise to increase the number of pages just yet, as the advertising expenses are so heavy but we must advertise as much as possible to get it thoroughly established.

I enclose cheque for five guineas. It has decided to pour with rain here most of the week. I hope you are getting better weather. News from Montreux is that the town is flooded so it seems a bad summer everywhere.

With again good wishes and thanks for letting us have the manuscript.

Yours sincerely,

Bryher.

❧

Gertrude Stein, continuing her battle for admission to the pages of the Atlantic Monthly, *submitted her "Portrait of Cézanne" to Ellery Sedgwick.*

FROM THE ATLANTIC MONTHLY

Boston, Mass., Aug 19, 1927

My dear Miss Stein:

It is not that I am unsympathetic with the present and the future. At any rate, I try to be preoccupied with modern things, and to resist in part the influences of the past. But I confess that I am lost in the mazes of your prose. I have read this "Impression" of Cézanne a dozen times at least, but I am so accustomed to thinking of words as conveying ideas, each with its little aura of suggestion, to be sure, but rather definite at the core, that to regard them as symbols of another kind is quite beyond me. The little rhythms which ripple through your picture do not, to my heavy wit, call up the faintest suggestion of the exciting impression of a Cézanne.

You have taken a friendly interest in my training, and as an example of adult education it is an experiment worth trying! Perhaps you would some day write me an entirely intelligible comment upon these paragraphs of yours. I ask this in all seriousness, for as I near my second childhood, I yearn increasingly to be educated. I am speaking, I beg you to believe, quite seriously.

Yours sincerely,
Ellery Sedgwick.

FROM SHERWOOD ANDERSON

[Troutdale, Va., Fall? 1927]

Dear Gertrude,

A dumb summer after a dumb winter. Have been in a continuous jam. Now I think I am getting out. Made up my mind that the grand trouble with me was that I was trying to live by writing. It is so easy over here and so difficult. I had begun trying to work on a schedule and was pressing, off my stroke etc. Up until two or three years ago, as I guess you know, I had always made my living by writing advertisements. Hated to go back to that but had made up my mind to do it.

Then something came up. Near me there is a count[r]y town named Marion, Virginia. It is a prosperous little town, county seat etc and had a weekly paper that makes money. It is filled with town news, who married, who went to visit Aunt Mary, who died etcetc. The man who owned it had to sell and I am buying it and hope to live by it.

That is my definite news. I did not want to write anything that was not fun doing. I knew that if I went on trying to make my living by it I would soon be a hack. I shall not try to do anything with the paper—I mean in the way of uplifting the town. I'll just run around and get the local news and stick it in. Have an idea it will be great fun.

Aside from that there is no news. We are in the country. It is gorgeous here now. Most of the year I can drive to my newspaper over the mountains. When the snow is deep I shall have to stay over there about four days a week.

Of course I am on a book but I am going to let it take its own time. Write me the news of yourself.

Sherwood A—

Bravig Imbs, in desperation, had returned to the United States to try to earn some money.

FROM BRAVIG IMBS

[New York] Day after Thanksgiving [1927]
Dear Gertrude Stein:—

Your long letter came so delightfully this morning for though I am never wanting in courage I am often depressed, especially in these perilous days, but you always remind me I am a person and then I feel better. Alas, after a week and a half of vain buffetting in newspaper offices and publishers' houses I have been reduced to taking a job at Macy's Department Store—in the toy section, $22.50 a week—in order to ward off utter starvation. I am quite out of funds and my friends are as poor as I.

But I have had so many adventures since I have begun living here I could amuse you throughout a whole tea. . . . I must tell you about the lecture bureau—Sherwood Anderson's—the Leigh-Emmerich. I went there heavily armed with introductions . . . [Mr. Emmerich] likes your work very much and seemed like quite an intelligent person. He offered me a large sum of money if I could persuade you to come over here on a lecture tour. I told him that I was pretty sure nothing less than an earthquake would dislodge you from France but he kept on. He said he would guarantee you would have no contact with the public at all if you did not want it, that your wishes would be followed implicitly in regard to travelling conditions and that he would make a contract for either ten or twenty appearances. Of course, his bureau is quite the leading one of New York and business-like. I told him I

would write to you and tell you what he had said and he has
since telephoned me to find if I have kept my word. . . .

. . . Thank you so much for your news of Paris as no one
else writes me despite all my letters. And thank you for your
good wishes. I send Alice and you the very best of mine, and
please . . . write me soon again.

Sincerely,

Bravig

*Although the Picasso-illustrated "Birthday Book" did not material-
ize, Kahnweiler, in December 1926, had published Miss Stein's*
A Book *with Gris's lithographs, and in 1927 he asked for a manuscript to be illustrated by his brother-in-law, the artist-friend of
Gris and Picasso, Élie Lascaux. She sent him* A Village.

FROM DANIEL-HENRY KAHNWEILER

Galérie Simon, 29 bis, Rue d'Astorg, Paris,

Dec 1, 1927

Dear Miss Stein,

Many thanks for your kind letter. I wrote you at once,
after receiving the Ms, thanking you, and telling you that I
liked it very much. Unfortunately it seems that my letter
didn't arrive.

Since, I have been reading the Ms again, and I like it still
the more. I told Lascaux about it. I am very glad to publish it,
and he, to illustrate it. I am going to translate it to him—
that is not easy—and, afterwards, perhaps, we could talk the
matter over with Lascaux at Boulogne, spending an evening
together. We could publish, then, the book at once.

Everybody is well, in spite of the cold weather. I am glad
you are, too.

Believe me, dear Miss Stein

Always yours

Kahnweiler

Mildred Aldrich sent a report on her recent reading, from Carl Van Vechten's Peter Whiffle *to Vivian Burnett's memoir of his mother* The Romantic Lady (Frances Hodgson Burnett). *The "little paper" to which she refers was a periodical entitled* The Mahogany Tree, *which appeared briefly in the 1890's.*

FROM MILDRED ALDRICH

La Creste, Huiry, Quincy-Ségy (S. et M.),
Dec 14, 1927

Dearest Gertrude;

Yes, I did bring "Peter Whiffle" down to Huiry, but I will mail it back at once if you want it. . . . I have just finished [the first of the "Cahiers de Marcel Proust"] . . . I can no longer read ALL the time as I used to. When I put it down I felt that I should throw a fit if I could not talk to some one about it. I was as full of words that I wanted to throw off as I used to be in the old days when I earned my living doing it . . .

I had such a lot of things to say about the Romantic Lady, which I did not have time to say. For example she showed how much she did *not* know Boston when she narrated the presentation of the Keats bust, the day she first met [Israel] Zangwill. She said "the presentation was made by a Mr Day." Imagine any one really in the know speaking of Fred Holland Day as "Mr Day," and dismissing like that the American man who probably owned more Keats and Shelley mss. than any one on the other side of the Atlantic, and who had spent his life and his money ferreting out all sorts of things—of no use to any one but enthusiasts and faddists. But, of course, Fred Holland Day would have had no use for Mrs Burnett. Those were the days when he and Herbert Copeland were publishing as "Copeland & Day," and getting out some rather nice books. It must have been in your time. Did you ever see any of them? There are two or three among my books, and

Fred did the wood-cut for the title page of my little paper on which I broke my heart. We say that, as a joke, but it seems that I really did.

Love to you both,
Mildred

❦

La Creste, Huiry, Quincy-Ségy (S. et M.),
Dec 25, 1927

Dear both of you;

I got up quite early this morning, and dolled myself all up. I went down to my coffee, in my best mauve kimono and my best sandals, with my Christmas cap—very becoming—on my head, with a new handkerchief . . . tucked into my sash, and my nose powdered and my eye-brows pencilled, and before I went in to my coffee I had a praise service—"Come all ye faithful"—a new disk . . . sung in the Metropolitan Opera House by the United Glee Clubs of America (850 voices), with the audience of 4000 singing the refrain. It shook the rafters—I have rafters to shake.

It was rather a pity no one saw me. I am not sure whether I looked like a perfect lady, or a perfect rip, but I knew that I was feeling better.

I hope you are both well and happy, and that your house is not too warm on this damp and wet extraordinary Christmas day. I did hope last week that it was going to be a real Christmas, cold and dry and sunny, but no such luck.

Lovingly
Mildred

❦

With the gift of her first book, Quicksand, *which was just being issued, there came a letter from the Negro novelist Nella Larsen.*

FROM NELLA LARSEN

2588 Seventh Avenue, New York,
Feb 1, 1928

Dear Miss Stein—

I have often talked with our friend Carl Van Vechten about you. Particularly about you and Melanctha, which I have read many times. And always I get from it some new thing—a truly great story. I never cease to wonder how you came to write it and just why you and not some one of us should so accurately have caught the spirit of this race of mine.

Carl asked me to send you my poor first book, and I am doing so. Please don't think me too presumptuous. I hope some day to have the great good fortune of seeing and talking with you.

Very sincerely yours
Nella Larsen Imes

✻

Joseph Brewer had succeeded in persuading his associates that their firm should publish Gertrude Stein's book in a series called "2 Rivers [of Manhattan]."

FROM JOSEPH BREWER

Payson & Clarke Ltd, New York,
Feb 17, 1928

Dear Miss Stein,

I have behaved absolutely monstrously and I don't know how to ask you to forgive me. I've never written to thank you for the grand blurb you sent for USEFUL KNOWLEDGE nor to tell you what a marvelous time I had with [William] Cook looking at Le Corbusier houses. (Could you send me Cook's proper name and address?) And you've not yet got any proofs of the book! It is all too horrible and I feel a very worm. . . .

We have been held up with the book, waiting for

McKnight Kauffer to design a 2 RIVERS gadget for it, and besides, there is a trade slump on (which seriously affects publishing) and we thought it best to wait a bit for things to pick up as being better especially for USEFUL KNOWLEDGE, but now it is in the works and before long I shall be showering you with proofs. . . .

Please remember me to Miss Toklas and believe me always,

Yours &c.,

Joseph Brewer

George Platt Lynes had opened a bookshop in New Jersey, but it did not prosper.

FROM GEORGE PLATT LYNES

Englewood, New Jersey, Mar 9, 1928

Dear Miss Stein:

It would take more than a calendar-promise of summer to persuade me that our dark, incorporeal, lustreless winter season would one day come to an end. Today, for example, there is fine, bitter snow, never reaching the ground, carried horizontally by a strong wind. No winter is always enough winter for me! Glenway [Wescott] writes that René [Crevel] has had a lung collapsed. How is he? Will he, by any chance, be in Paris when I arrive in May? Which reminds me that *I am* arriving in May. My shop is being sold. When that is finished I am off. And, though I will be in Paris only long enough to say hello, I will see you and the few. I am headed, so I am told, for a land of wasps and primroses! . . .

Always,

Geo.

Harold Acton had sent Gertrude Stein his book Cornelian, *published this year, which she had already seen in manuscript.*

FROM HAROLD ACTON

8 Adelphi Terrace [London] W C 2,
Apr 3, 1928

Dear Gertrude,

Ever so many thanks for your letter. I am so glad "Cornelian" still amuses you: it is entirely through you that I ever thought of sending it to a publisher. It seems to have shocked the stolid British reviewers, which is a good thing, and they complain bitterly of its exceedingly low "moral tone." I have also had a volume of poems published since I saw you last, and the publisher has quite deservedly gone bankrupt since their publication, but I was rather ashamed of them when I saw them in print so I did not send them to you.

Many . . . things have .happened since I so regretfully left Paris . . . I have been spending the last six months [in Florence] writing my laborious history of the last Medici. I am delighted to get away again, and enjoying my freedom tremendously, though I would enjoy it more in Paris. I have written a novel, very frivolous, and I hope it will bring me in some money . . . As soon as this materializes I shall return to France. The people here are so stupid I lose patience with them: no audacity, no ideas, the writers contemptible, the painters nil. Osbert and Sachie [Sitwell] have gone to Morocco: the failure of their play had a very depressing effect on them. Fortunately Edith is in London, and I see her often . . . [She] showed me her portrait by Tchelitchew, which I admire more than mine: it is one of the best I have seen, and certainly the best of Edith. She tells me he is coming to London this summer. . . . Raymond Mortimer, Clive Bell and Miss Todd have talked much of starting a new review, but nothing has happened about it yet. They none of them know their minds; Miss Todd would like to compromise with ordinary journalism, and Mortimer with the "grand old English traditions." Moreover they cannot find a financier. Desmond McCarthy, the enemy of all modern things and people younger than himself, is also to embark on a similar project. . . .

I have heard nothing of René [Crevel] for a long time; I do hope he is getting cured. I must return to Paris soon, as I would so like to see you and Alice again. Are you going to Belley this summer? I depend on "Transition" nowadays.

Yrs ever
Harold Acton

Tchelitchew had agreed with Diaghilew to do the décor and costumes for a ballet "Ode."

FROM PAVEL TCHELITCHEW [TRANSLATED]

Monte Carlo, May 6 [1928]

My dear friends

I was very very happy to receive your letter, for one feels so isolated from the rest of the world with this work that we have undertaken, which is not only difficult, but difficult at each step and requires the patience of an angel. Certainly this patience blows up sometimes like a volcano, and then what dramas, scandals, and funny stories! then once more all the ants return to their toil. . . . Happily we stop at night. But Father Diaghilew is the most capricious being in the world; he likes to be contradicted and at the same time detests all who contradict him . . . He loves to shout at and discharge the poor people like servants. He has already discharged two, his pianist and his secretary, and he shouted so much that the rats were frightened out of the basements and galloped around all the corridors of the casino. Diaghilew is very much afraid of them, but he is still very proud of having achieved such an uproar. He is very old and I believe this is the only moment when he feels his strength, shouting like an hysterical crazy old woman. I have some very funny stories to tell you, but at the moment I am completely worn out by the work and the

torture of having to work with so many people. . . . I should
so like to be able to rest here, for it's really so simple to rest in
the sun and on the sea-shore, but we hardly see the sun, just
for a few moments in the morning and during lunch. The
work here is almost finished, we shall return to Paris to complete it . . . I saw George Lynes; he is so changed that if I
had not known it was he, I should have passed him without
recognizing him . . . I didn't have much time to talk with
him for he has forgotten his French and I my English . . .
He is here with Glenway Wescott, who is the "rose of Villefranche" or rather the "Edelweiss" for he lives at the very top
of the mountain, which is quite high and hard to climb . . .
How go things in Paris, what is new? . . .

Yours,
Pavlik

*Shortly afterward, Gertrude Stein and Alice Toklas left to spend
the summer in the house which they had found at Bilignin, near
Belley.*

Paris, June 14 [1928]

Dear Gertrude and Alice—

I was very very sad and upset at your departure. You can
not imagine how I have missed you and how I should like to
know what you think of what I have done. I was even unhap-
pier, for you know I am so little liked in Paris—I have hardly
a friend in this city. Neither was Miss Sitwell there. I believed
at first that you thought what I have done for the ballet must
be very bad and you didn't want to be present at my fiasco.
Actually, despite all our efforts, the whole ballet is so badly
produced that it's an agony for me to have to see it two or
three times. Really I should tell you that I think even so it
was and is an entirely new thing and people do not know what
it is. It is even more difficult to judge because Diaghilew with
his scissors has chopped and rearranged everything to suit

himself. At the premiere it was a success and a great success
—it was *my* success just as if it were my birthday—all the same
it so astonished people that despite hatred and jealousy they
were amazed. Afterwards they thought, judged, discussed it
and certainly they say that it is only pretty, that it does not go
with the music nor with the dance, that much in it doesn't
come off (so as not to say that they wished to find the whole
thing a failure, etc.) Actually the second performance was
much better than the first, but yesterday, unluckily, when they
gave this ballet the same evening with the ballet of Stravinsky,
everything went so badly that I saw my strings and puppets
flying up to heaven, creaking, lights missing where they should
be and vice versa. I have never seen anything more piteous and
ridiculous. I think that the spirit of this ballet is so foreign to
all my contemporaries that I am surprised at even the success
that it did have. At bottom, the miscomprehension is general.
They find that it is too "pretty" (when actually it is ugly and
rather "tragic") that it is too music-hall, etc. I can say nothing
for of all the ballet and the things that I put into it only a
very small cake remains which Monsieur Diaghilew has cut
with his scissors as he wished. They stopped us from using
the luminous turning blue lines because they required 120,000
volts—the theatre would have exploded—so you see the end of
the ballet was cut, we had to arrange it as best we could.
Diaghilew gave us only two rehearsals—one of which was without costumes—the third was the performance—one hour before he changed all the lights—not even asking me what I
wanted done—I saw my sets lit up for the first time at the
performance.—I write you all this not to justify myself to you
but to show you what the situation was at the premiere. . . .

Bébé Bérard touched me very much, he told me with tears
in his eyes how astonished and touched he was by the spectacle, how it had surprised him. It was the evening after the
premiere. Afterwards certainly they have all changed their
opinions a thousand times. I think even so that I have opened
a new door, certainly no arc de triomphe—but I did not want

that—I have simply made a hole in a huge wall. And I think
that even so that is something. I am very sorry that you weren't
there for you are the only "young" ones eternally young and
tormented by the need for the new and for researches, and
Gertrude I am sure that you would have found it interesting,
new. . . . They've probably written you a great deal about
it, or perhaps they don't think it worth it? You know how
little that matters to me. I am even happy that my contemporaries are too backward to understand all that; and yet it
makes me sad for the more I go away the more I feel alone,
horribly alone, and not one of my painter-friends with whom
I can say a word. They are saying now that Bérard is a painter
by intuition ("French" excuse) and I a painter by rule of
head, very "cerebral" even rather intellectual. My God I, a
painter by rule, when each time I finish with yesterday brings
me another and a new law, but always an accident and always
post-factum even post picturam—a resolution that I abandon
and that people call the law—I who cannot produce even a
series of four pictures in the same style! Human stupidity ex-
asperates me Gertrude; people end by saying that my painting
is strange and eccentric, only not to be banal like all the rest.
And I seek for that banality without being able to find it!
With this ballet it's the same as with those bouquets of flowers
you have in your house. You well know that you can see things
which others do not see. . . . Write me your news, make new
things to burst and crush the silliness and stupidity of humanity. Embrace Belley and its mountains for me. Excuse
me for having written of nothing but myself. I had to write
you everything. Have a good rest, don't forget me. . . .

                                                    Pavlik

FROM MARIAN WALKER WILLIAMS

The Cosmopolitan Club, 133 East 40th Street [New York],
June 28, 1928

My dear Gertrude

I have been in Baltimore for two weeks—a ghost among
ghosts who were more real than the realities and the most
real of all was your own vigorous self, tramping across town or
into the country, swinging down the corridors, full of life and
sanity and humour. Too bad America lost you—but in a way
she did not for the younger generation here is being profoundly
influenced by your books. . . . I don't know how you feel
about youth. When it is intelligent it interests me greatly,
especially this younger generation which thinks so much
straighter than ours did.

I should like to see you and be sand-bagged on the head
when I didn't agree with you and sand bag you back again.
It was a good life we led, that student life, and it is still a
good life that we lead in our individual ways. The world—
whether in Paris or California—is a great place and full of
interest to actors and on-lookers.

Good bye Gertrude. Congratulations on all you have
achieved. I can't begin to talk about it or this would become
a letter instead of note.

As ever
Marian Walker Williams

FROM PAVEL TCHELITCHEW [TRANSLATED]

[Paris] July 13, 1928

Dear dear Gertrude and Alice!

I have not written to you for a century. Don't hold it
against me. You know that with all I was obliged to do and

all the stupid things I had to take part in—saying and saying again the same things in an effort to persuade Monsieur Diaghilew and company to give in to my ideas—all that tired and agitated me so extremely that life became frightful and stupid. The difficulty in all that was that I was too tired to work and at the same time wanted very much to work for myself [to paint], but had no patience with them, no respect. And so I was furious, furious as never before. . . . And so I was torn between dissatisfaction with the work and the boredom of seeing stupid people, my God and I've seen a lot of them! . . .

How do things go at Belley? Ah Gertrude Gertrude, I envy your being among the sweet mountains of Belley, watching Madame Mont-Blanc, seated in a green meadow with Alice. There you have the true wisdom of life. . . . Just now there is a show of my pictures in London. It is Edith [Sitwell] who arranged it. She is really a guardian angel for me in London. I sent 15 drawings and 16 gouaches and Pierre [Loeb] sent about ten canvases. I hope that it will go well, I've already received letters and telegrams from everybody. All London was at the opening. Edith in spite of all—and her brother—arranged everything for the best . . . I suffer a great deal to be so foreign to the French. Dear friends, you have no idea how one suffers. I understand very well the Negroes of America, as I am a Russian Negro among the French. Write me a little of your news. Embrace for me the mountains and grass of Belley. . . .

With all my heart
Pavlik

Virgil Thomson, the American composer, had been successful in creating a musical setting for Gertrude Stein's "Capital, Capitals," and had undertaken to write music for her "Four Saints in Three Acts," an "opera" which she had completed the previous year. She

was currently working on another opera entitled "Their Wills. A Bouquet," for which music was eventually composed by Lord Berners, and which was produced as a ballet with the title "A Wedding Bouquet."

FROM VIRGIL THOMSON

[Hotel] Etchola, Ascain, B. P.,
July 19 [1928]

Dear Gertrude

The opera is finished including the intermezzo and Act IV. That is to say it isn't finished by a long shot but all the composing is done. I am glad to have done the music before seeing Spain. My plan now is to go look and listen to Spain a bit because I've an idea that Spain makes a special kind of noise that will bear imitation orchestrally. Her tunes & her rhythms are too good to be interesting and there isn't anything to be done about them but I think her *timbre* may have possibilities. I shall not go immediately but maybe next month or so. In the meantime I have some violin pieces to write and that same symphony to finish. I love more and more [the] Pyrenees country. I plan to advance slowly on Spain, a little expedition one day to the monastery of St. Ignatius at Loyola, a little glimpse of beach, and finishing at Fontarabie, and then one day when nobody is looking I shall openly take a Spanish train and go somewhere. When your weather gets cooler, why don't you drive over and hear the opera. It's a swell trip. *Their Wills* has a nice sound. We shall certainly do the *Capitals* in N. Y. next winter. I hope you get your garden. Here are some clippings. And love,

Virgil

FROM ALYSE GREGORY

Chez Perrier Café, Les Esplantas, Belley,
Aug 11, 1928

Dear Miss Stein,

My husband, Llewelyn Powys, and I are staying in Belley, and we wondered whether you would be willing to let us come in and call on you some afternoon or evening for a few minutes when you are free. I was for some time Managing Editor of The Dial and I think we have a number of friends in common.

Sincerely yours,
Alyse Gregory

FROM FORD MADOX FORD

32 rue de Vaugirard, Xtmas Day 1928

Dear Gertrude

I wish you'd let my friend Allen Tate who is a very fine poet call on you with his wife. They're such nice people—residing at present in No 3 of your street: Hotel de Fleurus.

All good wishes
F M F.

FROM SHERWOOD ANDERSON

Marion, Virginia, Jan 15, 1929

Dear Gertrude Stein:—

I am ashamed that I have not written you any letters for a long time.

Everything of my routine of life has been disturbed for a long time now. I have been trying to work, but have not got much done. It has been very interesting and absorbing running the country weeklies during the last year—but they have taken a lot of time.

Now my son, Bob, who is twenty-one, is with me and will be able to do a lot of the work. I hope to be able to get free from so many of the details, that had piled up on me and that I shall have a book or two in the next year.

I think often of you in Paris and your house.

I think anyone who at all follows writing sees also your influence everywhere.

With lots of love and luck to you and your house.

Sherwood.

Laura Riding and Robert Graves, who were at this time publishing Gertrude Stein's An Acquaintance with Description *with their Seizin Press imprint, had written Miss Stein about Hart Crane, the American poet, whose* White Buildings *had appeared in 1926.*

FROM HART CRANE

Hotel Jacob, 44, rue Jacob [Paris]
Jan 31, 1929

Dear Miss Stein:

May I introduce myself as a friend of your friend, Laura Riding?

And on that presumption may I ask to see you some hour early next week—whenever it may suit your convenience to have me call—?

I am going away for the weekend, but shall probably be back by Monday evening. I hope I may hear from you.

Sincerely,
Hart Crane

In New York, Virgil Thomson continued in his work of publicizing the opera. Carl Van Vechten had agreed to try to sell some of Kristians Tonny's drawings, and Max Ewing was exhibiting his "Extraordinary Portraits."

FROM CARL VAN VECHTEN

150 West Fifty-fifth Street
[New York, Feb 18? 1929]

Dear Gertrude,

Virgil Thomson came & played "Four Saints in Three Acts" to a select crowd which included Mabel Luhan, Muriel Draper, les Stettheimers, Alma Wertheim, Witter Bynner etc. & everybody liked it so much that yesterday I cabled you. I liked it so much that I wanted to hear it all over again right away. Mabel liked it so much that she said it should be done & it would finish opera just as Picasso had finished old painting. Well I cabled you, but everybody loved it & I think your words are so right & inevitable in music. "Capital-Capitals" is being done next week.

I *did* receive [Georges] Hugnet's poems & I did write him, but *where* are Tonny's drawings? You wrote that they were arriving by a Capt. [Emmett] Addis who was sailing on Jan. 18 & I waited to get them before writing you & I am still waiting. *Where* are they? . . .

Max Ewing's exhibition is extraordinary. I think you have had a catalogue. & I am *very* well again, but am having all my teeth taken out. Some of us took Virgil to Harlem after the concert, & he behaved very well, but in spite of that I think he was a little astonished.

Love to you both from us,
Carlo.

We might come over any minute; so I hope the Tonny drawings come before we go after them.

The drawings arrived safely a few days later and Carl Van Vech-
ten eventually disposed of all of them.

Gertrude Stein's "Capital, Capitals" with Virgil Thomson's
music was performed this month in New York.

FROM VIRGIL THOMSON

140 E. 19 [New York] Feb 26 [1929]

Dear Gertrude

Capitals swell success. N. Y. talks of nothing else since
three days. Audience roared with laughter during and bravos
afterwards. Critics charmingly confused. Some thought it a
good joke, some a bad joke and one or so got quite angry. . . .
I enclose assorted clippings. Don't throw them away. Met
your friend [Henry] McBride. Liked him & him me & he heard
some opera and liked it. Theater Guild man [Philip Moeller]
not useful at present because he was mad he hadn't thought
of it himself and he bit his fingernails in fury all during. I
neglected to mention that at the Capitals show the poets were
all disgusted with the words and the composers thought the
music too low for anything. But the audience's way of taking
it proved to me the possibility of having a regular boob success with the opera, at least it might run long enough to pay
its expenses and it might just might (and without surprising
me at all) make a little money. I return on Île de France March
29, arriving April 3. I shall be glad.

Love

Virgil

I had after the concert a sweet and complimentary letter from
a person named Lindley Hubbell whom I gather to be an
acquaintance of yours. Terribly nice letter.

FROM CHARLES HENRI FORD

Blues, A Revue of Modern Literature, Columbus, Mississippi,
Mar 27, 1929

My dear Miss Stein,

If you have seen the March number of BLUES (No. 2), although I doubt if you have, you may recall the announcement of an Expatriate Number of BLUES to appear shortly. I admire your work intensely, but even if I did not, no Expatriate number of an American magazine (although such a thing has never appeared) would be complete without work by Gertrude Stein. Do you have a prose piece, long or short, or a poem that you could let me have for this issue? It will probably appear in the summer and will include work by Eugene Jolas (contributing editor of BLUES); Ezra Pound, more than likely; H. D., etc. I should be very grateful to you; especially since BLUES, at the outset of its very hazardous career, will not be able to pay for contributions.

If there are other young Americans in Paris whose work you are interested in and whose careers you would like to foster I should also be glad to see their work. And please send any biographical material about yourself, as well as the others, that you care to. . . .

Faithfully yours,
Ch. Henri Ford

The expatriate number of Blues *appeared in the spring of 1930 and contained "Evidence," a portrait of Bravig Imbs, by Gertrude Stein.*

Stuart Davis, the American painter, then recently arrived in Paris, had been taken to the rue de Fleurus by Elliot Paul, who had published an article on Davis's work, illustrated with reproductions of paintings, in Transition. *Gertrude Stein was interested and agreed to visit Davis's studio as soon as he had some work ready for her to see.*

FROM STUART DAVIS

50, Rue Vercingetorix, Paris, XIV,
May 1, 1929

Dear Miss Stein:

I have got some more paintings & lithographs done. It would be fine if you and your friend, Miss Toklis (pardon wrong spelling) could come here some afternoon and look at same. I know you are understanding about paintings and your ideas about them will be very interesting to me. I have wanted to ask you for months past but I am a slow worker and so had to wait to get something to show you. If you will set your own day & hour and let me know by mail I will be honored to see you.

Sincerely yours,
Stuart Davis

Georges Hugnet was at this time publishing in Paris, under the imprint "Editions de la Montagne," his own translation of selections from The Making of Americans, Morceaux Choisis de La Fabrication des Américains. *This volume was to contain, in the de luxe copies, a frontispiece reproduction of a drawing of Gertrude Stein by the French painter and designer for the theatre Christian ("Bébé") Bérard. Miss Stein had already gone to the country for the summer.*

FROM GEORGES HUGNET [TRANSLATED]

[Paris] Friday, May 24, 1929

Very dear Gertrude

I beg you to excuse me for having been so long in writing you. . . .

I shall have the third proofs of the book at the beginning

of the week (Monday or Tuesday) and I shall send them back at once since I shall be quite free (I hope) and there will be only a few mistakes to correct. But I still haven't the photos of your portrait by Bérard, and Georges [Maratier] doesn't answer my letters. . . . Would you, dear Gertrude, write him not harshly but firmly and pull his ears? We'll see if that won't get him. The book should be out in ten days if he gets busy about it. . . .

I am unhappy just now—without an incentive, even a futile one. Ah how I wish you were here: you could say the right things without my telling you what the trouble is, by intuition and true friendship. But writing you does me good and the idea of having a letter from you soon chases away my despondency. . . .

Oh yes I shall come to see you in September.

What a fine evening it was, do you remember, with Virgil [Thomson] and Picasso.

Dear dear Gertrude, don't leave me long without news of you. Best wishes with all my heart to you and Alice.

Georges

FROM STUART DAVIS

50 Rue Vercingetorix, Paris XIV,
June 1, 1929

Dear Miss Stein:

This is a letter asking for favors.

Elliot Paul told me that you were interested in one of my paintings, Egg Beater, and that you would buy it. I would consider it an honor to be in your collection and in addition to that my finances are missing on all cylinders. Therefore I would like you to have the painting in question for your own price and if you can arrange to do it I would appreciate it very much. I have to give up my studio July 15 and would leave the painting anywhere you say. My forced retreat to America will be followed by an exhibit in N. Y., next fall—from which I hope to get funds to return here at once. Now for the second favor. I conceived the idea that you might write a paragraph about your impression of my work which I could use as a fore-word in the catalogue of my exhibition. The use of your name in this way would be of great value. I hope you will excuse the disagreeable character of this letter and my only excuse is that modernistic painters in general have a tough time.

Best wishes for the summer

Sincerely
Stuart Davis

Gertrude Stein did not buy the Stuart Davis painting, nor did she write an introduction for his catalogue.

She had for some time been seeing Christian Bérard. He hav-ing done a drawing of her, she wrote a portrait of him.

FROM CHRISTIAN BÉRARD [TRANSLATED]

[Paris] Saturday [Summer 1929]

Dear Miss Stein,

I am deeply touched by your sending me this portrait and I am impressed by the feeling of truth which it contains. I keep it beside me and it heartens me as a continuing witness to your friendship which is so precious to me. I am happy to have made the drawing of you and shall be so proud to see it soon as the frontispiece of your book.

I should like to come to thank you in person and I hope that I may soon.

I am working a good deal and shall be very happy to show you my last pictures when they are finished.

Believe me, Miss Stein, I am most sincerely your friend,

Christian Bérard.

FROM BRAVIG IMBS

[Paris] June 25 [1929]

Dear Gertrude:

. . . Last night I had the privilege of seeing just how one of those Select fights develop from the beginning to the final ignoble ousting by the police. Georges Hugnet was in beautiful form having already dislocated his shoulder a week ago and feeling rebellious ever since.

First we dined at Sabin's which was delightful—they sent their love to you (meilleures amitiés) . . .

Then we went to a new bar in Montparnasse and danced until two or thereabouts and had a good time, except Georges who was nursing some grudge, abetted no doubt by the five martinis, two pernods, five vermouths, wine white and red and ginn fizz's consumed during the day.

Then we drifted on to the Select penniless or near it and had been there about a half an hour when along drifted Bébé [Bérard] with two millionaires and Boris Kochno. He did not deign to notice us though he sat nearby and this infuriated Tonny who began to shout gros légume, gros tonneau, answered by pauvre râté, and the bullyragging continued. Georges constantly assez assez. Then Bébé sidled over to us his two eyes like drooping orchids and his mouth a blown rosebud and saying with much pity but what have I done that you should treat me thus whereupon Georges screamed assez, lifted his chair with his good hand and flung it at Bébé. Women shrieked and a garçon got hold of Georges. I broke in because I feared he was going to hurt Georges' arm and it was very exciting and Boris tried to apologize and the gérant was very vile and we were all ousted to the accompaniment of some of the most magnificent Billingsgate I have ever heard. We had to walk home which was well as Georges needed calming . . .

Well that's that. Best of love to you and soon we'll be seeing you,

Bravig

An Acquaintance with Description *had appeared in April* 1929 *and Gertrude Stein had sent a copy to Bernard Faÿ. He and Bravig Imbs had finished the English translation of his* Benjamin Franklin.

FROM BERNARD FAŸ

Clermont Ferrand, July 29, 1929

Dear Miss Stein,

I have been terribly slow to thank you for the beautiful and divine book you sent me, terribly slow to write you. . . .

First I had to finish Franklin, then to hurry correcting the proofs, then to receive the thousands of Americans who kindly came to see me and nearly killed me. Finally I had to suffer from the baccalauréats, the terrific heat . . . And I leave tonight for Paris, Le Havre, New York, Boston, and Gambier (Ohio).

All these things have prevented me from finishing a great Essay: "Poésie" where there will be question of YOU, Monsieur Hugnet, Monsieur [Tristan] Tzara, and Monsieur [Paul] Eluard. Very, very hard work, as I should like to be "digne de vous" and I know it is not easy. And I should hate to write such rotten stuff as all our people do just now. For some reason they are all idiotic. Mr [André] Gide seems decided to beat them all. His last essays in the Nouvelle Revue Française are sad. He seems to have started a crusade against "L'Oeuvre de la Bonne Mort et des Ames du Purgatoire" and he attacks them with methods and means which are only too well fitted for his enemies, much more than for the esteem I used to have for Mr Gide. . . .

Really I am fed up with literature, politics and practically everything just now, I can only enjoy poetry, yours for instance, and Xth Century Churches. I have seen a lot of them since a fortnight and that kept me alive. . . . It is not simply "goût de la vieillerie," but these "preromanesque" churches have a certain rhythm which is more manly than the ogival and even much more spontaneous than the romanesque itself. And they have never been spoiled by literary critics and enlightened tourists. . . .

England is invading Paris and filling the atelier of Mr Tchelitchew. It seems that his genius appeals particularly to English minds and if [Ramsay] MacDonald does not destroy England before six months, if the sterling holds somewhat, Mr Tchelitchew will be rich. . . .

But we had a great excitement. You probably heard of it. Mr Hart Crane feeling that genius was coming into him and remembering that according to Plato "Poésis esti mikra mania" went to get a great deal of "mania" in a café. When he was thoroughly drunk he strongly refused to pay. The saloon keeper, who was a lady or at any rate a woman, discussed with him, but failing to persuade him called for the police. Indignant of that impolite action Mr Hart Crane began calling the lady a great number of names, and unfortunately drunkenness had broadened the circle, ordinarily rather narrow, of his French. The lady was indignant, the policemen too. And there followed a sad adventure. Mr Hart Crane, refusing to follow the police, was beaten, trampled under feet by them, and finally kicked and triumphantly carried away by them as the Trojans carried the body of Patroclus. The crowd was horrified and tried in vain to interfere. Fate was against Mr Crane. He stayed in jail ten days, and we had a lot of trouble to get him out. We had to persuade the old lady that he did not speak French. She would not believe us until we had given proofs. . . .

Mr Crane is free and has sailed for God's own Country.
. . . I shall write again. And if you had a minute to send

me some news I should appreciate it immensely. You can always write 16 rue St Guillaume.

    With deep respect, and most sincere "attachement," I am
Yours,
Bernard Faÿ

Le Grand Hôtel, Leysin, Suisse
[Late Summer 1929]

Dear Gertrud,

    After an hoffle operation on my leg, I am now and for how
many times, in mountains.

    Somebody comes to see me sometimes and it's my consola-
tion because I am staying all the time in a high lit à roulette,
the Godiva of the beds, Godivissima. Perhaps, you can go, a
day, to see me. Leysin is near Aigle, Aigle near Montreux,
Montreux near Lausanne, Lausanne near Genève, Genève near
Belley, Belley near Bilignin and Bilignin is Bilignin, and Leysin is Leysin (alas).

    It's raining and raining, and always raining.

    The Doctor does a cure of Tuberculine, and it all is good,
after one year you will have a René Crevel, with lungs and
legs and heart and all that is necessary for good life.

    I hope in a little time [to] begin (again) my translation,
but ill is lazy and I am the both.

    All my love for you both, for yoth (nice word)
René.

*The artist Eugène Berman had visited Gertrude Stein at Bilignin
during the brief period of her interest in his work.*

FROM EUGÈNE BERMAN [TRANSLATED]

[Paris] Oct 1, 1929

Dear Miss Gertrude and Miss Alice

I got back to Paris Friday night . . . I am going to get back to work tomorrow or the day after, spending a little time on my apartment, and I shall move probably after the 15th. I have not seen anyone yet . . .

Here I am once more at home, among my pictures, ready to begin work again. My holiday with you thanks to your invitation will have done me the greatest good. I speak not only of the physical well-being which the good life at Bilignin did me, the absolute quiet, calm of air and sun and all the attentions with which you surrounded me and for which I owe you my deepest gratitude, but also of a good of another order—new impressions, fine landscapes, perhaps even new subjects, new forms and above all the great impression made upon me by your words on the mixture of true and false, the need of separating them, of concentrating every effort on that. Naturally I felt that instinctively and that is why I have never worked easily, seeking blindly and making many attempts without results—only it was necessary that it be formulated as simply and as precisely as you did, and I believe that it will not again leave my head. . . .

With all my wishes for a fine end to your stay at Bilignin, I send both of you, dear Miss Gertrude and Miss Alice, all my gratitude and affectionate regards.

Eugène Berman

The Cooks had returned to spend the winter in Mallorca.

FROM WILLIAM COOK

15 Calle de los Banos, Terreno, Palma de Mallorca,
Nov 12, 1929

Dear Friends;—

Well here we are again looking at the cathedral of Palma. We have the house just over the last one we had; the house is considerably larger and we have a very good sized garden which is full of flowers at present. . . .

I can't see that things have changed so very much. Your old hotel Victoria has painted up and additioned and on the other side of us the hotel Mediteranneo towers up into the sky quite a bit. It is a very good hotel by the way with good food and good service. We stayed there while getting settled here. . . .

There is an English library which looks pretty good just at the tramway station at the top of the street. The road from Perpignan to Barcelona is magnificent. Better run down when you get too cold, but don't come into Barcelona after dark until you have become used to the mule carts and one thing and another and of course the Spaniard when he has a car doesn't see the use of running it at half speed when it is no more work to make it go as fast as it can, and the heavy trucks have a cheerful way of not carrying any lights which makes things a bit disconcerting.

There are lots of turkeys strutting about waiting for Thanksgiving and Christmas. I don't seem to see quite as many of them tied on the balconies and as for the formidable number of English inhabitants of the island they seem to be tucked away obligingly out of sight in obscure and economical corners . . .

Our love to you both;

Cook

During the summer of 1929, Marian Walker Williams, her husband having died of tuberculosis, had visited Gertrude Stein in Paris.

FROM MARIAN WALKER WILLIAMS

Hotel Palmato, Ravello (Pr. di Salerno) Italy,
Jan 21, 1930

Dear Old Gertrude

Is it too late to wish you and Alice and Basket a very happy New Year? Late or not I wish it to you. I have been here in Ravello since the middle of November. . . . I don't know yet whether I shall sail from Italy or go up to Cherbourg. The only advantage of the latter course is that in passing through Paris I should see you—and some pictures. Both of which I should like.

Your remark about liking to see people come and liking to see them go seems to me the true philosophy of life—not to possess any thing or to count upon possession but to ride life with light hands, taking with pleasure what comes one's way but never trying to hold it.

It was good to see you last summer, & find you still the same old Gertrude, batting all the heads that come your way. The reason we get on is that my head is tough and I too like the game of batting. But after 25 yrs. it is pleasant to find you again.

Do you know this heavenly spot on a hill top above Amalfi? I remember that years ago you went to Paestum so you may have come up here. It is as lovely as anything I know & the weather is heavenly—crocuses all out and almond blossoms beginning.

As ever
Marian W. W.

❧

Robert Coates was now writing for the New Yorker. *He had a scheme to make Furman of Macaulay's republish* The Making of Americans.

FROM ROBERT COATES

67 West 11 Street, New York, Jan 24, 1930

Dear Miss Stein,

I don't know when I'll ever get back to Paris. What we are doing now is building a house in the country. New York is such a helter-skelter place—bells ringing, parties, people calling up, people dropping in—that it is almost impossible to get any consecutive work done, and it takes me so long to start on anything, even hack work, that only by working consecutively can I finish anything quickly enough to make a living. That is the main reason for the house in the country. Moreover, in spite of the paradox, we feel we'll be less tied down than now with an apartment—lease, having to store furniture if we go away, and so on.

But the business of paying for the land and paying for the building, meanwhile, makes a pretty problem. I'm working away, doing profiles for the New Yorker, mostly, who are very nice people to work for, but it just doesn't leave time for anything else. Ideas, for another novel I've been planning for over a year, come into my head, and I have to put them over —while I finish something I'll get paid for—until they get stale. I think soon I'll have to let everything else slide and settle down to my own stuff. . . .

I begin to realize, what I knew but only theoretically before, that life for the artist nowadays must be a continual struggle—something like that of the religious men of pre-medieval times—not so much for his ideals as for his own interest, not against outside influences as against subtle little changes within himself.

You know, about the Making of Americans: I think it's

still likely that Furman may publish it, if you still want him to. Several of us have been arguing with him about it: with a publisher, of course, the whole question is a financial one, and that has been our argument. You must know, if you read any American publications at all, how your name is bandied about. I should think it would infuriate you sometimes—it certainly does me—to see your name used by critics who obviously have never read a line of yours as a tag for anything from 3 A.M. at the Select Bar to Communism. Well, it seems to me it would be amusing and might be profitable for Furman to put something of yours before these people to read. They aren't really, consciously, unfair, I think; it's simply that they have to write their columns every day, and in default of first-hand information, and to save time, they use clichés.

. . . For the rest, there isn't much news—a good deal of running around, seeing this person or that, and so on. . . . Best regards to you and Miss Toklas, and please write.

Sincerely,
Bob Coates—

FROM MARSDEN HARTLEY

Café des 2 Magots [Paris, Jan? 29, 1930]

Excuse the bourgeois crest—It is splendidly decreed that this gentleman will be most pleased to receive Miss Gertrude Stein in her own home—and to establish the exact shade of the 'even more' than auld lang syne. It is expected that all red carpets will be laid from curb to throne—and if it rains, the customary awning.

Much is to be made of this by all attending deities.

Approximately at 9— all bells will be rung.

Devotedly
Marsden.

Georges Hugnet, having published the Morceaux Choisis de La
Fabrication des Américains, *next issued the* Dix Portraits—*a collection of ten portraits by Gertrude Stein, printed both in
English and in French translation, and (in the de luxe copies) ap-
propriately illustrated. Miss Stein had written her own poetic version of Hugnet's poem "Enfances," and had sent Hugnet a copy.*

FROM GEORGES HUGNET [TRANSLATED]

Saint-Malo, July 9, 1930

Admirable Gertrude, what joy you give me in my solitude
of sand and rock! I laugh at the sea which breaks out into
white laughter all along the shore. This isn't a translation, it
is something else, *it is better.* I more than like this reflection
[of my poem], I dream of it and I admire it. And you return
to me hundred-fold the pleasure that I was able to offer
you. . . .

I love you with all my heart for so brilliantly translating
me and I send you the last thought of my 23rd and the first
of my 24th year.

Georges

FROM GEORGE PLATT LYNES

Englewood, New Jersey, Nov 29, 1930

Dearest Gertrude,

I wish you were really here, to be seen and talked to. Talking about you is the second best, but it only aggravates my
lonesomeness, making you seem especially far away. For I
have had the luck to be able to talk about you, often and ten-
derly, with Bernard Faÿ. And he is sailing away, within the
week, and I must stay behind. Next summer I mean to be in
France again. Then I shall pursue you into the depths of the

country, bearing with me gifts and the accoutrements of my profession. . . .

There must be new editions (although I haven't paid for the last one yet), more grammar or portraits. Bernard read me his piece about you. I was delighted with it. I should like to have a copy. Could you and he combine to send me one? For my letter will reach Paris only a few days before he does. You are so much a part of my history. Having known you, near and far, for more than five years, feeling impressively devoted, I want every scrap. And lovely long letters. . . .

My best love always,

George

Gertrude Stein and Georges Hugnet were having some disagreement about the proposed publication of their poems. Eventually the two were printed on opposite pages of the Winter 1931 number of the magazine Pagany, *Miss Stein's with the consciously alliterative title "Poem Pritten on the Pfances of Georges Hugnet." When her poem appeared in book form in 1931, the once happy relations which had existed between Hugnet and Miss Stein were commemorated by a new title,* Before the Flowers of Friendship Faded Friendship Faded.

FROM GEORGES HUGNET [TRANSLATED]

Dec 18, 1930

Dear Gertrude,

Your request surprises me. It surprised me this summer at Belley. And I thought that you would not follow up this proposition. Those whom I have questioned about the phrasing which you wanted on the prospectus, both poets and publishers, have all said that your name beside mine would give the impression of a collaboration, when, don't you agree, there is no question of that.

The sale of this book in America, if it interests me, will not force me to disclaim in this way a work for which, in spite of its faults, I intend to take complete and sole responsibility.

I understood your insistence that the word translation be replaced by another term like adaptation, transposition. Though the point seemed to me futile, I could only agree to it. I suggested to you at Belley: "free translation," which seemed to me exact and without pretension, but you rejected it.

You know, dear Gertrude, that I admire your translation, this "reflection" as you called it of my "Enfances," and nothing will take away the joy that I felt in reading what you had written in the margin, if you wish, of my text, still following it sufficiently so that I could make no objection, this summer, to the translation which you read me page for page almost, and which you yourself proposed, last March, a year after I had written my "Enfances" at Bruges. . . .

I dare believe, my very dear Gertrude, that you will understand and even approve of the importance which I attach to the responsibility for this work living in me and to my prior right . . . I dare believe also that an incident of this kind will not affect our friendship which I wanted to be alive and fresh. All good wishes to you

Georges

VI. THE COMING OF FAME
1931–MAY 1935

Gertrude Stein had grown weary of the long struggle to get her writing published. She had sold Picasso's Girl with a Fan, an important early painting, to Mrs. Harriman and with the proceeds had set up a plan for the publication of all her unpublished work. This was the Plain Edition, of which Alice Toklas was the editor. Miss Stein sent Kate Buss a proof of the cover of the first volume of the series, Lucy Church Amiably, *which was published on January 5, 1931.*

FROM KATE BUSS

[Medford, Mass., Jan 1931?]

Dear Gertrude,

Your letters are very rich and very pleasure giving. And such a lot of information that I was wishing for. Thanks so much. And as prettily as I know how great thanks for the azure page from Lucy Church Amiably. . . .

You're the principal character in the MS that I'm rewriting about writers in 1921 in Paris. Also what they're up to up to date. I shall tell some of the fun it was to be at hand while you were publishing Geography and Plays. That's the one book

of yours of which I have a personal knowledge of its transition
from MS to book. At that time you hadn't published for about
ten years, had you? And didn't seem to think the time ready.
But there was that great row of bound MS. Now what's left
of it going into Plain Edition. Is that right?

I shall never forget those hilarious evenings . . .

Love to you always
Kitty

*At about this time Gertrude Stein stopped seeing the entire Tche-
litchew-Berman-Hugnet group. (The break with Bravig Imbs was
soon made up.)*

FROM BRAVIG IMBS

7 rue du Chalet, Boulogne-sur-Seine, Seine
[Jan 1931]

Dear Gertrude:—

If I have said, done, or written anything which has displeased or hurt either you or Alice, I am heartily sorry and beg
you to forgive me. My conscience is not quite clear, and even
though this should be the last letter I write to you, I should
rather have made this apology and be straight with myself.

If I have become dull or uninteresting to you, that is another matter, and I recognize your right to drop me in such
a case. . . .

Losing friends is a sad matter for me, as I have so few of
them, and to lose such friends as you and Alice have been, is
doubly hard. I remember you said once that all the young men
went away, and I wondered at your statement, for I could not
believe it possible. Perhaps the young men should go away for
their own sakes, but I do not feel or care to be one of them.

Of course, you have your own reasons for your silence and
as you are much wiser than I, I must abide by them. Still, I

should like to thank you for all the kindnesses you and Alice
have shown me in the past, and to assure you of my loyalty. I
am really deeply grateful, and my admiration and respect for
you is limitless.

I know this letter may seem ludicrous to you, but I tell
you the feeling behind it is not, and so I make bold to sign
myself once more,

Your friend,
Bravig Imbs

FROM ROBERT M. COATES

67 West 11 Street, New York,
Feb 25, 1931

Dear Miss Stein,

Your letter had grand news: "Lucy Church Amiably" and
the Plain Editions plan. I've been doing book reviews for the
New Yorker the last couple of months and your announcement came just as I was getting together a piece about limited
and special editions. So I hope you won't mind that I put in a
notice about Plain Editions.

Have you made any arrangements to distribute the books
over here? I think you should, and please let me know if I
can do anything to help make arrangements with someone
suitable. . . .

Our great hope . . . is to get over to France this fall. It's
time, it seems. After too long here, one gets too caught up in
things, too hurried, too much concerned about money and so
on. I think it would be very healthy for us both to get away
for a time and forget about our accumulating responsibilities—
the house in the country, the job and all that. But we can't
leave the house this summer. I hope to finish off work on it this
season, and then go away in early autumn.

Here's hoping to see you then. Meantime, best wishes from

us both to you and Miss Toklas. And success to Plain Editions.
I think that is really important news to everyone. . . .

Sincerely,
Robert M. Coates.

Louis Bromfield was living with his family in nearby Senlis. Gertrude Stein had recently discovered the manuscript of her first book, "Q. E. D.," written before Three Lives, *and had let Bromfield have it to see what he thought about the possibility of publishing it. The book was eventually printed in 1950 with the title* Things as They Are.

FROM LOUIS BROMFIELD

Presbytère de St. Etienne, 2, rue St. Etienne, Senlis (Oise)
[Spring? 1931]

Dear Gertrude Stein:—

Thanks for your kind note about the book [*Twenty-Four Hours*]. I'm delighted that you discovered our community of language. I felt the same thing—or rather that the more experienced I grow the nearer I come to speaking your tongue. The book has met with a varied reception. I tried to write a statement, very simple, of a story, leaving the overtones entirely to implication, and I've been abused, as a result, because I'm a simple storyteller. I cannot see how logically I could have put high-sounding philosophies into the mouths of any character in the book. It makes me sick and inclined to take William Rothenstein's assertion that "much criticism is refined gossip" at its face value. . . .

I have finished the early book you gave me to read and find it vastly interesting not only for itself but for the presence in it of the ideas which later flowered in Lucy Church. Incidentally I sent Lucy Church among the list of recommended books to the N. Y. Daily Tribune (requested). Perhaps that will be an opening wedge. I'm thinking of the possibilities of publishing "Quod etc." There are great difficulties certainly but it's possible they may be overcome.

I'm sending this to the rue de Fleurus as I can't make out the Department you're in. I can't possibly accuse you of bad handwriting after my own. With the best of everything to you both,

Louis Bromfield

Michel Leiris, the French surrealist poet and anthropologist, was the brother-in-law of Kahnweiler and of Élie Lascaux.

FROM MICHEL LEIRIS [TRANSLATED]

Mission Dakar-Djibouti, Paris,
Apr 8, 1931

Dear Miss Stein,

I think you know that I am to leave for Africa with the Dakar-Djibouti scientific expedition. Our departure is now set for May 16, from Bordeaux. . . .

A rather amusing thing is to happen—one rather unusual for this kind of enterprise—the famous American Negro boxer Al Brown is making an appearance for our benefit at the Cirque d'Hiver on April 15. Many personalities from the American colony will be there, as well as a great number of painters whom you know, and writers like Raymond Roussel (the author of "Impressions d'Afrique" and one of the sponsors of our expedition) whom I hope to persuade to come.

I tell you very frankly that I should be delighted to have you agree to take part in our benefit. It would be a great joy for me to see poetry represented beside all the snobs and officials. . . .

I should be delighted too to have you see Al Brown who is a charming person.

Please give my best remembrances to Miss Toklas, and accept my thanks for anything you care to do.

Respectfully yours,
Michel Leiris

❧

Paul Frederic Bowles, a young American composer and writer, had shown some of his poems to Gertrude Stein.

FROM PAUL FREDERIC BOWLES

Munich, May 20 [1931]

Dear Miss Stein—

I am glad (gladder than that really) that you don't dislike all the poems as much as the first one. I was quite discouraged by the finality of: "He's not a poet. No. He's not a poet" that evening. Things look up. . . .

I am trying to think of a good excuse for being near enough to Belley to warrant my visiting you. Perhaps one will come along as the days go by. I love that section of the country, having first seen it when it was all pink with sun very early in the morning. I woke up not far north of the Lac du Bourget, and was tremendously excited by the strange aspect of the landscape. And it was all new then, even the little shrieks of the locomotive as it started up at each station, and especially just before it darted into a tunnel.

The festival ends tomorrow on Oedipus Rex and I shall return to Berlin. Shall return all wet with rain and with very little money.

Good bye,
Frederic

FROM HENRY McBRIDE

Hotel Roblin, 6, Rue Chauveau-Lagarde, Paris (8e),
Wednesday, June 1931

My dearest Gertrude:

I am broken-hearted not to see you and Alice. It is ridiculous to come to France and return sans vos nouvelles. I came unexpectedly for ten days only to see the Matisse show and the Colonial affair and depart for London next Tuesday and for the States on July 2. . . .

I saw Picasso last night at the Matisse vernissage, and again this afternoon at his studio. He tells me he is going to see you soon and I charged him to give you and Alice my love, and probably he will do so. He is in excellent spirits and has some marvellous pictures in his studio. Always the last one seems to be the greatest.

Matisse's vernissage was very mondaine. All sorts of picturesque specimens. I had dinner with Matisse preceding the party and he was most amiable and kind as usual. They say in America he is getting 6,000,000 francs for his Dr Barnes decoration. Even allowing for exaggerations he seems to be getting well paid.

In the pell-mell on Pablo's table I noticed the blue covers of Lucy Church Amiably and when I pointed it out Pablo smiled and said "Ah, oui, chère Gertrude." My address in London is Clarges Hotel, Half-Moon St. Don't empty any vials of wrath on me for not coming south—I feel sufficiently convicted of sin as it is.

With love to you both
Henri

Paul Bowles and Aaron Copland had visited Gertrude Stein during the summer.

FROM AARON COPLAND

bei Strub, Uhland Str. 3, Berlin—Charlottenburg,
Nov 10 [1931]

Dear Miss Stein,—

The proposed concert I mentioned to you at Bilignin has worked out. The British Music Society has agreed to sponsor a concert of American chamber music on Dec 16 at Aeolian Hall. Your Capital Capitals will be sung by the Tudor Singers with Virgil [Thomson] coming from Paris to play his own accompaniment. I think that assures a good performance. Other items on the program are Sessions' Piano Sonata, my Piano Variations, Carlos Chavez' Sonatina, Citkowitz's Songs to texts of Joyce, and very probably Freddy [Bowles]'s Sonata for Oboe and Clarinet. I expect Freddy will come to London to hear his piece—it will be his debut as composer, you know.

It occurred to me that there might be people in London who would not hear of the concert through the ordinary channels, but who would be glad to hear the Capitals if they knew they were being given. If you know of any such, I'd be glad to have their names and addresses and will see to it that notices are sent them. Any other suggestions you might have for the furthering of the concert would be welcome.

I'm sorry to say that I won't be able to pass through Paris on the way to London. I suppose it's too much to hope to see you in London.

Kind regards for Miss Toklas

Sincerely
Aaron Copland

Kate Buss had met John Dewey and discussed Gertrude Stein's work with him. It was at her suggestion that a copy of Lucy Church Amiably *was sent to the philosopher.*

FROM JOHN DEWEY

320 East 72nd Street, New York, N. Y.,
Feb 19, 1932

My dear Miss Stein

I am quite humiliated that I have let the receipt of your Lucy Church Amiably go without acknowledgment. . . . I read it of course & with great interest—I don't pretend to appreciate just what you are doing, but I am much interested —as well as perplexed. I enjoyed meeting your friend in Cambridge last spring, & she was good enough to show me copies of some of your correspondence with her which helped me. But I should prize an opportunity to meet you personally. While I don't understand, I have too much respect for the possibilities of aesthetic development to reject just because I don't grasp.

Thanking you, I am

Sincerely yours
John Dewey.

Lindley Hubbell sent Robert Coates' review of Lucy Church Amiably *to Gertrude Stein.* How to Write *had been issued in the Plain Edition in November 1931.*

FROM LINDLEY WILLIAMS HUBBELL

223 West 15th Street, New York,
Feb 25, 1932

Dear Miss Stein:

I am sending you a copy of the New Yorker which you would probably see anyway. But I don't want to take the slightest chance of your not seeing it, because it contains what I think is a very intelligent review . . .

I finished How to Write and liked it a lot. It is, if I count right, your eighteenth book, and what an interesting procession they make, from Three Lives to How to Write! I have been thinking about them a great deal lately. To tell the truth, one of the essays in How to Write—A Vocabulary of Thinking—is the first of your writings that I have ever found difficult. The unit of form is so huge that I felt like one who, accustomed to the slopes of Olympus, was suddenly invited to mount to the top of Kinchinjunga. When I finally got there I liked the view but felt dizzy.

Soon after I finished that book, I received Before the flowers of friendship faded friendship faded. Well, no difficulty there. . . . It's a great poem, I believe, and it's what a poem should be; that is, it is beautiful . . . simply because it is a beautiful thing. And, in my opinion, it's the loveliest format of any of your books. . . .

About the same time I received Haveth Childers Everywhere by James Joyce. I couldn't make head or tail of it, but it was interesting to read it along with yours, because most people say that you and he are the only two creative writers in English today. It is interesting because you and he started at about the same point (Dubliners isn't as good as Three Lives, but it *is* good) and from that point you started in exactly opposite directions; he toward greater complexity and you toward greater simplicity. And his is a blind alley, because the more complicated you get the more incomprehensible you become, until you reach a point where you are entirely incomprehensible (he's reached it. And I have to laugh at people who say that Work in Progress is witty. He has no more wit than a trout.) But the road which you took can't end until you reach the thing-in-itself. And whether there is a thing-in-itself I don't know, and neither do you. But at any rate, it's a long road, open under the sky, and good healthy travelling. The result is that everyone who has followed him has become sterile and finally stopped writing altogether; and everyone who has followed you—well, everyone who writes stories for Harpers or Scribners or the Atlantic is following you, so there can't be any harm in it! . . .

Yours with love and gratitude,
Lindley Hubbell

But still the Atlantic Monthly *was not persuaded.*

FROM THE ATLANTIC MONTHLY

Boston, Mass., Feb 26, 1932

Dear Miss Stein:—

We live in different worlds. Yours may hold the good, the beautiful, and the true, but if it does their guise is not for us to recognize. Those vedettes who lead the vanguard of pictorial arts are understood, or partly understood, over here by a reasonably compact following, but that following cannot translate their loyalties into a corresponding literature, and it would really be hopeless for us to set up this new standard.

I am sorry.

Yours sincerely,
Ellery Sedgwick.

Alexander Calder had just had an exhibition in Paris of some of his mobiles.

FROM ALEXANDER CALDER

14 rue de la Colonie, Paris 13e.,
Mar 9, 1932

Dear Miss Stein

Would you and Miss Toklas care to come to tea next Monday (Mar. 14)? We liked very much meeting you, and would like to do so again. I have arranged a few of the things from the show so that they work, here.

Will you please drop us a card as to whether you will come or not?

Very Cordially
Calder

❦

A copy of How to Write *had gone to F. Scott Fitzgerald.*

FROM F. SCOTT FITZGERALD

Hotel Rennert, Baltimore, Md.,
Apr 28, 1932

Dear Gertrude Stein:

You were so nice to think of me so far off and send me your book. Whenever I sit down to write I think of the line that you drew for me and told me that my next book should be that thick. So many of your memorable remarks come often to my head, and they seem to survive in a way that very little current wisdom does.

I read the book, of course, immediately, and was half through it for the second time (learning a lot as we all do from you) when my plans were upset by my wife's illness, and by an accident it was consigned to temporary storage.

I hope to be in Europe this summer and to see you. I have never seen nearly as much of you as I would like.

Yours always, admiringly and cordially,
F. Scott Fitzgerald

❦

The editor of Blues *was in Italy. The Young and Evil, which he had written with Parker Tyler, was going the round of the publishers in manuscript, and was eventually issued in Paris.*

FROM CHARLES HENRI FORD

[Italy] July 8, 1932

Dear Miss Stein,

Thanks for your nice letter. You are right, being in Italy for the first time is quite wonderful. . . .

I'm in the tiniest town I ever saw and strangely enough

do not miss Paris in the least (probably though because I know I'm going back). I'm working on the new book, have the general scheme well in mind and have completed the first 6000 words. I remember your telling me "make it from the inside" and it's from the very inside all right. . . .

Parker Tyler has finished a book of his own which he is submitting under a pseudonym. Liveright still silent about our book. Did I say it came back from both Cape and Gollancz in London and that Bradley, agent in Paris, now has that copy but don't know what he will do with it?

Remember me to Miss T. Thoughts both delicious and grave for yourself.

Faithfully,
Ch Henri

Bernard Fay had undertaken a new translation of extracts from The Making of Americans *selected by Gertrude Stein herself, and had worked on the book with her at Bilignin. It appeared in Paris in 1933 and the English text was published in the United States the following year.*

FROM BERNARD FAŸ

Genetines, Aug 31, 1932

Dear friend,

I have spent in Bilignin ten days of such a great and deep happiness that it is not easy to thank you. . . . I can't tell you how much I enjoy working with you. The Making of Americans is a very great book, and, sincerely, when I started the translation, I was a little afraid that the translation would be hopelessly inferior to the English text. Reading it aloud to you has made me feel that the French version will after all give a fair idea of the great richness and beauty of the English book. . . .

I am a little hurried, and I sha'n't write a long letter this time, but I shall write again before sailing. . . .

Affectionately yours
Bernard Faÿ

In the late summer of 1932, Gertrude Stein had written The Autobiography of Alice B. Toklas. *W. A. Bradley, now her agent in Paris, was alive to its commercial possibilities.*

FROM W. A. BRADLEY

5, rue Saint-Louis-en-l'Île, Paris 4,
Nov 13, 1932

Dear Miss Stein,

Of course I shall be *delighted* to see Miss Toklas' Autobiography and hope you will send it to me as soon as it is completely typed. Or, better still, you might send it in two instalments, so that I can get on with the reading as fast as possible. . . .

With all best greetings to you both & looking forward to seeing you soon, I am, as ever,

Sincerely yrs.
W. A. Bradley.

5, rue Saint-Louis-en-l'Île, Paris 4,
Nov 26, 1932

Dear Miss Stein,

The second part of the ms. has just arrived, and wild horses couldn't keep me from reading it at once!

I am now looking forward to seeing you both as soon as you return to Paris, next week.

Sincerely yrs.
W. A. Bradley.

Gertrude Stein had for some time been very much interested in the painting of the young Englishman Sir Francis Rose.

FROM SIR FRANCIS ROSE

La Porte des Îles, Mougins, A. M.,
Jan 1, 1933

Dear Miss Stein

Thank you for the lovely box & the chocolates. I was delighted with it.

I am also glad the little statues pleased you. (They have been cooked and won't melt). The only danger is they are very breakable. . . .

I deeply appreciate your having paid more for the last picture although the knowledge that I have, that you derive pleasure from my pictures is really compensation enough for me.

I am working very hard and hope some day that your confidence in me will be justified.

With all my love to you both for the happiest of New Years

Francis Rose

Bradley had no difficulty in selling The Autobiography of Alice B. Toklas *to Harcourt, Brace in New York, for American publication, and Gertrude Stein achieved a life-long ambition when the* Atlantic Monthly *decided to publish it serially.*

FROM THE ATLANTIC MONTHLY

Boston, Mass., Feb 11, 1933

Dear Miss Stein:—

There has been a lot of pother about this book of yours, but what a delightful book it is, and how glad I am to publish four installments of it! During our long correspondence, I think you felt my constant hope that the time would come when the real Miss Stein would pierce the smoke-screen with which she has always so mischievously surrounded herself. The autobiography has just enough of the oblique to give it individuality and character, and readers who care for the things you do will love it. . . .

Anything that we can do to help the success of the book, as well as the serial, will certainly be done.

Hail Gertrude Stein about to arrive!

Believe me,

Yours sincerely,
Ellery Sedgwick.

Boston, Mass., Mar 20, 1933

Dear Miss Stein,

As Assistant Editor of the *Atlantic*, I have fallen heir to the duty and pleasure of editing *The Autobiography of Alice B. Toklas* so that it might be published serially in four issues of the magazine. The limitation placed upon us by Mr. Bradley, that not more than sixty per cent of the text be used, and the agreement arrived at with Mr. Harcourt to the same effect, meant that the job of editing the manuscript was one of deciding what parts to omit, and I can tell you that it was no easy thing to decide. . . .

Your autobiography met with such an unusual reception in our office that I think I ought to tell you about it. Mr. Bradley addressed the manuscript to me, and sent with it a mysterious letter in which he refused to divulge the identity of the author other than to say that she was a well-known American writer living in Paris. I opened the package about ten o'clock of a very dull morning, rather annoyed by what I took to be a trick of Mr. Bradley's to pique my curiosity, and vastly bored by the prospect of having to wade through so many reams of anonymous wood-pulp. . . .

In this state of mind I settled down to *Toklas*. I read the first page, and right there you had me. I was instantly fascinated and went on reading, turning page after page automatically, not knowing that I turned them, so completely absorbed had I become in your story. At last I was recalled to awareness of the here and now by an increasing darkness in the room. There was hardly light enough for me to see the page before me. I thought a storm had come up and glanced out the window. There were no clouds, but the sky looked queer. I pulled out my watch. It was after five o'clock and the sun was setting! I could not believe it, but it was so. I had forgotten time, forgotten my lunch, forgotten a dozen things I had meant to do that day, so entirely had I been caught by the spell of your words. I rushed at once to Mr. Sedgwick and told him about it. "Such a thing never happened before in this office," he exclaimed, and he was right—it never had.

So we accepted the manuscript, and now it is about to be published. If you could do this to an editor, of all people the least susceptible to the magic of print, what, I wonder, will be the effect of your story on the general public?

Sincerely yours,

Edward C. Aswell

FROM CARL VAN VECHTEN

[New York] May 22 [1933]

Dear Gertrude—

And now Bennett Cerf tells me that Three Lives is to go into the Modern Library and has asked me to write a preface. I am *thrilled*! It is your year. You'd better come over & be photographed. . . . I photographed Matisse on Saturday.— The second number of the Autobiography is *grand*—I loved the story of M. Aldrich & the canaries! I can't wait till I see the whole thing!

Much love to you both,
C.

❦

FROM MATILDA E. BROWN

[Oakland, California] July 2, 1933

Many many years ago one Friday afternoon, during the rhetorical period in the Oakland High School, on the corner of 12th and Market Sts, a girl made what she considered a masterful talk—her subject was "Lighten the Ship." The closing lines were these:

> "If safe on the billows you fain would ride—
> Cast over for ever thy burden of pride
> Lighten thy heart of its fatal weight,
> Ere voices shall whisper, 'too late, too late'
> For the heavily laden shall never see
> The blessed port of Eternity"—

When she finished and tremblingly took her seat, a note was thrust upon her desk by a classmate. It read: " 'luna, lunae, feminine' Who do you think you are a preacher?"

Since the passing of these years, this classmate has won international fame, not only in the world of letters, but everywhere—

Would she deign to tell this would be preacher, girl friend that she still remembers? The girl waits—

Her name is Tillie E. Brown. She lives in Oakland, California at 600—29th St.

❦

Picabia's painting had not interested Gertrude Stein greatly when they first met in 1913, but now in the thirties she began to find his work more important. He and his wife visited her at Bilignin.

FROM FRANCIS PICABIA [TRANSLATED]

July 20, 1933

Very dear friends,

We had a very good trip to Cannes. . . .

Those few days spent with you did me enormous good; besides the very great affection I have for you, our conversations on painting again confirmed me in the certitude that my experiments are working out and will be, I hope, the expression of exactitude with me.

When I say "will be" it is modesty, for I know that I have got to that point in several of my last pictures.

Olga and I send you all our best affection.

Your
Francis Picabia

FROM GRACE DAVIS STREET

215, John Street, Oakland, California,
Aug 13, 1933

Dear Gertrude:

It pleased me very much that you answered my letter and sent a picture of you and your dog. It proves the truth of what you said in the letter—that nothing is really different, with friends, when they meet, either by letter or in person; friends begin right where they left off. Years do not matter. Everything fits in. . . .

When we were young high school girls, there was a party at Gertrude Stein's. I wonder if you remember it. Of all the jolly memories of that period, this party stands out as the merriest and most humorous of all. Every detail is etched on my brain and so long as I live I will be able to laugh, when I recall it.

It was like this: One afternoon, a few of us girls met at

your home. We found everything packed up to move and already in huge packing boxes. . . . Suddenly I proposed a *party*, meaning ice cream. Bertha was there, and Leo, Mary Cook and some others. I had just learned to make cake and Bertha took me right up, when I said I would make a banana layer cake. Our Chinese cook was cross, so Bertha said for me to make it at your house. So I *did*—in the afternoon. We then pooled our dimes and nickels and ordered a gallon of ice cream. Came the night, my mother would not let me go to the party unless my two little brothers, Sumner and Reeve, went along. I was against it for they were devils and I knew what would happen—John Cook, Simon and my brothers would simply raise hell, in some way. Now our idea was a bohemian party—sitting around on packing cases and eating and drinking with absolute careless abandon. But—enter the picture right here—Mike Stein, home from Harvard and held in awe by us little girls. Now Mike had no such Bohemian ideas as we did—No sir—Mike made us—Yes he *made us*— drag out of those packing boxes linen and dishes and we had (I can hear Bertha protesting now) to sit down, absolutely against our desires—to a set-table. All the joy was gone, for me, but I remember Mikie dished up the ice cream from the freezer on your back porch and Leo passed it around. We were sort of stiff and not happy but were getting on and were ready for the second round of ice cream when—well—Mike found the freezer *gone!!* No more ice cream but plenty of cake. Our worst fears were true—those four devils of brothers had stolen the ice cream and run off with it. We found the freezer in a vacant lot, next day.

But here is the most comical part. Your father got word that your rich uncle in New York was coming out to S. F. and you all hastily unpacked the household treasures—bought new gorgeous carpets, curtains etc.—got a cook and made ready for the Uncle. He came—stayed *one* night with you and then went to the Palace Hotel, where there were more *bath rooms*.

I often wonder if this lived in your memory as vividly

as it did in mine. My two little brothers are gone and Simon is gone and only the happy memory remains. . . .

Adieu—

Grace

FROM KATHARINE CORNELL

Haus Hirth, Untergrainau b. Garmisch,

Aug 20 [1933]

Dear Gertrude Stein—

I have just seen Thornton Wilder in Salzburg and he was full of thrilling things you had said.

There is a possibility that I may go through Geneva en route for my sailing on the Rex from Nice September thirteenth. Would you be in Belley on the twelfth? if so could I come out to you for the day?

I could catch the train from either Geneva or Lyon in the evening for Nice—

I start work in October with Romeo and Juliet in fact in Baltimore, then I plan to do St Joan by Shaw in February.

I hope you are having a glorious summer I am sure you are. Thornton was in wonderful form.

With love to you and Miss Toklas

Always

Katharine Cornell—

FROM CARL VAN VECHTEN

150 West Fifty-fifth Street [New York]

Sep 8, 1933

Dear Gertrude:

I have been rereading The Autobiography in book form and have nothing but words of praise for it. It seems to me, indeed, that I have talked about nothing else since the first part appeared in the Atlantic. What a delightful book it is! I am showering copies on my happy friends. I find we are alike in two important ways: our passion for breakable things and for pigs—this passion might be united in a painted Mexican porcelain pig! Have you ever seen one? They are banks, pottery banks, and you put pennies in them. Have you a passion for banks too? I have and I am sure you have. Anyway I loved every minute of the book and the second reading made it seem even fresher. I've also been reading Américains d'Amérique with Faÿ's preface which I liked very much. I was pleased that he spoke of your laugh. And this book is very convincing in French and in this abridgement. Why couldn't it be issued in English in this shorter form? . . .

Anyway it is a joy to know you and to shake your hand across the sea and I think you'd better come over and take the tribute due you and be photographed. . . .

Carlo.

❦

Robert McAlmon, in the early twenties, had introduced Gertrude Stein to the American poet, novelist, and physician, William Carlos Williams.

FROM WILLIAM CARLOS WILLIAMS

[Sep 16, 1933] I'll be 50 tomorrow

Dear Gertrude Stein,

You have been exceptionally thoughtful in having them send me your recent "Autobiography" and in sending me, with the words of greeting, the "Américains d'Amérique." It's pretty hard for me to say just the pleasure I have experienced. A rare pleasure. Too damned rare for a life of the sort I had imagined.

Nothing much ever gets said so why should I waste breath. Perhaps I should spend every bit of breath I have in the attempt. Many thanks. It would be worth while exchanging gifts with you if there were anything I could send.

Keep it up.

Yours

W. C. Williams

Thanks for being so exceptionally accurate as to put down the facts about Contact Press—the bastards make a virtue of forgetting.

W.

❧

Miss Mars and Miss Squire, habitués of the Stein salon in the early days, had been the subject of one of Gertrude Stein's best-known portraits, "Miss Furr and Miss Skeene," published in Geography and Plays *and later reprinted in* Vanity Fair.

FROM MAUD HUNT SQUIRE

Vence (Alp. Mar.) [Fall? 1933]

Dear Gertrude Stein and Alice B. Toklas,

I want to tell you how much we enjoyed your book—it was very delightful & took us back to those most interesting evenings in the rue de Fleurus, in fact it was just like living them over again. . . . The last time we were up there was during the Colonial exhibition and we called around to see you but the concierge said you were then out in the country. We were there only a few days—we can't stay away very long from our Siamese cat Wow & his mistress Min—he brought her home one day, a little gray colourless thing with a long rat tail, but a sweet disposition, & from our three canary birds.—

If you ever come down this way do come & see us. We hink Vence a beautiful place, & we have a villa here. I don't believe you liked Vence much—I believe you said it gave the impression of always walking up hill—but we like the scenery and being near Nice & the shore—which is gay & sophisticated.

You see Miss Furr still likes gay things & being gay & wanting everybody & everything else to be gay.

With lots of love to you both—

Miss Furr and Miss Skeene.

Max Ewing, who had met Gertrude Stein in Paris, sent her a postcard of a rose from Hollywood.

FROM MAX EWING

Roosevelt Hotel, Hollywood, California,
Sep 19 [1933]

To Gertrude Stein—this rose which is what a rose is! I wonder if you know that you are more discussed in Hollywood these days than Greta Garbo? The autobiography is delightful. And the performance of the Opera in Hartford is the one thing that makes me wish I were to be in the East this winter. Are you coming over? And will you come out West? I hope so. My best to you and Miss Toklas.

Max Ewing

The Hound & Horn *had been founded at Harvard by Lincoln Kirstein and, at his graduation, had moved to New York. Although Gertrude Stein agreed to his request, the article on Henry James was never written.*

FROM LINCOLN KIRSTEIN

545 Fifth Avenue, New York, Oct 7, 1933

Dear Miss Stein:

In the spring The HOUND & HORN is issuing a number dedicated entirely to the work of Henry James. We hope to make this more or less an international homage to his genius. In this country he is almost completely forgotten by our younger writers, and we hope this issue of the magazine will be in the nature of a testimony of faith in his innovations and genius.

I wonder if you would have any interest in writing about James? The passages in The AUTOBIOGRAPHY OF ALICE B. TOKLAS dealing with him struck us as so evocative that we hoped for the possibility of an extension of these remarks. Any ideas you might have on this subject would be extremely interesting to us.

Sincerely yours
Lincoln Kirstein

FROM HENRY McBRIDE

Herald Square Hotel (as usual) [New York]
Oct 27, 1933

Dearest Gertrude;

I suppose you thought me dead! I almost had the thought myself last summer and for that reason delayed writing. I wasn't quite sure that you cared for death-bed letters! . . .

The Autumn is no time to die, in America, anyway. The country is unbelievably beautiful. . . . Those last two weeks of summer in Pennsylvania are always the best of my vacance, and thinking to squeeze still another one from the lap of Fate, I thought I could make my first Sun page out of gleanings from your Autobiography, and do it down there. But would you believe it, the bright young publicity agent for Harcourt, Brace, refused me a copy, saying they already had had a review of the book in the Sun, and apparently didn't care for another. By the time I finally secured the book, I had to be in New York, and I actually wrote something about it and you before I found time to read it. Isn't that American journalism for you? But it explains the thinness of my article.

It was apparent, with the very first chapter in the Atlantic, that the book was doomed to be a best seller. (Doomed, is my word for it, not yours. I don't like giving you up to the general public and sharing you and Alice with about a million others). The most unlikely people came to me with praises on their lips, such as Mr. [Charles P.] Everitt, the bookselling dealer in Early Americana, who rather wanted to secure the rights. An individual not so highly pleased, however, was the great Henri Matisse, with whom I lunched about that time. . . . I tried to tell him that the recital of your frank and jovial relationship to artists would be a bonne réclâme in America, but he shuddered. He would prefer, it seems, to be spoken of sepulchrally, as though he were Poussin and you were Bossuet. Well, there are all sorts of ways of taking the world, and all sorts of attitudes towards fame. . . .

Love to you and Alice;

Henry

P. S. When I finally did read the book I thought it too short. I had the same feeling that I have so often had when walking down the Boulevard Raspail after an evening in the rue de Fleurus—that we had not threshed half the wheat I had intended.

FROM VIRGIL THOMSON

Hotel Leonori, New York, Dec 6 [1933]

Dear Gertrude—

Here is a newspaper article that will amuse you from the Hartford Times. The cast of the opera is hired and rehearsals begun. I have a chorus of 32 & six soloists, very, very fine ones indeed. Miss Stettheimer's sets are of a beauty incredible, with trees made out of feathers and a sea-wall at Barcelona made out of shells and for the procession a baldachino of black chiffon & bunches of black ostrich plumes just like a Spanish funeral. St. Teresa comes to the picnic in the 2nd Act in a cart drawn by a real white donkey & brings her tent with her and sets it up & sits in the door-way of it. It is made of white gauze with gold fringe and has a most elegant shape. My singers, as I have wanted, are Negroes, & you can't imagine how beautifully they sing. Frederick Ashton is arriving from London this week to make choreography for us. Not only for the dance-numbers, but for the whole show, so that all the movements will be regulated to the music, measure by measure, and all our complicated stage-action made into a controllable spectacle. . . . Everything about the opera is shaping up so beautifully, even the raising of money (it's going to cost $11,000), that the press is champing at the bit and the New York ladies already ordering dresses & engaging hotel rooms. . . . Rumors of your arrival are floating about and everybody asks me is she really coming and I always answer that it wouldn't surprise me. Certainly, if everything goes off as fancy as it looks now, you would be very happy to be here and to see your opera on the stage and I would be very happy to see it with you and your presence would be all we need to make the opera perfect in every way. (February 7th is opening date, I believe.) . . .

Always affectionately
Virgil

FROM CARL VAN VECHTEN

150 West Fifty-fifth Street [New York],
Jan 2, 1934

Dear Gertrude,

I guess nobody but me would have the nerve to turn a duchess into an errand boy, but I have done just that. The Duchesse de Clermont-Tonnerre is sailing Friday (probably on the boat which will take you this letter!) and she is accompanied by the BIG Painted Pig! She was extremely sweet about the whole thing and acted as if she considered it a favor to be permitted to be the go-between for two such charming people! It is to the Duchess too that you must turn for the latest news about the Opera. . . . I am staying away from rehearsals so that I may get an entirely fresh impression. I have booked seats for the two opening nights and will go to Hartford on a sort of pilgrimage. You will get a full report from me then. . . .

Carlo!

FROM W. G. ROGERS

R. F. D. #1, East Longmeadow, Mass.,
Jan 9, 1934

Dear Miss Stein—

I finished reading The Autobiography about a month ago and since then I have been trying to write a letter to you. For perhaps 10 years I have been trying to write a letter to you, and I should probably not be doing it now if you had not, in The Autobiography, wondered how many of the soldiers you met in Southern France knew today who you are. . . .

My name—it would be like a detective story if you had to wait until the signature to learn it—my name is William G. Rogers and I was in the Amherst College ambulance unit and came to Nîmes and the Hotel du Luxembourg in early December 1917. I went there because I wanted to see Roman ruins, or Roman structures, most of which happened to be ruins. . . . After a day or two you were good enough to speak to me and then later you and Miss Toklas took me for frequent trips, with me sitting on the floor of the car and my feet on the running board, and I remember we always had to get back before nightfall, but whether that was because you didn't like to drive at night or because you had no lights I don't remember. We went to Orange and Les Baux and Arles —that was before I had ever heard of Van Gogh—and to a rather wild place supposed to have been the site of Caesar's defeat of Vercingetorix and to the walled city from which St. Louis started on one of his crusades . . .

Then after I returned to the front I wrote several times to Miss Toklas and she wrote to me and two or three times after that, when I was passing through Paris, I called at 27 Rue de Fleurus but you were never there. Then after the War was over, I stopped writing . . .

Then several years later I saw your picture in a Sunday paper rotogravure section, and I compared it with the snapshots you had given me, or Miss Toklas had sent me, of you with the Ford or with wounded French soldiers or outside hospital gates in and near Nîmes, and I was sure it was you. . . . In the summer and fall of 1929 I was in Paris with my brother and I called on you but the concierge told me you were away. I felt I could have explained to you about writing and then not writing, but I still felt I couldn't write it. So I waited till now.

Early in February Mr. Austin of the Wadsworth Atheneum in Hartford, Connecticut, is planning to present your opera about the saints. Hartford is about 25 miles from Springfield, Massachusetts, where I am working on a newspaper. If you will allow it, I will write you how it is received. . . .

Most sincerely,
W. G. Rogers.

The Catalogue for Francis Rose's 1934 exhibition at Wildenstein's in London contained notes by Gertrude Stein dated 1932 and February 1934.

FROM SIR FRANCIS ROSE

La Porte des Îles, Mougins, A.M.
[Feb? 1934]

Dear Miss Stein,

I was delighted with your preface. Nothing could be better and I am so happy to be able to use the old one also. Thank you so much for it and it pleases me ever so much that you have written the first preface ever printed for an exhibition of

my pictures and thank you so much for all the good luck you
wish me and I sincerely hope all may come true. . . .

> As ever
> Francis Rose

*Among the many reports of the Hartford première, the first was
the one promised by Carl Van Vechten.*

FROM CARL VAN VECHTEN

> The Heublein Hotel, Hartford, Conn.,
> Feb 8, 1934

Dear Gertrude,

Four Saints, in our vivid theatrical parlance, is a knockout
and a wow. I cabled you when I got home from the invited
dress rehearsal last night (I mean you were invited to buy
seats). It was a most smart performance in this beautiful little theatre. People not only wore evening clothes, they wore
sables and tiaras. . . . I haven't seen a crowd more excited
since Sacre du Printemps. The difference was that they were
pleasurably excited. The Negroes are divine, like El Grecos,
more Spanish, more Saints, more opera singers in their dig-
nity and *simplicity* and extraordinary plastic line than *any*
white singers could ever be. And they enunciated the text so
clearly you could understand every word. Frederick Ashton's
rhythmic staging was inspired and so were Florine's costumes
and sets. Imagine a crinkled sky-blue cellophane background,
set in white lace borders, like a valentine against which were
placed the rich and royal costumes of the saints in red vel-
vets, etc. and the dark Spanish skins. . . . The manager who
is taking it to New York expects it to be a success and I am
sure it will be *something.* . . . I really think you should see,
hear, and feel Four Saints. . . .

> Love always,
> Carlo

FROM PAUL FREDERIC BOWLES

[New York, Feb 1934]

Dear Miss Stein—

Here is the stub of my ticket for the opening night of *Four Saints*. I have collected some of the notices about it. At first, at any rate, I cut them out. Later there were so many references to it I stopped. But since I don't know whether you have them all or not, I am sending those I have, in another large envelope. . . .

The smart thing among the younger artists is to be violently against it. Stieglitz decides also to side with them. Most of the defense must be taken for Virgil, against whom they allow themselves to rage for having had the audacity to give Gertrude Stein in modern dress. That is all I make of their fury, anyway. People walking on Broadway and sitting in Automats talk of "the Saints Play" and usually sound doubtful as to whether it would be worth while trying to get tickets for it. . . .

I am living in the city and doing music, which is not as much fun as doing it in the country. I have made songs out of two short things from Useful Knowledge, but no one has seen them yet, because I want to do more. I am glad to know that they are as different from Virgil's settings as anything could be. But I should like some more short romantic poems to make a group out of. What I want is to write several lieder on your words, but I can't find the right words to use. Would you at any time be interested in writing four or five lieder? Perhaps you would prefer hearing my music first. Still, I should like to have them all written when I return to Paris, and show them to you. I think you would like them very much. . . .

My Sonatina was played a while ago by the League of Composers, and got the best reviews of the evening. That made the Winter less harsh. And I think the Spring will be sweetened by a Symphonic piece about Berber tunes and Flamenco songs.

I send my best wishes to you and Miss Toklas.

Sincerely
Paul Frederic Bowles

FROM ALFRED HARCOURT

Harcourt, Brace and Company, Inc., 383 Madison Avenue, New York, [Mar 2, 1934]

Dear Miss Stein:

I was in Florida after a little spell of illness the night that "Four Saints in Three Acts" opened in New York, but I was able to see it last night just after my return. I can't refrain from writing you that it was a thrilling evening and a really splendid performance. . . .

The house was crowded last night with a really distinguished audience. Toscanini was in the orchestra chair behind me, and I noticed that he seemed completely absorbed in the performance and applauded vigorously.

It must be a good satisfaction to you to have had at last real recognition from an audience in America. I am delighted to have had some small share in it.

Sincerely yours,
Alfred Harcourt

FROM HENRY McBRIDE

Herald Square Hotel, New York, Mar 20, 1934

My dearest Gertrude;

Well, the Four Saints is finished, temporarily they say, but I fear permanently, and we are all somewhat depressed.

I am depressed to think of all those who did not see it, including yourself—for positively you can have had no conception of the way it visualized itself for us. When we went up to Hartford for the premiere we were expecting some kind of a good time, naturally, but we were totally unprepared for the unearthly beauty that the first curtain disclosed and which mounted and mounted as the thing went on and finally left all of the hard-boiled and worldly connoisseurs in tears at the end. I saw it four times in all and last Saturday's final performance was the finest of all. It has been years since I have cared to see anything in the theatre twice, but honestly I wanted to attend the Four Saints constantly; and sorry as I am for your having missed it entirely I am also sorry that I only saw it four times. It now ranks with the two or three exalted experiences that I have had, with Mei Lang Fang and the Mme. Sadda Yacco of years ago. The fact of the matter is that everybody connected with the presentation caught an inspiration, all of them had to create and all of them did —so that the word miracle is the only one that describes what happened. Even now, thinking it over in cold blood, I can't conceive how Virgil dared to do what he did . . . The incessant inventions in choreography supplied by Freddy Ashton seemed like some baroque dream of the eighteenth century (only far more finished and perfect than the eighteenth century itself could have dreamed of) and Florine Stettheimer's costumes and sets and the Feder lights that were flung upon them were simply unbelievable. Unite all this to the exotic effect of the beautiful Negro performers and their incredibly fine voices—and even then you haven't got the whole of it. It is, indeed, indescribable. With all this, the regular music critics (who know nothing of painting) did not "get" it; and quite a few people who were bowled over by the performance tried to repudiate their emotional collapse afterward, and keep ringing my telephone to "explain" it to them. "What is the real meaning underneath, for clearly it must mean something?" they ask. All this is tiresome. After twenty years of

cubism and abstract art, it seems that these unfortunate people have not yet heard of it. I loathe explaining any work of
art, and always insist that any work of art that can be "explained" is worthless; yet nevertheless, I suppose I must at
least bully some of these people into reasonableness. What I
really feel is, that people who do not feel greatness in the best
things of Picasso and Braque (now being shown here by Paul
Rosenberg) do not know what painting is; and those who
do not see poetry in your Four Saints do not know what
poetry is.

But I mustn't tire you with shop talk. When I see you, if
I do this summer, I can tell you why the run of the play was
so short. The commercial management were not up to it.
They hadn't the faintest idea of what it was all about. Even
so, the event has upset New York as nothing else has this
winter. I thought last autumn when the Autobiography made
such a terrific success that I was finished with you and that I
would have no further occasion to write about you (for all
the population seemed delighted to have established contact
with Gertrude Stein) but this confusion about the Four Saints
shows me there is still some work to be done by somebody.
Did Carl [Van Vechten] send you one of his photographs of
your name in electric lights on Broadway? It seems to me
that ought to content you with fame. Love to Alice. Love to
you. Perhaps I'll be coming over, in spite of the dear francs.

Henry

FROM SIR FRANCIS ROSE

La Porte des Îles, Mougins, A.M.
[May? 1934]

Dear Miss Stein
    I received your letter and I regret that you do not like the
picture that was sent to you.

I am surprised that you judge the entire [content] of my London show from one picture.

I suggest therefore that you return the picture to me and I will send you another which I hope will please you more. . . . I am not sure which picture you have as there were four or five I think of the same subject exactly. One original painted in a sunny day and one a grey day. The rest were copies I made in my work room of the original picture, in order to have enough landscapes. Naturally the copies may lack the vigor of original creations and are only constructed rather than constructive. Perhaps you have one of these. I told the gallery to pick from the best, but I believe when the choice was made Sir Robert Abdy was no longer in London. . . .

I agree with you about the second Paris show not being all it should. There were shown pictures which should never have left the studio. . . . Naturally I will not have any such mistakes reoccur in New York and I only expect to show pictures of my finest quality. Fewer if necessary but carefully chosen. I hope you will agree if this plan is followed the American show should justify the faith you expressed in your letter for my work.

As ever
Francis Rose

Gertrude Stein had at last agreed to make a lecture tour of the United States. The Kiddie, on a trip to Europe, had visited her at Bilignin, and they had discussed plans for the Fall. Eventually, Miss Stein dispensed with managers, and Alice Toklas handled most of the business details herself.

FROM W. G. ROGERS

Springfield, Mass., June 4, 1934

Dear Miss Stein,

I have put off writing to you principally because I thought I might hear further word from Mr. Bradley in New York, and I have. He says in substance that, according to a letter from you in his office, you are sufficiently committed to a lecture tour in this country this fall for Colston Leigh to be free to make definite dates for you.

That's fine! . . .

I stopped in to see Stieglitz to tell him you wished to be remembered to him. He was surprised, and pleased, to hear you were coming to lecture. He said, however, that he had never really believed you would come, and he discussed at length . . . how Sherwood Anderson had felt his tour was not a success, how wise Geo. Bernard Shaw had been in staying in England, and so forth. . . .

Please let me know what else I can do to help this fall.

Sincerely,
W. G. Rogers.

A young American writer Max White had sent Gertrude Stein the number of the one-man periodical Plowshare *devoted to his short stories of Spain.*

FROM MAX WHITE

Woodstock, New York, June 12, 1934

Dear Gertrude Stein,

Your note concerning my number of The Plowshare reached me a few days ago and I can say without exaggeration that no letter has ever pleased me more.

I was glad to see you thought I had gotten down on paper something of the special brand of realism that is Spain's own. And your saying it led me indirectly to the discovery of America. I have been seeking to discover it with my own eyes for some time now. Your phrase "realism of Spain" gave me the clue I have been wanting a long time now.

The stories in The Plowshare are the only work of mine up to date that I care to have you see. I have completed two novels but they are not the thing. However I am doing some work now that I should like to have you see when it is done if you are still interested.

Will you write me again? I should very much like to hear from you.

Respectfully yours,
Max White

Mrs. Charles Goodspeed, introduced by Fanny Butcher of the Chicago Tribune, *had visited Gertrude Stein in the country and, as President of the Arts Club of Chicago, had made a selection of paintings for an exhibition of Sir Francis Rose's work in Chicago.*

FROM MRS. CHARLES GOODSPEED

[Hotel] George V, Avenue George V, Paris
[July 10? 1934]

Dear Miss Stein—

What a red-letter day for me—July 8th. I can't tell you how I appreciate all you did for me. . . . I had absolutely no idea of your taking me way to Montreux, or I would have arranged to take a later train so as not to hurry you so. Do forgive me. All I can say is that you are a splendid driver, & I am glad that I was in your excellent hands. Thank you a thousand times.

I telegraphed your brother [Michael] & he was awaiting me this morning. We had a delightful seance in your apartment, where I revelled in your gorgeous paintings, and we picked out 13 (that is my lucky number, so I hope it won't do Sir Francis any harm!) paintings, the list of which I enclose. If you can tell me anything more about them do. I took them right in the car immediately over to Lefebvre-Foinet, where I know they will be well taken care of.

I do hope that you will feel like writing a little foreword for our catalogue of the exhibition, as it would be a great

Gertrude Stein and Basket I at Bilignin (1934)

honor to us to have it. If you do care to, would you please
send it to me . . .

It was such a great privilege to me to meet you & I am
looking forward with great anticipation to the pleasure of
your visit with us. . . .

Most gratefully yours,
Bobsy Goodspeed

FROM BENNETT CERF

Random House, 20 E 57, New York,
July 26, 1934

Dear Miss Stein:

. . . I spent last evening with Carl Van Vechten and we
devoted a great part of the evening to talking about you and
your plans. It should hardly be necessary for me to tell you
how happy we would be to become the American publisher
of all of your books. Carl assures me that your visit here this
Fall is now certain, and I daresay that we will have lots of
occasion to discuss this entire subject in person. I am writing
this letter, however, just to make sure that you know how
anxious we are to do your books.

I have two suggestions to offer at this time. First, it seems
to me that one new book should be published to coincide
more or less with your lecture tour in America. Carl tells me
that you are going to deliver six lectures at Columbia. Might
it not be possible to collect these six lectures into one volume
and to publish them with some intriguing title? It seems to
me that such a volume should not only receive reams of publicity, but should really achieve an excellent sale throughout
the country. . . .

That brings me to my second suggestion to you which
refers to the copies you have left of the "Plain Editions." . . .
If you would like to send several copies of each of these old
editions to us here, we might be able to stimulate some de-

mand for them by the time you come to America, and sell them at the regular published price less the usual 40% discount to dealers. I would be willing to take care of this matter for you as a friend, and would be glad to turn over to you the entire proceeds realized from such sales.

I will be very glad indeed to hear from you again.

Cordial best regards to Miss Toklas and yourself.

Sincerely,

Bennett A. Cerf

Donald Sutherland, then eighteen and a Princeton undergraduate, had written a novel, which he sent to Gertrude Stein. Her comment after having read the manuscript was that going on depended on what came next.

FROM DONALD SUTHERLAND

[Princeton, N. J., Summer? 1934]

My dear Miss Stein:

I remember and you may remember that you and my friend [Arch P.] Kepner had a correspondence in February about Princeton and the young generation. Now I have written a story about Princeton and the young generation and I have told how the young men I know matter. . . . I am very anxious indeed to know if I should go on writing because it is often very sad to think you are making a lot of effort doing nothing. It will be no secret from you if you find the time to read my story that I have read the Making of Americans and been very much delighted and impressed, though I fail to make accomplished rhythms most of the time. . . . My story is not so long nor so good as your book but I think it is a twentieth as both and so it should interest you and you should like it I think a little. I beg you not to trouble to return the manuscript but do send me a good criticizing letter . . .

Mr. Kepner also sends you his love as I do.

Donald Sutherland

❦

FROM JEAN COCTEAU [TRANSLATED]

Roquebrune, A.M. [Aug? 1934]

My very dear Gertrude

The book came in one of those periods when life was making only nightmare gestures and grimaces at me. Since then I have read it as I like to read you, in detail, here and there, as the bird flies—before plunging into the soul of the matter. These are my only travels. Have you received in exchange my "Enfants terribles?" I sent it to Pernollet (at the end of July). Certainly they will have forwarded it? Dear Gertrude I embrace you, I feel myself nearer to you than to all those who come around me and our hearts are united by a special thread.

Your
Jean

❦

Janet Scudder felt that Gertrude Stein should not go to America and made her reasons clear in the postscript of a letter.

FROM JANET SCUDDER

279 rue de Vaugirard [Paris] Aug 4, 1934

Dear Gertrude;—

. . . I don't at all approve of your going to America. I think that you should follow your usual serene habits and allow America to come to you. In other words the oracle on the mountain top should *stay* on the mountain top. Anyhow you have been away too long. You and Alice will be like two Rip van Winkles over there. It's too *late* to take this step, just as it was too late for St Gaudens when he returned to France after many many years' absence. He couldn't stand it and he couldn't *under*stand it—over here I mean, and he was very unhappy in Paris though it had been the dream of his life to come back to his native country.

FROM JULIAN SAWYER

280 Fort Washington Ave., New York, N. Y.,
Aug 31, 1934

My dear Miss Stein:

I do not know whether or not you are familiar with my name at present but you were kind enough to write me a highly gratifying letter concerning my review of your opera which Sheed & Ward had seen fit to send you.

I am writing you now . . . to inform you that I have designed and executed a version of "Four Saints in Three Acts" which I believe would interest you. With the simplest of props . . . I have already presented this monologue version of the opera for my friends and such persons as Mr. Lincoln Kirstein . . . Mr. A. Hyatt Mayor . . . Mr. Julien Levy . . . Mr. Gorham B. Munson and Mr. Sheed of Sheed & Ward, all of whom were tremendously impressed by the production and my memorizing of the text and music.

I do not wish to make this venture of mine pretentious when it is not so but, on the other hand, I . . . am certain that if you were to witness it you would be pleased by the way I have captured the philosophical and spiritual aspects of the text both in the production and performance. (Incidentally, with the use of an illuminated aquarium off-stage, I have contrived a lovely background representing the water synonymous with the purgatorial first and third acts, with the fish floating back and forth against the wall during the disciplinary episodes. Other outstanding features of the production are the thirty symbols used in the first act to illustrate St. Therese's spiritual progress . . . the ballet of the fallen angels in the second act (seventh scene), the sailor ballet in the third act as well as the "saints' procession," and the altar designed for the last act.) . . .

When you are in New York City your time will doubtless be very much occupied . . . I am informing you of it now in hopes that during your sojourn here you will be able to find one free evening . . . to attend it. . . .

Faithfully yours,
Julian Sawyer

P. S.: Knowing of your fondness for young writers and people who read, appreciate and understand your work, I modestly inform you that I am nineteen years old.

FROM JAMES LAUGHLIN

Hôtel Windsor, Ouchy-Lausanne, Lausanne,
Sep 2, 1934

Dear Miss Stein—

I am very happy to know that I shall soon know you. I have wanted to talk to you for a long time.

First I was reading what you were publishing in *transition* & after that all the things I could find. I have never been bored by anything you have written.

I am 19, born in Allegheny, was a year at Harvard, where I worked with Dr. Whitehead who is the great man now alive, and now I am working at stories and poetry.

It is a very good thing for me that I may come to see you, and I want to thank you as much as I can. And M. Faÿ, as well.

I shall be at Culoz with the train of 15.39 Tuesday.

Servissimus
James Laughlin IV

Gertrude Stein and Alice Toklas sailed from France on the
SS Champlain *on October 17, 1934, and arrived in New York on
October 24th. Alfred Harcourt, whose firm had published* The
Autobiography of Alice B. Toklas, *did his part in helping Gertrude
Stein to renew her acquaintance with America.*

FROM ALFRED HARCOURT

383 Madison Avenue, New York,
Oct 26, 1934

Dear Miss Stein:

I have had one further idea for the weekend which I hope
you and Miss Toklas will spend with us November fourth.
That is this: Would it amuse you to come out a little early on
that Saturday and go with me to the Yale-Dartmouth football
game at New Haven? . . . The game is considered one of the
big ones of the season, and as a pageant of American youth, is
something to see that I am sure will amuse you, especially if
the day is fine. There are apt to be sixty to eighty thousand
young folks at the game, and it's quite stirring. . . .

I have tickets for the game, anyway, by way of some of our
young people, so the decision can wait until the last moment.
But I thought I'd mention it now, as it might be fun for you
to see what has come to be an American institution.

Sincerely yours,
Alfred Harcourt

*Gertrude Stein went to the game with Alfred Harcourt and en-
joyed seeing this aspect of American life.*

*Dorothy Norman was editing a volume of tributes to Alfred
Stieglitz entitled* America *and Alfred Stieglitz. Gertrude Stein's
contribution was solicited and inserted as the book was being
printed.*

FROM DOROTHY NORMAN

1075 Park Avenue, New York,
Oct 31, 1934

My dear Miss Stein:

What you wrote for the Stieglitz Book is so fine in every sense of the word that I cannot refrain from writing to you. It *is* so much what is so often called a breath of fresh air but which isn't necessarily, that I hesitate to use the phrase—but only the simplest most essential phrase will serve—even though the phrase itself is corrupt—since the essence of what I refer to is not—but is *reality*, is *pure*.

What you wrote adds a positive note because it is in itself so positive in its vision—in its intuition—in its clarity and perception.

Thank you for your spontaneity and your *action*. How easy to tell the *doers* from the *others*. . . .

When I showed your "Stieglitz" to Stieglitz he was really moved—and I know deeply touched. Not because it was about *him*, but because of what it represented as an affirmation of that thing which in my mind *relates* you two.

Sincerely,
Dorothy Norman

Gertrude Stein saw Four Saints *at last in Chicago.*

FROM FLORINE STETTHEIMER

80 West 40th Street, New York,
Nov 11, 1934

Dear Gertrude Stein,

I am so pleased you decided that our production of the Four Saints Opera was not the way you do not like it. Many thanks for your telegram.

Perhaps you will find time to come to my studio during

the week? Why not call me up some day at two o'clock and say when you could come.

Greetings to you and Miss Toklas

Florine Stettheimer

Greetings upon her arrival in America came from William Saroyan, who had heard a radio broadcast which Gertrude Stein had made.

FROM WILLIAM SAROYAN

348 Carl Street, San Francisco,
Nov 15, 1934

Dear Gertrude Stein:

My visit to my native land is very pleasant too. I still cannot figure out how it happened and why I should be so very lucky. Everyone seems to have forgotten what a miraculous thing it is to be alive but I am afraid I won't begin to forget until I am dead and after that I will be a long time forgetting. . . .

I cannot tell you what a fine thing it was to hear you talking so naturally and easily and sensibly over the radio. I am sure Manhattan must be fantastically splendid in 1934. It is hard to say which is the dream and which is the reality of this amazing race. Those skyscrapers are hard to believe even when you are standing in the street at the foot of one. I am writing a swift novel American Glory because Cerf & Klopfer have the idea I am a born glutton for work and am loafing if I do not write a novel in a month which is nearly the truth too. I have only fifty five pages written but the writing of these pages is unlike any other writing in English and maybe very good but I find the pleasantest thing about such writing is that a man doesn't care if it is never printed just so he writes it and to hell with what is loosely called art. The way I see it art is not only what is made but the *way* it is made and I think I have run pellmell into a pretty fine way of making it which is very much like the way God Almighty makes snow maybe or maybe rain and probably ultimately the only way, inevitably. . . .

Some critics say I have to be careful and not notice the writing of Gertrude Stein but I think they are fooling themselves when they pretend any American writing that is American and is writing is not partly the consequence of the writing of Gertrude Stein and as the saying is they don't seem to know the war is over. Even when a writer has never read the writing of Gertrude Stein if he writes America his work will show something maybe differently but show it just the same that is already in the writing of Gertrude Stein. So help me. I will very much want to meet you and Alice B. Toklas when you reach San Francisco but I hope it will not be at a place where there are many people because I get muddled when there are many people and cannot see straight let alone think and what I generally do is talk my head off and shout everybody else down and afterwards everybody thinks of me with a shudder of horror O that crazy Armenian who shouts all over the place especially when he talks about his own writing. Which is a thing never to do I am sure and a thing a young writer is always doing. So very sincere good luck to each of you and very sincere good wishes:

William Saroyan.

FROM BERNARD FAŸ

The Bienville, New Orleans, Louisiana,
Nov 30, 1934

Here I am quietly, dear friend, and I want to chat a little with you. . . .

It is a great joy for me to find you everywhere, all over this big continent, to find you as I know you, and to find you as I did not know you. . . .

I feel that what is going on now in America—what this trip of yours is doing is tremendously important in the mental life of America. What you bring them, nobody had brought them since Walt Whitman . . . And they know it, they feel it. You know I have watched them very closely since 1919— and seen them get excited over all kinds of things: the new Ford cars, Mr. Hoover, Al Smith, air-travel, the Queen of Rumania, speak-easies, etc.; but I have never seen them act as they do now with you.—It is something deeper and more personal. What your work and yourself stir up in them had not been stirred up for decades. It is a fine and fascinating sight for a historian, who is in love with America and who loves you. . . .

With my deep affection,
Bernard.

During their first stay in New York, Gertrude Stein and Alice Toklas had been christened Baby and Mama Woojums by Carl Van Vechten, himself Papa Woojums.

FROM CARL VAN VECHTEN

[New York] Monday [Dec? 1934]

Dear dear DEAR Woojumses! (pronounced Woo-Jums-Ez, please!)

You seem to be having all the excitements what with blizzards and squad cars and marathons. Have you ever seen a wrestling match? It is the only thing I can think of to compete with your excitements. If you haven't I'll see that you do when you return. Such a tour! No one except Sarah Bernhardt and William Jennings Bryan has ever seen so much of our country. You will have fabulous stories to tell for years and when some one mentions Blue Bell City, Maine, or Sight Unseen, Idaho, you will pipe up and say I spent several weeks there during the Great Freeze of 1934. It's too wonderful. . . . I can't

wait until I photograph the Woojumses, after their Mar-
copoloesque journey . . . I'd like to see you both this
minute! . . .

178,968 yellow irises, singing Hallelujah to you!

Carlo!!!

❦

*Gertrude Stein's "I came and here I am"—her impressions on ar-
riving in America—had been sold through Random House to the
Cosmopolitan.*

FROM BENNETT CERF

Random House, 20 E 57, New York,
Dec 18, 1934

Dear Gertrude:

I was delighted to receive your sweet note this morning
from Indianapolis. Rather than take any chance of missing
you on your flying tour, I am going to address my answer to
Pikesville.

First news, and the best news, is that the check came in
from Cosmopolitan and has been mailed to Morgan et Cie
in Paris, to be deposited to your account. The sum is $1500.00
as agreed upon.

In the second place, the books are all selling nicely and
when the final figures come in you will be pleased. I sent out a
publicity note to the effect that THREE LIVES was the best selling book in the Modern Library in November, and that has
caused a great deal of comment.

The arrangement of the book of lectures sounds fine to me,
and we will count on bringing it out sometime late in February. We will depend upon Alice to turn in the manuscript to
us the beginning of January.

We miss both Alice and you very much indeed. Merry
Christmas to you and love.

As ever,
Bennett

Gertrude Stein spent Christmas with relatives in Baltimore and renewed her acquaintance with the Fitzgeralds.

FROM F. SCOTT FITZGERALD

1307 Park Avenue, Baltimore, Maryland,
Dec 29, 1934

Dearest Gertrude Stein:

It was a disappointment to think that you would not be here for another meeting. I was somewhat stupid-got with the Christmas spirit, but I enjoyed the one idea that you *did* develop and, like everything else you say, it will sing in my ears long after everything else about that afternoon is dust and ashes. You were the same fine fire to everyone who sat upon your hearth—for it was your hearth, because you carry home with you wherever you are—a home before which we have all always warmed ourselves.

It meant so much to Zelda, giving her a tangible sense of her own existence, for you to have liked two of her pictures enough to want to own them. For the other people there, the impression was perhaps more vague, but everyone felt their Christmas eve was well spent in the company of your handsome face and wise mind—and sentences "that never leak."

All affection to you and Alice,

F. Scott Fitzgerald

Gertrude Stein spoke at the Choate School in Wallingford, Connecticut, on January 12, 1935, on the subject "How Writing is Written."

FROM DUDLEY FITTS

The Choate School, Wallingford, Connecticut,
Jan 18, 1935

Dear Miss Stein

I hope you weren't disgusted with us; that you didn't leave us thinking that I was certainly right about there being a fog in New-Haven County. I think you would be very happy if you could know all the things you did for us: how much your lecture, and your conversation, and yourself meant, and mean, to us. . . . Mrs St John has asked me to ask you, and we all want you more than I could ever express, if you and Miss Toklas won't please come back sometime before you go to Chicago, or in the Spring after you come back from the Coast, and spend a few days at the Headmaster's house. It would be a swell place to rest between engagements: you wouldn't have to see anybody you didn't want to see, or do anything you didn't want to do; but there are so many boys who were bitterly disappointed in not having been able to talk to you, or listen to you . . . that I think you would not feel that it was wasted time. Won't you please consider it? . . .

The stenographer who took down your lecture had difficulties which I have tried to iron out, but I'm not sure I've been successful. Unless you object, Vanderbilt wants to print it in the next issue (22 February) of the *Lit*. He is sending you the proofs next week sometime, so that you can (if you will be so kind) correct us where the stenographic transcript baffled us completely. . . .

It was a good week-end. . . . I shall probably be first tarred and then feathered, and then lynched very painfully on the central playing-field, if you don't come back.

Gratefully yours,
Dudley Fitts

❧

The program in California included a party given by Gertrude Atherton, whom Gertrude Stein had met in Paris through Avery Hopwood. The meeting with Mrs. Luhan did not take place, although the two ladies exchanged greetings by telephone.

FROM GERTRUDE ATHERTON

2101 California Street, San Francisco,
Mar 16 [1935]

Dear Miss Stein

The other day a friend of Mabel Luhan (who is staying at Carmel, an artists' colony near Monterey) called me up and said that Mrs. Robinson Jeffers was very anxious to bring about a "reconciliation" between you and the High Priestess of Taos. I suggested that Mrs. Jeffers write to you and find out whether you cared to meet Mrs. Luhan or not. If you did I'd ask her to the cocktail party. Now, please tell me frankly how you feel about it. If you don't want her she doesn't get asked; that is certain. I like Mrs. Luhan, but this is your party and I want no jarring note. I have asked the most interesting and distinguished persons in San Francisco and environs—at least all that would be likely to interest you, and it promises to be the most notable cocktail party that has been given for years. Not one regret have we received! They fairly sputter over the telephone when asked. Already we are up to seventy-five, and hope to stop there, for if there are too many few will get a chance to talk to you.

Several will stay on to supper, and you and Miss Toklas will stay also or go home to rest before your lecture; whichever you think best. I have emphasized the fact that the party begins at four on account of your lecture—hoping that the majority of the guests will clear out earlier than usual.

Very sincerely
Gertrude Atherton

❦

Through Sherwood Anderson, Gertrude Stein had met Lloyd Lewis in Chicago and had lent him the manuscript of her Four in America, *a work—then unpublished—which concerns George Washington, Ulysses S. Grant, Henry James, and Wilbur Wright.*

FROM LLOYD LEWIS

The Chicago Daily News, Chicago, Apr 5, 1935

Dear Gertrude Stein:—

I am returning "Four In America." I hate to, for I would like to read it many more times, but if I don't get it to you I will hang onto it too long.

The main thing about it to me is that it determines me to go off to Paris or Florence or Leadville, the three far-off places I like best to be, when the time comes to write the life of Grant which I have been collecting for, across the past six years.

Your apartness from Grant's country while you thought about him gives your book a clairvoyance that I would pray for. . . .

My mind harps on Grant and religion ever since I began reading your ms. . . .

Morale was stiffened upon his every advent. This is not much different than a conviction of salvation. People didn't star him as a savior, nor perhaps as the worker of miracles at all. But they did begin to believe in themselves . . .

He could do this without sermons or oratory of any kind. I don't know how he did it. . . .

Your religious concepts of the situation are the best I have read on this puzzling point. Of course your saying that wars are over before they are fought is the best thing I ever read about war. . . .

With warmest thanks for your kindness in lending me the ms., I am,

Faithfully,
Lloyd Lewis

FROM DuBOSE HEYWARD

Follywood, Folly Beach, So. Car.,
Apr 6 [1935]

Dear Miss Stein:

Thank you so much for your thoughtful note about seeing Porgy. I am glad you saw it, and liked it.

We liked you in Charleston, tremendously—even if we did not always understand you—and we hope ever so much that you're coming back some day.

As ever
DuBose Heyward

Gertrude Stein had made an extremely favorable impression upon the gentlemen of the press. She and Joseph Alsop met and argued interminably about the role of intelligible communication in modern literature—arguments at least partially recorded in some of her later books.

FROM JOSEPH W. ALSOP, JR.

New York Herald Tribune [Early 1935?]

Dear Miss Stein:

I enclose this letter, which I am asked to forward to you, more as a pretext to write and thank you for the pleasure it has given me to cover you for my paper, than because I believe it will please you to receive the letter. . . .

Your lectures have been a revelation to me in many ways. The chief revelation has been yourself. You may possibly have gathered from my reports, if you have troubled to read them, that I have conceived a real admiration for you and for your work. I must beg your pardon, also, for my inadequate reporting of your lectures, and offer my poor excuse that they are extremely hard to get down verbatim. At the same time unless they are set forth in quotation they lose much of their flavor, and therefore I have thought it better to quote you as nearly as I could, and thus mangle probably your sense and certainly your verbal form, rather than to give none of their true effect.

Could I, perhaps, call on you some time before you leave New York? I want awfully to get a story on your impressions of this country after the long interval of your absence, but if you do not care to be interviewed again I should like more than I can say merely to see you.

Gratefully & sincerely,
Joseph W. Alsop Jr.

In Richmond, at the request of her friend Carl Van Vechten, Ellen Glasgow entertained Gertrude Stein, and they later met briefly in New York. To Miss Glasgow, Miss Stein sent a copy of her Lectures in America.

FROM ELLEN GLASGOW

One West Main Street, Richmond, Virginia,
Apr 30, 1935

Dear Gertrude Stein,

It was charming of you to send me your book of lectures, which I found awaiting me when I reached home yesterday. I am delighted to have the book from your own hand, with the most kind inscription.

That glimpse of you in New York was a great pleasure, and I hope that the three of us may meet soon again.

My love to Miss Toklas and to you,

Ellen Glasgow

The American tour came to an end, and Gertrude Stein and Alice Toklas sailed from New York, once again aboard the Champlain, *on May 4, 1935.*

VII. THE LATE THIRTIES
SUMMER 1935–JULY 1939

The lectures had also gone to Francis Rose.

FROM SIR FRANCIS ROSE

La Porte des Îles, Mougins, A.M.
[Summer? 1935]

Dear Miss Stein

Thank you so much for the book. I was delighted to receive it. I have read a part of it and it delights me very much —especially about painting and English literature.

I am working every day and feel in very good form . . . I do not know if you will like my new pictures as they are quite unlike my last pictures and one would have to go back a very long way to find any resemblance in what I am aiming at. I have tried to eliminate every possible literary trick or idea and produce . . . what I hope are the simplest truths (I mean by this those which are the least obvious to the eyes and the most important to the inside of the picture.) I work a great deal but very slowly. . . . The more I paint the more

I realize how little one can know about painting in one's life time and the more one loves to paint and the more one is tormented with the desire to do much better, much much better. . . .

As always yours very affectionately
Francis Rose

❦

Gertrude Stein had stayed at Frank Case's Algonquin Hotel while she was in New York. Back in France, she left Paris almost at once for the country and from there wrote Mr. Case a letter of appreciation.

FROM FRANK CASE

[New York] June 21, 1935

Dear Miss Stein

That is the nicest note you wrote me, you know the one in which you say over there is unreal & over here is real, because I think that very seldom happens. When I leave N. Y. for a few days I always think of it as closed up, no street cars running, no policemen directing traffic or anything going on. Either that or I don't think of it at all. My imagination doesn't get outside the small circle of which I happen to be the center at the time. And I think most people are like that. So for you to think of N. Y. and the Algonquin as real is so complimentary & gratifying that I am delighted.

We miss you and Miss Toklas and speak of you nearly every day.

Frank Case.

❦

James Laughlin was among Gertrude Stein's visitors again this summer.

FROM JAMES LAUGHLIN

Lausanne, July 19, 1935

Dear Miss Stein:

I want to send you a little word of thanks for the nice visit which you gave me the other day. And it isn't just habit that prompts me to thank you. I *get* something out of my talks with you, a sort of freshening up of the mental process. . . .

You would be surprised to know how much I have thought about your work and how much I have written about it. And the more I write and think about it, the more I know what a sloppy thinker and hopeless writer I am, and at the same time, the surer I become that you are reliable. I have come to feel that I can rely on you, and on your work, that I can be sure to find it always hard at the center and moving on the surface. . . .

I'm asking my NYC booksellers to forward you a copy of my first NATURAL HISTORY. It has more of the story thing in it than the others are having. It has also a sort of cheapness that I hope in the others to rise above. America is a little bit that way, but I think there is a better way of putting it.

With kindest wishes to Miss Toklas & again thanks for a pleasant visit.

Jay Laughlin

FROM HENRY MILLER

18 Villa Seurat, Paris (xiv), July 24, 1935

Dear Gertrude Stein:

I had a letter recently from James Laughlin iv. suggesting that I send you a copy of my book, Tropic of Cancer. I have just requested my publisher to mail you a copy—to this address. If you have anything good or bad to say about it I should be pleased to hear it.

Sincerely yours,
Henry Miller

✻

*The Arts Club of Chicago was planning an exhibition of the work
of Élie Lascaux for early 1936. For the catalogue Gertrude Stein
wrote a foreword, which Kahnweiler translated for Lascaux.*

FROM ÉLIE LASCAUX [TRANSLATED]

Villa Monette, Avenue du Général Maiziore, Antibes
[Aug 1935]
Mademoiselle:

Kahnweiler has just translated your preface for my American exhibition.

May I first try to thank you, Mademoiselle, for your great
kindness to me (as always) and then for the charming way in
which you present me to your country?

I owe this exhibition to you, and I am deeply touched.
I do not ask that my pictures, going to Chicago, please, but
that they appear young and thus confirm that white light
which you have so well described. . . .

Please give my respects to Miss Toklas, and, Miss Stein,
please be assured of my humble and profound admiration.

Lascaux

✻

*Gertrude Stein had got to know Thornton Wilder very well during
her visit in the United States and he had given her the use of his
apartment during her second stay in Chicago. She had lent him
the manuscript of* Four in America *to read.*

FROM THORNTON WILDER

American Express Company, Kärtnerring 14, Vienna I,
Sep 23, 1935
Dear Friends:

I cast myself out into the open seas of friendship and hope
to be supported and understood. So: there are long long

stretches of the *Four in America* where I don't understand a word. . . . The movement of the poetical opening—the autumnal mood—*that* I got and then I was lost. The Grant I followed best of all and it is full of beauties—on religion and war and America, though even that slips away from me in the last quarter. The first part of Henry James was the clearest of all, because there I could follow the ideas from my memory of your expressing them in other places. So that degree to which I can express my happiness and confidence in the whole of the work, is bound up with my mortification and my rueful apology of my inadequacy to so much of it.

Anyway it's no news to you that I am a slow-poke plodder in so many ways, still stuck in the literal XIXth Century; but very proud every time I feel I have made more progress and have been given more and more flashes of insight into the endlessly fascinating individual expression which is Gertrude's style. Unless you want the MS back soon I shall keep it near me and get deeper and deeper into it.

Still I haven't settled down. A morning work-routine began in Salzburg after the Festival closed, but it wasn't clean-cut enough. And now in Vienna such floodgates of Viennese hospitality open up that concentration is impossible. Not only something Mediterranean flows through the air of this town, but something Oriental as well. The endless café-sitting, the headwaiters who are indifferent as to whether one has ordered or not, the relaxed idea of time. . . . They put a determined will into café-sitting.

That's not my tempo. So I'm going out Thursday to stay at that hotel forty-five minutes away. There I'll take my walks and read my Grillparzer and write my plays. . . .

But it's a fascinating town. It has the eleven great Breughels in it. And an impoverished Graf Czernin has just loaned his Vermeer to the Kunsthistorische Gallerie here—a wonderful thing.

So again *la vita commincia domani.* I'll write you next week when I'll feel that I have my feet finally squarely on a road. And feet is here no metaphor—walking is bound up with any existing I am permitted to do.

All my best, best, best from your

devoted
Thornton

❧

Gertrude Stein had just completed a new manuscript, The Geographical History of America, or The Relation of Human Nature to the Human Mind, *to which Thornton Wilder had agreed to write an introduction.*

At the Hotel Schloss Cobenzl on Monday Oct 7 [1935] at 2.06 p.m.
overlooking Vienna and the Danube
DEAR ONES:

What a book! I mean What a book! I've been living for a month with ever-increasing intensity on the conceptions of Human Nature and the Human Mind, and on the relations of Master-pieces to their apparent subject-matter. Those things, yes and identity, have become cell and marrow in me and now at last I have more about them. And it's all absorbing and fascinating and intoxicatingly gay, even when it's terribly in earnest. . . .

Don't be mad at me if I say again there are stretches I don't understand. This time it doesn't seem important that I don't understand, because there's so much that I do understand and love and laugh at and feed on. . . .

Anyway, lissen. There's something else I'm excited about, too.

Something's happened to me. I'm crazy about America and I want to go home. I'm going to leave here in about three weeks. If you're still in Bilignin can I stop off at poor vexèd Geneva and come and see you at Bilignin, or by then—about Oct 30—will you be in Paris again?

I've got so much to ask, I've got so much to say.

Yes, I'm crazy about America. And you did that to me, too. . . .

So, I've got two bonfires in my being—one: your great big book that's as big as an alp and yet as homely as a walk in the village; and my return to my country. And my two excitements send a thousand messages to one another. MORE SOON: for the present I knock my forehead on the ground and rejoice that I am

Your friend
Thornton

American Exp Co., Kärtnerring 14, WIEN I,
Oct 14, 1935, a beautiful autumn afternoon

Dear Friends:

So I shall see the Rue de Fleurus at last and my friends in it. And the pictures around them.

I still don't know when. . . . There's so much in town here that vexes me, the kind assiduities of authors, playwrights and stage directors . . .

There are compensations. Prof Freud was told that I had expressed (under pressure, but certainly true) a wish to see him, and he asked me to go yesterday at 4:15 to his villa in Grinzing. I was all alone with him for an hour and a half, and it was fine. He's seventy-nine. He talked of many things: "I don't do anything any more—loss of interest—satiety—impotence." . . . "I could not read your latest book [*Heaven's My Destination*]—I threw it away. Why should you treat of an American fanatic; that cannot be treated poetically." "My sister-in-law admires your *Cabala* the most; I do not think so." (One of the characters makes a slighting reference to Freud in it!) "I am no seeker after God. I come of an unbroken line of infidel Jews. My father was a Voltairean. My mother was pious, and until 8 I was pious—but one day my father took me out for a walk in the Prater—I can remember it perfectly—and explained to me that there was no way that we could know there was a God; that it didn't do any good to trouble one's head about such; but to live and do one's duty among one's fellow-men." "But I like gods" and he pointed to handsome cases and cases full of images—Greek, Chinese, African, Egyptian—hundreds of images! . . . "Just these last weeks I have found a *Formulierung* for religion." He stated it and I said I had gathered it already from the close of *Totem and Tabu*. "Yes," he said, "it is there, but it is not expressed. Hitherto I have said that religion is an illusion; now I say it has a truth—it has an historical truth. Religion is the recapitulation and the solution of the problems of one's first four years that have been covered over by an amnesia." . . . "My daughter Anna will be so sorry to have missed you. You can come again? She is older than you—you do not have to be afraid. She is a sensible reasonable girl. You are not afraid of women? She is a sensible—no nonsense about her. Are you married, may I ask?"!!!

Really, a beautiful old man. . . .

For my own help and for the pleasure of it I have begun a vast apparatus of pencilled glosses on the margin of your MS; but I shall erase it all before you can see it. That's the way I close in on it and really digest. And the more I see, the more I see. . . .

The trouble with me is that I can't be soul-happy outside of my beloved U.S.A. and that's a fact. So I think I'm sailing from Havre or Southampton on Nov. 2. But first I'll have five days in Paris and every day I'm going to pay a call on two of my most loved Americans in the world. Oh, say can you see what I mean. So . . . Küss die Hand, Küsse die Hände

Thornton

FROM SIR FRANCIS ROSE

c/o Hong Kong & Shanghai Bank, Hong Kong
[Dec? 1935]

Dear Miss Stein

Your letter which I have just received has given me great encouragement. How glad I am you find my work more complete. I have done a lot more since. . . . Until the false ideas of mode & surrealist talk is crushed or more reasonably cleared up, I am afraid I must wait. I am not afraid as nearly always waiting and hard work win. My painting after all is my whole life and if it does take time for me to be recognised I will always have better and more complete work to show then. I can only spread out very slowly step by step. I must say travelling has opened my eyes to many new things.

I do however hope things will turn for the good soon as it would give me so much bigger scope and perhaps I would not be so lonely, so alone. I suppose you know what it is to depend on oneself for every idea every conversation.

I have just finished the 4 seasons as fruit & flowers. Hong Kong is like a Midland town in a glorious landscape. It is run on the fanatic ideas of bored drunken stupidity and missionary false virtue. It is stodgily mad and the idea of every one is to play at having nothing to do.

I hope you both will have a very very Happy Christmas & New Year

As ever affectionately
Francis.

Gertrude Stein, on her tour, had met and liked Donald Sutherland.

FROM DONALD SUTHERLAND

Nassau Inn, Princeton, N. J., Dec 22, 1935

My dear Miss Stein:

Nothing came of all that fussing with the publishers as I really should have been sober enough to know, but anyway there it is, nothing came, and by now I am fairly glad because if something had been published in a book it would have hung over me the rest of my life, and really I see now it was pretty bad and should not have been printed, as it was not. I say its youth as I see it is justified because I was younger, but having to justify it is pretty sickening and perhaps I will always be justifying what I have already done, but then perhaps not . . .

I have seen Carl Van Vechten now and then who has advised me and teased me and listened to me and sent me away full of good scotch. As I have explained before, since you pulled me into the edge of your limelight I have met a great many people and more people through them and some of them quite important to me, some of them wonderful . . . It is late to hope your Christmas will be merry, I shall have to hope it was and that your new year will be full of delight. And I hope so fervently I may see you before too long either here or there.

Yours ever,
Donald Sutherland

Gertrude Stein had written to her publishers about a young writer, Wendell Wilcox, whom she had met in Chicago through Thornton Wilder.

FROM WENDELL WILCOX

1120 East 55th St., Chicago, Ill. [Jan 2, 1936]

Dear Gertrude Stein

Here it is the second day of the new year and the snow is falling very thick and lovely though a little gray from all the smoke and soot, and I'm a little the latter half of that myself.

And this morning the letter came from Harcourt Brace saying that in the light of your remarks they were very anxious indeed . . . They were really the last people I ever expected to hear from. They're such an old solid firm and though they always get everyone in the end they don't usually want them in the beginning.

The letter and the book arrived just in time to make Christmas very exciting and I was very glad the book was the How to Write one. I was glad too it was one of the Plain Edition Books. It is probably much nicer for you to have others printing your books, but myself I like the Plain Edition. Other people are always giving your outsides a mite too much elegance, or the wrong sort of elegance, or something. I have just finished reading your Chicago lectures and the inside of the book is fine but the outside is too orange. Of all the books that I have read about today (and incidentally about yesterday as well) I think that this one of yours and the one of Freud's called Civilization and its Discontents get the most of it said, and the strange thing is they are both such short books.

Somewhere along the line I've heard you don't like Freud so perhaps you don't want to be seen sitting next even in a letter, but maybe some time you will like him. For me it has always been that the ones I have liked the longest have been the ones that I have opposed the hardest in the beginning. Every new theory of Freud's makes me quite sick the first time I read it, but by the time there is a new one to make me sick I am reconciled to the old one, and Matisse made

my stomach turn over the first time I saw one of his pictures.
I like the long process of being persuaded and the final feeling
of giving in. . . .

We always open all of our Christmas presents on Christmas Eve, and that evening there was a little colored artist
named Sebree here to dinner. . . . His painting is very pure.
He has no trouble at all working directly from himself onto
the canvas without the intervention of who knows how many
other minds and hands, and if there is any law for creation
the first one is I am sure directness. We have had so many
competent writers and painters in this country but with most
of them there has always been that inability to go directly
out of themselves and down onto the paper. There are always
influences. There always must be I suppose, like the medium
at the seance, but in the end it is no good if you can't get the
current to flow directly down your own arm. The actual physical space between oneself and the paper is so short and I have
often wondered what it was (what the thing was made of)
that could stand so solidly between.

And so I think that perhaps I had better try to thank
you a little more directly. I am a terrifically bad thanker. I can
never say the things I really do feel in the way I want them
said. Out of the ones left living now there are so few I can
trust, and I do trust you, and to have the ones you trust say
yes even a little bit is a very important thing.

I have been talking for such a long time. I am always very
long-winded, and this for me is really a very short breath.

Much love and many thanks,
Wendell Wilcox

*In January, Gertrude Stein went again to England to lecture at
Oxford. Lord Berners invited her to stay with him at Faringdon
House in Berkshire.*

FROM LORD BERNERS

Faringdon House, Berks., Jan 6, 1936

Dear Miss Stein

I am so very glad to hear from Diane Abdy that you and Miss Toklas will come and stay with me for your Oxford lecture which is quite near here—I mean Oxford—and I hope you will stay as long as you can as there are some very interesting things to be seen in the neighbourhood as well as some very uninteresting ones.

I will write and let you know about trains getting here as the time approaches.

Yours very sincerely

Berners

FROM ALFRED HARCOURT

Harcourt, Brace and Company, Inc., New York, Feb 21, 1936

Dear Miss Stein:

By a great turn of fate, I am now in the position of a go-between between you and Mabel [Dodge Luhan]! I assume you have seen her two INTIMATE MEMORIES volumes—the girlhood volume which she called "Background" and the second volume which she called "European Experiences." She has now sent on to us a volume which she calls "Makers and Shakers" covering the American period, and to me it seems much the best of the three—perhaps because I knew more of the people and the events she describes. In it she wants to print the enclosed batch of letters from you. Of course, letters belong to the person who wrote them rather than to the recipient, and where Mabel is reprinting letters, she is asking the authors of the letters if it is all right. She has asked me to ask you about the enclosed. I find them most interesting, and I hope it will be all right by you. Will you let either me or Mabel know?

Sincerely yours,
Alfred Harcourt

❧

Gertrude Stein gave her permission and some ten of her letters were printed in Mrs. Luhan's Movers and Shakers *(the book's published title).*

Meanwhile the English visit had come and gone, and Lord Berners had agreed to write the music for A Wedding Bouquet, *a ballet to be made from a text by Miss Stein.*

FROM LORD BERNERS

Faringdon House, Berks., Mar 1, 1936

Dear Gertrude

(I hope I may use Christian names it's so much more like that and Bertie [Abdy] does). Thank you so much for sending Operas and Plays. I think They must. be wedded. to their wife. looks very suitable for music. I will start on that when I've finished The Camel. I'm reading [Dashiell Hammett's] The Maltese Falcon, the book you recommended and am enjoying it enormously. . . .

Have you been to the Corot exhibition at the Orangerie yet? Look at my little picture of Venice. I think it is very charming. The Comte de Bieville is being very active—he had Dali to lecture and Lifar to dance, though it would have been more original if Lifar had lectured and Dali danced and perhaps more appropriate. . . .

Yours
Gerald Berners

Alexander Woollcott had met Gertrude Stein through Thornton Wilder and had been much interested in Basket I, her white French poodle.

FROM ALEXANDER WOOLLCOTT

Carlton Hotel, London, S. W. 1,
Mar 18, 1936

Dear Stein:

Kindly have Basket all cleaned by the morning of March 30th when I arrive on your door-step. I expect to see him (to use the words of a New Jersey farmer I once knew) as pure as the drivelling snow.

I shall be getting into Paris some time on Sunday and shall be descended, as you Parisians put it, at the Chatham.

A. Woollcott

Francis Rose was traveling in Indo-China.

FROM SIR FRANCIS ROSE

20 Rue Ngu Vien, Hué, Annam, May 1936

Dear Miss Stein

At last I am settled and really able to write and tell you lots of things which I have been longing to do for so long but have been prevented to by moving perpetually.

Saigon was amusing as it remains a charming provincial town of about 1910, but still it is the first glimpse of China which one has. Singapore is really only a vast Luna Park. Just outside of Saigon there is an old Chinese town built by Chinese merchants of the Ming Dynasty and once ruled by a Chinese governor. Today it is a mass of shops, bridges, canals

& barges—shops full of paper toys, wonderful tailors where one can buy silks as one can hardly believe still exist.

It was at Cholon I bought my first lotuses and made my first drawing of them. They are the most beautiful flower I have ever seen, and of a white more wonderful than white walls stained—with damp, a "matière" between wash opaline & whipped cream and fresh as drops of dew. When the petals fall off, the pods are almost as beautiful as the flower. In this town one can also buy fine turquoise & many blue fishes each in a tiny bowl, & around the city are fertile plains of damp marshy gardens. Each garden is built up like a platform of earth divided by paths, each platform is covered with the brightest green vegetables, all the land is composed of bright greens on browns and the people are all dressed in shiny black or dull blue, with occasional touches of magenta, purple & yellow green. . . .

The people of the Saigon market are so amazing & so beautiful in just the way you would find them beautiful & real that I was unhappy to think you were not with me. There is something very near to your work in the whole working of this land, of the way of living, of the way of looking, of the way of moving, of the way they live because of their lives. I can only say it is a land like a picture when it does not need a frame. This is what I believe people call the mystery of the Chinese. I do not know why it is called mysterious because it is really only very real, for the landscape & the people do not separate and life & climate, flower & man, animal & friendship are one. . . .

I left Saigon for Cambodia along a flat ever so flat road across an ever so flat country except for tombs everywhere (which however end in Cambodia as they cremate there) one might be crossing Russia as I imagine Russia. Goldy brown fields & pale blue sky heavy with shadowy white clouds, no trees & few villages until one comes to the ferry of the great green grey river the Mekong. On the further bank of the Mekong is born a wonderful new land, a landscape of big tufts of bamboo not bamboo as we see it in Europe, but rich thick bamboo, vivid & green as any northern green. Everything is so green & fresh & so wonderful that it becomes huge. It is a huge landscape in a huge land & with a huge sky. The kapok tree leafless is like a Noah's Ark tree in silver filigree, the sort of tree the Aztecs must have made for the gardens of El Dorado. . . . The birds & the butterflies are really colours. The only impression I have ever had of so rich a landscape was when I saw the background of Van Eyck's Adoration of the Lamb in Ghent. It seemed so bright & impossible on that grey Flemish day & the birds of so many varieties & of so rapid a flight . . . & yet I have seen here at least a 1000 swallows leave one tree, fly across the sky in a design & alight on the next tree again. . . .

I hope you will write to me about Paris & my work & what you think is the best for me to do as it is really only you who now have any direct contact with my work & I am happy that the last things please you & hope to send soon many more. I have lots & lots of drawings & gouaches.

As ever

Yours affectionately
Francis Rose

The son of the great bull-fighter Belmonte had appeared in the ring at Palma.

FROM WILLIAM COOK

55 Calle de la Salud, Terreno, Palma de Mallorca,
May 7, 1936

Dear Gertrude and Alice;—

It was too bad you weren't here last Sunday, for it was one of the days you remember. The youth Belmonte is too lovely. It might have been Belmonte père that day at Valencia. . . .

Will try to get you some photographs and am promised some good ones but haven't seen any as good as the one of little Belmonte in the Ultima Hora which I think will take both of you back to the days of his father. To me, he is a bit more elegant than his father, and with just that elegance gained he loses somewhere else, although looking at him you don't know where it is. He did several passes which seemed about the most beautiful things you had ever seen. And the illusion that it must be his father over twenty years ago is almost fantastic. . . .

Our love to you both;

Cook

Jeanne nearly threw her new straw hat at Belmonte. It was very exciting.

❦

Gertrude Stein's review of Lloyd Lewis's Oscar Wilde Discovers America *appeared in the* Chicago Daily Tribune *for August 8, 1936.*

FROM LLOYD LEWIS

The Chicago Daily News, Chicago, Ill.,
June 26, 1936

Dear Gertrude:—

. . . Your review of the book was better than the book, which had handicaps, one being the sickness of my collaborator during the last stretch, and his death just as the proof reading started. . . .

Your review meant more to me than all the other reviews for it was like hearing you talk, and I could hear you talk the other evening, too, when Thornton [Wilder] was telling Alexander Woollcott and me about his visit to you. We could see the serenity of the life you and Miss Toklas lead, the neighbors thinking about you and coming to see you, and Wilder listening as you talked on walks. . . .

The presidential campaign is warm now, with Roosevelt

becoming more and more of a preacher, an earnest, eloquent preacher, speaking over the radio as from a pulpit, straight to his listeners, doing with inflection and sympathetic tones, what the newspapers cannot do. He is an artist, possibly a very great artist, speaking via the air machinery. The masses are for him, the wealthy are against him. Politically speaking, he has made just the right enemies. We are much interested in your French situation. New Dealism seems world wide. The old social and financial order seems going. I'm too steeped in American pasts to understand Communism, but as a Jeffersonian, I feel Roosevelt is restoring the old agrarian civilization in so far as it can be restored in the age of automobiles.

Kathryn joins me in affectionate remembrances to Miss Toklas and you,

As always,
Lloyd

Gertrude Stein praised Samuel Steward's Angels on the Bough, *a book for the writing of which its author was discharged from his teaching position at the State College of Washington.*

FROM SAMUEL M. STEWARD

47—17th Ave., Columbus, Ohio,
July 9, 1936

My dear Gertrude Stein,

Indeed your letter did make me most happy and I am glad that you liked the book because I liked writing it so many years ago, 1932 I think it was, yes 1932, and since then I have written very little but I am now once more beginning to write this hot summer here in Columbus and I envy you the snow which you say is around, but particularly I liked what you said about the "unity without connecting" and the problem of time which was a very real problem to me, and also about the "level"—yes, I am most pleased and happy over your opinion, and just two weeks from today I will be twenty-seven years old.

I had wanted very much to be able to come to France this summer but if you will read the clipping with my picture on it you will [understand] why I must stay here to see if I cannot find another job. The brackets on this clipping indicate the customary journalistic embroidery and it was wholly because of the book I was discharged at such short notice . . . But in 1937 in the summer certainly I will be able to come to France if you are still there, and oh I want more than anything else to have some long talks with you . . .

So let me thank you once more, my dear friend, for the pleasant things you said of my book . . . I am so pleased and devotedly yours, always.

Sam Steward

❦

The Cooks had been obliged to leave Mallorca at the outbreak of the Spanish Civil War.

FROM WILLIAM COOK

Marseille, Aug 7, 1936

Dear Gertrude and Alice;—

It was if possible more of a pleasure to have your letter this morning than usual. . . . Mallorca went right, so we were rebels. Barcelona bombed us twice a day for ten days. We had been under martial law for two weeks. No mail or any communications in or out. Your letter not received. . . .

Since all the banks had failed with our deposits some months ago none of us got money down for more than a month at a time and everything happened at the end of the month. This was perhaps the most annoying part of the thing. . . . The British cruiser took off 676 people of all nationalities except Spanish of course and did things beautifully. I preferred to leave on an American boat, and we left the next day. . . .

Quite selfishly we are nicely fixed here. Nice rooms and good pension at special prices at the restaurant of the brother of our next door neighbor in Palma who slept with his family, his beds, his chairs and crucifixes in our cellar for two weeks before we left. Things have been very nice and people more so. Some of the people have found everything wrong, but we have found the human race quite nice. . . .

Our love to you both,
Cook.

FROM LORD BERNERS

Faringdon House, Berks., Nov 16, 1936

My dear Gertrude

I am delighted to get your letter. The Wedding Bouquet is going on nicely. The music is now finished and I am orchestrating it. Everyone seems to like it, and Fred Ashton is keen about it and will I am sure make something very charming and Constant Lambert is a very intelligent conductor of orchestra. I hope it will be done at the Sadlers Wells in March. Not before, I'm afraid, as Ashton has other things he has to do before then.

I have been here most of the time with occasional excursions to London. It is very pleasant in the country: the loveliest time of year in England I think. . . . I would love to come over to Paris and see you but don't want to move from here till I have finished the orchestration. . . .

Best love to yourself and to Alice. I have invented a rather pleasing new "plat" (or perhaps it's as old as the hills) pastry pies—same as mince pies—filled with very soft steamed vegetables—carrots, cabbage & chopped onions—served with hollandaise sauce—ask Alice to try it!

Love again from
Gerald

❧

Faringdon House, Berks., Feb 9, 1937

My dear Gertrude

Many thanks for [your] letter which I was delighted to get. Do you want it called 'A Wedding Bouquet' or just 'Wedding Bouquet.' Personally I favour the first, but what do you wish? . . . The work as regards music, orchestration and copying is now complete, and I hope it will be done in March —probably towards the end. You and Alice must come and stay with me in London for it. I will let you know at once as soon as a definite date is fixed.

I don't think, alas, I shall be able to get to Paris before that. I have got a horse running in the Grand National—will you please pray for it on March 19th? Don't forget.

. . . Lady [Sibyl] Colefax is in America. I had a row with her about an elephant. But it is too long to tell you on paper, to make it as funny as it really was. A report got into the newspapers that I had sold her an elephant and she was continually being rung up about it and besieged by press-photographers asking if they could photograph her with her elephant. She was very angry. And now I see that she was knocked down in New York by a pig at one of Miss Elsa Maxwell's parties.

Much love to Alice and yourself

Yours
Gerald

❧

FROM LLOYD LEWIS

The Chicago Daily News, Chicago, Feb 21, 1937

Dear Gertrude:—

As I was leaving, weeks ago, for Mexico, I got your most exciting letter—with its mountain-to-Mahomet suggestion that you would like to collaborate with me on Grant.

Excited though I was, I couldn't answer for the simple reason that there was hanging at that moment a proposition for me to change employers and jobs—a change that would make it likely I could get at Grant, which I cannot now. . . .

I have heard nothing but continued hints . . . Returning from Mexico I find things still at a standstill . . .

To collaborate with you would be a constant joy . . . But with my situation what it is, and my plodding scheme of research what it cannot help but be, I see time as the great obstacle, checking me in what would be a great opportunity for me as well as intellectual delight. You see into Grant more clearly than anyone, and you have already collaborated far more than you know, in my concept of the man. . . .

Thanks once more for your letter which contained the finest compliment my writing ever received. Love from us both,

Lloyd

Max White had written another novel, and had sent it to Gertrude Stein in advance of publication.

FROM MAX WHITE

64 Horatio St., New York, N. Y., Feb 28, 1937

Dear Gertrude;

This letter has been a little long in getting started and I hope you will not hold it against me that I have not written you sooner to thank you for the wonderful letter you wrote me about my book.

I transcribed it in typewriting and took a copy of it to . . . the editorial head of Stackpole Sons. He read it and was nearly as pleased as I. He used most of it in one form or another to advertise the book. . . .

Certainly I must tell you all over again that your writings have had a large part in my book. I would doubtless have written the book if I had not known your work but certainly it would have had a somewhat different form. No other writer gave me such an idea of the sentence as a unit of composition as have you or had I ever seen thoughts pass before a writer's eyes and make the same quiet sound on the page that was almost a sight as do yours. It's something like a "stream of reader's consciousness" rather than like a "stream of writer's consciousness." Besides I've always said you were just the opposite from Joyce whom I don't enjoy. . . .

Love to you and I'd love to hear from you again soon.

Max

❧

Gertrude Stein went again to London for the première of A Wedding Bouquet *at Sadler's Wells on April 27, 1937.*

FROM SIR OSBERT SITWELL

2, Carlyle Square, S.W.3, May 3, 1937

My dear Gertrude,

Thank you so much for your letter.

. . . I was awfully disappointed to miss you at the station when you left for Paris. It was a curious experience. I concluded that you were going by the 4:30 train, and walked to Victoria. On my way, William and the Rolls flashed past me, with you and Alice inside. I therefore felt quite happy about it, and, arriving at the station two minutes later, bought myself a platform ticket and walked up and down the platform looking for you in the train. I examined every compartment four or five times, but not a sign, and in the end the train left without my finding you.

It was a great disappointment, but I hope to see you either in Paris or at Belley.

May I, as they say in business letters, "subscribe myself"

Yours affectionately,
Osbert

Bennett Cerf had persuaded Gertrude Stein to write, as a sequel to
The Autobiography of Alice B. Toklas, *an account of her 1934–*
1935 visit to America, Everybody's Autobiography. *An instalment*
from it was to appear in the Atlantic Monthly.

FROM CARL VAN VECHTEN

101 Central Park West, New York,
June 22, 1937

Dear Baby Woojums,

At LONG LAST, Bennett let me read the manuscript, over a
weekend as the Atlantic had to have it back, and it seems
to me that Everybody's Autobiography is one of your finest
works. It is not as amusing or as gossipy as the Alice B. Toklas
opus, but it is much more of an integrated work of art and
much more in line with the rest of your work. Don't you
agree with me? I think you give the effect of living it as you
write it; it all flows with your consciousness and the reader
is exhausted* by YOUR vitality. I am sure this work will have a
most notable success, whatever the press, which is unimpor-
tant. I am pretty sure, however, you can count on a good press!

Bennett wants me to illustrate it with photographs. Of
course I have hundreds which are suitable, but you may not
like the idea at all and if you don't, PLEASE SAY SO. If you do,
I think Thornton Wilder and the Kiddie (I don't even know
this number's name) ought to be in it . . .

I have taken many interesting photographs lately, Thomas
Mann, Thomas Wolfe, and Scott Fitzgerald, among others.
I told George (at the Algonquin) he was in the book and he
nearly DIED with pleasure.

My warmest enthusiasm and my heartiest congratulations
and lots of love to you and Mama Woojums,

! Carlo !

* pleasantly! [CVV's note]

At the end of the year Gertrude Stein and Alice Toklas moved from 27, rue de Fleurus to an apartment at 5, rue Christine, not very far away.

FROM MRS. CHARLES GOODSPEED

2430 Lake View Avenue, Chicago, Illinois,
Jan 4, 1938

Gertrude dear:

Happy New Year to you both. How nice it was to have your long newsy letter.

We are delighted to hear that you are so comfortably settled in your new quarters. I can't wait to see them, and do hope that I may be in Paris some day to see you in them. It does seem strange though, not to be writing to you at Rue de Fleurus. . . .

I spoke to Massine about "The Wedding Bouquet," and he is very much interested, and said he would write directly to Lord Berners. You see, I told Lord Berners last summer in Paris to get into communication with Massine in London, but apparently he didn't do this. Now between you and me, I think it would be much better to have the new Massine Co. do "The Wedding Bouquet," if they will. So, I am now leaving it in Massine's hands. I told him I would write to you and tell you all this and I think it would help if you could write to Lord Berners and tell him what I have done, so that he may be ready when Massine's letter comes. I do hope this all works out. It would be such fun to have "The Wedding Bouquet" here in America.

Thornton [Wilder] went flying through here the other day, only long enough to see his adaptation of "A Doll's House," which was excellent, by the way. . . .

The hectic life here doesn't seem to let up for me, as the

Arts Club is a continuous night and day job. But as long as I have the strength it's great fun. . . .

Our very best to you,

Affectionately,
Bobsy

FROM MAX WHITE

Imperial Beach, San Diego County, California,
Jan 30, 1938

Dear Gertrude,

We got your card quite a while back and, as you mentioned you might be writing again soon, I have been thinking I might hear again at greater length. . . .

There's a young Negro writer we saw a few times before we left New York. His name is Richard Wright and he says he has been immensely influenced by your writings. We haven't seen anything of his but he is at least a very smart person. I went as a delegate to the Writers' Congress and he was there too. There was a huddle of novelists on Sunday morning and I must say his was the clearest and hardest of the minds present. I might say it was the only one. Anyway Harper's are going to bring out his first book before long. I think he is doubtless a left-wing writer. I know he's class-conscious to a degree and I'm looking forward to seeing what he writes. I was wondering whether you know him.

I hope you find time and are moved to write us before long. It's always a pleasure to hear from you and always stimulating. Our love to you both and do write.

Max

Gertrude Stein's Picasso *appeared first in a French version in Paris.*

FROM WILLIAM COOK

3 Piazza del Popolo, Rome, Italy,
Mar 27, 1938

Dear Gertrude and Alice;—

We are delighted, charmed and fascinated with the new "Picasso." With the dedication we are more than pleased. Thanks kindly.

When [André] Malraux's "Voie Royale" came out, it struck me that the French write French so well that the writing isn't very good. My impression is that your French is good. Of course I don't know enough about French to have anything but an impression, but a number of your passages struck me as very beautiful. Haven't had time yet to go over it carefully. It came this morning. . . .

Palma it seems keeps going. Am afraid it will be a different Spain when we get around to go back. It was a beautiful Spain as you say.

Our love to you both, as always;

Cook

P.S.—

It's always better to read a book before talking about it, so I've read the Picasso now.

It runs along with a swing in which there isn't a hitch, it jumps and bounds at times and beyond a doubt you have done the Picasso legend and it will stay that way.

It's as it should be, for I have always maintained that you made Picasso; without you he would have melted off somewhere, into something else, you have kept him and made him Picasso, so, now it is only right that you should have made Picassoism, and you have. . . .

Maybe the Picasso is better than the Autobiography in that it is more compact or maybe it's the new medium or maybe it isn't and it's because I've just read it. At any rate it's good writing and hasn't that Malraux fault of being so good that it isn't.

And, they will keep on reading it, because it's our time and will be all times, because one time is like another only different, but they will have to read it to find out what our time was like. In fact you can't imagine their not reading it.

The whole point is there. Just as you can't imagine their reading Hemingway, so you can't imagine their not reading the Autobiography. Because people weren't like Hemingway's not even in our own time. Damn it. I've been in my way of our time and I know. They never were like Hemingway's. That's what I hated about his Spain, people weren't like that, although he wrote well about them. That's all right, and I think we owe him that, but they won't keep on reading him.

Now, I can say with King Agrippa, Gertrude, almost thou persuadest me to be a Picassoite; and say it in all seriousness. Even if not quite, you won't care; there will be enough you will persuade completely, and look at all those you have before the book; for as I have always said, you made him. And he is not a mean thing to have made, nor is the book.

Affectionately
Cook

FROM JANET SCUDDER

Paris, Apr 3, 1938

My dear Gertrude;—

You wrote that if I do not know how artists work, every day and all day and always alone, I am not an artist. Don't be foolish—you very well know that I myself work every day and all day and alone. If doing that settles in your mind the status of an artist, then you should look upon me as a very great artist indeed because no artist living or dead ever worked harder than I have done. But as you have never shown any particular interest in my work, you see your theory about what you think of dogs for work is faulty.

I repeat—I think myself that your pet artist [Picasso] has

been great, very great indeed, but I also think that for some years he has been working with his tongue in his cheek to see what he could make you and the rest of his public swallow and he certainly has got away with murder. Ask Picasso yourself if he does not work with his tongue in his cheek.

I invited you and Alice to dinner . . . the 24th at 7 o'clock. You failed to reply to my invitation in your letter. Aren't you coming? Or are you going to pout because I do not share your enthusiasm for Picasso's later work?

Affectionately

Janet.

Gertrude Stein had liked the head that Lipchitz had made of her in the spring of 1921, and in 1938 there were plans for more sittings. These resulted in two drawings, but various complications rendered the making of the bust at that time impossible.

FROM JACQUES LIPCHITZ [TRANSLATED]

9, Allée des Pins, Boulogne-sur-Seine,
May 15, 1928 [*i.e.* 1938]

Dear friend,

Everything is ready to begin the sittings that you promised me. I am delighted at the prospect of seeing you over several days in succession, and beg of you to say when we can begin.

Friendly greetings to you both from us both, and I hope to see you soon.

Your

J Lipchitz

Lord Berners had come to Paris, and Gertrude Stein had shown him part of a new opera, "Dr. Faustus Lights the Lights," which she had just begun to write.

FROM LORD BERNERS

Faringdon House, Berks., May 17, 1938

My dear Gertrude

Thank you so much for Doctor Faustus. I like it *very* much. I wish I could start on it at once but I have my present work to orchestrate and it won't be done for a month or two. But it is nice to have it by me and I can think about it.

I saw Daisy [Fellowes] who is over here—also Tchelitchew, who was calmer than last time I saw him. He says he is determined not to be "drawn in to surrealism." But "surrealist" is now the fashionable adjective; if you upset a cup of tea it is surrealist—just as in the old days anything out of the ordinary was considered "futurist." So I fear poor Pavlik may be surrealist malgré lui.

Please give my love to Alice and much to yourself

Gerald

❦

B. T. Batsford Ltd. was to publish the Picasso in English in London and the firm's associates in New York, Scribner's, got the contract for the American edition of the book, to the disappointment of Random House. Gertrude Stein offered Bennett Cerf "Dr. Faustus" as consolation.

FROM BENNETT CERF

Random House, Inc., New York, Aug 4, 1938

Dear Gertrude:

I am probably more distressed about the Picasso situation than even you are. We have endeavored—and I think succeeded—in creating the impression that we were your exclusive publishers in America. Now, to have another firm bringing out so important a book as this one breaks down, in one stroke, the whole structure that we were building so carefully. In my opinion, Batsford should have been told, when he bought the

English rights, that he could sell sheets to us and to nobody else in America. This would have precluded the possibility of his sending a cable—as he did on June 24th—demanding an immediate decision on the offer that he made us, concluding his cable "Otherwise must close with other offer." All this could have been worked out to everybody's satisfaction if it had been clearly understood at the beginning that he had no *right* to deal with anybody else but ourselves on this book. Just how this other offer developed is a mystery to me. It would seem to indicate that the book was offered to more than one other publisher in America.

At the moment, I cannot see any point in publishing the Faustus play. If it is ever produced on Broadway, that will be the time to bring it out in book form. Simply to publish it without an actual stage production to back it up would be a mistake, in my opinion. Without a question of a doubt your book in America for next year will be the Picasso, and we feel that anything else of yours during that time is bound to suffer by comparison.

I want you to know that I realize quite well that this mixup is absolutely no fault of yours . . . I propose that we all forget about it as quickly as we can. I hope that Scribner's will do a bang-up job for you and that the book will sell 100,000 copies!

With my best love to Alice and yourself, I remain,

As ever,
Bennett

The French poodle, Basket I, died. Gertrude Stein had just finished a children's book, which was to be published in New York by William R. Scott and in London by B. T. Batsford.

FROM CARL VAN VECHTEN

101 Central Park West, New York,
Dec 2 [1938]

Dearest Gertrude,

I am awfully upset about Basket. It seemed to me he was an immortal dog and would be eternal. I always love animals so much more than people and I have a pang whenever I recall any of my dead cats. When they die it is agony and anguish for months. That is why I don't have them any more. There are people who take these things more lightly and get a new dog every time one dies and of course it is possible to love a new animal, though it never takes the place of an old one. I am so very sorry, sweet Baby Woojums, and I know what a heartbreak it is. . . .

I think The World is Round will be a favorite child's book and can't wait to find out. I shall send copies to all the children I know. I met [Alexander] Smallens on the street yesterday and he asked "What about the opera Gertrude Stein and Berners are doing? I want to conduct it." I told him I didn't think it was ready yet. . . .

We have a love[ly] new picture of St Cecilia charming the animals, painted by Roelandt Savery (Flemish) circa 1600. We got this at an auction. And I think your picking up Hemingway on the Faubourg St H[onoré]. will result in literature on BOTH SIDES. I can't wait to see what you write about this. I'm glad you met all the Orientals and liked them! It seems to me that since there is so much race prejudice one meets more races than one used to. . . .

Love to you and Mama Woojums,

[Unsigned]

FROM ALEXANDER WOOLLCOTT

Bomoseen, Vermont [Dec 25, 1938]

Dear Gertrude Stein,

Here I am, after several years of indulgence in the heady vice of broadcasting, settled down at last to the resumption of my original trade, which was putting words down on paper. More specifically, here I am committed, among other things, to writing that deathless work on the French poodle. Indeed, committed to having it ready for publication in the Atlantic in the Spring. And just when I was planning to complete my material by asking for the latest word of Basket, I got the news here in New York that Basket had died. I am sad when I think that I shall not see him again and I am sending you this word today—writing you on Christmas Day in a New York hotel—hoping that you will write and tell me all about the last hours of Basket. Carl Van Vechten is letting me see a letter he has from you and I hope you will say, too, that I may quote the part about Basket from that.

The ineffable [Thornton] Wilder has just gone through what would be to a more normally constituted person the harrowing experience of having had his second play [*The Merchant of Yonkers*] turned into a good deal of a bore by unfortunate casting and heavy handed direction. He thought he was writing an adaptation from the Viennese but all unbeknownst to himself his good American ancestry took possession of him and what he really wrote was a pure Charles Hoyt farce of the 1885 vintage. If this had been given to any American stock company prior to 1900, it would have presented no problem and they would have put it on the following Monday with great success. Under Reinhardt's hand it all went faintly Launcelot Gobbo. Or so it seemed to me when I watched the tryout in Boston last week. Now it will come to New York and I suspect be trampled upon. If all this bounces off Wilder like a rubber ball thrown at Gibraltar, it is because his thoughts are really engrossed in Play Number Three and he hardly notices what they are doing to him.

There is some talk that he and I will venture overseas the latter part of March if you haven't all gone to war by that time. Meanwhile my island in Vermont is as good a refuge as any and that is where you will write me if you write me at all.

Bonne Année.

Alexander W.

❧

Gertrude Stein was eager to interest Kenneth Clark, then director of the National Gallery in London, in the painting of Francis Rose.

FROM SIR KENNETH CLARK

30, Portland Place, W. 1., Jan 5, 1939

Dear Miss Stein,

Thank you very much for your kind letter. We have not yet left this house as we cannot sell it, and when you come over for Francis Rose's exhibition I expect we shall still be here. I hope you will come and see our pictures.

There is one young English painter called Graham Sutherland that I think outstandingly good, and I believe that you would like his work. I do not yet know quite what I feel about Francis Rose's painting. The pictures and drawings I saw in your house I liked very much, but I did not get on so well with the ones at the Salon d'Automne. I very much hope I like his exhibition here, and I look forward to meeting him.

Yours very sincerely,
Kenneth Clark

❦

The Museum of Modern Art opened its 53rd Street building on
May 10, 1939.

FROM CARL VAN VECHTEN

101 Central Park West, New York, Sunday,
May 14 [1939]

Dear Baby Woojums,

I was THRILLED to receive the new photographic stamp
(you were the only one who thought of sending it!) and I'm
very pleased with the French government to have thought of
it. As times get worse at least we can be diverted with stamps
and the American government thought of this a few years ago
and now we have a new stamp every month and love 'em! . . .

The opening of the new Museum of Modern Art was
something: Bobsy Goodspeed, Brancusi, Marsden Hartley, and
Anne Lindbergh all in the same room together! Cars were
stalled all the way up and down Fifth Avenue as Piccadilly is
when there is a Drawing-Room and inside the Museum I discovered that when they are crushed together in a heated room
rich people smell a little worse even than poor people. The
show begins with Ryder and Eakins and Cézanne and comes
down to Miró, Picasso, and even Dali. The arrangement is
good and it looks like a smash hit. Sculpture is in the garden
and in the basement is a moving picture theatre (for old films)
which is most amusing. On the opening night they were showing Theda Bara in A Fool There Was. Then Dudensing has
Picasso's Guernica and when I wandered in the opening day
somebody asked me to be photographed and pushed me over
next to a nice Spaniard in front of the picture and when it was
over we were introduced and it was General Negrin. There
are a lotta important shows here on account of the Fair and I
think the two most generally represented artists, curiously
enough (I mean in combination) are Picasso and Eakins. I
haven't been to the Fair yet but we expect to go tomorrow if

it doesn't rain, which it generally does. Everybody raves about the Fair and says it is beautiful and FUN.* The Lin Yutangs are back and were here for a (partly) Chinese dinner one night. And I am addressing this letter to Bilignin with the idea that you will be there by the time it arrives! . . .

P!

*But it is not yet successful. [*CVV's note*]

Thornton Wilder had visited Gertrude Stein again at Bilignin. He was about to go to England, where he had been invited to stay at Lady Colefax's in the country.

FROM THORNTON WILDER

Thursday evening 10:37 Bilignin-time [June 1939]
Dear Friends:

After visits like ours I long to know what you, what they, did after I left.

Whenever I finish a good book I at once turn back and begin it again, and so I wish I could with the visit, and so I wish I could know *what happened next.*

I stood for a long while in the corridor of the train looking at Le Bugey, and then I returned to my place and read *Everybody's Autobiography* until dinner time (Seconde service 8:p.m.) Better than ever. Better than ever.

(This afternoon I met Marie Laurencin, and she spoke of how displeased she was with passages in the Autob. of A. B. T.; "but," I said, "what beautiful things you said to explain your displeasure—all that about a painter being unable to see his past, etc." And then she looked very pleased to think that her displeasure had been turned to such good profit, and we became very good friends.)

This morning I did the shopping that would help me look less like an absent-minded American brought up so stringently that he was not accustomed to nice things, and yet so neatly that he was not driven into a passion, or even an observation, of nice things; I have been assembling the disguise, the fancy-dress that I must wear at Mells. I enjoy masquerades, but not those in which one must disguise one's-self *in order to be recognized.* . . .

I shall report to you soon from England, and always with lots of love

Thornton

For a number of a French review in homage to Max Jacob, Gertrude Stein had written a short tribute.

FROM MAX JACOB [TRANSLATED]

St. Benoît s/Loire (Loire In.), June 14, 1939

Dear Gertrude—

Intelligence is the view of the whole. There can be no picture without a whole, no truth without the picture. In your style, which comes from the bowels of the earth, you relate the years to the century, and the century to the human type. Your twenty lines leap out of this too indulgent review like a bas relief on a triumphal arch.

Thank you.

Faithful and constant friendship
Max Jacob.

Gertrude Stein had decided to write a book on Paris, which Batsford would publish in London and Scribner's would issue in New York.

FROM B. T. BATSFORD LTD.

15 North Audley Street, London, W.1,

June 15, 1939

Dear Miss Stein,

. . . Francis [Rose] is in England and has been in several times to work out the detail of the illustrations for "The World is Round." I think we shall be able to make an extremely pretty book of it, and the fact that he is willing to do the drawings within two or three weeks will make it possible for us to get it out in September, which, failing crises, is a very advantageous time for an autumn book.

By the way, I had a charming letter from Charlie Scribner saying how pleased he was that we had settled on the Paris idea and that they would be handling another book of yours.

It was so delightful to see you in Paris and I very much appreciated your kindness in taking me round to see Picasso, who I thought so very charming and simple.

Yours sincerely,

Charles Fry

Director.

FROM THORNTON WILDER

The Manor House, Mells, Frome, Sunday morning 10:30 a.m.

[June 18, 1939]

Dear Girls:

It is raining and Somersetshire is polishing up its profound greens.

A little inadequate American is being permitted to see, in a pure state, The English Week-end.

I keep saying to myself, "Relax, boy, relax."

It's all perfect.

I can see Henry James on his knees before it.

But the ease of it, their ease, the ripple that does service for conversation, the being willing to accept this courtesy-deep emotion-hidden interchange as the social sufficiency is hard to understand—I have to keep, strange to say, the memory of the War before me. The tablets in the beautiful church at the very door of the house are my bridge into our table-talk. I cling to the days of the War when agony lived here. Lady Horner's daughter, beautiful and composed, was married to Asquith's oldest son, dead in the War. Brothers, cousins, nephews, died in the War. Gardeners, farmers, delivery boys, died in the War. If they could read my thoughts, as with great kindness they talk to me of the strawberries this year, or the village doctor who was very good last week in a performance of *The Mikado*, wouldn't they be surprised to read in capital letters: You lived through the War.

Two days later—London.

Well, well.

What do you suppose happened?

That Sunday I fell in love with everybody in the house. . . .

That strange phenomenon LOVE that pops up in the strangest places, that hurdles the most obstinate barriers, that refuses the most pressing invitations; there it was.

It popped up again yesterday, too, at Max Beerbohm's. And Sunday night at dusk there it was, as for a few minutes our car stopped in the roadway before Stonehenge.

And here it is, as usual, on my shoulder as I write to you. I pass to him the pen and we both sign this letter.

LOVE
Thornton

For the Picasso exhibition at the Museum of Modern Art in 1939, Alfred Barr, then in Paris, tried to persuade Gertrude Stein, in Bilignin, to lend at least her portrait.

FROM ALFRED BARR

c/o Chase Bank, 41 r. Cambon, Paris,
July 17, 1939

Dear Miss Stein,

Thank you for your very nice and very prompt reply. I sympathize keenly with your desire to keep your paintings on your walls though naturally I am very much disappointed for we needed them badly.

Rereading your letter I find some slight suggestion that you might have been persuaded to lend the "Portrait of Gertrude Stein" were there time to send it to America after your return to Paris late in October. Were we to make a special shipment I think there would be time for the picture to reach New York, for the exhibition will not open until the second week in November at the earliest. Even if the picture arrived late it would be welcomed with special celebration.

Won't you let us know if under these circumstances you would be willing to let us have just the Portrait? I hope that I am not exasperating you by repeating this request—the Portrait would be such a great addition to the show for it would link in visible form the artist with his most distinguished American patron.

We have had a most interesting time putting the show together though it's not been altogether "lovely."

Sincerely
Alfred Barr

VIII. WORLD WAR II AND AFTER

AUGUST 1939–1946

Among other visitors at Bilignin in the summer of 1939 were Clare Boothe and Henry Luce.

FROM CLARE BOOTHE LUCE

The House, King Street, Greenwich, Connecticut,
Aug 16, 1939

Dear Miss Stein,—

We are home now and the important thing is that it is very very hot. Nobody cares very much about anything over here now except how to feel cool . . . so nobody in New York cares a hoop about hearing our experiences in Europe. And that's humiliating to both of us, so I'm writing you about them back in Europe.

I'm sick afraid that you're wrong about the war. Everywhere, in Poland and in the Balkans they've got too many guns, and now nobody can think what to do with them but shoot them off. That's 'raisonable' too, isn't it? We were in Warsaw and the Ukraine. The average Pole is a square short blond fellow with a head that looks bullet-proof. He hasn't a pocket-book, so he has both hands up under his chin. He has nothing but his life to lose. When men are reduced to such ignominious poverty they generally fight. We think they'll fight, and we think we won't. Ours is still an audience psychology. We hoot the villains and cheer the heroine, and pray she'll be rescued, and we fancy because we suffer with her vicariously that we are part of the plot, but we're not, we're still sitting where we feel it is proper to sit on our comfortable fundaments on the plushchaired side of the footlights. What is going to change that in time? We don't know, and as I say, because there's been a bad heat wave, we don't care a lot.

We came back on the Normandie. The sea was so smooth we couldn't imagine why the boat didn't sink. There was nobody on board, except three or four hundred people who were not at all used to the clothes they had just bought in Paris, and now when I think about them they didn't have faces, because we never looked at their faces. . . . One night, though, we had to dine with the Captain, and there were some faces which we finally focussed on. One, and a pretty dark one, with a petulant mouth belonged to a girl . . . [who] was doing something in Paris which she never made very clear to us, but we were glad she did it, because that way she had gotten to know you and Miss Alice and that gave Harry and me something to make speeches at dinner about. She asked me if I thought you were a genius and I said I didn't know, but that you said you were and I thought your opinions about such things were often surprisingly accurate. She said could a person *be* a genius and be a person who *would* say he was a genius? And I said I don't know why not. Why should a genius be required to lie about himself, and besides all the geniuses I had ever read about generally had gotten the talk about their being geniuses started first, and often they had talked about it when everybody else kept still or just said The man's mad, or What bad taste. And she said Oh, but do you know any other *live* geniuses, because dead geniuses do, naturally behave differently. And I said I knew Einstein and I had found him modest because perhaps I don't speak German, but Toscanini I've met, and Roosevelt, and Thomas Wolfe, and Saroyan, and Clifford Odets, and Hemingway, and Maurois and Morand and Maugham and Shaw and Augustus John and Wells and O'Neill and lots of others, and maybe *they're* no geniuses but heavens knows they're no shrinking violets. So she seemed very sad, and that confused her even more about you. So then she wanted to know if you could *get* to be a genius by just saying you *were*, and I said, that's the way most of the geniuses in Hollywood got to be that, but that sometimes it didn't seem to last. So she just said Oh to nearly everything I said after that. But the next day she told me she wrote! So I said Oh to everything she said after that. And it was all very pointless except that I enjoyed to hear myself saying how I knew Gertrude Stein and had not been surprised or disappointed but had had a lot of fun, just as if she weren't a genius, but a person. Imagine that.

So then I got back to The House and . . . I was very glad to see my desk. It's got too many things on it I don't need, but I get attached to little boxes and clocks and things even tho they keep catching my eye and making me think sometime I must *really* write, I must write on a smooth empty flat top. . . .

What you said about my plays made my spirit a lot tougher. I needed to have you say something good so very much. Please understand that. . . .

Affection and greetings.
Clare Luce

The New Yorker's *"Genêt" compared notes on the war.*

FROM JANET FLANNER

[Paris] Oct 16, 1939

My dearest Gertrude:

Your letter was sublime. Few ladies in these times have the concentration to ignore the war, and heaven knows it's true that in the end that's all that prevented . . . me coming down and eating mushrooms with you and Alice.

Through someone, I've forgotten whom, I hear you have Arabians and horses billeted on your property. This must be extremely stimulating. . . .

What do you and Alice plan to do? . . .

What a new kind of life this all makes, and how tragically undesirable!

My best love to you and to Alice, and even to Basket [II]. Bless you both.

Yours always very affectionately,

Janet

FROM BENNETT CERF

Random House, Inc., 20 East 57 Street, New York,
Oct 17, 1939

Dear Gertrude:

I received your letter this morning and, as usual, loved hearing from you. We have only done one new detective story this Fall, but it is going out to you at once along with a few other of our new novels, and I hope that both you and Alice will be amused by our latest efforts at Random House.

George Kaufman and Moss Hart's hilarious play about Woollcott opened last night. It is called THE MAN WHO CAME TO DINNER, and you are in it! I am enclosing the review from the Times, which will give you a rough idea of the play. One of the scenes takes place on Christmas Eve and [Montie]

Woolley gets a Transatlantic call from Gertrude Stein. He explains to his listeners that Gertrude Stein calls him up every Christmas Eve, no matter where he is, so he can hear the chimes of Notre Dame. "Last year," he says, "she found me walking on the bottom of the Atlantic Ocean with William Beebe." It got a great laugh from the audience.

Write soon again. My love to you both.

As ever,
Bennett

Gertrude Stein reported progress on Paris France *to her English publishers.*

FROM B. T. BATSFORD LTD.

Walton Villa, Malvern Wells, Worcestershire,
Nov 20, 1939

Dear Miss Stein,

Thank you very much for your letter. I am glad we agree so well on the matter of illustrations, and that you are going ahead so steadily, and expect the book to be finished soon. Fifteen more pages would just do, but I think if you could possibly extend the second instalment to about the length of the first it would really be better, and would prevent the book looking pamphletish rather than a real full-length book. Of course, I am not asking you to spin words just for the sake of lengthening it, but if you *could* let it come out as long as possible it would be all to the good. I am particularly anxious that Scribners won't be able to say that they are getting less than they bargained for.

I will write to Francis [Rose] and ask him if he will do a jacket. What you suggest sounds very appropriate.

Yours sincerely
Charles Fry

FROM LORD BERNERS

The Warden's Lodgings, Wadham College, Oxford,
Dec 3, 1939

My dear Gertrude

I was delighted to get your letter and to hear that things are not too bad with you. What I want to say is, and it makes me very sad to say it—that all inspirational sources seem to have dried up: I can't write a note of music or do any kind of creative work whatever and it's not for want of trying and I don't believe I shall be able to as long as this war lasts. I feel confronted with the break-down of all the things that meant anything to me and the thought of it has got into my sub-conscious and filled it up to the exclusion of anything else. Not being able to find a note of music is driving me mad. I don't know when I shall be able to go on with Faust. That is why I very reluctantly suggest that you give it to someone else, Virgil Thomson perhaps. It makes me miserable to think of anyone else doing it, but it is unfair to you if I keep hold of it when I can't do it, and I really feel at the present moment that I shall never be able to write music again. . . .

Love

from
Gerald

Much later, after the deaths of Lord Berners and Gertrude Stein, Virgil Thomson did consider writing the music for "Dr. Faustus," but he eventually decided against it. For its production at the Cherry Lane Theatre in New York in December 1951, incidental music was written by the young American composer Richard Banks.

Gertrude Stein and Alice Toklas were still at Bilignin.

FROM NATALIE BARNEY

Villas Trait-d'Union, Beauvallon, Dec 3, 1939

My Dears,

I see by the Herald of Dec 1st that we have to have our passports "validated before January 1st 1940—for six months at a time," and no matter where they were issued, or when they expire, and that validation will only be granted to those who cannot afford to go home, have residences abroad; "substantial evidence will be required to prove the bona fides of each case." So hie ye to the nearest consul of USA before the beginning of the new year—and let us sit tight, and not be shooed home. If you are returning to Paris I may do likewise, but remaining here—or going, if need be to Italy, more tempting otherwise: the Herald adds that "requirements will be less strict for persons desiring to visit or reside in Spain, Portugal, Italy, Switzerland etc." I mention all this in case you have not seen it—or been warned of this new regulation. Last war being worse, they hadn't time to bother us, this way! . . . Do let me know what you intend doing. . . . Would love to see you & hear you—do write to

Yours ever
Natalie.

Bravig Imbs sent the latest news from the United States as a slightly delayed, birthday greeting.

FROM BRAVIG IMBS

23 Seventh Avenue, New York, Feb 6, 1940

Dear Gertrude,

Many happy returns of the day. I should have remembered sooner and forgive me for having been so tardy. I am only just catching up on my correspondence. . . .

You will be amused to hear I have become a 100% American, in love with my country to the point of being chauvinistic, mad about New York in particular. I don't regret having lived in Paris—not at all—but I am very very happy to be here. It has the feel of Paris in the twenties—but different. Everyone is hard at work or hard at play and there are great doings in the air. . . .

Business is on the whole very bad or feverishly good; everyone is scared to death that Roosevelt will plunge us into war. If the people have anything to say America will stay out whether Hitler wins or not. If the Allies had paid their debts people would feel differently but all that bitter feeling about money has come up again, especially as taxes are going up and relief is such an item in so many states. . . .

Do give me your news and I'll promise to answer right away,

Best to you and Alice,
Bravig

Robert Haas, for whose engagement to Louise Antoinette Krause Gertrude Stein had written a poem, was now preparing a volume to contain the English lectures, etc., to be titled What Are Masterpieces.

FROM ROBERT HAAS

Culver Military Academy, Culver, Indiana,
Mar 1, 1940

Dear Gertrude:

So long it has been since I have had a moment to write to you. I sent over, more than a month ago, contracts for the Oxford-Cambridge volume but I never got them back from you. Since I think you would not hesitate to tell me if the arrangements were not entirely satisfactory to you, I conclude that they somehow went astray. I am, therefore, enclosing another set which I have just made up myself. If you will sign

and return them to me, I will return your one copy to you
fully endorsed later. I have time to prod the thing along here,
there is no need to bother you with the details. They had already some layouts made and all the estimates taken on the
work, but the delay in the contracts scared the backer out for
the present. But we'll manage it. I am doing everything with
Hal Levy, he is the . . . responsible one, and he is doing
the right thing.

I have so much else to tell you . . . but this is in a hurry
about the contracts.

Love from Bobolink

The English edition of Paris France *appeared in 1940 and was
soon followed by an American edition published by Scribner's.*

FROM CARL VAN VECHTEN

101 Central Park West, New York,
Mar 19 [1940]

Dearest Baby-Woojums,

I LOVE Paris-France, which I ate up at one sitting last night.
For me Paris is smell, and this piece of yours has the true smell
of Paris. It has the sounds too. Somehow, it just IS Paris and
it made me feel very nostalgic to read about the way the
French ARE. Sometimes they can be most aggravating being
that way, but it is nice to read about it afterwards and makes
me feel very homesick. . . .

I talked to Bennett [Cerf] about the motion picture possibilities of The Autobiography which are ENORMOUS, but
motion picture people are peculiar. You can't approach *them*.
They must approach *you*. I think the time to take this up is
when you are lecturing in Hollywood. Of course you both
would have to appear in the picture. Even Greta Garbo and
Lillian Gish couldn't be you and Alice. . . .

Bennett says he has part of a novel by you. You haven't

written me about this. . . . And about lecturing, I don't know what to say. Maybe you wouldn't like it! you see this time you would be with a professional bureau and the pace would be more strenuous (they think nothing of sending you from New York to Denver) and if you were making money they would want you to lecture every day for MONTHS. . . .

Fania is on an actors' committee that is getting up a big ball for French soldiers and all the time now I take color pictures, but I have no color pictures of Baby and Mama Woojums, which is a source of unhappiness for your loving

Papa Woojums!

Nothing came of the Hollywood suggestion, but the writing of the novel Ida *advanced rapidly.*

FROM BENNETT CERF

Random House, Inc., New York, Apr 2, 1940

Dear Gertrude:

I am delighted that you have gotten so much of a novel written. It must be many years now since you have written a novel, and everybody who loves you and admires you will be impatient to read it. I enjoyed everything that I understood about the part that you have sent us and I really understood a lot of it, which, as you know, is a new record for me. In fact, I have fallen in love with Ida and can't wait to hear the end of her adventures. Please hurry up and finish the book.

I'm returning the part of the manuscript that you sent me and ask you to please go over it very carefully, because there are a lot of words missing where Alice, for very understandable reasons, probably couldn't figure out your handwriting. There are also a number of typographical errors that I think you will want to correct yourself. I hope that you will write just about as much more to finish the book as you have sent us here, because that will make just about the right size from a commercial point of view. Get it finished and send it to me, and we'll publish it in just as lovely a format as we can devise for it. It's a long time since we've had a new Gertrude Stein book on our list and I'm rarin' to go!

My deep love to you and Alice. . . .

As ever,
Bennett

The Germans invaded France in the middle of May and occupied Paris on June 14th; but a report came out of the enemy-held city.

FROM BERNARD FAŸ

16, rue Saint-Guillaume, Paris, July 18, 1940

Dear friend,

I was very glad to hear from you and to know that you are in good health. I think you were and you are very wise to stay in Bilignin for some time. Paris is quiet, the Germans behave politely, but life is not easy. Gasoline is scarce, no busses, and tho' there is enough food, it takes some time to gather daily what one needs. . . . I did not leave Paris and organised an Ambulance service for the refugees and for our prisoners, which did and does much useful work.

Many of my friends are getting big government jobs—but, for obvious reasons, I prefer to do some writing and thinking and lecturing—at least for the coming months. I had planned to go to the U. S. A. in the fall. I doubt if it will be possible.

Let me hear of you again—

Faithfully yours,
Bernard

Communications became increasingly difficult, particularly with America.

FROM KATE BUSS

[Medford, Mass.] July 30 [1940]

Dearest Gertrude and Alice,

I am wondering about you constantly, asking myself if these last terrible weeks in France have brought you great distress in Bilignin; if you have lost your paintings in Paris (too awful for belief); if the new regime is going to drive you out of France and, maybe, into the U. S. A. It seems as though Gertrude would have turned aside, would have been able to turn aside invaders near the Rhone—if they got that near—you see we know all of nothing over here of what may be happening to you in France. Thus I am trying to get through to you via the air in order to persuade you when you can to send me word of your safety. . . . The day of France's mourning, I had just received Paris, France, and I spent the day alone with this 'love-letter' for France, in sorrow, in enchantment, in anguish, as I read, remembered, realized. This book is such a tribute to France as few persons will ever be able to equal.

But with all the deep delight of reading your book is mingled the anxiety of what may be happening to you—you will tell me of yourselves when you can. Meanwhile, very much love

Kitty Buss

Gertrude Stein's "The Winner Loses, A Picture of Occupied France" appeared in the Atlantic Monthly *for November 1940. For the contribution, Miss Stein was paid two hundred fifty dollars, the* Altantic's *top price.*

FROM MR. AND MRS. W. G. ROGERS

The Springfield Union, Springfield, Mass.,
Jan 6, 1940 [*i.e.* 1941]

Dearest Gertrude:

Well I can never tell you how surprised and delighted deeeelighted we were to get, after a long and ominous silence,

one letter a week ago and then three more all in a batch . . .
Mildred and I thought perhaps we ought to read them at one-
week intervals, to dilute the fun and spread it well into the
new year; or that's what I thought. But Mildred likes her fun
all at once so we opened and read them at one sitting. . . .

That was a mean business, that Atlantic check. I think the
Satevepost would have made it two or three times as much,
because it was a fascinating story, and a long one too. The
Atlantic is, I have heard, trying to be economical.

We'll start some magazines to you, and keep them
coming. . . .

And you keep clean with all your precious soap, and keep
warm with your wood stoves, and keep well fed, and keep out
of auto accidents, and keep thinking of the Kiddies who miss
you, and everything will come out all right in the end, as the
best of the seers has revealed, for you and Alice . . . and also
for the

Lonely Loving Kiddies

FROM SHERWOOD ANDERSON

The Hotel Royalton, 44 West 44th Street, New York,
Jan 26, 1941

Dear Gertrude:

I was very much delighted to get your letter and hear the
news of your house, of Alice and of how you are spending your
days. . . .

Eleanor and I are now planning to go off to South America late in February. We have a passage engaged on a boat
and plan to take a long sea voyage and land far down somewhere on the west coast, probably in Chile. We may stay
down there several months.

I dare say you have heard of Hemingway's huge success
with his new book [*For Whom the Bell Tolls*] and of the
sudden death of Scott Fitzgerald. I guess poor Scott has had

a rather rough time. His wife went insane and he himself rather went to pieces, overdrinking badly. He has for some time been making his living as a movie writer out in Los Angeles.

I keep hoping that you may be heading back to this country, one of these days, and perhaps living with us over here.

In the meantime, all our love to you and Alice.

Sherwood Anderson

Sherwood Anderson did not get to Chile, but was taken off the boat at Colón and died on March 8, 1941. His letter did not reach Miss Stein until later, when it was reforwarded by Mrs. Anderson.

Natalie Barney had gone to Italy.

FROM NATALIE BARNEY

17 via Saint Leonardo [Florence] Jan 31, 1941

My Dears,

You see it's like playing "musical chairs": when the music stops you settle down where ever you happen to be, and only move on when the music begins again. However I've written to U. S. A. for "visas" for France or Switzerland . . . "B. B." and your brother [Leo] (the one we don't see!) are still here— so we suppose that, for the time being, it's as "all right" as anywhere else; plenty to eat & people to see.

Si non en cet endroit
Où voulez-vous qu'on soit?
Celui où l'on se voit:
Est le meilleur endroit.

But how get there? and if I become homesick I hope to be able to read your "Paris-France!" In the meantime & ever, with love to both from both

Your not unhappy exile (as the verses enclosed prove!)
Natalie C. Barney

P. S. So glad to get your letter & now your post card. Let's keep in touch—as ever and much

Natalie.

FROM ARNOLD RÖNNEBECK

435 Clermont Street, Denver, Colorado,
Apr 23, 1941

Dear Gertrude Stein:

It seems that I am spending my life defending you. They always say Yes, but . . . and we keep on yes-butting. Paris France makes me feel extremely homesick. What would we feel if we were there *now*! It's all too unbearable.

When I think back on pp. 120 and the following of Alice B.'s Autobiography, pages on which my name appears many times, I smile, because I know you know it was not true, and I will not sue you. Our diaries (and I kept one too in those years) are concurring, only that you skipped two years in date to make it sound more real. . . . What has become of 27 Rue de Fleurus?! I shudder in the shadow of such memories . . .

Why am I writing to you? Because I have spent many a mentally great Saturday evening at 27 Rue de Fleurus, Gertrude Stein, when you had just written the Portrait of Mabel Dodge—when I translated it into German and into French . . . because I owe to *you* many great hours. *Quand même*, Gertrude Stein: we *have* those hours. Let me, somewhat wearily, take your hand over PARIS, FRANCE! My best regards to you and to Alice B.

Arnold Rönnebeck

FROM LINDLEY WILLIAMS HUBBELL

67 Charles Street, New York, June 5, 1941

Dear Gertrude:

I have thought of you so often, and wondered how you and Alice were getting on. . . .

I heard Four Saints last week—given, as you know, in concert form—like an oratorio. I was almost apprehensive about going; the original production had been so enchanting—but do you know I think I liked it better this way—scenery and costumes and dancers are all very well in their way, but damned if I don't think now that they got in the way. Given in concert form, nothing gets in the way of the words and music. It was all clear and simple and permanent.

What an ovation afterward! Virgil [Thomson] and Smallens and the singers had to keep coming back for five minutes. Only you were lacking.

With love and gratitude and every good wish for you both.

As always,
Lindley

Bernard Faÿ had accepted from the Pétain Government a post as head of the Bibliothèque Nationale.

FROM BERNARD FAŸ

Vichy, Sep 13, 1941

Dear Gertrude,

How nice it was to hear from you and to get this fine book which gives me the proper ideas and indicates the means of getting really rich. It's very appropriate as I am spending 200 millions to house your future books and to build a musical library, a business library and a geographical library. I have a great fun in doing all that, tho' I don't want to stay more than 4 or 5 years as boss of the B. N. There are too many books there, you don't have time to read them or to write new ones. And I am full inside of new ones to be written—a very good novel also called "La Croix de Paille"—which is a good title, isn't it? . . .

I spend a week every month in Vichy to call on the Marshal and advise him how to run his business. He is very nice, and says "yes, yes"—and I go home feeling great. We do it every month. Unfortunately that keeps me too busy to go and see you—which would be a great joy to me. Maybe if October is not too stormy?

My love to you, & to Alice too—

Bernard.

FROM W. G. ROGERS

Springfield, Mass., Oct 13, 1941

Dearest Gertrude:

Here are a couple of odd items.

One: Last Friday or Saturday night Mildred & I turned on the radio to get the CBS broadcast of war news. The N. Y. announcer said that, among other speakers, there would be a report direct from London by Alexander Woollcott! Imagine. And sure enuf, there was, in his best radio voice telling how, planes being too small for him and his luggage, he crossed the ocean in a British battleship. And, says he, explaining that London was still a cosmopolitan place, just before I came to this studio, he said, whom should I see but Thornton Wilder getting onto a bus in Piccadilly!—You may have known all about it, or he may be visiting you now—if so, our best to him.

Two: Going over notes on reading I did last summer, I discovered one underlined passage pointing out—or did I tell you at the time?—that along in the late 1880's Odilon Redon lived, of all places, at 27 rue de Fleurus. . . .

By the way, it always bothers me to run into coincidences, and I couldn't help but be amazed to get from you, just a week after I wrote asking what you ate the meal before & the meal after getting my letter, a letter telling me several of the vegetables available in your garden. Maybe your prophecies, if they are supernaturalism of the same kind, do deserve study after all. (But I still hope for answers to my questions). . . .

The Kiddie

❦

Now and then news from Paris filtered through. A French transla-
tion by Mme. d'Aiguy of Paris France had just been published in
Algiers.

FROM HENRI DANIEL-ROPS [TRANSLATED]

Aix-en-Provence, Dec 27, 1941

Dear Friends,

A short trip into the free zone allows us to send you—better
than by "inter-zone" card, our affectionate and best thoughts.
What should one hope for in these hours of misery? Little
happinesses, simple and modest—to find oneself again in dear
Bugey with the same warm friendship—that is our Christmas
wish.

Yesterday, in the train which carried us across the snowy
Alps, I read "Paris-France" with joy, and Madeleine and I
(and Claudine! [*the dog*]) are proud at finding ourselves in it.
There are truly a great many profound things in this book,
dear Gertrude; the observation that you made à propos of
Picasso and me struck me particularly: it is true that, for me,
the conscience of that which is vital and necessary is one of
the psychological fundamentals without which one can build
nothing sure. I think that your book will be successful (I am
only sorry that it is so badly printed!) and will find many
friends.

Goodby, dear friends. May your winter be not too bad.
It will be all right with us. How I should like to talk with you
about the war in the Pacific. What do you think of it? Madeleine's and my truest affection, and Happy New Year!

Daniel-Rops.

P. S. If you will answer by return of the courier, your letter
will be sure to reach me before my departure.

FROM FRANCIS PICABIA [TRANSLATED]

Golfe Juan, A. M., Dec 27, 1941

Dear Gertrude,

What has become of you? If you are still at Bilignin and this reaches you or finds you, Olga and I would be happy to have news of you. Life here is rather difficult—I work from morning to evening . . . I have done a good many pictures—they are in Algeria. My painting is more and more the image of my life and of life itself, but of my life which does not wish to and cannot regard the world in its cupidity and monstrousness. All that fixes the world is dead, happily! It is the only service that the cataclysm which surrounds us has rendered.

Olga and I embrace you and Alice. With our best wishes,

Francis—Olga

Gertrude Stein had consented to the publication of her letter to Scott Fitzgerald about The Great Gatsby *in a posthumous volume edited by Edmund Wilson,* The Crack-up.

FROM EDMUND WILSON

Wellfleet, Mass., Apr 17, 1942

Dear Miss Stein:

Thank you very much for your letter.—I am having Scribner's send you a copy of Scott [Fitzgerald]'s unfinished novel, *The Last Tycoon,* which you may not have seen.—Scotty is in her last year at Vassar. She looks like Scott & Zelda in about equal proportions. Zelda lives with her mother & sister in Montgomery.—The tragedy is so complete. Scott, you know, had stopped drinking & was working very hard at the time of his death. . . . His serious literary ambitions had reasserted themselves, & he was working on a book about Hollywood,

which I believe would have been one of his best things. He
had had a heart attack a few weeks before his death. The doctor hadn't taken it particularly seriously; but one afternoon,
when he had been sitting talking, he got up & suddenly fell
dead. He had been feeling rather happy about the progress he
was making with his book.—I think you are right: that he had
the constructive gift that Hemingway doesn't have at all—&
I feel sure that some of his work will last.

Yours sincerely,

Edmund Wilson

FROM W. G. ROGERS

[Springfield, Mass., Sep 1942]

Dearest Gertrude:

Here's September, the edge of the heat has gone, and, worst
of all, there are rumors that there'll be a restriction on airmail-
ing letters. If mine stop coming thru, you'll know it's the post
office and not me.

Our most interesting vacation experience was a stop on the
way out, in Connecticut, to spend evening, night and morning
with Sandy Calder, maker of stabiles and mobiles. He lives in
the hills & the country, perhaps 50 miles from N. Y. . . .

Among the people there, mostly writers and artists, were
. . . André Masson, who with his little French wife has
settled in that vicinity. Masson, who's boyish and pleasant,
had some very kind words to say about you, and hadn't forgotten some kind words you said about him. He remembered
that you once called him a "vrai naïf," and remembered it
with pleasure. He also remembered a time when you charged
him with keeping bad (surrealist) company; he admitted, he
said, that he didn't belong in that group, and he remembered
his defense: "Gertrude," he said he told you, "I stay around
with them because they praise my work." Which really does
make him a "vrai naïf." . . .

We hope you're all perfectly all right, but we have had no word since before vacation. Keep working hard on the new book and think often of the Kiddies, who think of you always

The Kiddie

FROM MRS. CHARLES GOODSPEED

["Weeping Willows," Osterville, Mass.] Sep 9, 1942

Gertrude dear—

I can't tell you how glad we were to have your card although it was dated March 27th & the news is quite old by this time. Still we are happy to have news of you up to that date. I can't understand why you have heard nothing from me for I have written all during the winter at least 3 or 4 times and sent the letters by clipper. I do hope you get this one. . . .

I had lunch today at Mrs. Murray Crane's and Somerset Maugham was there. He said he had so enjoyed your article about France. I am so glad the "Paris-France" is going so well in French. We all love it here. It was so good to see the pictures & article about you in the Harper's Bazaar. It made me homesick not only for you but also for Bilignin. . . .

By the way, I want to ask a strange thing. I remember so well a record you played on the gramophone when I was there —you said it was a Beethoven Trio & I loved it and have tried ever since to find it but cannot. Do you know which Beethoven Trio it was or have you Trios by other composers on your records? It was for piano, violin & cello. This sounds crazy in these dreadful days but one has to keep up on the little things in life when one can't help much in the big ones. . . .

I hear Thornton [Wilder] is doing work for the Intelligence Dept. I wonder where he is. Do you hear from him? Léger was down here visiting the James Sweeneys the other day & he is just as amusing as ever. Marcel Duchamp is in New York. . . . Fanny Butcher . . . [is] well, and that's all I can think of at the moment.

How is Alice? She looked well in the pictures. Do give her my love & keep lots for yourself from us all . . . and do write & tell us how you are.

Affectionately,
Bobsy—

Mme. d'Aiguy's translation of part of Everybody's Autobiography *was to appear in René Tavernier's magazine* Confluences.

FROM RENÉ TAVERNIER [TRANSLATED]

Confluences, Lyon, Apr 14, 1943

Dear Miss Stein,

On the trip back I have just finished reading Chapter Three. As I am writing to Madame d'Aiguy, that is the one which I prefer and it is even with all that I know of you one of the best things which has ever been given me to read; I found in it once more that extraordinary verve, that life of the sentence which fills it with movement and lets singularly acute reflections appear. It seemed to me also that a new grave accent is sometimes heard and that the depths that you reveal seem to permit a better understanding not only of your way of writing but of your method of thought, of judgment, and I hardly dare say philosophy, that word would horrify you so.

Before I finish this letter which I am writing just before I leave for Paris, I want to tell you again what great pleasure my short visit at Culoz gave me, and that I was quite confused by the rapid departure after lunch. I hope not to be one of those young men you spoke of whom it is a pleasure to see once but who afterward are all alike.

Please remember me kindly to Miss Toklas, and believe me, dear Miss Stein, yours most respectfully,

René Tavernier

Bernard Faÿ on a trip to Vichy had paid a brief visit to Gertrude Stein at Le Colombier, the chateau at Culoz to which Miss Stein had moved at the beginning of the war.

FROM BERNARD FAŸ

Chambéry, May 1, 1943

Dear friend,

It was a great joy to see you and to see you in such good shape. It was marvellous to talk with you. I get so bored with peoples' emotions and stupidity, and emotional stupidity and stupid emotions. I can bear bad food, but silly emotions make me mad.

I'll do my utmost to come again in August. I'd love to stay a few days with you, but that's not easy. My responsibilities are growing and will grow steadily in the coming months. It's not dull.

Thanks again—and love.

Bernard.

P. S. . . . You'll find inside some bread-tickets, with renewed thanks.

FROM RENÉ TAVERNIER [TRANSLATED]

Confluences, Lyon, June 23, 1943

Dear Miss Stein

How can I thank you again for your welcome, your advice, and your collaboration.

I am rather overwhelmed to have all at once the responsibility of publisher, magazine editor, poet, and the pleasure of being your host. . . .

These days are sadly wanting in piquant anecdotes, charming escapades, and diverting events. . . . And above all one does not have ravishing Bugey, your terrace so beautifully framed with green, and your conversation which is tonic for the spirit. . . .

We have great need of all that. Believe me, dear Miss Stein, I admire you deeply. Please remember me to Miss Toklas and thank her for me.

René T.

P. S. Did I forget to tell you that in order not to have to interrupt the Autobiography by the number on the novel, I plan to begin it right after that number; otherwise our readers would have had to wait for the continuation from June until September. . . .

❦

A son of neighbors of Gertrude Stein had been sent to Germany under the Germans' plan for recruiting labor for the homeland.

FROM CHARLES DE LA FLÉCHÈRE [TRANSLATED]

Gössnitz [Germany] Sep 10 [1943]

Dear Miss Gertrude,

How touched I was by your good letter and how happy one is to feel in touch when one has left one's country. One would like to have faster postal service so that the exchange of ideas could be made more easily. How happy I should be to have you as guide in this German literature which does merit being genuinely appreciated. As for the language, I am following your advice and talking as much as possible especially with children whose thoughts are expressed in so simple a way. It would be an exaggeration to say that I am making great progress but I am beginning to get the idea.

At Culoz, the grapes must have ripened and the harvest should be taking place; it is hard not to be able to help, but after all the good wine of Bugey is not made in a hurry and cannot be drunk for several months. François of Magdeburg and Marc Dastarac of Vienne write me that they are coming soon to taste it. Courage is necessary but morale is good.

I hope that you are well and Miss Alice also. Please remember me kindly to her and to all those around you.

With my best wishes,

Ch. de la Fléchère

FROM BERNARD FAŸ [TRANSLATED]

Vichy, Hotel Mondial, Jan 4, 1944

Dear Gertrude,

I don't want to let the first of January go by without sending you my best wishes and a testimony of my affection. In the difficult year which has just gone by the 2 days spent with you were an oasis, a great joy which I am still experiencing. I was so happy to find you as you were—in good health and humor, strong, creative, active.

Now 1944 has begun. May it reunite us. I want this year to finish my Lafayette, my Vergennes and a novel which I have begun. I shall try to come to talk with you about them when good weather is with us again.

For the moment I hardly move out of Paris, except for tiring visits to Vichy, and sometimes a week-end at my country place. The family is well.

Best wishes to Alice, and to you, once more, my deep affection.

Bernard Faÿ

FROM RENÉ TAVERNIER [TRANSLATED]

Lyon, June 13, 1944

Dear Miss Stein,

I am writing you just a word in haste to tell you that we are all well here, that we survived the bombardment unharmed and the various trials of which daily life is composed.

Confluences has had a hard time as a result of the closing of the shop of its printer by the occupying authorities; our paper, our copy for the next numbers are all sealed and the next number had to be improvised.

I should have been very happy to have news of you and to know if all goes well there. I do not dare say that we shall see you soon for the trains are in the habit of not arriving or even of not leaving, and to cover the 60 kilometers which separate us we might have to take two days! We should nevertheless have liked to come to spend a good day at Le Colombier.

Our kindest regards to you, dear Miss Stein. Please remember us warmly to Miss Toklas.

René Tavernier

People are shooting each other up with machine-guns around the house each night and this morning as I am writing. There is no more bread, no telephone (I am one of the few to have one still thanks to Confluences). One feels free in spirit and I am taking advantage of it to write some poems and a play. The autobiography of wars will be enriched!!

❧

On August 14, 1944, American, British, and French troops landed along the south coast of France.

FROM RAYMOND ESCHOLIER [TRANSLATED]

Malachite, Mirepoix—Ariège, Sep 7, 1944

Dear Gertrude Stein,

The American radio today takes away a weight which has been pressing on me night and day. Your region had seemed to me so threatened that I feared for your and Alice Toklas's life. And here you are, as always, very much alive and even writing about the maquis. I too, on my part; for our maquis of the Pyrenees yield in no respect to yours of the Ain.

What has happened to your Picassos? When are you going back to the rue Christine?

Well, we shall see each other there. I embrace you for America, for France, and for dear old England. . . .

Your respectfully devoted
Raymond Escholier.

FROM LIEUTENANT GENERAL A. M. PATCH, U. S. ARMY

Headquarters Seventh Army, APO 758,
Sep 17, 1944

Dear Miss Stein:

Major Quello has just delivered to me your kind note inviting me to visit you in Culoz. I have regretted deeply that our rapid advance has prevented me from visiting the area of the Lac du Bourget and Aix les Bains of which I hold so many happy memories of a delightful, if short, vacation during the last war. The opportunity of meeting the lady whose literary works and humanitarian achievements I have long admired, together with the tempting offer of a chicken dinner, have convinced me that I cannot long postpone a trip to your delightful countryside. I shall make every effort, as soon as the military situation permits, to accept and thank you in person for your thoughtful invitation.

Sincerely,
A. M. Patch

Letters began to arrive once more from old friends.

FROM CECIL BEATON

British Embassy, Paris, Sunday, Oct 29 [1944]

Dearest Gertrude & Alice,

This is such an enthralling moment for me—to be able to write to you & feel that you may receive the letter . . . to feel even that I may receive a reply. I wrote about three years ago when I was in Lisbon—but there is every possibility that the letter never arrived. You can imagine how much I have thought about you both hoping that you were withstanding with certain calm, all the rigours & horrors of the last years. There have been so many rumours—that you had arrived in New York—that you had left New York—& now I have heard of you over the Radio as being still in Bilignin where I have imagined you all the time. That wonderful house must have been the greatest comfort & joy to you.

I have arrived here to arrange an exhibition of Press Photographs showing Britain at war. It may be interesting to Parisians who have been denied all English papers. It will keep me occupied here for 2 weeks at least—& I am thrilled to be here again though finding Paris a sad city in many ways. It has never looked more beautiful. . . .

I have only recently got back from a tour that lasted almost a whole year & took me to China & India—& on my way home to New York. Thus I have seen more places in the last years than most. China was a big disappointment. I had expected so much & did not realise that *all* the most interesting places have been taken by the Japs—that all that is left is about as uninteresting as any town in the Ozark mountains. Also I was disappointed to find their war effort sabotaged by so much dishonesty & corruption. I have been working for the Ministry of Information—writing reports & taking photographs by the million. I have been very lucky to survive without greater horrors happening to me—& it has been a great experience to see so much—I do trust I may soon receive a word to know you are both in fine spirits. With love from

Cecil

FROM BRAVIG IMBS

United States Information Service, APO 887, U.S. Army,
Nov 2, 1944

Dear Gertrude,

At last I can write to you! I have been in France since early in June and have often thought of you and wondered how you and Alice were faring. I understand from Georges [Maratier] that your pictures are all right, which is an incredible piece of luck. I am staying in Francis [Rose]'s flat which has been pillaged only slightly—a few tables, andirons, a Picasso and some miniatures and the chauffe-bain. Everything else is there.

I am a civilian attached to the army—wear an officer's uniform—as a radio man. I am on the air regularly—but I don't think you can hear me yet. I set up the first radio station in free France—in Cherbourg, shortly after its liberation. And I had the honor of opening the station. In the States, I worked for the Office of War Information and spoke to France every night. I wonder if you ever heard me. . . .

I couldn't write a line in New York but now that I am in this town I feel like writing again and have a book in mind. It is a positive rejuvenation to be back here and alone. And I like being with the army very much.

Do let me know how you are, love to both,

Bravig

An American friend, a neighbor in the Quarter, who had been placed by the Germans for a time in a concentration camp, reported on events in Paris.

FROM KATHERINE DUDLEY

13 rue de Seine [Paris] Nov 14 [1944]

Dear Gertrude

Ferren came to see me yesterday with news of you. He thinks perhaps you may not return to Paris immediately. So I have told Svidko to finish cleaning the kitchen and your bed-room & bath and to verify the gas & test the radiators and to await your word before continuing the cleaning. . . . I went with him the first day and saw the condition things were in. Fortunately as far as I could see all the pictures on the walls were unhurt though several of the small Picasso heads had been thrown on the floor. We put them back in their places & none are harmed. . . . But it's a miracle that your collection is still there for about 2 weeks before the Boches left 4 men of the Gestapo came, demanded the key of the concierge who protested in vain that you were American. The young girl who is secretary in the Bureau Weil heard steps overhead, rushed up, banged on the door until they opened it, pushed in past them and asked by what right they were there—that the proprietor was American, that she had charge of the house. They tried to put her out but she stayed. They were lashing themselves into a fury over the Picassos saying they would cut them to pieces and burn them. 'De la saloperie juive, bon à bruler.' The big pink nude 'cette vache.' They recognized your Rose portrait—they had a photo of you with them—and the other Rose heads in the long gallery, 'Tous des juifs et bon à bruler.' The girl rushed downstairs to her office, telephoned the police and in 10 minutes there was the Commissaire & 30 agents before the door much to the excitement of the street. By this time they—the G.s—were trying on your Chinese coats in your bed-room. The Commissaire asked them for their order of perquisition which they had neglected to bring with them and they had to go but taking the key with them. So she waited before the door until a menuisier could be found to change the lock. They opened the coffre with the rugs & tore the papers but Svidko doesn't remember how many packages he did up in '39. Also they opened one or two other boxes of ornaments. But I doubt if much is missing—the only thing is the carpet cleaner but it is more likely the workman on the roof who took that. I think it was left in the salon. Picasso has several radiators. There are 3 left in the apartment of which one only needs a little repairing. I'm sending this letter through Ferren who says regular mail to your region is long. Write me or try to telegraph if you want S. to continue. Naturally the place is filthy, all the woodwork needs to be washed. I doubt if you could find anyone better to do it. He is very efficient and very careful. He had the electricity turned on & the man said considering what you consumed in the past you would still have a fair allowance. This is the longest letter I've ever written. My best to you & Alice.

Katherine D.

FROM SIR FRANCIS ROSE

2 Rossetti House, Flood Street, Chelsea, London, S.W.3,
Nov 27, 1944

Dear Dear Dearest Gertrude,

It is not necessary for me to say what I feel writing this letter, so much delayed by events. I have never stopped thinking of you, and worrying about you and Alice, and it was with the greatest joy that I received your messages through [Eric] Sevareid. I wonder if you received any of my letters via the Red-Cross—one of them was returned (just before the fall of France) because I had drawn roses on the border; with it was a purple slip saying that it was forbidden to send drawings of planes! We pinned the letter & the slip on the board in our mess, & it was a great joke during those days of the battle of Britain. I was in the R. A. F. for nearly three years. . . .

It is so wonderful writing to you, & there is so much to

say that I can think of nothing more to say, except to Alice; & will you tell her that all this is for her too, & that you both have been ever in my thoughts. . . .

As ever
Francis

FROM CARL VAN VECHTEN

101 Central Park West, New York,
Nov 29, 1944

Dearest Baby Woojums!

How excited we were to get your radiogram on Sunday. I have not been too sure where you were and sent postcards both to Paris and to Culoz (I wasn't even sure before that Culoz was in Ain). However, it was a long time forbidden to send picture postals to France (and may still be) and I didn't know this rule and sent several picture cards which may reach you just the same in time. It is just now possible to send letters, but no airmail yet. I can't tell you how exciting it was to get the letter you sent through Bennett [Cerf] by the newspaper man, but your radiogram was more exciting still. . . .

Florine Stettheimer is dead after a brief illness and her sister Carrie followed her this summer within a month. I have been helping Ettie, the remaining sister, arrange her affairs and one of the things that has resulted is the Modern Museum has promised her a show in the fall. Virgil [Thomson] had some of his portraits performed by the Philadelphia Orchestra recently: he conducted them himself. . . . I'll write you more later about the Stage Door Canteen etc. and tell you what has been going on as fast as I think of it. Did you know for instance that Alexander Woollcott had died? I dare say many pleasanter things have happened which I will think of gradually. In the meantime Fania and I send Love and Kisses to YOU and MAMA Woojums!

Papa Woojums!

❦

Katharine Cornell and Guthrie McClintic were touring with The Barretts of Wimpole Street *for the U.S.O.*

FROM KATHARINE CORNELL

[Hotel Crillon, Paris] Tuesday, Jan 9, 1945

Dear Gertrude Stein—

We had such a heavenly luncheon with you and Miss Toklas we will never forget it. It is always an experience of rare stimulation.

Unfortunately we have a matinée on Sunday here in Paris . . . Could we have luncheon instead of Sunday, the following Wednesday, that is our day off and I think we leave Paris the next day.

However in the mean time perhaps you will let us know that you could come to the Barretts—we open in Paris Friday the 12th and play every night through Tuesday the 16th.

I am taking it very easy and resting most of every day till I leave for Versailles each evening so I could be reached in my room by telephone 123—that is my room number at the Crillon.

Again our thanks and looking forward to seeing you soon.

Love

Kit.

We do play matinées Sunday the 14th and Tuesday the 16th—I think that the evenings are more exciting as audiences. But whatever you want.

Kit.

❦

The first newspaperman to reach Gertrude Stein had taken back to America—besides letters—a copy of her account of her experiences during the occupation, Wars I Have Seen. *Two instalments appeared in* Collier's *before the book itself was published by Random House.*

FROM CARL VAN VECHTEN

101 Central Park West, New York
[Feb? 1945]

Beloved Baby Woojums,

I have been reading Wars I Have Seen in the greatest state of excitement . . . It is an amazing book in which you have imprisoned your feeling about all the world in the microcosm of a small French village. Never has your "style" been so perfectly wedded to your subject matter or to the effect you planned to make on your reader. The end of course sent me up in an airplane; it explodes like a rocket and fills the sky with showers of pink and blue and silver stars! Dear Baby Woojums your love for America, as expressed in those pages, is as alive as Nijinsky at top career. You DANCE your way out of this superb book and I wish Gershwin were alive to write music about these pages! Some one is sure to do it. . . . Somebody told me that Richard Wright, the Negro who wrote Native Son, had reviewed the book in last Sunday's PM. I was curious about this review although I didn't expect it to interest me much. To my surprise, it is more understanding than any other review of the book that has yet appeared. . . .

I am not quite sure which Corporal has written you because I have sent the whole American Army so far as I know it STRAIGHT TO 5 Rue Christine! . . . Everything you say about American soldiers in this war IS true. They are entirely different from the last war. They are the best and most charming soldiers in the world! So Love and Kisses to you and Mama Woojums and WRITE SOON!

Carlo

I went to a cocktail party for (of all things!) Marcel Duchamp last week and in the middle of it a man got up and yelled: "I can't stand another second of this. It's just like 1912!" And of course it was except in 1912 cocktail parties were a novelty.

Gertrude Stein at 5, rue Christine (1945)

Gertrude Stein consented to sponsor an exhibition in a Paris gallery of recent paintings by Sir Francis Rose and sent special invitations to various prominent individuals in Paris to attend.

FROM THE AMERICAN AMBASSADOR TO FRANCE

Paris, Mar 10, 1945

Dear Miss Stein:

There is such a pressure of work at the moment—and I see no surcease of this in the near future—that I am obliged to limit myself to activities within the Embassy. However, I thank you very much for your invitation to attend the opening of the SIR FRANCIS ROSE Exhibit, and I should like very much to have someone from the Embassy represent me.

Sincerely,
Jefferson Caffery

FROM PFC. JOHN BREON

In Germany [Schloss Blankenheim] Mar 17, 1945

Dear Miss Stein,

From time to time, I have had news of you, via newspaper clippings and letters from my mother, and I have meant to write before. Since college, I have had a deep interest and a profound admiration for you and for your work.

Although "Ida" is the latest of your books I have read, I look forward with interest to the book, I believe called "Mrs. Reynolds" and the others you have done since the war. With me, I have always had "Makings of Americans."

I'm writing this from the rather fantastic grimness of a German castle, in which I happen to be living at the moment.

As I'm only twenty-one, I hope this won't sound very presumptuous. I just wanted you to know.

My sincere admiration and with every good wish,

Yours truly
John W. Breon.

FROM BENNETT CERF

Random House, Inc., New York, Mar 27, 1945

Dear Gertrude:

I am at a complete loss to understand why my several letters to you have evidently gone astray. Maybe by the time this reaches you, at least one or two of them will have turned up.

At any rate, I am sure you know by this time that WARS I HAVE SEEN has been accorded a perfectly wonderful press and that the sale is already over the 10,000 mark. This will undoubtedly be by far the most popular success you've ever had in America. The $2000.00 that you receive from Collier's for use of parts of the book will be invested in war bonds, in accordance with your request. Under separate cover, I am · sending you copies of some of the reviews of the book and I am sure they will make both you and Alice very happy. I hope to hear from you as soon as you have had a chance to examine a copy of the book itself. It's a beautiful job, I think, and I know you will be pleased with it. . . .

Write soon again and know that I love you both very deeply. I wish you were coming to New York some time this year. You'd find it plenty exciting, I promise you. . . .

As ever,
Bennett

Robert Haas had been planning an anthology of Gertrude Stein's writings.

FROM ROBERT HAAS

Apr 2, 1945

Dear Gertrude:

Liberation, glory be. My copy of Wars and your postal card came the same day—April Fool's day at that, Easter-time, the most beautiful California spring days I have ever seen. No, I sent you several postals, some to Belley, some to Culoz, some to Paris. They came back again and again as the service was not certain as yet. At least you have had one now, and at last letters are possible. To catch you up on two years of news will be a job. Your letter to me must do the same, but especially about the writing . . . I am determined to go on with the Anthology, as I have interested some one very competent to help. I will tell you about that. All this year you and I must think of letters to send, to Carl, to Thornton, to everyone who might contribute, and get them to do their bits. Do you suppose Picasso would do a short statement on Gertrude Stein and Painting, perhaps a page or two, to intro-duce that section? Francis Rose or Picabia or anyone you might suggest, failing that. I will get busy soon typing out a detailed plan of the thing as I see it lately. It could be won-derful. Perhaps you could write to Bennett Cerf to see whether it would be possible to put it out in some such form as a Modern Library Giant. Do you think I could interest him in looking over the prospectus and giving suggestions? . . . Let me know and write soon. All our love as ever

Bobchen

FROM SIR FRANCIS ROSE

2, Rossetti House, Flood Street, Chelsea, S.W.3,
Apr 16 [1945]

Dear Dear Gertrude

Again with a pen I address you, wondering if this time you will receive my letter. One letter after the opening of the show has arrived from you, & it was a letter of joy & good tidings. My heart felt sad for I longed so much to be in Paris; in fact ever since I have been in a bad temper—seeing so many people go over. But I cannot go however much I want to; at least not at once. I must first find something to do in Paris which will keep us alive; until I do this I am tied here.

I must give you some idea of my life since I was invalided out of the R.A.F. I was very ill at the time, & none of my friends did anything to help my work or get me a job; actually some did their best to suppress me. I fought through with the help of my very wonderful wife, who never for one moment failed me, or lost confidence in my abilities. Withstanding terrible financial difficulties & illnesses she managed to get me back to work, & the result was the "Le Nain" exhibition which met with violent attack & insults. As you know I do not care about such things, but it was a serious problem to know how to get enough money. I was lucky in being able to get dress materials & furnishing textiles to design; 3 or 4 books to illustrate, & books to write (2 are in print, & a 3rd under contract). This gives me a lot of work & the day seems too short, as there is one thing I will not allow & that is interference with my serious painting. All is well & as it should be, but I would like to get back to France—I miss you, & the stimulation of the French language. . . .

I have undertaken to prepare an exhibition for the autumn & I feel that at last my best work is coming out. Locked in my studio it is not much difference than if I were in Paris;

it is only afterwards that one feels it. This summer I shall
paint landscapes in my own country. We are going to Sutherland. What a long letter, but there is so much to say! . . .

Love from us both & love to you & love to Alice

Francis

⁂

*Gertrude Stein had written to Richard Wright about his auto-
biographical best-seller* Black Boy. *Later, when Wright did come
to Paris, Miss Stein was a member of the reception committee
that welcomed him.*

FROM RICHARD WRIGHT

89 Lefferts Place, Apartment C-23, Brooklyn, New York,
May 27, 1945

Dear friend Gertrude Stein:

It was indeed pleasant to get a letter from you and from
a country I have never visited but always wanted to visit. . . .

The things you said about Black Boy made me very
glad. . . . I can well understand why the American soldiers
are worried about Negroes. And why you wonder about them.
America has made Negroes into a strange people. Negroes are
free now, on their own, and they live in a land where everywhere they turn they see mean images of themselves. They
live and move and walk through the white world with fear
in their hearts, and many feel that they are not wanted anywhere, and others feel that it would be lowering themselves
to speak to whites unless they are spoken to first. It is all like
a nightmare. But for writing, it is great. Negro life as it relates to white life shimmers with a thousand little dramas and
I've been able to get only a shadow of what I've seen and felt
on paper. . . .

We have made for ourselves a very tragic thing in America, and we are afraid of it. I get many, many letters from
white people; they ask me, Tell me what to do. And I can-

not tell them what to do, for I know that they know what to do about Negroes. They know what to do and they would rather die than do it. So, what can you say to people like that? They come to me and want to talk, want to hear what Negroes feel, and when I tell them, they are distressed and sad. They say, If I felt like that I'd kill myself. To most of them I say as your Melanctha said in your Three Lives, If I ever killed myself, it would be by accident, and if I ever killed myself by accident, I'd be awful sorry. I expect them to laugh with me when I say that, but they don't; not one has laughed so far. So guilt and fear stand staring at each other, each knowing that something is going to happen, each waiting for something to happen. . . .

Is it bad in France now? Is there enough food? Was there much destruction? What do the American boys think of the Nazi prison camps where so many people were killed? Over here most people refused to believe that such things were happening; but when they saw the pictures, they wanted every last German killed. I predicted that many of the leading Nazis would live to write their memoirs; also I told my friends that many of them would be photographed and interviewed. They were. I don't know what we can do with the Germans; I'll guess that we will help them to start all over again. Of course, everybody now is talking about the next war, that it will be against Russia. All day the radio talks of it. The death of Roosevelt simply knocked all the optimism out of people. The world looks so bleak they are scared. We want to get back to work and buy cars and radios. No doubt we will.

But books are selling like mad. I don't know why. . . . My own Black Boy has sold more than 450,000 copies since March first. And the weekly sales at present total more than 3,000. Frankly I don't know why people read my work; it upsets them terribly. . . . It may be that they like to be upset. Not knowing what to do in life about feeling and living, they can feel and live with a book.

Your Wars I Have Seen had some very very funny things

in it; I've seen copies of it in the subway, people riding and reading it. . . .

Really next year I want to bring my wife and child to France, to Paris. I'm going to try my best to do that. . . .

As ever,

Dick Wright

P. S. Did you know that your book hit the best seller list? Well, it is there and I hope a great many folks read it.

R. W.

❧

Gertrude Stein had discovered a new Spanish painter upon her return to Paris, and she wrote an introduction (in French) to the catalogue of his first exhibition. By Katharine Cornell, Miss Stein had sent Carl Van Vechten a copy of the French translation of her First Reader, *but the book had somehow been lost.*

FROM CARL VAN VECHTEN

101 Central Park West, New York,

June 21, 1945

Dearest Baby Woojums,

I was enchanted to receive the two catalogues of Riba-Rovira. What a charming introduction and how proud this young man must be to have received your accolade! . . . The new copy of Petits Poèmes is here and I am very happy to have this and what a delightful book! Poor Kit [Cornell] was very distressed that she couldn't find this book. When she returns from her vacation, I'll ask her to look in the pocket of her army coat. . . . You and your Glen Miller Bands and your Jitterbugs are having such a time! Paris will never be the same again and our Wars bring a great deal of pleasure to you one way or the other. Last war it was the Kiddie and this year it is a whole Regiment of Kiddies. . . . So lots of love to you and Mama Woojums from Fania and

Carlo

Papa Woojums!

Gertrude Stein began to be a popular lecturer to American Army groups.

FROM THE GROUND FORCES REPLACEMENT CENTER

Hq., G. F. R. C., APO 887, U.S. Army,
June 27, 1945

Dear Miss Stein:

This is a very brief note to express to you the appreciation of members of our command for your discussion on April 25th. Any number of the men have told me that many viewpoints were expressed which will help them more adequately to think through the great problems facing us, more sanely.

My personal appreciation for your cooperation goes with this, also.

Sincerely,

. . .

I & E Officer.

The mothers of the G.I.'s appreciated the interest Miss Stein took in their sons.

FROM MRS. JESSIE BREON

408 Albert Avenue, Rockford, Illinois [Summer? 1945]

Dear Miss Stein,

I am very happy to have your letter telling of John's evening with you, and am especially pleased that you liked him. He has been one of your most ardent admirers, spending many happy hours with such of your writings as he possesses. To have you say he is "completely the young boy," after all he has experienced as a soldier, rejoices my heart. He is inexpressibly dear to me and we have been very close in the mother-son relationship.

When he wrote of your receiving him in the evening, and of the lovely walk, the artist, and the tea, and later dinner with you and Miss Toklas, he said he hoped you both knew how very much it had meant to him to be with you. To quote him, "For one evening it was as though I were home again, in America." For that I thank you both, humbly and gratefully, for I know his longing for home has been very great. . . .

Thank you so much, Miss Stein, for your dear letter that tells me so very much of all the things a mother wishes to hear.

Sincerely and gratefully yours,

Jessie Breon.

Donald Sutherland had seen a good deal of action as a footsoldier and reconnaissance scout in the war in France and Germany. While waiting to be sent on to Japan, he was assigned the task of helping to compile the history of his regiment. He had seen Gertrude Stein recently in Paris, and she had given him a copy of the Petits Poèmes.

FROM DONALD SUTHERLAND

Camp Oklahoma City, France, July 16, 1945

Dear Miss Stein and Miss Toklas—

I am in a tent but my typewriter ribbon is both black and red, so I am full of a silly sense of luxury and leaving the Regimental History to settle while I write a thank you note. But I can't really tell you how much I enjoyed the time I spent with you, or how it all reassured me. Naturally I had to face the dreary realisation of how much I have, since the war, backslid from civilisation, but it was something and something very exciting, even eupeptic, to know that what I mean by civilisation is still on and not being treated as a lost cause. . . .

I am reading the Petits Poèmes little by little and liking them very much. The French translation does a funny thing to what I imagine the English must be—it restores for me the shock of verbal novelty as against normal French procedure —since it is a long time since I had the pleasure of reading your work as a contradiction to normal English. Now, since I really do not read much English any more, normal English least of all, I do get a nice reminiscent feeling of the first delighted shock I had when I was 13 or 14 and came across Tender Buttons in the Library of Congress. At any rate by this time, because I do read a good many languages without referring them to English, I read Stein as Stein just as I read Herodotus as Herodotus . . . They used to say that Herodotus was for children and philosophers, and it is true as well as snobbish to say so, and I think the same thing goes for Petits Poèmes. At least I feel the same way about it. It is the same sort of lucid steady excitement and rare enough.

So thank you very much for everything, for the talk and the reading and the wonderful food. And for all the reassurance. . . .

Love,
Donald

FROM SIR FRANCIS ROSE

Invershin Hotel, Sutherland, Scotland,
July 19, 1945

Dear Dear Gertrude,

At last I am in my own country & I love it. It is quite wonderful here, & I paint all day long, & it is like the old days in Bilignin . . . The colour here is grey green—rich, and black —very deep—and all the browns are purple & the reds have turned to pink. The sky is very pure but much covered with strange shaped clouds. It is warm & watery & it is summer in climate—not like England thank God. The only bother are the gnats.

I rather want to settle in Scotland, when I can get a home; I mean a cottage. It is after all good to be, for part of [the] year, in the place one comes from.

I have not had a word from you for months. . . . Do let me know if it will ever be possible for me to live in Paris again? . . . So much depends on my show in London—that hateful vile place: I did not think I could ever hate any place so much. I feel that some capital must be my centre & as my own battle of London is in full swing with the critics, I feel I must go on until I win or lose. Do you agree? Please give me your opinion, as five years of exile does separate one so much. I have no idea of what is happening in Paris, as everyone brings conflicting views. . . .

Bébé Berard was over here just before I left & it was a happy event to see him.

Frederica sends you both all her best wishes.

With love . . .

Francis

❧

In June, Gertrude Stein and Alice Toklas had flown with a group of G.I.'s on a tour of Germany, and Miss Stein had written up the trip for the magazine Life.

FROM MAJOR GENERAL F. H. OSBORN

Headquarters Army Service Forces, Information and Education Division, Washington 25, D. C., Aug 10, 1945

Dear Miss Stein:

I was simply delighted when I learned that you had actually made that trip into Germany in company with some of your enlisted friends. The article you wrote about it is immensely valuable; the public badly needs to be shaken up and start doing some thinking. For five years we have been fed headlines as hard to digest as dynamite. So much has been going on that we don't know anything about. It all looks too big for us to fit into our own limited view, so we have been getting into the habit of accepting orders on the big, important things and making terrific kicks about the small personal things that bother us. With any of us it needs a shock to make us think about what we are really trying to do in Germany. That's why I think your article is so valuable. It will be more widely read in LIFE than it could have been in anything else over here. Do keep on and give us some more. We need it.

    With warm personal regards to yourself and Miss Toklas, I am

Yours sincerely,
F. H. Osborn
Director

A friend from the Savoy set himself up as couturier in Paris. Gertrude Stein and Alice B. Toklas took Cecil Beaton to his show, and Miss Stein's brief article about him was published a few months later in Vogue.

FROM PIERRE BALMAIN [TRANSLATED]

44, rue François 1er, Paris, Sep 7, 1945

My dear Gertrude

    I am sending you an invitation to the first showing of my first collection . . . I am counting absolutely on you. All the French and American press and several Parisian personalities will be there—there will be photographers and it would flatter me very much if the American magazines published you at the opening of a new maison de couture. I believe Vogue or Harper's Bazaar would be interested in the short article which you so kindly spoke to me about.

    As for me, I do not sleep any more. I am already in a very nervous condition, but I have such confidence in my future that I am sure I shall make a success of this establishment . . . And you know, my dear friend, that Savoyards in general succeed in life!

Do you know any American journalists or photographers who should be invited so that they would speak of my establishment? The young designer of Liberated France!

My best and most respectful regards to you and Alice

Pierre

❧

Miss Stein was at this time writing a book about the G.I.'s and their ideas. One of her friends figured in the title, Brewsie and Willie.

FROM FRANKLIN H. BREWER

Weinheim, Germany, Sep 24, 1945

Dear Miss Stein—

I was so sorry to have had to leave Paris without seeing you and Miss Toklas once again. Not that I could have succeeded in making you know how much it meant to me to have been made so welcome, but I should like to have tried. So, you see, you were spared a great deal after all.

I arrived back in the Company in a blaze of publicity, due, as you will probably guess, to that bit in TIME coupled with the tall young lieutenant who came to your lecture. . . . He told everyone back here, of course, about meeting you through me, and when TIME came out the men quite accurately put two and two together. I have denied till I'm blue in the face that I'm the "hero" of the book, but it's no use. Rumor has even gone so far that "Willie" is supposed to be my battalion commander since his first name happens to be William. In all this palpable mangling of facts I see only one bright spot for you—every man in the Company, and many in Battalion and Regiment, is impatiently waiting to purchase the book. And that will be very good for them. . . .

Never having had immortality conferred upon me before I am uncertain as to what one should say, but I'm naturally most happy and pleased that the name my GI comrades gave me should have its place in your book about GIs and their worries. And since during the past year I've been made all too aware of mortality, I'm all the more grateful for the immortality you've given me.

I shall write Miss Toklas later to thank her again for that unforgettable chocolate ice cream.

My thanks, and kindest wishes to you both, and to Basket.

Most sincerely,
Brewsie

Bernard Faÿ was eventually tried on charges of collaboration with the Germans and sentenced to imprisonment and indignité nationale.

FROM BERNARD FAŸ

Oct 15, 1945

Dear Gertrude,

How nice of you it was to write to me such a nice letter . . .

You have sent me some very good food—some very good candy—which is the greatest luxury in jail—and you have sent me messages that are worth millions. I feel and enjoy from my cell your affection and your vitality. As soon as you can, send me some of the things you have written recently. I am terribly eager to see it. "American literature" is the great fad now all over France and particularly here. I have been talking a lot about American writers and most of all about you here with a lot of people . . . (you cannot know how much talking and discussing there is in jails and concentration camps. It's incredible. Writing is a lot more difficult, because the main trouble of being in jail is the impossibility of dismissing a caller who calls on you. Manners and customs forbid to dismiss anybody. Consequently there is always a chance of having somebody to listen—or even to talk to—but it's a

great luxury to have a day by oneself. It costs a lot of cigarets
—cigarets are the only money here.)

Nevertheless I've written a good deal—some good stuff—
some bad stuff. . . . But of course nothing of that is for
speedy publication. In my life there is no more speed now.
And after so many years of terrific speed this slow-moving
pace of life is in a way a kind of rest. But I have never been
fond of rest, and had always hoped I should not rest as long
as I lived. Rest has come in a queer way and maybe also in a
useful way. I have rested since September 44. I am resting
now. I shall rest as long as I am here, but my, as soon as I
get out of here, there won't be any more rest. I'll have to rest
from that exaggerated rest!

Now, dear friend, I send you my best, to you, to Alice
also, and I bless you.

Affectionately
Bernard.

John Breon too became a character in the G.I. book.

FROM JOHN BREON

Bremerhaven, Germany, Oct 22, 1945

Dear Miss Stein,

Back in Bremerhaven, very tired, but very happy with the
memories of Paris. I want to thank you again for all the times
and the kindness you showed to me. I hope I can return your
hospitality someday, for you gave me the most wonderful
times and the happiest, I've known since coming into the
Army.

Miss Stein, I have practically decided to take a discharge
here in Europe. While coming back on the train, I thought
and thought about all that you told me, and I know now, it
is the right thing and the wisest. There *are* government jobs
available, although I'm a little afraid of being tied down to

anything concerning the Army, as it might be just like the
Army. However I shall take one if I can be sure of being in
Paris, for, unless one can prove he has a definite job available
here, a discharge in Europe is impossible. . . . I'll shine shoes
in Paris before I'll go back to the routine of Rockford. I'm
afraid to go back now, for I'd never leave—trapped there
forever.

Oh, incidentally, by the time you get this letter, the vita-
min pills [for Bernard Faÿ] will be well on their way to you.
I wrote to my mother . . . and told her to send them to you
immediately. Hope it won't take too long. . . .

Thank you again for everything, Miss Stein. These are
times I'll never forget, that you gave to me. 'Bye for now.

Sincerely yours,
John.

*The Theater at the Biarritz American University (set up for Amer-
ican soldiers) had planned to do Gertrude Stein's play "Yes Is For
a Very Young Man," but certain liberties which they intended to
take with the text came to Miss Stein's attention and caused her
to request the return of the script.*

FROM THE BIARRITZ AMERICAN UNIVERSITY THEATER

APO 772, U. S. Army, Oct 27, 1945

SUBJECT: Cancellation of Play
To   : Gertrude Stein

1. In accordance with the telephone conversation with
Miss Toklas, the proposed production of "Yes, is for a Very
Young Man" was immediately cancelled.

2. The original script and the designs sent by M. Robina
[*i.e.* Riba-Rovira] are being returned by messenger to you.

3. The University Theater regrets that this interesting experiment could not have been concluded.

. . .

Head, University Theater

APO 562, Oct 30, 1945

Dear Miss Stein,

Mme Bille-DeMot of the Education Branch, Brussels Garrison, British Army wrote to this office to say that while in Paris she spoke to you, and learned that you have been speaking to groups of American soldiers in Paris and Germany. She suggested that the American soldiers stationed in Brussels would enjoy hearing you speak.

This letter is to tell you that there are Americans in Brussels who are desirous of attending one of your lectures, and to ask if it will be possible for you to come to Brussels to speak to them.

If you decide that you wish to make the trip to Brussels, arrangements as to transportation, and lodging will be made in cooperation with Mme Bille-DeMot.

We hope that you wish to come to Brussels, and speak to us.

Sincerely,

. . .

I–E Officer

Gertrude Stein went to Brussels and it was there that she suffered the first serious attack of intestinal trouble, which proved eventually to be cancer.

At the death of his brother, Harold Acton had returned to his father's home, the Villa La Pietra in Florence. From there he wrote about conditions in Italy.

FROM HAROLD ACTON

La Pietra, Florence, Nov 12, 1945

My dear Gertrude,

Thank you so very much for your kind letter, which I have just received. I would have written before but that I felt so depressed. . . . I came out through the R. A. F. on "compassionate leave." We are practically camping in the villa, with a minimum of everything at enormous expense. La Pietra had a remarkable escape, considering that it is surrounded by ruins, and that mines are still being removed from the poderi and the Ponte Rosso at the bottom of Via Bolognese. A few arms, legs, heads of statues have been blown off by shells, but the gardeners collected the fragments; the wine cellar was emptied (maddening to think of those soothing wines being poured down hunnish throats); several fine rugs and most of the porcelain were removed—but none of the finer objects. We have a great deal to be thankful for. The garden never looked better, and the chrysanthemums, dahlias and zinnias are in exceptional splendour. Now that I am here I dislike the thought of moving, though a certain degree of comfort must be sacrificed to beauty, and the house is extremely cold.

I am afraid I have little news of other Florentines, as I have hardly moved outside the villa except for a brief visit to Rome. Without a car at one's disposal it is not too easy to get to Settignano, to visit B. B. and others. . . . None of the English have returned; they are not encouraged to until conditions become more normal. Rome appeared far more gay, on the surface.

I gather that you live in a whirl, which I wish I could share. I look back nostalgically to my moments of escape from the Scribe-Chatham, and whenever I leave Florence I hope it will be for Paris where I left my best friends.

Best love to dear Alice and you,

Yours ever,
Harold.

⁂

Because of the uncertain nature of mail deliveries to Europe, Carl Van Vechten had been sending his letters and packages to Miss Stein in care of some member of the American armed forces, who passed them on to her.

FROM CARL VAN VECHTEN

101 Central Park West, New York,
Nov 19, 1945

Dearest Baby Woojums,

Do you realize we have no Mercury? Joe Barry writes me he is no longer in the army and that he has no address and not to write him until he gets one, but even when he gets one I can't send packages to him as he will no longer be in the army and it would be the same as sending packages to YOU. So Please get a Mercury for US right away. Dick Wright has something waiting to go to you and so has Papa Woojums. You shoulda received THREE packages of coffee and rice in one of which were dishcloths. I hope all three got through . . . I asked Bennett to let me see the ms of Brewsie and Willie and he said he was sending it to the printer as fast as possible but he would let me see the proofs, so I can't report on this. I ran into Rogers at a cocktail party and I told him all your news. . . . I've seen Virgil since he got back and he seems awfully happy that you may collaborate again and Susan B Anthony seems a swell idea. . . . The Mother of us All is a natural for a title. . . .

Don't you think it is about time you made another visit to the United States, and everybody asks, "Is Gertrude coming over?" and I always say YES, maybe in the Ides of March, and maybe I can bring it about that way. so, please answer this at once and send me the address of a Mercury where I can address packages, and write me all about the play. Love to you both from Fania and

Papa Woojums!

Joseph A. Barry had told Gertrude Stein the story of picketing for
some cause in his student days and being arrested, charged with
loitering. As Jo the Loiterer he appears in a major role in The
Mother of Us All, *the opera about Susan B. Anthony upon which*
Miss Stein and Virgil Thomson collaborated. Joe Barry sent Miss
Stein and Miss Toklas a post-card from Marseille.

FROM JOSEPH A. BARRY

[Marseille, Nov 30, 1945]

Dearest two—

Do you know Marseille? It's a dirty, vicious, exciting place.
I'll be back about this weekend.

Yours,
Joe Barry
the loiterer

A group of actors on tour with the U.S.O. production of "Kind
Lady" had called on Gertrude Stein and secured her permission to
give the world première of "Yes" at the Pasadena Community
Playhouse in California. She had agreed to make whatever changes
they found were needed.

FROM ROBERT CLABORNE AND LAMONT JOHNSON

[New York, Jan 11, 1946]

DELIGHTED WITH LAST LETTER AND ADDITIONS. NOW ONE MORE
REQUEST: DIRECTOR FEELS NEED FOR BRIEF SEQUENCE AT BEGIN-
NING OF SCENE TWO TO CLARIFY TIME LAPSE AND TO AVOID HAV-
ING TWO FERDINAND-CONSTANCE SCENES FOLLOW ONE UPON
ANOTHER. WE THOUGHT PERHAPS YOU MIGHT INSERT AN OLYMPE-
CLOTHILDE SCENE CONCERNING GERMANS DEMANDING GARDEN
KEY, POSSIBLY OPEN SCENE WITH SERVANTS THEN GERMAN ENTERS
DEMANDS KEY SERVANTS SUMMON CONSTANCE WHO DEALS WITH

HIM AS YOU DID. GERMAN GOES FERDINAND ENTERS AND PRESENT
SCENE AS WRITTEN FOLLOWS STOP PLAYHOUSE WANTS 200-WORD
FOREWORD FOR PROGRAM STOP PEOPLE MAY BE SUSPICIOUS BUT
THEY'RE MIGHTY EXCITED STOP LOVE

BOB AND MONTIE

FROM ROBERT CLABORNE

[Pasadena, California] Feb 14, 1946

Dear Miss Stein
Dear Miss Toklas,

Happy Valentine's Day to you both—how we do wish you
both were here so we could get a greeting to you before its
time was so far past! and for a lot of other reasons, too!

But really, I must say that the way *you* manage to get
changes, additions and forewords to *us* in practically no time
at all is just miracle working. . . .

We're working very hard, thank you, and do feel that we're
progressing the right way, too, we think—because Tom [*the
director*] . . . has accepted the play as a "perfectly simple,
straightforward" play about *people*! and any little tendencies
we may have to complicate things theatrically (how we *hate*
to leave out anything you told us about the 4 characters! and
how that makes for complications) are immediately slapped
in the teeth and back we go to the simple, natural attack, and
everything straightens out again. I'm glad we have a director
who loves the show as much as we do. . . .

I'm sitting on the roof of the YMCA . . . and it's just as
hot as it can be—the sky's clear as a bottle of spring water,
and the mountains look like they're just about a foot away—
but as a woman once said (I forget *exactly* where I heard it)
"I'm home-sick for the quays of Paris and a roasted chicken"
—well, I'll settle for a roasted chestnut and *one* quay—or even
an old curbstone . . . So, as much as we wish you were here,

we *certainly* understand that a little sun is a poor substitute for No. 5 [rue Christine].

Your letters are wonderful to get, so do write us again now and then—and we'll write & let you know everything that's going on . . .

Our love to you both
The four of us.

FROM VIRGIL THOMSON

222 West 23rd Street, New York,
Mar 15 [1946]

Dear Gertrude

Carl says the opera is nearly finished. I hope so. I want to see it. I pine for it. I shall be leaving here sometime between the 15th of April and the 1st of May. It would be nice if I had it before I left. A theatrical producer has offered $1000. for an option on the completed work, sight unseen. I am looking into the matter; and if it seems proper to accept, I shall write or wire for your approval. My lawyer can make the contract, since you have no agent here; and we can split his fee, which will be reasonable. I spoke to Carl about this today, who approves my procedure. I think I have an engraver for *4 Saints*.

I have a can-opener for Alice and a book for you. Write for what else I can bring you. And do send me *The Mother of Us All* if it is done. Or a couple of acts. I like to look at things a while before I start writing music to them.

Affection
Virgil

Daisy Fellowes, an old friend in London and Paris, had been the victim of a robbery.

FROM THE HON. MRS. REGINALD FELLOWES

19, rue St. James, Neuilly-sur-Seine, Paris,
Mar 28 [1946]

Dear dear Gertrude

Your nice thought has given me a great deal of pleasure.
A *little horror* has remained with me since that unpleasant
night. I don't feel quite myself and miss my usual things—
my hands feel bare and too light. You see the things that were
stolen were all part of a sentimental past that has left me long
ago, but slowly, so that I didn't notice it and now I have got
to notice it, and I feel rather sad and lonely. The people in my
past are all dead some a long time and some not and lots of
me is dead too and no one now remembers me when I was not
dead and now I have nothing left of those dead people except
the streets where they lived which very much remind me of
them. But the chauffeur knows never to pass in those streets.
Perhaps I should tell him to pass there now, but would it be all
right?

My bad memory will arrange things presently dear Gertrude and thinking of you often.

I am coming back in April. Will you dine with me on the
29th? I want to try and have a birthday dinner.

I love you very much and Alice

Yours
Daisy.

FROM VIRGIL THOMSON

[New York] Apr 15 [1946]

Dear Gertrude

The libretto is sensationally handsome and Susan B. is a
fine rôle. I am sailing on May 1. Shall be at 17 Quai Voltaire
on the 8th or 9th. I am having more copies made of [the]
libretto. Sending one to Columbia University. Douglas Moore,

their music head, is writing you to ask where you want your money sent. Arnold Weissberger is writing you about the offer of [X] . . . to pay us $2500 (the price has gone up) for first option on producing the opera after Columbia Univ., this money not to be charged against royalties. He is a high-class producer, will give us free hand in the production. The offer is most advantageous, and I hope you will agree with me that we should accept. . . .

And certainly Susan B. comes out a noble one. She is practically St. Paul when she says "let them marry." And the whole thing will be easier to dramatize than 4 *Saints* was, much easier, though the number of characters who talk to the audience about themselves, instead of addressing the other characters, is a little terrifying. Mostly it is very dramatic and very beautiful and very clear and constantly quotable and I think we shall have very little scenery but very fine clothes and they do all the time strike 19th century attitudes. Agnes de Mille will be useful for that; she is after all a granddaughter of Henry George. À bientôt and full of affection

Virgil

FROM DOUGLAS MOORE

Department of Music, Columbia University in the City of New York, Apr 25, 1946

Dear Miss Stein:

Virgil Thomson has shown me your libretto "The Mother of Us All" which he proposes to use for his commissioned opera to be performed at Columbia in May, 1947. We all like the libretto tremendously and believe that this should be a most happy collaboration. All of us appreciate the honor of the opportunity of producing the work and I write now to offer you the customary commission for the libretto. You will note that it consists of $500 for the librettist on the condition that the rights for the first production be given to the University. If you approve of this arrangement, will you please sign both copies of the agreement and return one of them to me for filing? . . .

I hope that by some miracle you may arrange to be present at the performance next year.

Yours sincerely,
Douglas Moore

An old friend who had lived for several years at nearby Senlis was now devoting himself to agricultural pursuits in Ohio.

FROM LOUIS BROMFIELD

Malabar Farm, Lucas, Ohio [Spring? 1946]
Dear Gertrude and Alice—

We loved your letter and as usual were delighted to hear the news. . . .

I'm glad you liked "Pleasant Valley" so much. It goes on selling and selling here and has even penetrated in the English version into most countries in Europe. It is also being translated everywhere. I have sent you a copy of the new book "A Few Brass Tacks" . . . which deals with economics, agriculture, philosophy, politics, etc. I think you may like some of the ideas.

The Farm is doing very well and looks lovely just now. We lead much the same life as at Senlis but on a much bigger scale in all senses. People come and stay from all over the U. S. as well as from Europe and the Far East. And Sunday we have rarely less than a couple hundred visitors—mostly farmers, schools, Four-H clubs etc to see the experiments we are carrying on in soil. It is a fascinating experience and a full life—too damned full at times. But Mary is happier than she has ever been.

I long to see old friends in Europe but rather dread seeing

Europe itself. I might come over any time on some sort of mission but have no plans. I may fly to China and India for the Department of Agriculture in the late summer. . . . In the meanwhile much love from us all.

Louis

Other friends returned to Paris.

FROM NATALIE BARNEY

74, Rue Raynouard, Paris—16,
End of May, 1946

Dear Gertrude and Alice dear,

Here I am at last, but with my sister in the 16th, instead of 20 rue Jacob in the 6th with my souvenirs—and near you! But I am near you all the same as I've "Wars I have seen." . . . My half faithful servant Berthe (her other half is occupied by dress-making) greeted me at the station (Gare de Lyon: Florence-Paris direct) with "il pleut sur le lit de Mademoiselle" —so as I'd been most comfortable in my wagon-lit I decided not to rough it until my old pavilion is put in comparative order and repaired. I long to be your 'voisine' again and resume our night-walks—and be greeted by Alice, and revisit your lovely home rue Christine in the meantime;—when shall that be? The newly arrived have very little to do, except moon about, and like the newly married reacquaint themselves with things strangely familiar, realized as in a dream. I have dreamed of getting back to our old quarter so long, that, like a somnambulist, I shall find my way to your door, and see the doves of your bedroom flutter, and the easy chairs contain us as before, and your portrait seating you above us looks down: uniting past & present to whatever future we have yet to live through—may it be in Paris—although my visa is only *via* France! . . .

"Au revoir" is a nice word, and let it be soon. Just tell

Berthe or telephone or send me a note to say when I can find
you in. And ever most attentively and appreciatively your
friend

Natalie

*Gertrude Stein, just before she died, received from Lamont John-
son a cable announcing that arrangements had been completed to
give her play a New York production. Actually this plan too fell
through, but the Johnsons and the Clabornes did realize their
hopes to have "Yes" produced in New York, if not on Broadway,
when the play was presented at the Cherry Lane Theatre in the
spring of 1949.*

FROM LAMONT JOHNSON

NEW YORK [July 24, 1946]

JUST SIGNED AGREEMENT . . . GUARANTEEING BROADWAY PRO-
DUCTION OF 'YES' . . . PRODUCTION OPENING FIRST WEEK OCTO-
BER. THIS NECESSITATES EXTENSION OF PRESENT DRAMATISTS
GUILD OPTION TO NOV 1ST TO COVER THAT PRODUCTION SCHED-
ULE. . . . NOW WE ARE SURE OF GREAT EVENT CAN YOU COME
OVER END OF SEPTEMBER TO BE HERE THRU FINAL REHEARSALS
AND OPENING? WE SO NEED AND WANT YOU AND MISS TOKLAS. CAN
ARRANGE HIGHLY LUCRATIVE RADIO APPEARANCES FOR YOU ON
EXCELLENT PROGRAMS THREE OF WHICH WOULD TOTAL UPWARDS
OF DLRS 1500 IN FEES. ANXIOUSLY AWAITING YOUR CABLED AN-
SWERS. SALVOES OF CONGRATULATIONS. WE'RE WINNING. LOVE
ALWAYS

MONTIE

*Gertrude Stein died at the American Hospital in Neuilly on July
27, 1946. Among the many letters of condolence which came to
Alice Toklas was one written from prison by a faithful friend.*

FROM BERNARD FAŸ

Aug 1, 1946

Dear Alice,

I know how much you are suffering and I want you to feel my deep and affectionate sympathy. I know what you have lost—maybe I know better than anybody else. For years and years I have so much admired and loved Gertrude, and I have enjoyed her so much, so genuinely, so thoroughly. She has been one of the few authentic experiences of my life—there are so few real human men and women—so few people really alive amongst the living ones, and so few of them are continuously alive as Gertrude was. Everything was alive in her, her soul, her mind, her heart, her senses. And that life that was in her was at the same time so spontaneous and so voluntary. It is a most shocking thing to think of her as deprived of life. I trust that God in some way, somehow has given her His Life as a reward for all the life she spread around her, for the lives she welcomed, stimulated, cared for and glorified through her genius of understanding and of describing.

During these long days I am dreaming of her. My bed is facing west. My window always open is looking over a rather wide and open country with trees and bushes and the wind which blows through the foliage gives me a deep feeling of freedom.

The memories of Culoz—1943—come back to me. What a heavenly place you were living in, and what a heavenly weather we enjoyed during those days—the last ones I was going to spend with her. T'was like New England's Indian Summer.

She is radiant and happy in my last image of her. . . .

It is a very bitter sorrow for me to think that I shall not see her any more. For the last 6 months I had kept her book "Wars" next to my bed, and was reading it very slowly "back and forth"—as I used to talk and discuss with her. And I felt as if I had been conversing with her and I could hear once in a while one of those fits of laughter which were familiar to her, and which swept away all nonsense and all sadness—all the silly ideas and the dull objections.—

Dear Alice I can still hear her voice—I shall hear it as long as I live. May I see you soon. Anyhow most faithfully and affectionately yours,

Bernard.

INDEX

[Page references to an individual's letters are in bold face]

Abdy, Sir Robert, 280, 313
Abdy, Lady, 312
Acton, Arthur, 62, 186
Acton, Harold, ix, 186, 217, **218–219**, 391, 392
Addis, Emmett, 228
Aldrich, Mildred, ix, 51, **59–60**, **77–78**, 82, 83, 99, 101–102, 103, 109, 126, 129, 139, 148, 167, 168–169, 176, 181, 214–215, 263
Algonquin Hotel, New York, 301, 324
Alsop, Joseph W., Jr., ix, **298–299**
Altman, Benjamin, 88
America and Alfred Stieglitz, 288, 289
American Express Co., Paris, 125–126
American Fund for French Wounded, 113, 117, **119–120**, 150
American Hospital, Neuilly, 401
American Mercury, The, 160
Americanism, 22, 30, 41, 144, 145, 153, 154, 157, 291, 292, 305–306, 307, 348, 374
Amherst College, 273
Anderson, Robert, 227
Anderson, Sherwood, ix, **138–139**, **142–143**, **144–145**, 150, **152–153**, **155–156**, 158, 178, 179, 191–192, 201, 211–212, 226–227, 281, 297, 353–354
Anderson, Mrs. Sherwood, ix, **201**, 353, 354
Anthony, Susan B., 393. *See also under* Stein, Gertrude, her writings: *The Mother of Us All*
Apollinaire, Guillaume, 79, 80, 111, 175
Appleton-Century-Crofts, xii
Arensberg, Walter, 137
Argonaut, The, 126, 127
Armory Show (1913), 70–72, **74**

Arts Club of Chicago, 303, 326
As Stable, 190–191
Ashton, Frederick, 272, 275, 278, 320
Asquith, Lord, 339
Aswell, Edward C., ix, **261–262**
Atherton, Gertrude, ix, 296
Atlantic Monthly, The, 129, 130–131, 210–211, 255, 256, 260–261, **261–262**, 267, 270–271, 324, 333, 352, 353
"Auntie," 117, 121–122, 126
Aurel, Mme., 200–201
Austin, A. Everett, Jr., 274

Babb, James T., xii
Bachrach family, 14
Balmain, Pierre, ix, **386–387**
Balston, T., 194, **195**
Banks, Richard, 346
Bara, Theda, 335
Barker, Dr. Lewellys F., ix, 22, **24**
Barker, Mrs. Lewellys F., ix
Barlow, Samuel L. M., ix, 128, **173**
Barnes, Dr. Albert C., 252
Barnes Foundation, Merion, Ohio, 34
Barney, Natalie C., ix, 163, **200–201**, 347, 354, 400–401
Baron, M. & Mme. François, x
Barr, Alfred H., Jr., ix, 339, **340**
Barretts of Wimpole Street, The, 373
Barry, Joseph A., ix, 393, **394**
Basket I, 240, 314, 331, 332, 333
Basket II, 344
Batsford, B. T., Ltd., ix, **330–331**, 337, 338, 345
Beach, Sylvia, ix, **138–139**, 183
Beaton, Cecil, ix, **368**, 386
Becker, Charlotte, 72
Beebe, William, 345
Beerbohm, Sir Max, 339
Beethoven, Ludwig van, 361

Beffa, 110, 125, 126
Bell, Clive, 218
Bell, Mrs. Harmon C., ix
Bellevallée, Fernande. *See* Olivier, Fernande
Belmonte, Juan, 316–317
Bender, Albert, 37
Bennett, Arnold, 47
Bérard, Christian, 205, 221, 222, 231, 232, **233**, 234, 385
Berenson, Bernard, ix, 18, 19, 25, 54–55, 62, 66–67, 81, 354, 392
Berenson, Mrs. Bernard, 22, 25, 62 81
Berger, Norma, x
Bergson, Henri, 140
Berlitz School, 81
Berman, Eugène, ix, 205, 237, **238**, 247
Berner, Mr. & Mrs. Pincus, xii
Berners, Lord, ix, 225, 311, **312**, **313**, **320**, **321**, 325, 329, **330**, **332**, 346
Bernhardt, Sarah, 116, 292
Bernheim, Jeune & Cie., Paris, 63, 85
Biarritz American University Theater, 390
Bible, The, 154, 189
Bibliothèque Nationale, Paris, 356
Bieville, Comte de, 313
Bille-De Mot, E., 391
Bing & Hoyashi, 91
Bird, William, 190
Black family, 27
Blood, Florence, ix, **49**, 62–63, 79–81, 109–110
Bloomsbury Group, 94
Blues, 230, 257
Bobbs-Merrill Co., xii
Bodley Head, The, xi, **134–135**, 203–204
Boni, C. & A., 188–189
Boni & Liveright, 170–171, 178, 179
Bossuet, J. B., 271
Boston Browning Club, 6
Boucher, François, 48
Bowles, Paul Frederic, ix, **251**, 252 253, **276–277**
Bradley, Florence, 60–62
Bradley, W. A., ix, 258, 259, 260, 261–262, 280–281
Bradley, Mrs. W. A., ix

Brancusi, Constantin, 335
Braque, Georges, 111, 279
Brausen, Erica, x
Breeskin, Adelyn D., xii
Brenner, Michael, ix, 104, **105**, 111–112, 112–113
Breon, Jessie, ix, **382–383**
Breon, John, ix, **375–376**, 382–383 389–390
Breton, André, 180
Breughel, Pieter, 304
Brewer, Franklin, ix, **387–388**
Brewer, Joseph, ix, **199**, **216–217**
British Music Society, 253
Bromfield, Louis, ix, **249–250**, **399–**400
Bromfield, Mrs. Louis, 399
Brooks, Romaine G., 200
Brooks, Van Wyck, 153
Broom, 142, 146–147
Brown, Al, 250
Brown, Edmund R., **143–144**, 150
Brown, Matilda E., ix, **11–12**, **263**
Browning, Robert, 6, 121
Brustlein, Janice Biala, x
Bry, Doris, xi
Bryan, William Jennings, 292
Bryher, Winifred, ix, **161–162**, 208, **209–210**
Bryn Mawr College, 132
Bull fighting, 94, 316–317
Burke, Claire Marie, 95
Burnett, Frances (Hodgson), 214
Burnett, Vivian, 214
Buss, Kate, ix, 142, 143, **149–150**, 180, **246–247**, 253, 254, 352
Buss, Mr. & Mrs. Walter H., ix
Butcher, Fanny, 282, 361
Bynner, Witter, 228

Caesar, Julius, 273
Caffery, Jefferson, ix, **375**
Calder, Alexander, ix, **256**, 360
Cambridge University, 184–185, 186 197–198
Cambridge University Press, xii, 140
Camera Work, 57, 64, 66, 67–69, 93, 186
Cape, Jonathan, 258
Carlock, 65
Case, Frank, ix, **301**

Cassa-Miranda family, 48
Cather, Willa, 182
Century Magazine, The, 149
Cerf, Bennett, ix, 262, 283–284, 290, 293, 324, 330–331, 344–345, 349, 350–351, 372, 376, 377, 393
Cézanne, Paul, 28, 62–63, 85, 86, 91, 106, 112–113, 125–126, 164, 210, 335
Chanor Base Section, 391
Chapman, Mrs. Gilbert W. (formerly Mrs. Charles Goodspeed), x, 282–283, 325–326, 335, 361–362
Charles IV, of Spain, 59
Chase, William M., 93–94
Chavez, Carlos, 253
Cherry Lane Theatre, New York, 346, 401
Chicago, University of, 14, 171, 310
Chincho, 91
Choate Literary Magazine, The, 295
Choate School, 294–295
Christine, 5 rue, 325, 370–371, 374, 396, 400
Citkowitz, Israel, 253
Claborne, Robert, x, 394–396, 401
Claborne, Mrs. Robert, x, 394–396, 401
Claire Marie, 95–96
Clark, Harriet F. See Hanley, Harriet (Clark)
Clark, Sir Kenneth, ix, 334
Clermont-Ferrand, University of, 193
Clermont-Tonnerre, Duchesse de, 272–273
Close Up, 208–210
Coady, R. J., 104, 105, 112–113
Coates, Robert M., ix, 175, 176, 241–242, 248–249, 254
Coburn, Alvin Langdon, ix, 78, 82, 97, 98, 194
Cocteau, Jean, ix, 138, 285
Colefax, Lady, 321, 336–337, 338–339
Colette, 200–201
Collier's, 59, 373, 376
Collins, J. P., 98
Colt, Mrs. J. Edith, ix
Colt, LeBaron C., ix
Columbia Law School, 13
Columbia University, 283, 397–399

Cone, Dr. Claribel, ix–x, 45, 93–94, 176
Cone, Etta, ix–x, 30, 45, 46, 93, 176, 191
Confluences, 362, 363–364, 366
Congress, Library of, 384
Constable and Co., Ltd., ix
Contact, 141
Contact Collection of Contemporary Writers, 161–162
Contact Editions, 170, 190, 268
Cook, John, 265
Cook, Mary, 265
Cook, Mrs. Robert, x
Cook, William, x, 126, 127, 145–146, 216, 238, 239, 316–317, 319–320
Cook, Mrs. William, 126, 127, 238, 239, 317, 319–320
Copeau, Jacques, 94, 123–124
Copeland, Herbert, 214
Copeland & Day, 214
Copland, Aaron, x, 252, 253
Cornell, Katharine, x, 266, 373, 381
Corot, J. B. C., 313
Cory, Daniel, xi
Cosmopolitan, 293
Covarrubias, Miguel, 207–208
Coward-McCann, xii
Craig, Gordon, 124
Crane, Hart, x, 227, 236
Crane, Mrs. W. Murray, 361
Crédit Lyonnais, 125
Crevel, René, 193, 197–198, 199, 217, 219, 237
Criterion, The, 161, 164, 165–166, 172–173, 185, 194
Crown Publishers, xi
Crowninshield, Frank, 123, 160
Cruttwell, Cecilia M., x
Cruttwell, Maud, x, 107
Curonia, Villa, Florence, 51, 53, 60–62, 65, 79
Czernin, Graf, 304

D., H. See Doolittle, Hilda
d'Aiguy, Baroness, 358, 362
Dali, Salvador, 313, 335
Daniel & Cruttwell, xii
Daniel-Rops, Henri, x, 358
Dartmouth College, 288
Dastarac, Marc, 364

Daumier, Honoré, 63
Davidson, Jo, 60–62, 74, 148, **149**, 157, 159, 160
Davidson, Mrs. Jo, x
Davidson, Yvonne, 60–62, 148–149
Davies, Arthur B., 71, 85
Davis, Stuart, x, 230, **231**, **232–233**
Dawson, Emily F., **47**
Day, Fred Holland, 214–215
Delacroix, Eugène, 28
Delarue-Mardrus, Lucie, 200–201
Delaunay, Robert, 77
de Mille, Agnes, 398
Demuth, Charles, 106
Dent, J. M., & Sons, Ltd., xii
Derain, André, 111
Dewey, John, x, 253, **254**
Dewey, Mrs. John, x
Diaghilew, Sergei P., 219
Dial, The, 144, 189, 196, 226
Diamand, Mrs. A. P., x
Dickens, Charles, 122
Dodge, Edwin, 51, 54, 62, 63, 66
Dodge, Mabel. *See* Luhan, Mabel Dodge
Doolittle, Hilda, 208–209, 230
Dostoevski, F. M., 162
Doucet, 111
Draper, Muriel, 62, 65, 228
Draper, Paul, 62
Draper, Ruth, 71
Dreier, Katherine S., x, 129, **130**
Dreier, Mary E., x
Dreiser, Theodore, 153
Dubois, 74
Duchamp, Marcel, x, 116, 129, 130, 137, 151, 361, 374
Duckworth, Gerald, & Co., Ltd., x, 82, **194**, **195**
Dudensing, 335
Dudley, Katherine, x, 369, **370–371**
Duffield, Pitts, x, 32, **33–34**
Duffield, Mrs. Pitts, x
Duffield & Co., **33–34**
Duncan, Isadora, 116
Durand-Ruel, 28

Eakins, Thomas, 335
Edgerly-Korzybska, Mira. *See* Korzybska, Lady
Edinburgh, University of, 19
Edward VII, of England, 60

Einstein, Albert, 342–343
Einstein, William, xii
Eliot, T. S., x, 161, 164, **172–173**, 185, 194
Elliott, Major. *See* Eliot, T. S.
Eluard, Paul, 235
Emmerich, F. J., 212
English Review, The, 73
Epstein, Jacob, 115
Erving, Dr. Emma (Lootz), 23, 24, **25–26**, 28, 29, **41–42**, 46
Erving, Dr. William, 25, 41
Escholier, Raymond, **366–367**
Eulalia, Infanta of Spain, 47–48
Evans, Donald, **95–96**, 97
Everitt, Charles P., 271
Ewing, Doris I., x
Ewing, Max, x, 228, **269**
Ex Libris, 178, 179

Fabbri, Egisto, 62–63
Farmer, Dorothy, xi
Faÿ, Bernard, x, 193, **235–237**, 243, 244, **258–259**, 267, 287, **291–292**, 351, **356–357**, 363, 365, **388–389**, 390, 401, **402–403**
Fellowes, Hon. Mrs. Reginald, x, 330, 396, **397**
Ferren, 371
Fifield, Arthur C., **58**
Finnie, 11
Firbank, Ronald, 151
First and Merchants National Bank of Richmond, Va., xii
Fiske, Mrs., 59
Fitts, Dudley, x, **295**
Fitzgerald, Frances. *See* Lanahan, Mrs. Samuel J.
Fitzgerald, F. Scott, x, 174, 198, 257, 294, 324, 353–354, 359–360
Fitzgerald, Zelda, 198, 294, 359
Flanner, Janet, x, 343, **344**
Fléchère, Charles de la, **364–365**
Flechtheim, Alfred, 175
Fletcher, Constance, x, 53, 62, 68–69, 75
Fleurus, 27 rue de, 25, 28, 48–49, 85, 86, 88, 90, 99, 152–153, 158, 227, 268, 271, 306, 355, 357
Foote, Mary, 60–62
Ford, Charles Henri, x, 230, **257–258**

Ford, Ford Madox, x, 158, 159, 162, 163–164, 165–166, 167, 226
Four Seas Co., Boston, 143–144, 145, 150
Francis, Saint, of Assisi, 195
Frank, Waldo, 147
Freud, Anna, 307
Freud, Sigmund, 306–307, 310
Friedman, Dr. Leo V., x, 10
Friend, Krebs, 163–164, 165–166, 167
Friend, Mrs. Krebs, 167
Fry, Charles, ix, 338, 345
Fry, Roger, x, 75, 76, 78, 82, 94, 134
Fuerstenberg, Eugenia M., xi
Furman, Lee, 241–242

Gallimard, Librairie, xii
Galsworthy, John, 47
Gamberaia, Villa, Florence, 49, 79
Gans, Howard, x, 113–114, 117–118, 191
Gans, Mrs. Howard, 74, 113–114
Gans, Marion S., x
Garbo, Greta, 269, 349
Gautier, Théophile, 59
George, Henry, 398
Gershwin, George, 374
Gestapo, 370–371
Gibb, Harry Phelan, x, 92, 114–115, 132–133, 143, 178, 182–183
Gibb, Mrs. Harry Phelan, x, 183
Gide, André, 235
Gish, Lillian, 349
Glasgow, Ellen, x, 299
"Godiva," 147, 149, 237
Gogarty, Dr. Oliver St. John, x, 92–93
Gollancz, V., 258
Goodspeed, Mrs. Charles. See Chapman, Mrs. Gilbert W.
Gorer, Geoffrey, x, 197, 198–199
Gourmont, R. de, 200
Goya y Lucientes, Francisco de, 59
Grafton Press, 42–43, 43–44, 142
Grant, Duncan, x, 94, 95
Grant, Gen. U. S. 297, 321–322
Graves, Robert, 227
Greco, El, 275
Gregory, Alyse, x, 226

Grillparzer, F., 304
Gris, Georges, 201, 202
Gris, Josette, x, 201, 202
Gris, Juan, x, 104, 111, 114, 147–148, 161, 172, 175, 176, 177–178, 201, 202, 206–207, 213
Ground Forces Replacement Center, 382
Guevara, Alvaro, 205

Haas, Robert Bartlett, x, 348–349, 377
Hammett, Dashiell, 313
Hanley, Harriet (Clark), ix, 25, 29, 30, 38, 67, 131
Hapgood, Charles H., x
Hapgood, Hutchins, x, 30, 31–32, 48–49, 59, 74, 79, 89, 97, 182
Hapgood, Mrs. Hutchins, x, 30, 43–44, 59, 182
Harcourt, Alfred, x, 261, 277, 288, 312–313
Harcourt, Brace & Co., xii, 260, 270, 310
Harper & Brothers, 326
Harper's Bazaar, 361, 386
Harper's Magazine, 255
Harriman, Margaret (Case), ix
Harriman, Marie, 246
Harrison, Austin, 73
Hart, Moss, 344–345
Hartley, Marsden, x, 64–65, 70, 84–86, 87–88, 89–90, 106, 141, 143, 162, 183, 242, 335
Harunobu, 91
Harvard Medical School, 12
Harvard Psychological Laboratory, 3, 10–11
Harvard Psychological Review, The. See Psychological Review, The
Harvard University, 3, 6, 9, 10–11, 13, 17, 19, 50, 265, 287
Havemeyer, Mrs. H. O., 85
Haweis, Mrs. Stephen. See Loy, Mina
Hayden, Charles H., 38
Heap, Jane, x, 152, 153, 161, 164, 170–171, 188–189
Heber-Percy, Robert, ix
Helmholtz, H. L. F. von, 4
Hemingway, Ernest, x, 142–143, 145, 158, 159, 160, 162, 163–164,

Hemingway, Ernest (*continued*)
164–165, 166–167, 170, 173–174,
178, 179, 191, 328, 332, 343, 353,
360
Hemingway, Mrs. Ernest, 142–143
Hennessey, Joseph, xii
Herald, Paris, The, 347
Herald-Tribune, New York, The,
249, 298–299
Hermitage House, Inc., x
Herodotus, 384
Hessel, 63
Heyward, DuBose, x, 298
Heyward, Mrs. DuBose, x
Hitchcock, F. H., 42–43, 43–44
Hitler, Adolf, 348
Hodges, Dr. Fletcher, x
Hogarth Press, 193
Holly, Flora M., 34, 38–39
Holt, Nora, x, 196, 197
Hoover, Herbert, 292
Hopwood, Avery, 108, 151–152,
154, 156, 195, 207, 296
Horner, Lady, 339
Houghton Mifflin Co., xii
Hound & Horn, The, 269–270
Hoyt, Charles, 333
Hubbell, Lindley Williams, x, 229,
254–255, 355–356
Huebsch, B. W., 171, 179
Hugnet, Georges, x, 228, 231–232,
234, 235, 243, 244–245, 247
Hutchinson & Co., Ltd., xii

Ibsen, Henrik, 325
Ignatius, Saint, of Loyola, 225
Imbs, Bravig, x, 201, 212–213, 230,
234–235, 247–248, 347–348, 369
Imes, Nella (Larsen), xi, 215, 216
Irish Statesman, The, 189
Irwin, Will, 59

Jackson, William A., xii
Jacob, Max, x, 337
Jaffa, Dr. Adele, xi
Jaffa, Aileen R., xi
James, David, xii
James, Henry, 46, 97, 98, 269–270,
297, 338
James, William, x, 7, 9, 13, 18, 19–
20, 50–51
James, Mrs. William, 20, 50

Jeffers, Mrs. Robinson, 296
John, Augustus, 343
Johns Hopkins Medical School, 8, 12,
14, 15, 16, 17, 18, 20, 22–24
Johnson, Lamont, x, 394–395, 401
Johnson, Mrs. Lamont, x, 394–396,
401
Jolas, Eugene, 230
Jones, Howard Mumford, ix
Josephson, Matthew, 147
Josephson, Mrs. Matthew, xii
Joyce, James, 92, 154, 159, 162, 188,
253, 255, 323

Kahnweiler, D.–H., x, xi, 86–87, 89,
104, 105, 159, 161, 175, 177–178,
201, 206–207, 213, 250, 303
Kandinsky, Wassily, 77
Kauffer, E. McKnight, 217
Kaufman, George, 344–345
Keats, John, 214
Kennerley, M., 72
Kepner, Arch P., 284
Kiddie, The. *See* Rogers, W. G.
Kind Lady, 394
King, Georgiana G., 132
Kipling, R., 65
Kirstein, Lincoln, x, 269–270, 286
Klopfer, Donald, 290
Knoblauch, Mrs. Charles, 42, 43–
44, 56, 57, 67, 130, 141, 153
Knopf, Alfred, xii, 151, 153–154,
157–158, 160, 161, 172
Knopf, Blanche, 172
Kochno, Boris, 234
Kohn, Estelle (Rumbold), x, 25, 27,
28, 29, 30
Kohn, Robert, 27, 28, 29, 30,
Korzybska, Lady, x, 139, 140
Korzybski, Count Alfred, x, 139,
140–141
Krause, Louise Antoinette, 348
Kreymborg, Alfred, x, 142
Kuninaga, 91

Lachman, Dr. Arthur, xi, 17
Lafayette, Marquis de, 365
Lambert, Constant, 320
Lanahan, Mrs. Samuel J., x, 359
Lane, John, xi, 76, 134–135, 203–
204
Lang, Cecil, xii

Larsen, Nella. *See* Imes, Nella (Larsen)
Lascaux, Élie, xi, 177, 213, 250, 303
Lathrop, Isabel, 113, 119
Laughlin, James, xi, 287, 301, 302
Laurencin, Marie, 133, 134, 175, 176, 177, 336
League of Composers, New York, 276–277
Lebender, Lena, 15, 33, 39, 46
Le Corbusier, 216
Lefebvre-Foinet, 282
Léger, Fernand, 111, 361
Legion of Honor, 148
Leglaye, Abel, 120, 124, 127–128
Leglaye, Lucie, 120
Leigh Emmerich Lecture Bureaus, Inc., 212
Leigh, W. Colston, 281
Leiris, Michel, xi, 250–251
Lemaître, Jules, 121
Le Nain brothers, 378
Levy, Hal, 349
Levy, Harriet, 59
Levy, Julien, 286
Lewis, Lloyd, xi, 297, 317–318, 321–322
Lewis, Mrs. Lloyd, xi, 318, 322
Lewis, Wyndham, 115
Liberty Loan, 118
Lifar, Serge, 313
Life, 385–386
Lin Yutang, 336
Lindbergh, Anne, 335
Lipchitz, Jacques, xi, 137, 138, 329
Literary Digest, The, 122
Little, Brown & Co., ix
Little Review, The, 152, 161
Little Review Gallery, The, 170–171
Liveright, H., 160–161, 258
Loeb, Harold, xi, 142, 146–147
Loeb, Pierre, 224
Loeser, Charles, 54–55, 62–63
London Mercury, The, 169
Longhi, Pietro, 69
Longmans, Green & Co., xii
Lootz, Emma. *See* Erving, Dr. Emma (Lootz)
Louis, Saint, 273
Loveman, Samuel, xii
Lowell, J. R., 3, 4
Loy, Mina, 65, 171

Luce, Clare (Boothe), xi, 341–343
Luce, Henry, 341–343
Luhan, Antonio, 153
Luhan, Mabel Dodge, xi, 51, 52, 53, 54–55, 59, 60–62, 63, 65–66, 70–72, 74, 79, 89, 90, 95, 96–97, 151, 152, 153, 156, 157, 160, 181–182, 228, 296, 312–313
Lynes, Carlos, Jr., xii
Lynes, George Platt, xi, 190–191, 217, 220, 243–244

McAlmon, R., xi, 141, 161, 162, 170, 188, 189–190, 208, 267
Macaulay's, 241–242
McBride, Henry, xi, 78, 82–83, 123–124, 137, 143, 229, 252, 270–271, 277–279
McCarthy, Desmond, 218–219
McCausland, Elizabeth, xii
McClintic, Guthrie, 373
McClure's, 39, 42
MacDonald, Ramsay, 236
MacKay, Frances W., xii
MacLeish, Archibald, 198
Macmillan Co., xii
Macpherson, Kenneth, xi, 208–209
Macy, Gertrude, x
Mahogany Tree, The, 214–215
Mall, Dr. Franklin, 22, 24
Malraux, André, 327
Man Ray, xi, 149, 180
Manet, Edouard, 27, 63, 125
Mann, Thomas, 324
Maratier, G., 232, 369
Marie, Queen of Rumania, 292
Marin, John, 85
Marinoff, Fania, xi, 97, 106, 108, 116–117, 154, 172, 197, 207–208, 350, 372, 381, 393
Marne, Battle of the, 103
Marriage, 8, 14, 23–24
Mars, Miss, 268–269
Martin Secker & Warburg, Ltd., xii
Maryland Trust Co., Baltimore, ix
Massine, Léonide, 325
Masson, André, 176, 177, 360
Masson, Odette, 177
Matisse, Henri, xi, 36, 37, 40–41, 48, 50, 57, 58, 66, 67–68, 78, 81, 82, 84, 86, 93–94, 106, 180, 186, 252, 262, 271, 310–311

Matisse, Mme. Henri, 36
Matisse, Pierre, xi
Maugham, Somerset, 343, 361
Maurer, Alfred M., xi, 158
Maurois, André, 343
Maxwell, Elsa, 321
Mayor, A. Hyatt, 286
Medici family, 218
Mei Lang Fang, 278
Meller, Rachel, 154
Methuen & Co., Ltd., 76
Metropolitan Opera House, 215
Meyer, Albert, 37
Mikado, The, 339
Miller, Glen, 381
Miller, Henry, xi, 302
Miller, Townsend, xii
Miró, Joan, 335
Modern Library, The, 262, 293, 377
Moeller, Philip, 229
Molière, 124
Montagne, Éditions de la, 231
Monticelli, Adolphe, 48
Montross Galleries, The, 106
Moody, William Vaughn, 3
Moore, Douglas, xi, 397, 398–399
Moore, Marianne, xi, 141, 196
Morand, Paul, 343
Morgan, Harjes & Cie., Paris, 169, 293
Morgan, J. P., 88
Morosov, I. A., 86
Mortimer, Raymond, 218
Moscow, Museum of Modern Western Art, 86
Moses, Jacob, 33
Moses, Mrs. Jacob, 33, 39
Münsterberg, Hugo, xi, 3, 4, 15
Munson, Gorham B., 286
Munsterberg, Ella, xi
Munsterberg, Margaret, xi
Museum of Modern Art, New York, 110, 335, 339, 340, 372
Mutts, R. J., 116

Napier, Mrs., 65
Nation, The, London, 83
National Gallery, London, 21, 28, 334
Negrin, Gen., 335
Neish, Howell & Haldane, xi

New Criterion, The. See Criterion, The
New Republic, The, 150
New York Mornings, 106
New Yorker, The, 241, 254, 343
Nietzsche, F. W., 174
Nijinsky, V., 374
Norman, Dorothy, xi, 288, 289
Norton, Allen, 95, 96, 107
Nouvelle Révue Française, La, 235

Oakland High School, 11, 263
"Ode," 219–222, 223–224
Odets, Clifford, 343
Office of War Information, 369
O'Keeffe, Georgia, xi
Olivier, Fernande, 34, 36, 41, 110, 175
Omega Workshops, 75, 76, 94
O'Neill, Eugene, 343
Oppenheimer, Adele, 4
Orangerie, Paris, 313
Oregon, University of, 17
Osborn, Gen. F. H., xi, 385–386
Oxford Fortnightly, The, 75
Oxford University, 50, 75, 185, 186, 311, 312
Oxford University Press, xii

Pagany, 244
Pall Mall Gazette, The, 98
Palmer, Frank, 73
Paris, Bombardment of, 125–126
Pasadena Community Playhouse, 394–396
Pascin, Jules, 123
Patch, Gen. A. M., xi, 367
Patch, Mrs. A. M., xi
Paul, Elliot, 201, 204–205, 230, 232
Payson & Clarke, Ltd., 199
Péguy, Charles, 50
Perlman, Philip B., ix
Perry, Ralph Barton, xii
Pétain, H. P., 356–357
Phidias, 115
Philadelphia Symphony Orchestra, 372
Photo-Secession, 56, 57, 64
Picabia, Francis, xi, 72, 74, 106, 263, 264, 359, 377
Picabia, Olga, xi, 263–264, 359
Picasso, Eva, 110

Picasso, Fernande. *See* Olivier, Fernande

Picasso, Pablo, xi, 34, **35–36, 41,** 48, 57, 64, 66, 67–68, 72, 76, 79, 80, 86–87, 89, 91–92, 94, 106, **110–111,** 112, 133, 157, 159, 172, 175, 186, 213, 228, 232, 246, 252, 279, 327–329, 335, 338, 339, 340, 358, 367, 369, 370–371, 400

Plain Edition, The, 246–247, 248–249, 254–255, 283–284, 310

Plato, 236

Plowshare, The, 281–282

Polk, Willis, 83

Pollak, Francis D., xi, **13**

Pollak, Mrs. Francis D., xi

Pound, Ezra, 158, 162, 165, 230

Poussin, Nicolas, 271

Powys, Llewelyn, 226

Princeton University, 6, 284

Prints, Japanese, 27, 91

Proust, Marcel, 154, 214

Psychological Review, The, 10–11, 15–16

Quello, Major, 367

Quinn, John, 158, 159

Radcliffe College, 3, 4, 6–8, 9, 18

Radcliffe Philosophy Club, 6–7

Raffel, Bertha (Stein), 3, 12, 39, 202, 265

Raffel, Daniel, xi, 202, **203**

Random House, Inc., xii, 293, 330, 344, 373. *See also under* Cerf, Bennett

Ray, Man. *See* Man Ray

Reconnaissance Française, Médaille de la, 150

Red Cross, 119–120, 371

Redon, Odilon, 357

Reinhardt, Max, 333

Rembrandt van Rijn, 88

Renoir, P. A., 28, 45, 63, 86, 91

Reviewer, The, 157, 159, 160

Reynolds, Paul R., & Son, x

Riba-Rovira, 381, 390

Richards, Grant, xi, **53–54,** 151

Richards, Mrs. Grant, xi, 53

Richards, J. M., xii

Richardson, Dorothy, 154

Rideout, Walter, ix, xii

Riding, Laura, 227

Rinehart, Mary Roberts, 151–152

Rivera, Diego, 113

Robeson, Mr. & Mrs. Paul, 179, 183

Robinson, Mrs. Bestor, xii

Robinson, E. A., 96–97

Roché, H.–P., xi, 34, **40, 55–56,** 129, 130, **133, 134**

Rönnebeck, Arnold, xi, 64, **77,** 84–85, 88–89, 90, 182, 355

Rogers, W. G., xi, **121–122, 273–274,** 280–281, 324, **352–353, 357,** 360–361, 381, 393

Rogers, Mrs. W. G., **352–353, 357,** 360–361

Rogue, 95, 107, 108

Romeike, 47, 48

Ronnebeck, Mrs. Arnold, xi

Roosevelt, F. D., 317–318, 343, 348, 380

Rootham, Helen, 185, 206

Rose, Sir Francis, xi, **260, 274–275,** 279–280, 282–283, **300–301, 308,** 314–316, 334, 338, 345, 369, 370, 371–372, 375, 377, **378–379, 384–385**

Rose, Lady, 378–379, 385

Roseboro', Viola, 39, 42

Rosenbach, A. S. W., 188, 189

Rosenberg, Paul, 111, 279

Rosenfeld, Paul, 144, 153

Rosson, John B., xii

Rothenstein, William, 249

Rothermere, Lady, 161, **164,** 172

Roussel, Raymond, 250

Royal Air Force, 371, 378, 392

Royce, Josiah, xi, **6–7**

Royce, Stephen, xi

Rubens, Peter Paul, 21

Rumbold, Estelle. *See* Kohn, Estelle (Rumbold)

Russell, Bertrand, 25

Russell, Mrs. George S., ix

Russell, John, xi

Ryder, A. P., 335

Sadlers Wells, London, 320, 323

Safe Deposit and Trust Co. of Baltimore, ix–x

St. Gaudens, Homer, 285–286

St. John, Mrs. George C., 295

Samuels, Oscar, xi

Sanborn, Alvin F., 42–43
San Francisco Fair, 83
Santayana, George, xi, 6, 7, 67
Sarkar, Benoy Kumar, 140
Saroyan, William, xi, 290–291, 343
Satie, Erik, 133–134
Saturday Evening Post, The, 83, 118, 353
Savery, Roelandt, 332
Sawyer, Julian, xi, 286–287
Schilling, Alexander, 27
Schuchardt, Charlotte, x
Schukin, S. I., 86
Scott, Sir Walter, 59
Scott, William R., 331
Scribner, C. A., 174, 338
Scribner's, 330–331, 337, 338, 345, 349
Scribner's Magazine, 255
Scudder, Janet, 77, 167, 168, 285–286, 328–329
Sebree, Charles, 311
Sedgwick, Ellery, xi, 129, 130–131, 210–211, 256, 260–262
Seizin Press, 227
Sessions, Roger, 253
Sevareid, Eric, 371
Shadowland, 180
Shakespeare, W., 121, 266, 333
Shakespeare and Co., 138
Shaw, G. B., 47, 266, 281, 343
Sheed & Ward, 286
Shelley, P. B., 214
Simonson, Lee, 65
Sitwell, Dr. Edith, xi, 184–185, 186, 193, 205–206, 218, 220, 224
Sitwell, Sir Osbert, xi, 193, 206, 218, 224, 323
Sitwell, Sacheverell, 193, 206, 218
Smallens, Alexander, 332, 356
Smith, Alfred E., 292
Smith, Logan Pearsall, xi, 75, 135
Snyder, Margaret Sterling, 7–8, 16
Société Anonyme, 129
Soil, The, 113
Solomon, Joseph, xi
Solomons, Leon, xi, 3, 4, 10–11, 12, 15–16, 17, 18, 19–20
Spanish Civil War, 319–320
Squire, Sir J. C., 169
Squire, Maud Hunt, xi, 268–269
Stackpole Sons, 322

Stage Door Canteen, New York, 372
Star, Toronto, The, 158
Stearns, Harold, 160
Steichen, Edward, 85
Stein, Allan D., 12, 14, 17, 18, 39
Stein, Bertha. See Raffel, Bertha (Stein)
Stein, Fred, 5
STEIN, GERTRUDE:
  her art collection, 27, 28, 34, 36, 37, 38, 47–48, 63, 64, 78, 82, 84, 86–87, 91–92, 94, 106–107, 125–126, 130, 175, 176, 177, 186, 228, 232–233, 237, 246, 260, 263, 264, 279–280, 282–283, 294, 303, 306, 316, 327–329, 334, 339, 340, 352, 367, 369, 370–371, 400;
  her attempts to get her writings published, 33–34, 38–39, 42–49, 58, 82, 105–106, 129, 130–131, 137, 141, 143–144, 153–154, 157–158, 159, 160–161, 162, 169–171, 172–173, 182–183, 184–185, 188–190, 194–195, 241–242, 246–247;
  her conversation, 21, 53, 55, 182, 223, 266, 267, 294, 317, 402–403;
  her early life: in California, 3, 264–266; at Radcliffe, 3, 6–13; at Johns Hopkins Medical School, 14–17, 20–24, 223; in Paris, 25–401 passim;
  her influence, 52, 72, 74, 133, 137, 138, 151–152, 156, 162, 165, 174, 178, 182–183, 184–185, 192, 196, 212, 218, 223, 227, 230, 232–233, 238, 242, 244, 249, 255, 257–258, 264, 281, 291–292, 294, 295, 302, 322–323, 326, 327–328, 385–386;
  her lectures: in England, 184–186, 193–194; in America, 212–213, 280–281, 283–299; to Army groups, 382, 387, 391;
  her method of writing: 15–16, 24, 31–32, 40, 42–44, 55–56, 136, 141, 350;
  her writings (alphabetically): "Accents in Alsace," 205; An Acquaintance with Description,

Stein, Gertrude (*continued*)
227, 235; *Américains d'Amérique*, 267; *The Autobiography of Alice B. Toklas*, xii, 259–263, 266–271, 273–274, 288, 324, 327–328, 336, 349–350, 355; "Aux Galéries Lafayette," 108; *Before the Flowers of Friendship Faded*, 244–245, 255; "Birthday Book," 159, 160, 172, 177, 213; *A Book*, 172, 201, 202, 213; "Braque," 123; *Brewsie and Willie*, 387–388, 389, 393; "Capital Capitals," 224–225, 228, 229, 253; "Cézanne," 210; "Christian Bérard," 233; *Composition as Explanation*, 193, 194, 196, 203; "Constance Fletcher," 75; "Cultivated Motor Automatism," 15–16; "Dan Raffel a Nephew," 202; *Descriptions of Literature*, 190–191; *Dix Portraits*, 243; "Dr. Faustus Lights the Lights," 329–331, 346; "Élie Lascaux," 303; *An Elucidation*, 204–205; "England," 141; *Everybody's Autobiography*, xii, 324, 336, 362, 364; "Evidence," 230; "The Fifteenth of November," 172–173, 185; *The First Reader*, 381; *Four in America*, 297, 303–304; *Four Saints in Three Acts*, 224–225, 228, 229, 269, 271–279, 286–287, 289, 356, 396; "The Gentle Lena" see *Three Lives*; *The Geographical History of America*, 305–306; *Geography and Plays*, 143–145, 147–148, 150–151, 246–247, 268; "The Good Anna" see *Three Lives*; *Have They Attacked Mary, He Giggled*, 123–124; *How to Write*, 254–255, 257, 310; "How Writing is Written," 294, 295; "I Came and Here I Am," 293; *Ida*, 349–351, 375; "Idem the Same," 152–153; "If You Had Three Husbands," 146–147; "An Indian Boy," 159, 160; "Ireland," 130–131; "Jo Davidson," 149; *Lec-*

Stein, Gertrude (*continued*)
tures in America, 283, 293, 299, 300; "Letters and Parcels and Wool," 113; "The Life and Death of Juan Gris," 206–207; "Lipchitz," 138; "A List," 153–154, 156; "A Long Gay Book," 170–171; *Lucy Church Amiably*, 246–249, 252–254; *The Making of Americans*, 51–54, 132–133, 151, 153–154, 156, 157–159, 160–167, 170–172, 174, 181–185, 188–190, 191–192, 196, 231–232, 241–242, 258, 284, 375; "Matisse," 57, 66–69, 93–94, 186; "Melanctha" see *Three Lives*; "Miss Furr and Miss Skeene," 268; *Mrs. Reynolds*, 375; "Mrs. Th——y," 113, 141; *Morceaux Choisis de La Fabrication des Américains*, 231–232, 243; *The Mother of Us All*, 393, 394, 396, 397–399; *Narration*, 310; "Normal Motor Automatism," 10, 11; *Operas and Plays*, 313; *Paris France*, 337, 338, 345, 349, 352, 354, 355, 358, 361; *Petits Poèmes*, 383–384; "Picasso" (1909), 57, 66–69, 93, 186; *Picasso* (1938), 326–328, 330–331; plays, 82–83, 95–96; "Poem Pritten on the Pfances of Georges Hugnet," 244–245; "Portrait of F. B.," 79–81; *Portrait of Mabel Dodge at the Villa Curonia*, 65–72, 74, 89–90, 92, 135, 186, 355; "Portrait of R. D.," 77; portraits, 55–56, 71, 79–81; *Portraits and Prayers*, 194–195; "Q. E. D." see *Things As They Are*; review of Lloyd Lewis's *Oscar Wilde Discovers America*, 317; "Sir Francis Rose," 274–275; "Stieglitz," 288, 289; *Tender Buttons*, 96–99, 384; "Their Wills," 225; *Things As They Are*, 25, 249–250; "Three Histories" see *Three Lives*; *Three Lives*, 28–34, 38–40, 42–51, 53–54, 69–70, 76, 123, 134–137, 142, 162, 170–171, 203–204,

Stein, Gertrude (*continued*)
209, 216, 249, 254–255, 262,
293, 380; "Three Sitting Here,"
209–210; "Two Women," 162;
Useful Knowledge, 199, 216–
217, 276; "Van or Twenty Years
After," 157; *A Village*, 213;
Wars I Have Seen, 373–374,
376–377, 380–381, 400, 402–
403; *A Wedding Bouquet*, 225,
313, 320–321, 323, 325; *What
Are Masterpieces*, 348–349;
"The Winner Loses," 352, 353,
361; *The World Is Round*, 331–
332, 338; *Yes Is for a Very
Young Man*, 390, 393–396, 401
Stein, Leo, xi, 3, 5–6, 8, 9, 10, 12,
14–16, 18, 19, 21, 22–23, 25–26,
27, 28, 30, 33, 34, 36, 39, 40, 45,
46, 48, 49, 51, 57, 58, 62–64, 67,
74, 81, 86, 90, 91–92, 114, 118,
119, 131–132, 135, 136, 265, 354
Stein, Michael, xi, 4, 6, 9, 10, 12,
14, 17, 18, 32–33, 36, 37, 39, 41,
63, 93, 106–107, 125–126, 265,
282
Stein, Mrs. Michael, xi, 4, 12, 14–
15, 17, 18, 30, 32, 33, 36, 37, 39,
125
Stein, Simon, 33, 265–266
Stephens, James, 77–78, 83, 99
Sterne, Mabel Dodge. *See* Luhan,
Mabel Dodge
Sterne, Maurice, 153
Stettheimer, Carrie, 228, 372
Stettheimer, Ettie, xi, 228, 372
Stettheimer, Florine, xi, 151, 154,
228, 271–273, 275, 278, 289–290,
372
Steward, Samuel M., xi, 318–319
Stieglitz, Alfred, xi, 56, 57, 64, 66–
68, 70, 74, 85–86, 87–88, 89–90,
106, 116, 153, 276, 281, 288, 289
Strachey, Lytton, 94
Stravinsky, Igor, 221, 251, 275
Street, Grace Davis, 264–266
Street, Reeve, 265–266
Street, Sumner, 265–266
Sun, The, Baltimore, 94
Sun, The, New York, 78, 82–83, 270
Sutherland, Donald, xi, 284, 308,
309, 383–384

Sutherland, Graham, 334
Svidko, 370–371
Sweeney, J. J., 361
Swinnerton, Frank, xi, 134, 135–136

Tanner, Allen, 198, 201
Tate, Mr. & Mrs. Allen, 226
Tauchnitz, 175–176
Tavernier, R., xi, 362, 363–364, 365–
366
Tchelitchew, Choura, 201
Tchelitchew, Pavel, viii, xi, 186,
187–188, 190, 197–198, 201, 204–
205, 218, 219–222, 223–224, 236,
247, 330
Thackeray, W. M., 174
This Quarter, 191
Thomson, Virgil, xi, 224, 225, 228,
229, 232, 253, 271–272, 276, 278,
346, 356, 372, 393, 394, 396, 397–
398
Three Mountains Press, 190
Time, 387
Times, Hartford, The, 271
Times, New York, The, 74, 95, 344
Todd, Miss, 218
Toklas, Alice B., vii, x, xii, 48, 59,
63, 74, 77, 80–81, 83, 86, 89, 90,
93, 97, 99–403 *passim*
Tonny, Kristians, 228, 234
Toscanini, Arturo, 277, 343
Transatlantic Review, The, 158, 159,
161–167, 174
Transition, 202, 204–205, 206, 219,
230, 287
Trend, The, 105
Tribune, Chicago, The, 317
Trollope, Anthony, 175–176
Tschaikowsky, P. I., 116
Tudor Singers, The, 253
"291," 85, 88, 116
Tyler, Parker, 257–258
Tzara, T., 235

Ullman, Alice (Woods), xi, 47, 48,
51
Ullman, Allen, xii
Ulrich, Mabel, 196
United Glee Clubs of America, The,
215
University College, London, 185

Vallotton, F., 47–48
Vanderbilt, R. T., Jr., 295
Van Doren, Irita, x, 197
Van Eyck brothers, 316
Van Gogh, Vincent, 273
Vanity Fair, 123, 149, 156, 157, 159, 180, 268
Van Vechten, Carl, ix, xi, xii, 74, 79, 95, 97, 105–106, 107, 108, 115, 116–117, 150, 151, 152, 153–154, 156–158, 159, 160, 161, 171–172, 179, 182, 196, 197, 214, 216, 228, 229, 262–263, 266–267, 272–273, 275, 279, 283, 292–293, 299, 309, 324, 332, 335–336, 349–350, 372, 374, 377, 381, 393, 396
Van Vechten, Fania (Marinoff). *See* Marinoff, Fania
Vauvenargues, 40
Venice, Accademia di Belle Arti, 68–69
Vercingetorix, 273
Vergennes, 365
Vermeer, Jan, 304
Verrue, Elmer R., ix
Vienna, Kunsthistorische Gallerie, 304
Vieux Colombier, Paris, 94, 123–124
Vogue, 386
Vollard, A., 112–113
Von Auw, Ivan, Jr., xii

Wadsworth Atheneum, 274
Walker, Marian. *See* Williams, Marian (Walker)
Washington, G., 297
Washington Square Gallery, 104
Washington State College, 318
Watters, Mrs. Wellington M., x
Weber, Brom, x
Weber, Max, 78
Wedekind, F., 116–117
Weeks, Mabel Foote, xi, 18, 20, 21, 25, 27, 29, 30, 42, 44, 46, 67–68, 74
Weininger, Otto, 45
Weissberger, Arnold, 398
Wells, H. G., xi, 47, 69–70, 343
Wells, Marjorie, xi
Wertheim, Alma, 228
Wertz, Miss, 11–12

Wescott, Glenway, xi, 171, 217, 220
Whistler, James A. M., 93
White, Max, xi, 281–282, 322–323, 326
"The White House," 25, 28–30
Whitehead, A. N., xi, 99, 100, 140, 287
Whitehead, Jessie, xi, 99, 100
Whitman, Walt, 292
Whittaker, 189
Wilcox, Wendell, xi, 309, 310–311
Wildenstein's, London, 274–275
Wilder, Isabel, xi
Wilder, Thornton, xi, 266, 303–307, 309, 314, 317, 324, 325, 333–334, 336–337, 338–339, 357, 361, 377
Willett, B. W., 203–204
Williams, Dr. Allen, 23, 45, 240
Williams, Dr. Russell, xi
Williams, Dr. Marian (Walker), 23–24, 44–45, 223, 240
Williams, W. C., xii, 141, 267–268
Williams, Mrs. W. C., xii
Wilson, Edmund, xii, 156, 359–360
Wilson, Woodrow, 118
Wolfe, Thomas, 324, 343
Woods, Alice. *See* Ullman, Alice (Woods)
Woojums family, 292–293
Woolf, Leonard, xii, 184, 193
Woolf, Virginia, 184, 185, 193
Woollcott, A., xii, 314, 317, 333–334, 344–345, 357, 372
Woolley, Montagu, 344–345
Wordsworth, W., 16
World War I, 101–128, 339, 347
World War II, 341–392
Wright, Richard, xii, 326, 374, 379–381, 393
Wright, Wilbur, 297

Yacco, Sadda, 278
Yale Collection of American Literature, ix
Yale University, 288
Yale University Library, vii, ix

Zangwill, Israel, xii, 25, 134, 135, 136, 214
Zangwill, O. L., xii
Zorn, Anders L., 38

A NOTE ON THE TYPE

This book was set on the Linotype in ELECTRA, *designed by W. A. Dwiggins. The Electra face is a simple and readable type suitable for printing books by present-day processes. It is not based on any historical model, and hence does not echo any particular time or fashion. It is without eccentricities to catch the eye and interfere with reading — in general, its aim is to perform the function of a good book printing-type: to be read, and not seen.*

The typographic and binding designs are by W. A. Dwiggins.

The book was composed, printed, and bound by The Plimpton Press, Norwood, Massachusetts.